Reverse Engineering Armv8-A Systems

First Edition

A practical guide to kernel, firmware, and
TrustZone analysis

Austin Kim

‹packt›

Reverse Engineering Armv8-A Systems

First Edition

Copyright © 2025 Packt Publishing

Portfolio Director: Rohit Rajkumar

Relationship Lead: Tanisha Mehrotra

Project Manager: Sandip Tadge

Content Engineer: Anuradha Vishwas Joglekar

Technical Editor: Tejas Mhasvekar

Copy Editor: Safis Editing

Indexer: Pratik Shirodkar

Proofreader: Anuradha Vishwas Joglekar

Production Designer: Pranit Padwal

Growth Lead: Namita Velgekar

Marketing Owner: Nivedita Pandey

First published: August 2025

Production reference: 1170725

Published by Packt Publishing Ltd.
Grosvenor House
11 St Paul's Square
Birmingham
B3 1RB, UK.

ISBN 978-1-83508-892-0

www.packtpub.com

To my wife, Helen, for encouraging me when I needed it and for standing by my side throughout my life.

— Austin Kim

Foreword

The era of **artificial intelligence** (**AI**) is here, capturing the attention of tech enthusiasts, innovators, and students everywhere. With AI at the center of tech discussions, many people, from new developers to experienced professionals, are eager to learn its complexities. But is this the right path? Is AI really the ultimate answer – the "super-hero" of technology? Should every new developer and even those already established focus only on AI? These questions remain as we move through this exciting time.

Alongside the AI excitement, another important topic is emerging: protecting personal information. In our connected world, people highly value their privacy. Yet, everyone knows that once personal data goes to the cloud, it's no longer fully secure. The best way to keep personal data safe is to store it locally, on embedded devices rather than sending it to the cloud.

This reality shows the growing importance of embedded systems, where Arm processors are already the most widely used technology. As the need for secure, local computing grows, Arm processors will become even more common, and the demand for Arm experts will rise. Moreover, while AI is strong in many areas, system software engineering, especially in reverse engineering, where AI often struggles, remains a vital and expanding field. Skills in this area will become even more essential as industries focus on secure, efficient, and reliable embedded solutions.

Here enters Austin Kim, a well-known writer in South Korea's tech community, famous for their insightful books on Arm architecture and the Linux kernel. Having read all of his books, I can say their greatest strength is how easy they are to read. Many technical books, even if full of great information, sit unread because they're hard to follow. But Kim's books are engaging and simple to understand. This ease doesn't mean they lack depth; it helps readers grasp complex ideas effortlessly. When I heard Austin Kim was writing a book in English, I wondered if their clear style would carry over. After reading this new book, I'm happy to say that he has a special talent for writing clearly and engagingly, no matter the language.

I strongly recommend this book to anyone wanting to learn more about Arm processors, system software engineering, or embedded systems in today's AI-driven world. Whether you're a new developer exploring this field, an experienced engineer shifting to embedded systems, or a professional aiming to stay ahead in a fast-changing industry, this book offers valuable knowledge. This book is a must-read for those eager to master a field that will only grow in importance, delivered with the clarity and engagement that only Kim can provide.

Bojun Seo

Software Engineer, LG Electronics

Contributors

About the author

Austin Kim has more than 14 years of experience in embedded Linux BSP development. He has worked on many tasks, such as board bring-up, crash and performance troubleshooting, and bootloader development for Arm-based devices. He has strong skills in binary analysis and has analyzed many memory dumps using TRACE32, Crash Utility, and ftrace. He has solved various kernel issues, including crashes, system lockups, and watchdog resets. Currently, he works as a Linux kernel BSP engineer and technical lecturer at LG Electronics. He enjoys sharing practical debugging skills, especially in areas such as Armv8-A architecture and kernel crash analysis.

I sincerely thank my wife, Helen Song, for her patience and support. Her dedication gave me the strength to complete this work. I'm also grateful for the guidance from mentors and leaders: Mike Seo, Dr. Reddy, Dr. Namseok Kim, and Dr. Gunho Lee. I also sincerely thank the technical reviewers: Bojun Seo, Rafiuddin Syed, Namhyung Kim, and Youngmin Nam. Lastly, I thank the Packt team, who supported me with great patience and professionalism.

About the reviewers

Bojun Seo is an open source developer at LG Electronics, developing advanced developer tools leveraging eBPF (extended Berkeley Packet Filter). He has an interest and experience in various fields related to computer science engineering, which include computer architecture, software architecture, parallel computing, **General-Purpose Computing on Graphics Processing Units (GPGPU)**, memory management, algorithms, security, open source culture, and so on. He actively engages with other developers, enjoying presentations on his current tools at C++ Now, LG Software Developer Conference, and the Korean Linux Kernel Developers Meetup. He lives in Seoul and enjoys traveling around the world.

Rafiuddin Syed is an embedded systems engineer with expertise in real-time computing, virtualization, and low-level software development. He has held various roles at Texas Instruments, Intel, NVIDIA, Harman, and Drako Motors. His work spans hypervisors, Linux kernel development, PCIe, USB, and secure IPC, with contributions to both industry and open source projects.

Namhyung Kim is a staff software engineer at Google. He's been working on the Linux kernel and other open source projects for more than 15 years. His main interests are low-level infrastructure such as operating systems, toolchains, performance monitoring, tracing, and binary instrumentation. Now he co-maintains the Linux perf tools and uftrace project, and also enjoys traveling all over the world.

Youngmin Nam is a seasoned software engineer with over 15 years of experience in embedded systems and low-level software development. At Samsung Electronics, he has led Linux kernel and Android BSP development for ARM-based SoCs, including the Exynos2400 platform used in Galaxy flagship devices. He played a key role in the Google Pixel project, collaborating directly with Google's Pixel team to bring up essential system drivers and ensure platform stability. More recently, he has been working closely with Google's kernel team and upstream maintainers to apply **Generic Kernel Image (GKI)** support to the Exynos kernel. His expertise spans kernel bring-up, memory management, platform integration, and upstream contributions to both Linux and Android kernels. Youngmin is passionate about reverse engineering, debugging complex system-level issues, and contributing to the open source community.

I would like to thank my family for their continued support and encouragement throughout my professional journey.

Join our community on Discord

Join our community's Discord space for discussions with the authors and other readers: `https://packt.link/embeddedsystems`

Table of Contents

Preface   **xxix**

Part 1: Fundamentals of Armv8-A Architecture   **1**

Chapter 1: Learning Fundamentals of Arm Architecture   **3**

Technical requirements 4

Introduction to the Arm architecture 4

What is the Arm architecture? • 4

Cortex® processor and architecture • 5

Armv8 profiles • 6

Registers 7

General-purpose registers • 7

Special registers • 9

   SP_ELx • 9

   ELR_ELx • 10

   PC • 10

Program status registers • 11

   PSTATE • 11

   SPSR_ELx • 13

System registers • 13

   Lowest exception levels • 13

   How to access the system register • 15

Key registers related to reverse engineering • 16

Procedure Call Standard for the Arm Architecture (AAPCS) **16**

Background • 16

Introduction to AAPCS • 17

Register used for AAPCS • 17

BL instruction • 18

Exception levels **20**

Exception levels and privilege levels • 21

EL0 with PL0 • 21

EL1 with PL1 • 22

EL2 with PL2 • 22

EL3 with PL3 • 22

Instructions to switch exception levels • 24

How to determine the current exception level • 26

Example routine to read CurrentEL • 27

Exceptions **28**

Key principles of exceptions • 28

Types of exception • 28

Exception vector table • 29

Details of exception vector table • 30

EL1 with SP_EL0 • 31

EL1 (current EL with SPx) • 31

EL0 (AArch64) • 32

EL0 (AArch32) • 32

How an exception is generated with the big picture • 33

Step 1: Indicating the cause of exception • 33

Step 2: Updating registers • 34

Step 3: Switching the exception level • 34

Step 4: Branching to exception vector address • 34

Step 5: Exception handling • 35

How an exception handler works • 35

Synchronous exception handler • 35

IRQ and FIQ exception handler • 36

SError exception handler • 36

Summary 36

Chapter 2: Understanding the ELF Binary Format   39

Technical requirements 39

Introduction to ELF 39

Why do we need to learn about ELF? • 40

What is ELF? • 40

Layout of an ELF file • 41

ELF header 42

How to identify an ELF header • 42

How to view the ELF header • 44

Exploring the ELF header • 46

The e_ident field • 46

The e_type field • 47

The e_machine field • 48

The e_entry field • 49

The e_phoff and e_shoff fields • 49

The e_shstrndx field • 50

Section headers 50

Layout of section headers • 50

Exploring section headers • 53

The sh_name field • 54

The sh_type field • 54

The sh_flags field • 56

The sh_addr field • 56

The sh_offset and sh_size fields • 57

Sections 57

The .text section • 58

The .bss, .data, and .rodata sections • 58

The dynamic section • 59

The .init section • 60

The GOT section • 60

The PLT section • 60

Program headers **61**

Layout of the program header • 62

Exploring program headers • 64

The p_type field • 65

The p_flags field • 65

The p_offset, p_vaddr, and p_paddr fields • 66

Summary **66**

Chapter 3: Manipulating Data with Arm Data Processing Instructions   67

Technical requirements **67**

Move operations **68**

The MOV instruction • 68

Examples of the MOV instruction • 68

The MVN instruction • 69

Examples of the MVN instruction • 69

Arithmetic operations **70**

The ADD instruction • 70

Examples of the ADD instruction • 71

The ADC instruction • 72

Example of the ADC instruction • 73

The SUB instruction • 74

Examples of the SUB instruction • 74

SBC instruction • 75

Examples of the SBC instruction • 75

Bit-shift operations 76

The LSL instruction • 76

Examples of the LSL instruction • 77

The LSR instruction • 78

Examples of the LSR instruction • 78

The ASR instruction • 79

The ROR instruction • 80

Case study – bit-shift operations in assembly code • 80

Logical operations 82

The AND instruction • 82

Example of the AND instruction • 83

The ORR instruction • 84

Example of the ORR instruction • 84

The ORN instruction • 85

Example of the ORN instruction • 85

The BIC instruction • 86

Examples of the BIC instruction • 87

The EOR instruction • 88

Examples of the EOR instruction • 88

Practicing logical operations • 89

The AND operation • 90

The OR operation • 90

The XOR operation • 91

Practicing data processing instructions 91

Initializing variables • 92

Checking the state • 93

Clearing a bit • 93

Handling the else part • 94

Summary 94

Chapter 4: Reading and Writing with Memory Access Instructions   97

Technical requirements 98

The LDR instruction 98

Syntax: LDR instruction in basic form • 98

LDR instruction with offset addressing mode • 100

The STR instruction 102

Syntax: STR instruction in its basic form • 102

STR instruction with offset addressing mode • 103

Extension: Memory access operation 105

Various load operations • 105

Various store operations • 106

The secret behind load operations • 106

Practicing memory access instructions 107

Introducing example code • 107

Analyzing assembly routine: STR and LDR • 109

Summary 111

Chapter 5: Controlling Execution with Flow Control Instructions   113

Technical requirements 113

Branch instructions 114

The B instruction • 114

The BL instruction • 115

The BR instruction • 116

The BLR instruction • 116

Analyzing an example routine • 117

Comparison operations 118

The condition flags in PSTATE • 118

The CMP instruction • 119

CMP instruction example • 120

The CMN instruction • 120

CMN instruction example • 121

The TST instruction • 122

TST instruction example • 122

Conditional codes • 123

Introducing conditional codes • 123

Analyzing an example routine with conditional codes • 124

Conditional branch operations 125

The CBZ instruction • 126

The CBNZ instruction • 126

The TBZ instruction • 127

The TBNZ instruction • 128

Analyzing assembly routines for reverse engineering • 129

The CBZ instruction • 130

The CBNZ instruction • 132

The TBZ instruction • 133

System control operations 135

The SVC instruction • 136

The HVC instruction • 137

The SMC instruction • 138

Summary 140

Part 2: Background Knowledge for Binary Analysis   **141**

Chapter 6: Introducing Reverse Engineering   **143**

Technical requirements 143

Why reverse engineering is necessary 143

Library and firmware debugging • 144

Legacy systems • 145

Improving debugging skills • 145

Case study – how reverse engineering skills enhance debugging abilities • 146

Methods of reverse engineering **146**

Static analysis • 147

Dynamic analysis • 148

Dump analysis • 149

Introducing binary for dump analysis • 149

Advantage of dump analysis • 150

Compilation process **150**

What the compiler does • 150

The breakdown of compilation • 151

The compiler option – optimization level • 152

Assembly instructions and machine code **153**

Opcode and instruction • 153

Background knowledge of reverse engineering **155**

Assembly instructions • 156

Linux kernel • 156

ELF format • 156

Summary **157**

Chapter 7: Setting Up a Practice Environment with an Arm Device   159

Technical requirements **159**

Raspberry Pi **160**

Introducing Raspberry Pi • 160

Arm processor profile in each Raspberry Pi • 161

QEMU **162**

User-mode emulation • 163

Full system emulation • 165

Summary **167**

Chapter 8: Unpacking the Kernel with Linux Fundamentals 169

Technical requirements 169

Architecture overview 170

What is the Linux kernel? • 170

Resource manager • 171

Supporting the execution environment • 172

Understanding system calls • 172

User space and kernel space • 172

How the system call works • 174

System call number and system call handler • 176

Monitoring system call operations • 176

Process management 177

Introducing processes • 177

The data structure of the process • 179

Understanding the call stack of the process • 180

Multiprocess management • 181

Introducing threads • 185

Memory management 186

Key memory features in the Linux system • 186

Introducing the virtual memory system • 190

Virtual addresses in user space and kernel space • 190

Understanding the virtual memory area • 193

Key security hardening features 194

LSM • 194

Address sanitizer • 196

Why the Address Sanitizer was introduced • 196

Understanding the KASLR feature • 196

Summary 197

Part 3: Unlocking Key Binary Analysis Skills for Reverse Engineering 199

Chapter 9: Understanding Basic Static Analysis 201

Technical requirements 201

Introducing static analysis 201

What is static analysis? • 202

Programs used for static analysis • 203

Identifying binaries 204

Introducing binary utilities to check binary files • 204

The file utility • 205

The readelf utility • 206

The xxd utility • 207

Identifying the raw data of binary file • 207

Identifying the raw data of a text file • 208

Case study of the corrupted binary file • 209

Analyzing the control flow with if statements 210

Basic if statement • 211

The if-else statement • 212

The else-if statement • 214

The if with return statement • 216

Analyzing the control flow with for loops 218

Basic for loop • 218

A for loop with a break statement • 222

A for loop with a continue statement • 224

A for loop with a return 0 statement • 226

Identifying log output patterns 228

Why do we need to understand log output routines? • 229

Analyzing the call to the printf function • 229

When printf becomes puts • 230

Summary 230

Chapter 10: Going Deeper with Advanced Static Analysis 233

Technical requirements 233

Methodology for static analysis 234

Setting clear and flexible goals • 234

Techniques for analyzing instructions • 235

Line-by-line analysis • 235

Control flow analysis using function calls • 235

Understanding the limitations of static analysis • 236

Comparing static analysis and dynamic analysis • 237

Introducing advanced static analysis 238

Key features of kernel binaries • 238

Selecting kernel binaries for analysis • 239

Debugging program for kernel binaries • 240

Structure of kernel binaries 240

Exploring vmlinux • 240

How to generate vmlinux • 240

Inspecting header sections in vmlinux • 241

Understanding *.ko files (kernel modules) • 243

Types of device drivers • 243

*Why is it important to analyze *.ko files? • 244*

*Checking header information in a *.ko file • 244*

Inspecting metadata in the .modinfo section • 246

Key features of kernel binaries 250

Accessing system registers • 250

Handling exceptions in the kernel • 251

Managing sp_el0 and current macro • 251

Instructions to identify exception levels • 253

Understanding the pattern of struct data structures 254

Understanding the offset of fields in struct • 255

Instructions for accessing fields in a struct • 256

Summary 258

Chapter 11: Analyzing Program Behavior with Basic Dynamic Analysis 261

Technical requirements 262

Introducing dynamic analysis 262

What is dynamic analysis? • 262

Limitations of dynamic analysis • 262

Introducing basic dynamic analysis • 263

Exploring the GDB program 264

Introducing GDB • 264

Using GDB • 264

Running the GDB program • 265

Launching GDB • 265

Setting breakpoints • 265

Debugging information commands • 266

Inspecting memory contents • 266

Introducing GEF • 266

Understanding the virtual address range 268

Virtual memory system • 268

Examples of the virtual address pattern • 269

Analyzing stack memory content 270

Understanding the call stack • 270

Debugging a corrupted stack • 272

Exploiting stack corruption • 274

How to identify stack corruption • 275

Introducing the debugging patch • 275

How to use the stack debugging code • 276

Mitigation method • 277

Return-oriented programming analysis 278

Key concept of ROP • 278

Using compiler options to prevent this symptom • 281

Memory corruption: buffer overflow case study 282

Introducing the example code • 282

Debugging with a patch • 282

Buffer overflow over multiple layers: case study • 285

Buffer overflow from another software layer • 285

Buffer overflow in a struct • 286

The mitigation method • 286

Summary 287

Chapter 12: Expert Techniques in Advanced Dynamic Analysis   289

Technical requirements 290

Introducing advanced dynamic analysis 290

What is advanced dynamic analysis? • 290

Debugging program for kernel debugging • 291

vmcore and the Crash utility 292

Debugging approaches for the kernel binary • 292

Understanding the KDUMP feature • 293

Analyzing vmcore files using the binary utility • 293

Understanding the layout of the vmcore file • 293

NOTE section of the program header • 295

Understanding the Crash utility • 297

Stack area of the process 299

Background on the stack of a process • 300

The overall layout of the process stack • 300

Analyzing the memory contents of the process stack • 302

User process stack versus kernel process stack • 304

Code review on the stack magic value • 305

Summary of the magic value inside the binary • 307

Tracking the start address for a struct using the address 307

Understanding the task_struct structure • 307

How to find the address of the task_struct structure • 308

Reviewing the thread field in the task_struct structure • 311

Identifying a structure using a function pointer **313**

Data structures that store function addresses • 313

Finding the address of bcm2835_mmc_irq • 314

Understanding the irqaction structure • 315

Finding the address in the irq_desc structure • 316

Summary of the analysis • 317

Summary **318**

Chapter 13: Tracing Execution with uftrace   319

Technical requirements **319**

Introducing log-based debugging **319**

Why do we need logs or tracing? • 320

The importance of logs in real-world projects • 320

Introducing uftrace **320**

Why was uftrace designed? • 321

Key features of uftrace • 321

How to install uftrace • 322

Basic features of uftrace **323**

Simple "Hello, World!" project • 323

Why -pg is added when compiling the code • 324

Format of uftrace output • 324

Practical features of uftrace **324**

Library debugging • 325

Argument tracing • 326

Return value tracing • 328

Summary **329**

Part 4: Security Features in Armv8-A Systems 331

Chapter 14: Securing Execution with Armv8-A TrustZone 333

Technical requirements 333

Introducing TrustZone 334

Why was TrustZone introduced? • 334

What are the primary features of TrustZone? • 335

Why we need to learn about TrustZone • 335

Key concepts of TrustZone 335

Understanding the Non-secure world • 336

Software scenario of the Secure world • 338

Secure monitor call 338

Non-secure world to Secure world • 339

Secure world to Non-secure world • 341

Exception handlers for TrustZone • 342

Implementation of TrustZone in real systems 346

How does a trusted OS run in the Secure world? • 346

Examples of security implementations using TrustZone • 347

Analyzing Arm Trusted Firmware 348

Analyzing the exception handler at EL3 • 348

Exception handler for the SMC instruction • 349

Hardware features related to TrustZone 352

AWPROT and ARPROT signals • 352

Hardware features supporting TrustZone • 355

Summary 356

Chapter 15: Building Defenses with Key Security Features of Armv8-A 357

Technical requirements 357

Privileged Access Never (PAN) 358

The motivation behind PAN • 358

Registers for configuring PAN • 359

    The PAN system register • 359

    The SCTLR_EL1.SPAN field • 360

Code review of PAN initialization in the Linux Kernel • 360

Implementation considerations in the Linux system • 361

Pointer Authentication Code (PAC) **362**

Introducing PAC • 362

    Understanding the PAC authentication code • 362

    The layout of the virtual address for storing PAC • 364

How the PAC feature is applied • 365

    A common use case for PAC • 365

    The execution flow when using the branch operation • 366

Assembly instructions on PAC • 367

The components of the PACIASP and AUTIASP instructions • 368

More PAC instructions • 370

Compiler support • 371

How to use PAC in Linux using the GCC compiler • 372

PAC exception: Fault on FPAC • 374

Key system registers for PAC • 375

Branch Target Identification (BTI) **376**

Why was BTI introduced? • 376

Understanding BTI • 377

The workflow of BTI • 379

The guarded page • 379

The BTI instruction and PSTATE.BTYTE • 380

    The BTI instruction • 380

    PSTATE.BTYPE: A new processor state • 381

Using the BTI option via a compiler • 381

BTI exceptions • 383

Code review of BTI • 384

Memory Tagging Extension (MTE) 385

Introducing MTE • 385

How tags are handled • 386

The virtual address layout used to store the address tag • 387

Memory tag • 388

MTE's tag checking operation • 389

Summary 389

Other Books You May Enjoy 393

Index 397

Preface

Today, Arm processors are used in a wide range of systems, such as smartphones, AI SoCs, the automotive sector (for autonomous driving and infotainment), cloud servers, and MacBooks. These processors are mostly based on Armv8-A 64-bit architecture, including popular Arm processors, such as Cortex-A53, Cortex-A57, and Cortex-A78.

In system software development, Armv8-A architecture is now one of the most important topics that engineers should understand.

This book, *Reverse Engineering Armv8-A Systems*, was written to share practical ways to analyze binaries on Armv8-A systems. My goal is to help readers learn how Armv8-A architecture works and also build real skills through hands-on experience.

The book covers practical content that can be used directly in real-world projects. It is designed for readers who want to start learning binary analysis from the basics and move forward to a deeper understanding of low-level systems in Armv8-A systems.

Why I wrote this book

Reverse engineering means analyzing a system without access to the original source code. When you hear the term "reverse engineering," you might think of binary analysis, security research, or exploit development. These are important skills and are often seen as core skills. Many blog posts and articles talk about using reverse engineering to create exploits from a security point of view.

However, for many system software developers, reverse engineering is usually used for a different purpose: to find bugs, analyze crashes, or investigate system failures, rather than to develop exploits. This book focuses on binary analysis skills that are useful for firmware developers and system software engineers. This book is not written for offensive security. Instead, it explains detailed binary analysis methods and practical debugging techniques.

I believe that the ability to analyze binaries is a core skill for becoming an advanced engineer in embedded systems. With this book, you will learn about the key concepts of the Armv8-A architecture and gain practical experience in analyzing binaries on Armv8-A systems.

Who this book is for

If you are interested in binary analysis, reverse engineering, or debugging on Armv8-A devices, this book is for you. It is especially helpful for system software engineers, security consultants, and ethical hackers who want to expand their binary analysis expertise. To get the most value, you should have a basic understanding of C programming. Familiarity with computer architecture, Linux systems, and security concepts will also help you follow the material in this book more effectively.

What this book covers

Chapter 1, Learning Fundamentals of Arm Architecture, introduces the basic concepts of the Armv8-A architecture, such as exception levels, register usage, AAPCS, and exception handling. These fundamentals will help you understand system behavior and prepare you for binary analysis.

Chapter 2, Understanding the ELF Binary Format, introduces you to the ELF binary format, including the file header, section header, and program header. You will learn how to use the readelf command to check binary structure and how each header helps during reverse engineering.

Chapter 3, Manipulating Data with Arm Data Processing Instructions, explains data processing instructions for arithmetic, logic, and bit shifts. You will learn how to reconstruct assembly instructions into C. These skills are key background knowledge for binary analysis.

Chapter 4, Reading and Writing with Memory Access Instructions, covers how memory access works in Armv8-A using LDR and STR. You will learn how they move data between registers and memory.

Chapter 5, Controlling Execution with Flow Control Instructions, explains flow control instructions that change how a program runs based on conditions with comparison and branch instructions.

Chapter 6, Introducing Reverse Engineering, introduces reverse engineering, a way to understand software without source code. You will learn about static and dynamic analysis, as well as the compilation process, which are important for binary analysis.

Chapter 7, Setting Up a Practice Environment with an Arm Device, covers how to set up a practice environment using an Arm device such as the Raspberry Pi or QEMU. With these tools, you will perform binary analysis.

Chapter 8, Unpacking the Kernel with Linux Fundamentals, focuses on Linux basics: user space, kernel space, system calls, and process management. You will also learn about memory management and security features such as LSM and KASLR.

Chapter 9, Understanding Basic Static Analysis, covers basic static analysis for reverse engineering by using binary utilities. You will learn how to check the type of a binary file and how to examine a corrupted object file. You will also learn how to read assembly code and understand how to convert it into C code.

Chapter 10, Going Deeper with Advanced Static Analysis, covers advanced static analysis for kernel binaries such as *.ko and vmlinux. You will learn about the ELF structure, typical kernel binary patterns, and how to recognize elements such as the .modinfo section.

Chapter 11, Analyzing Program Behavior with Basic Dynamic Analysis, discusses basic dynamic analysis, including its benefits and limitations. You will use tools such as GDB and GEF to debug various user-space binaries. This chapter also provides case studies related to memory corruption issues.

Chapter 12, Expert Techniques in Advanced Dynamic Analysis, covers advanced dynamic analysis of kernel binaries using the Crash utility. You will learn how to identify kernel structures such as task_struct using stack patterns and memory addresses. These skills are a key feature of this book.

Chapter 13, Tracing Execution with uftrace, explores uftrace, a powerful open source tool to monitor process execution. You will learn how to install and use uftrace with a simple example that traces function calls and return values.

Chapter 14, Securing Execution with Armv8-A TrustZone, explores TrustZone in Armv8-A. You will also learn how software switches between the non-secure and secure worlds using the SMC instruction. It also explains hardware features that support TrustZone, such as the AxPROT signal.

Chapter 15, Building Defenses with Key Security Features of Armv8-A, explains the latest security features in Armv8-A, including PAN, PAC, BTI, and MTE. These features are used to protect systems by controlling memory access and verifying addresses.

To get the most out of this book

To get the most benefit from this book, we recommend the following:

- You should be familiar with using Linux, especially with the command-line interface (shell).
- You should have basic knowledge of the C programming language.

We have tested all the example code in this book using the following platforms:

- x86_64 Ubuntu 22.04 LTS as a guest OS (running on Oracle VirtualBox 7.0)
- Raspberry Pi 4 Model B (64-bit Arm), tested with both the standard distribution kernel and our custom 6.6 kernel (lightly tested)

If you are using the digital version of this book, we advise you to type the code yourself or access the code from the book's GitHub repository (a link is available in the next section). Doing so will help you avoid any potential errors related to the copying and pasting of code.

Everything will be explained step by step. Whether you are a beginner or an experienced developer, this book will guide you through the interesting and practical world of binary analysis for reverse engineering.

Download the example code files

The code bundle for the book is hosted on GitHub at `https://github.com/PacktPublishing/Reverse-Engineering-Armv8-A-Systems`. We also have other code bundles from our rich catalog of books and videos available at `https://github.com/PacktPublishing`. Check them out!

Download the color images

We also provide a PDF file that has color images of the screenshots/diagrams used in this book. You can download it here: `https://packt.link/gbp/9781835088920`.

Conventions used

There are a number of text conventions used throughout this book.

`CodeInText`: Indicates code words in text, database table names, folder names, filenames, file extensions, pathnames, dummy URLs, user input, and Twitter handles. For example: "The `MOV` instruction is used to copy the value of an operand into the destination register":

A block of code is set as follows:

```
struct task_struct {
    int flags;
    int state;
    char task_name[15];
};
```

Any command-line input or output is written as follows:

```
crash> rd ffffff8040238018
ffffff8040238018:    ffffffc008028000
```

Bold: Indicates a new term, an important word, or words that you see on the screen. For instance, words in menus or dialog boxes appear in the text like this. For example: "**[3] Callstack** shows how function calls are made by processes.

> Warnings or important notes appear like this.

> Tips and tricks appear like this.

Get in touch

Feedback from our readers is always welcome.

General feedback: Email feedback@packtpub.com and mention the book's title in the subject of your message. If you have questions about any aspect of this book, please email us at questions@packtpub.com.

Errata: Although we have taken every care to ensure the accuracy of our content, mistakes do happen. If you have found a mistake in this book, we would be grateful if you reported this to us. Please visit http://www.packtpub.com/submit-errata, click **Submit Errata**, and fill in the form.

Piracy: If you come across any illegal copies of our works in any form on the internet, we would be grateful if you would provide us with the location address or website name. Please contact us at copyright@packtpub.com with a link to the material.

If you are interested in becoming an author: If there is a topic that you have expertise in and you are interested in either writing or contributing to a book, please visit http://authors.packtpub.com/.

Share your thoughts

Once you've read *Reverse Engineering Armv8-A Systems*, we'd love to hear your thoughts! Scan the QR code below to go straight to the Amazon review page for this book and share your feedback.

https://packt.link/r/1835088929

Your review is important to us and the tech community and will help us make sure we're delivering excellent quality content.

Download a free PDF copy of this book

Thanks for purchasing this book!

Do you like to read on the go but are unable to carry your print books everywhere?

Is your eBook purchase not compatible with the device of your choice?

Don't worry, now with every Packt book you get a DRM-free PDF version of that book at no cost.

Read anywhere, any place, on any device. Search, copy, and paste code from your favorite technical books directly into your application.

The perks don't stop there, you can get exclusive access to discounts, newsletters, and great free content in your inbox daily.

Follow these simple steps to get the benefits:

1. Scan the QR code or visit the link below:

https://packt.link/free-ebook/9781835088920

2. Submit your proof of purchase.
3. That's it! We'll send your free PDF and other benefits to your email directly.

Part 1

Fundamentals of Armv8-A Architecture

In this part, you will learn about the fundamentals of the Armv8-A architecture that are necessary to begin binary analysis. This part provides practical knowledge that you can use in real debugging or reverse engineering tasks in Armv8-A systems.

This part includes the following chapters:

- *Chapter 1, Learning Fundamentals of Arm Architecture*
- *Chapter 2, Understanding the ELF Binary Format*
- *Chapter 3, Manipulating Data with Arm Data Processing Instructions*
- *Chapter 4, Reading and Writing with Memory Access Instructions*
- *Chapter 5, Controlling Execution with Flow Control Instructions*

1

Learning Fundamentals of Arm Architecture

Founded as a joint venture in 1990, Arm® Holdings has become one of the dominant forces in the IT industry. Arm processors are used everywhere, from smartphones and tablets to servers and IoT devices. Arm processors are also the most dominant players in the automotive industry. With its vast ecosystem, a lot of chipsets are based on Arm processors. Arm's position in the semiconductor market is strong.

This first chapter covers the following topics:

- Introduction to the Arm architecture
- Registers
- **Procedure Call Standard for the Arm Architecture (AAPCS)**
- Exception levels
- Exceptions

In this chapter, we will primarily focus on the **Armv8-A** architecture because it is the most popular architecture. Smartphones, MacBooks, and automotive systems are all based on the Armv8-A architecture.

Armv8-A offers more features, including the **Instruction Set Architecture (ISA)**, **Application Binary Interface (ABI)**, virtualization, and memory architecture. This chapter covers the necessary fundamentals of Armv8-A to perform reverse engineering.

Let's begin this chapter by introducing the Arm architecture.

Technical requirements

To learn more about Armv8-A, you can check the following materials:

- Armv8-A Reference Manual: `https://developer.arm.com/documentation/ddi0487/gb`
- Programmer's Guide for Armv8-A: `https://developer.arm.com/documentation/den0024/latest/`

Introduction to the Arm architecture

An Arm processor is a semiconductor composed of transistors in terms of hardware. From a software engineer's point of view, how can we control the Arm processor? There are a number of Arm processors available in the market but software developers are often in situations where they need to configure Arm processors in different ways depending on the requirements of the project.

What is the Arm architecture?

The Arm architecture is how the Arm company describes the Arm processor from a software point of view. The key elements of the Arm architecture include registers, assembly instructions, exceptions, and TrustZone®, which software developers need to understand.

Let's take a look at the following screenshot:

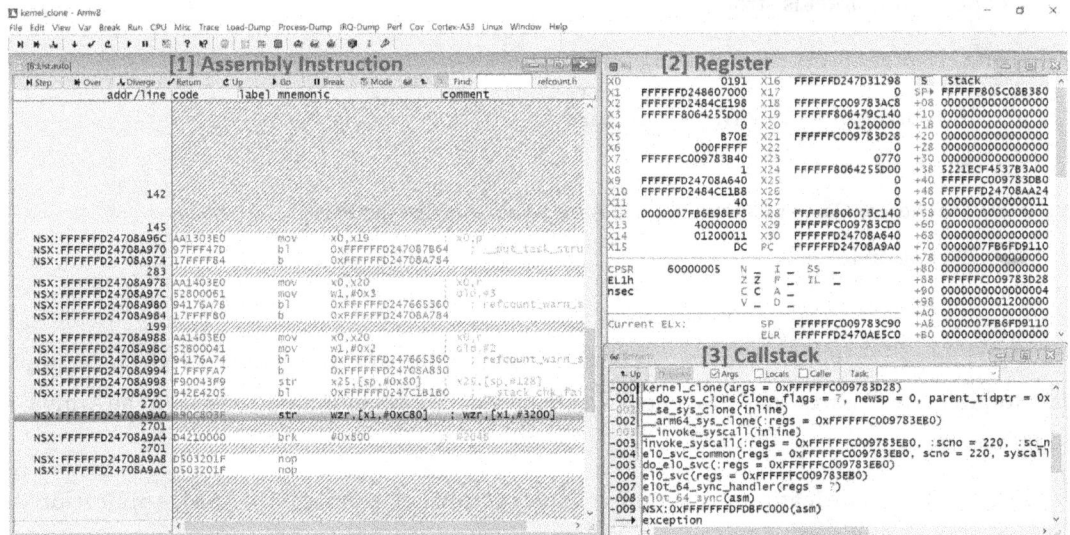

Figure 1.1: TRACE32 debugger window

Figure 1.1 shows the key elements of the Arm architecture. **[1] Assembly Instruction** shows the assembly instructions that the Arm processor can decode and execute. The Arm architecture defines the ISA, which describes the syntax of assembly instructions that the processor can execute.

The window labeled **[2] Register** reveals a set of general-purpose registers and the PSTATE. The assembly instructions can be executed using general-purpose registers. Whenever an assembly instruction is executed, the input or output is saved into a register. Software engineers examine the values of the registers when performing reverse engineering or debugging.

[3] Callstack shows how function calls are made by processes. The callstack is closely associated with the AAPCS. This standard defines a set of conventions for how subroutines are called and how parameters are passed between functions.

What you can see in *Figure 1.1* is from a software point of view. So, you can think of *Figure 1.1* as a simple view of the Arm architecture.

In practice, software engineers use various debugging tools depending on the features and requirements. Tools such as GDB or TRACE32 help you debug assembly instructions, check registers, and look at the callstack.

Cortex® processor and architecture

The Armv8-A architecture supports high-profile Arm processors such as the Cortex-A72 and Cortex-A73. The following table outlines the specifications for the Armv7-A and Armv8-A architecture with Cortex processors:

Architecture	Cortex Processor
Armv7-A	Cortex-A5
	Cortex-A7
	Cortex-A9
Armv8-A	Cortex-A32, Cortex-A35
	Cortex-A53, Cortex-A57
	Cortex-A72, Cortex-A73

Table 1.1: Architecture and processors

Each Arm processor has its own hardware design, including a **Memory Management Unit (MMU)**, cache, and internal clock configuration. For example, the cache configuration is different between Cortex-A73 and Cortex-A78. If you visit the Arm home page, you can find detailed specifications for each processor.

Despite the variations in hardware design among Arm processors, they share the same Armv8-A architecture. This means that assembly instructions, registers, AAPCS, and exception handling are compatible across all Arm processors within the same Armv8-A architecture. As a result, code written for Cortex-A53 processors can typically run on other Arm processors, such as Cortex-A57, without modification. From a software developer's perspective, the Arm architecture is more important than the specification of Arm processors.

Armv8 profiles

There are three profiles in the Armv8 architecture. You can see the details of each profile here:

- **Armv8-A**: With Armv8-A-based processors, chipset makers can design various application processors. Armv8-A is designed to support multimedia applications in operating systems such as Linux or Windows. It's widely used in various devices, from smartphones and tablets to servers and IoT devices. Additionally, Armv8-A offers support for virtualization, which allows hypervisors to manage the resources of guest operating systems. In the automotive sector, hypervisors are widely used.

- **Armv8-R**: This is the *real-time* profile designed for real-time systems. Armv8-R-based processors are commonly used in automotive systems, medical systems, robotics, and other real-time applications where precise timing and reliability are essential. R-profile processors run 32-bit code and support a much more limited memory architecture compared to the A-profile.

- **Armv8-M**: This is the *microcontroller* profile designed specifically for **microcontroller units (MCUs)** used in embedded systems. Armv8-M is used in IoT devices, wearables, automotive systems, and industrial automation, which require low power consumption.

If you start reverse engineering, you will find the appropriate version of the Arm architecture that matches the binary. Therefore, it is important to know the terminology related to the Arm processor and its associated architecture version.

Now that you understand the primary concepts of the Arm architecture and Cortex Arm processors, let's explore registers, which are a key feature in Armv8-A.

Registers

Whenever you read an assembly code, you will notice that there are registers that are used as the input or output of instructions. If you do not understand how registers are used, it is difficult to analyze the assembly routine. Therefore, it is important to learn how the registers are used.

In this section, you will learn how registers in Armv8-A are organized, as follows:

- General-purpose registers
- Special registers
- System registers

At the end of this section, you will learn about the key set of registers when performing reverse engineering. First, let's explore the general-purpose registers.

General-purpose registers

When you begin to learn about registers, the first registers you'll encounter are the **general-purpose registers**. Let's look at the list of general-purpose registers in Armv8-A and learn how each register is used:

X0	X4	X8	X12	X16	X20	X24	X28
X1	X5	X9	X13	X17	X21	X25	X29
X2	X6	X10	X14	X18	X22	X26	X30
X3	X7	X11	X15	X19	X23	X27	

Figure 1.2: General-purpose registers

General-purpose registers in the Armv8-A architecture are shown in *Figure 1.2*. The name of a general-purpose register consists of an X character and a number, such as X0, X1, and X29.

When you analyze assembly instructions, you should examine the registers, since general-purpose registers store the input and output values of assembly instructions. In theory, general-purpose registers are similar to local variables in a function.

You can also view general-purpose registers using various debugging tools. Here are the general-purpose registers shown in the TRACE32 program; these are commonly used in practical development:

N N	X0	0	X16	10	S	Stack	
Z _	X1	0A	X17	1	SP→	FFFFFFC010053BD0
C C	X2	FFFFFFC0	X18	10	+08	FFFFFFC01067E110
V _	X3	FFFFFFFF	X19	0	+10	0000000000000000
	X4	FFFFFFC011132A808	X20	FFFFFF8967F6E400	+18	FFFFFF8967F6E410
	X5	1	X21	FFFFFFEA	+20	FFFFFFC01129B078
	X6	FFFFFFC011327000	X22	FFFFFF89684E0000	+28	0000000000000000
	X7	01FC	X23	FFFFFFC010BA2420	+30	FFFFFFC01129B078
	X8	3	X24	FFFFFFC010BA2470	+38	0000000000000000
	X9	0	X25	FFFFFFC010F868D0	+40	FFFFFFC010053BD0
	X10	5D31202020203A30	X26	FFFFFFC0110220B0	+48	736B003406956500
	X11	205D4F4950475B20	X27	FFFFFFC010FA0478	+50	FFFFFFC010053C00
	X12	675F6E6F6D6D6F63	X28	0	+58	FFFFFFC01067BAAC
I ▪	X13	705F6C6172656E65	X29	FFFFFFC010053B80	+60	FFFFFF8967F6E410
F ▪	X14	202C2928656262F72	X30	FFFFFFC0106B3C6C	+68	FFFFFFC0115B34B8
	X15	FFFFFF89684E0510	PC	FFFFFFC0106B3C7C	+70	0000000000000000
					+78	FFFFFFC0115B34B8
	SP	FFFFFFC010053B80	CPSR	A0C00005	+80	FFFFFFC010053C40
EL1h	ELR	0			+88	FFFFFFC01067BE84
nsec	SPSR	10			+90	FFFFFF8967F6E410

Figure 1.3: General-purpose registers

You can see registers from X0 to X30. These are the general-purpose registers defined by the Armv8-A architecture. Any of these general-purpose registers can be used to hold the temporal data when running instructions. However, some specific registers—such as X0 to X7 and X30—are commonly used to control the execution flow of a program.

If you look in the assembly code, you may observe a W0 register rather than X0. When software reads from the W0 register, it can access the lower 32 bits of the corresponding X0 register.

X0 (W0) is any of the general-purpose registers. When applying this example to other general-purpose registers, we can say that reading from Wn is identical to accessing the lower 32 bits of the corresponding Xn register, where the value of n ranges from 0 to 31, as shown in *Figure 1.4*:

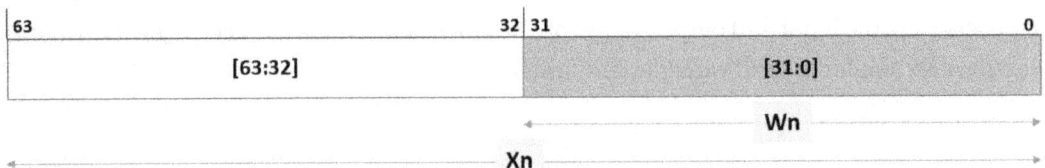

63	32	31	0
[63:32]		[31:0]	
		← Wn →	
← Xn →			

Figure 1.4: Format of the Xn and Wn registers

If the software writes data to W0, you will see that bits [31:0] of the X0 register are updated. This is because W0 represents the lower 32 bits of the X0 register.

Now that you understand the general-purpose registers in Armv8-A, let's learn about the special registers.

Special registers

Armv8-A defines special registers that manage the execution flow of a process. For example, when a subroutine call is made, the SP_ELx register is updated to hold the stack address of the process. The ELR_ELx register is updated when an exception occurs:

XZR/WZR				Zero register
PC				Program Counter
SP_EL0	SP_EL1	SP_EL2	SP_EL3	Stack pointer
	SPSR_EL1	SPSR_EL2	SPSR_EL3	Program Status register
	ELR_EL1	ELR_EL2	ELR_EL3	Exception link register
EL0	EL1	EL2	EL3	

Figure 1.5: A list of special registers in Armv8-A

From the list of special registers, let's learn about the SP_ELx register.

SP_ELx

The SP_ELx registers (e.g., SP_EL0, SP_EL1, SP_EL2, and SP_EL3) are stack pointer registers used at each exception level. SP_ELx is a combination of SP (which stands for *stack pointer*) and ELx (which stands for *exception level*). In this name, ELx is the suffix and shows the exception level, such as EL0, EL1, EL2, or EL3. For more details, please see the *Exception levels* section.

For example, SP_EL0 points to the top of the stack address of a process running at EL0 (execution level 0). SP_EL1 points to the top of the stack of a process running at EL1 (exception level 1).

Armv8-A provides two options to set up stack pointers:

- Each exception level has its own stack pointer, denoted as SP_EL0, SP_EL1, SP_EL2, and SP_EL3. Modern operating systems such as the Linux kernel and Xen hypervisor use this option.
- Share a stack pointer for all exception levels.

Remember that modern operating systems such as the Linux kernel are run with the first option.

ELR_ELx

Let's take a look at the ELR_ELx register. ELR_ELx stands for *exception link register*. It stores the address to return to after an exception is handled. Typically, the ELR_ELx register is updated to hold the return address at the time the exception is generated.

Let's look at an example. When an exception is taken to EL1, ELR_EL1 stores the return address where the exception occurs. Once the exception handling routine is complete, the process refers to ELR_EL1 to return to the address where the exception occurred.

What happens when the exception is taken to EL2? Likewise, ELR_EL2 stores the address at the time an exception occurs, where ELR_EL2 is used to perform the exception return. Remember that many software engineers refer to the ELR_ELx register to examine the return address for debugging purposes as well as for reverse engineering.

PC

The **Program Counter (PC)** register contains the address of the instruction currently being executed by the processor. In Armv8-A, PC is defined as a special register. It cannot be modified by running specific instructions such as ADD or SUB. The reason is that if attackers modify the PC register using arithmetic instructions, it can be used in a harmful way from a security point of view.

PC can be updated in the following scenarios:

- After an assembly instruction is executed on the PC register, PC automatically increments to point to the next instruction.
- When the branch instruction (e.g., BL or BLR) is performed, PC is set to the address specified by the branch instruction. Usually, the branch instruction (e.g., BL or BLR) is used during function calls.
- When an exception occurs, PC jumps to the exception vector address for the corresponding exception.
- When the RET instruction is executed, the value in X30 is moved to PC.

When performing reverse engineering, identifying the execution flow of a process often involves examining registers such as SP_ELx, ELR_ELx, and PC. So, understanding the special register is essential.

Program status registers

Armv8-A offers program status registers, including the **Processor State (PSTATE)** and the **Saved Program Status Register (SPSR_ELx)**. Now, let's understand the PSTATE and SPSR_ELx registers and see how these registers are used.

PSTATE

Armv8-A provides PSTATE, which is similar to CPSR in Armv7-A. PSTATE has a similar bit assignment map to CPSR.

> **Note**
>
> If you're familiar with the Armv7-A architecture, you may recognize the **Current Program Status Register (CPSR)**, where CPSR consists of processor mode, exception mask bit, and conditional flags.

If you glance at PSTATE, you may assume that it is a register, but this is not true. The Arm reference document does not specify PSTATE as a register. Instead, it describes PSTATE as an abstraction that provides the processor state. PSTATE cannot be directly written using a single assembly instruction. Instead, it provides several system registers that allow indirect access to PSTATE.

Let's take a look at bit flags for PSTATE:

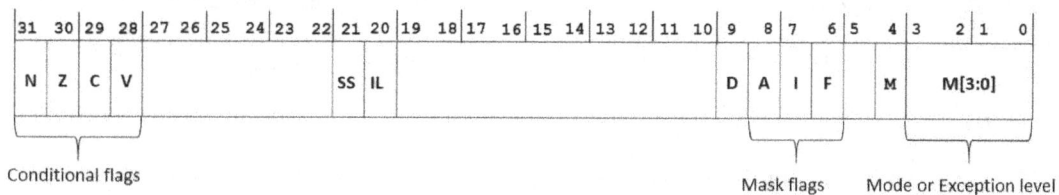

31	30	29	28	27 26	25 24	23 22	21 20	19 18	17 16	15 14	13 12	11 10	9	8	7	6 5	4	3	2 1 0
N	Z	C	V				SS IL						D	A	I	F		M	M[3:0]

Conditional flags   Mask flags   Mode or Exception level

Figure 1.6: Bit flags for PSTATE

As seen in *Figure 1.6*, PSTATE flags include conditional flags, mask flags, and mode or exception levels.

Let's first take a look at **conditional flags**. The meanings of the conditional flags are as follows:

- N: The arithmetic operation yielded a negative result
- Z: The arithmetic operation yielded a zero
- C: The arithmetic operation yielded carry
- V: The arithmetic operation yielded a signed overflow

When a comparison instruction is executed, the result is updated to conditional flags. The value of the conditional flag may affect the execution of the next conditional branch instruction. It is necessary to check condition flags because they are associated with the control flow of the assembly routine.

The **mask flag** is a bit flag that allows enabling or disabling exceptions as follows:

- D, bit [9]: Debug exception mask bits
- A, bit [8]: Asynchronous exception mask bits
- I, bit [7]: **Interrupt Request (IRQ)** mask bits
- F, bit [6]: **Fast Interrupt Request (FIQ)** mask bits

IRQ is a signal from peripherals that notify it of an event that needs immediate attention. FIQ is a type of IRQ with higher priority, used for urgent or time-critical events.

The mask bits can be denoted as PSTATE.<D,A,I,F>, which can be used as follows:

```
PSTATE.<D,A,I,F> = '1111';
```

The preceding sudo code reveals that it will be masking (disabling) all of the exception setting bits.

> **Note**
>
> What does it mean when a bit is being masked? You can think of *being masked* as *being disabled temporarily*. The mask bits can be set to either 0 or 1.
>
> 0 means the exception is not masked (not disabled).
>
> 1 means the exception is masked (disabled).

M[3:0] stores a bit that indicates the current exception level. The M[3:0] bits of PSTATE can be only accessed through the CurrentEL system register.

Once you are familiar with PSTATE, you may look into instructions to monitor the value of PSTATE. Keep in mind that you cannot find any instruction that accesses PSTATE directly.

SPSR_ELx

As the name of this register implies, SPSR_ELx is used to save the value of PSTATE before the exception is taken. Since SPSR_ELx is designed to hold the value of PSTATE, the bit flag of SPSR_ELx is identical to that of PSTATE.

The SPSR_ELx register is accessed especially in the context of exception handling. When an exception occurs, the corresponding exception handler is called. Generally, it reads the value of SPSR_ELx to identify PSTATE before the exception is taken.

You will find more material on how SPSR_ELx is used in exceptions in the *Exceptions* section of this chapter.

System registers

When you hear the term *system registers*, you may wonder about the difference between system registers and general-purpose registers. As discussed earlier in this chapter, general-purpose registers are used as input or output when executing assembly instructions. System registers, on the other hand, are only accessible when you are setting up the system configuration.

Armv8-A defines a system register to provide an interface for system configuration such as MMU, IRQ, cache, and trap handling. When configuring the system register, you should consider the following:

- The suffix of the system register tells us the lowest (minimum) exception level.
- The system register can be accessed using the MSR and MRS instructions. These are explained in the next subsection.

Since the system register name ends with the lowest exception level, we need to explore the lowest exception.

Lowest exception levels

When you look at the names of the system registers, you'll see a suffix that indicates the access level. TTBR0_EL1 is TTBR0 followed by the suffix EL1.

Let's consider the TTBR0_EL1 register as another example. With EL1 as the suffix, you might assume that only EL1 can access TTBR0_EL1. However, this assumption is wrong.

Figure 1.7 shows the lowest exception level that can access TTBR0_EL1.

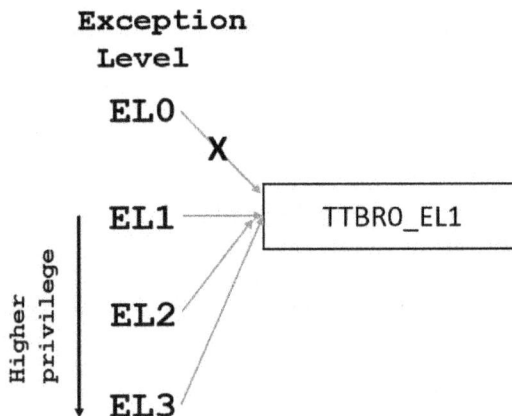

Figure 1.7: The lowest exception level that can access TTBR0_EL1

As seen in *Figure 1.7*, EL1, EL2, and EL3 are allowed to access TTBR0_EL1.

While EL1 appears to be the lowest exception level that can access TTBR0_EL1, it's important to note that this register can also be accessed from higher exception levels such as EL2 and EL3.

What happens when TTBR0_EL1 is accessed from EL0? The Arm processor throws a synchronous exception, which is considered a privilege violation because the lowest exception level for accessing TTBR0_EL1 is EL1. Remember that EL1 has a higher privilege level than EL0.

The following table shows key system registers defined in the Armv8-A architecture:

Register	Full name	Description
SCTLR_ELx	System Control Register	Controls key features of the memory system such as MMUs, caches, and alignment checks
ACTLR_ELx	Auxiliary Control Register	Manages various auxiliary functions and features
TTBR0_ELx	Translation Table Base Register 0	Holds the base address of the first-level page table
SCR_EL3	Secure Configuration Register	Holds secure state and controls the operation of trap handling at EL3

HCR_EL2	Hypervisor Configuration Register	Controls the operation of virtualization and trap handling at EL2
MIDR_ELx	Main ID Register	Provides information about the processor's main ID and revision
MPIDR_EL1	Multiprocessor Affinity Register	Provides configuration associated with the affinity of the processor
CTR_EL0	Cache Type Register	Provides information about the configuration of the cache

Table 1.2: A list of system registers that are commonly used in practical development

How to access the system register

If you consider reading or writing system registers, you might think of LDR or STR instructions. System registers are only accessible using specific instructions such as MSR and MRS.

Let's take a look at the following code to see how MSR and MRS instructions are executed:

```
01 MRS X0, TTBR1_EL1
02 MSR TTBR1_EL1, X0
```

We can analyze the preceding assembly code as follows:

- Line 01 stores the value of the TTBR1_EL1 register into the X0 register
- Line 02 stores the value of the X0 register in the TTBR1_EL1 register

> **Note**
>
> In general, primary system registers (e.g., VBAR_EL1) are configured at boot time. Some system registers can be updated during runtime. When writing a specific value to a system register, you need to consider using a barrier right after this operation. This is because, after a system register is configured, the result must be synchronized across all CPU cores. The barrier ensures this synchronization.

Key registers related to reverse engineering

Now that you understand the registers that Armv8-A supports, let's discuss key registers that are examined during reverse engineering. When performing reverse engineering, it is highly recommended that you do the following:

- Check the X30 register because X30 holds the return address
- Check the X0 to X7 registers as these registers are used to pass parameters to the function
- Examine SP_ELx, which points to the stack pointer for the process in each exception level

As mentioned in this section, you will encounter registers in any instructions when performing reverse engineering. Therefore, it is important to understand how registers are utilized during program execution. Some registers are utilized when function calls are made, which will be covered in the next section.

Procedure Call Standard for the Arm Architecture (AAPCS)

Program code consists of multiple functions. On your system, a lot of libraries generated by different compilers are integrated to run multiple functions for the application as well as drivers.

This section covers AAPCS, which specifies the standard across function calls.

Background

Let's begin this section by taking a look at the following example code:

```
01 int add_func(int x, int y)
02 {
03     int result = x + y;
04     printf("x:%d, y:%d \n", x, y);
05
06     return result;
07 }
```

If you write the preceding add_func function, you may expect it to execute as follows:

- Any function can call the add_func function
- After the task of the add_func function is completed, it returns to the instruction that called the add_func function

Also, the add_func function can be called from the assembly routine. For this, we need a standard to manage interactions between functions such as the following:

- How a function passes arguments to another function
- How the return is made to the instruction after the calling point

These standards are called calling conventions supported by different CPU architectures, including Armv7-A, Armv8-A, and RISC-V. In this section, let's explore the AAPCS.

Introduction to AAPCS

The Arm architecture supports AAPCS as part of the ABI. AAPCS defines the way to interact between subroutines, which is considered an important aspect when performing reverse engineering and debugging over binary. Arm defined the AAPCS using other terms, as follows:

- Arm Procedure Call Standard (APCS)
- Thumb Procedure Call Standard (TPCS)
- Arm-Thumb Procedure Call Standard (ATPCS)

If you refer to the Arm reference document in the previous version, you can find the preceding terms, which have the same meaning.

Register used for AAPCS

As discussed in the previous section, we know that general-purpose registers are used to store input or output to instructions. There are specific general-purpose registers across function calls. AAPCS defines the standard to save the arguments passing to functions, as seen here:

- X0~X7: Argument registers
- X0: Return register

First, let's take a look at the following figure to see how arguments are passed to registers:

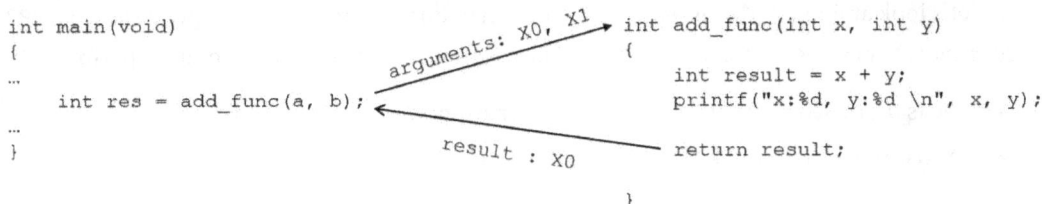

```
int main(void)                              arguments: X0, X1    int add_func(int x, int y)
{                                                                {
...                                                                  int result = x + y;
    int res = add_func(a, b);                                        printf("x:%d, y:%d \n", x, y);
...                              result : X0                         return result;
}                                                                }
```

Figure 1.8: How arguments are passed to registers

Figure 1.8 shows that the call to the add_func function is made inside the main function. The add_func function takes two parameters as an integer type described as follows:

- The first parameter is saved into X0.
- The second parameter is saved into X1.

In *Figure 1.8*, you can also see the return result; statement, which is responsible for returning the result of the function. The value of the result is saved into the X0 register because the X0 register is the return register.

In addition, let's explore the instruction associated with AAPCS.

BL instruction

Now, let's take a look at assembly routine by compiling the example code in C:

```
01 0x10000 <main>:
02 {
03 0x10000:    f81e0ffe     str x30, [sp, #-32]!
04     int res =  add_func(x, y);
05 0x10004:    52800061     mov w1, #0x3 // #3
06 0x10008:    52800040     mov w0, #0x2 // #2
07 0x1000c:    97ffffef     bl  0x20000 <add_func>
08 0x10010:    b9001fe0     str w0, [sp, #28]
09     printf("add res = %d \n", res);
```

First, let's examine lines 05 and 06. Before the bl   20000 <add_func> instruction in line 07 is executed, W0 and W1 are updated as 0x2 and 0x3, respectively. Why are these values moved to W0 and W1? Because parameters passed to the function are stored as follows;

- W0: 2 (first parameter)
- W1: 3 (second parameter)

Now, let's look at line 07. The assembly instruction in line 07 consists of BL opcode and 0x20000 <add_func>. When the instruction in line 07 is executed, the following actions are performed:

- PC is branched to the 0x20000 address corresponding to <add_func>
- X30 is updated to hold 0x10010, which is the address to return

Note that the preceding two tasks are performed by Arm hardware simultaneously. If you use GDB or TRACE32 debugger, you will notice how PC and X30 are updated. Since X30 is holding the address to return, its value is pushed into the stack area after the function call is made. If you examine the memory contents of the stack, you will find the data of X30 during this operation.

Note

> **Note**
>
> When performing reverse engineering, many application developers look into the X30 register to check the symbol of the caller function (which calls the current function).

It is time to review the add_func function in the following assembly code to see how the value of X30 is pushed:

```
01 0x20000 <add_func>:
02 {
03 0x20000:    a9bf7bf3    stp x19, x30, [sp, #-16]!
04     int result = x + y;
05 0x20004:    0b010013    add w19, w0, w1
06     printf("result: %d\n", result);
07 0x20008:    2a1303e1    mov w1, w19
08 0x2000c:    f0003ea0    adrp    x0, 188000
09 0x20010:    91182000    add x0, x0, #0x608
10 0x20014:    97ed3258    bl  1fe948 <printf>
11 }
12 0x20018:    2a1303e0    mov w0, w19
13 0x2001c:    a8c17bf3    ldp x19, x30, [sp], #16
14 0x20020:    d65f03c0    ret
```

Let's take a look at line 03 first. When stp x19, x30, [sp, #-16]! is executed, it will perform the following tasks:

- Push the value of x19 and x30 onto the stack.
- The SP register is decremented by 0x10 because the stack grows from higher to lower addresses.

After the add_func function completes its task, it will pull the return address off the stack. The assembly instruction on line 13 performs this operation by loading the data into x19 and x30.

> **Note**
>
> From the preceding example code, you can notice that data of X30 is pushed into the stack area. This means that stack memory should be already reserved before a function call is made. Note that the core job of the start-up code is to set up SP per each exception level.

Let's summarize what we have learned so far by looking at the following figure:

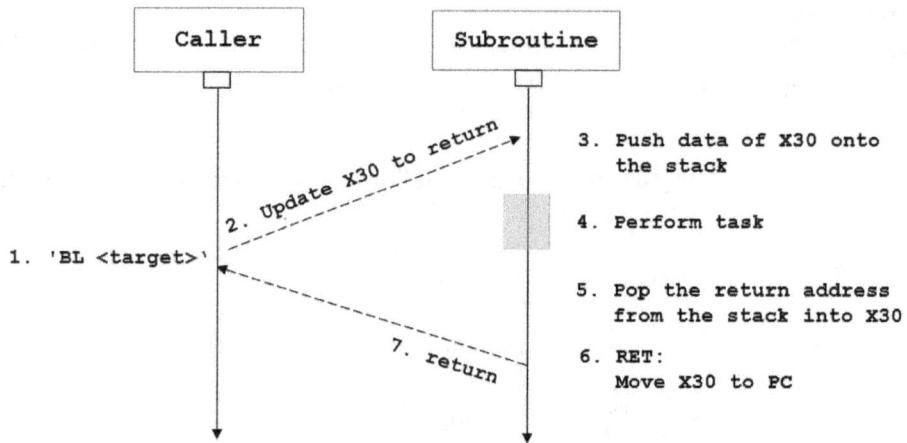

Figure 1.9: How the subroutine is called and returned

The preceding figure highlights the example code we have analyzed so far:

1. The program branches to <target>, where <target> is the starting address of the subroutine.
2. While branching to <target>, the return address is updated to X30.
3. The data of X30 is pushed onto the stack where the first instruction of the subroutine performs the push operation.
4. The given task is performed inside the function.
5. When the function is about to exit, it will pop the data in X30 from the stack.
6. The value of X30 is moved to PC by performing the RET instruction.
7. Return to the address.

This section covered the principles of AAPCS, which are the standards for subroutine and function calls. Understanding AAPCS is important during reverse engineering because we can predict the control flow without source code.

Exception levels

One of the most important features of Armv8-A is **exception levels** (**ELs**), as exception handling and registers are organized based on exception level.

Exception levels and privilege levels

What is an exception level? When you look into the Linux kernel or RTOS code, you will notice that several system registers are suffixed with EL1 or EL2:

```
01 MSR TTBR0_EL1, X1
02 ADD X0, X0, #0x800
03 MSR VBAR_EL2, X1
```

The preceding example shows that TTBR0_EL1 is suffixed with EL1 in line 01, and VBAR_EL2 is suffixed with EL2 in line 03.

In practice, an exception level is written as ELn or ELx, where the n or x characters are suffixed to EL and the value of n or x can range from 0 to 3. EL0 is called *exception level zero* and EL1 is called *exception level one*.

When you hear about exception levels for the first time, you may assume the exception level is related to the exception, as the name implies. However, exception levels correspond to privilege levels rather than exceptions.

Armv8-A defines exception levels, which correspond to privilege levels. As stated earlier, exception levels range between EL0 and EL3. This integer value of the exception level is equivalent to the **Privilege Level (PL)**. EL0 is equivalent to PL0, and EL1 is equivalent to PL1.

EL0 with PL0

First, let's understand EL0. Code running at EL0 is usually a user application with an unprivileged level or PL0. The software running at EL0 has the following limitations:

- EL0 cannot configure the interrupt, MMU, or cache.
- EL0 cannot access the address in kernel space.
- EL0 cannot set up system registers.

If software running at EL0 accesses hardware resources in the preceding examples, the exception occurs.

What happens if the software running at EL0 accesses the resources of EL1? The Arm core generates an exception because EL0 has a lower privilege level than EL1, which is considered a privilege violation. On the other hand, software at EL1 can access the resources of EL0 because EL1 has higher privilege levels than EL0.

EL1 with PL1

EL1 corresponds to PL1 and has higher privileges than EL0. Software running at EL1 (PL1) can configure hardware resources such as interrupts, the MMU, and caches. Typically, the Linux kernel or an RTOS kernel runs at EL1 because it has the privilege level to control hardware resources.

EL2 with PL2

Like EL1, EL2 corresponds to PL2. Usually, the hypervisor runs at EL2 to control multiple guest operating systems running at EL1 by managing the system resources of the guest operating systems. Since EL2 has a higher privilege level than EL0 or EL1, it can directly access the code and data running at EL0 or EL1.

The specification document also states that *"EL0 and EL1 are required to be implemented, while the implementation of EL2 and EL3 is optional."*

> **Note**
>
> Please refer to this link to find documentation—*Arm Architecture Reference Manual Armv8-A, for A-profile architecture, D1.1 Exception levels*: https://developer.arm. com/documentation/ddi0487/gb.

How can we implement EL2 or EL3? In order to implement EL2 or EL3, the following actions should be taken:

- Configure SP_EL2 or SP_EL3
- Set up VBAR_EL2 or VBAR_EL3
- Set up HCR_EL2 or SCR_EL3

Since the key feature of each exception level is exception handling and the use of SP_ELx, the preceding setup should be done.

EL3 with PL3

Since EL3 has the highest privilege level in the system, software running at EL3 can manipulate all of the resources at EL2, EL1, and EL0.

Note

During the booting process on Arm systems, the initial exception level is typically set to EL3. At EL3, secure boot and system initialization are performed. This includes setting up secure memory regions, configuring system registers, and enabling secure settings.

After initializing critical system components and security features at EL3, control is often transferred to EL2. Once the configuration is completed at EL2, EL2 is switched to EL1 during boot progress.

In general, the typical usage model of exception levels is as follows:

- EL0: User application
- EL1: Linux or RTOS kernel
- EL2: Hypervisor
- EL3: Secure monitor

The following diagram shows how different software runs at each exception level:

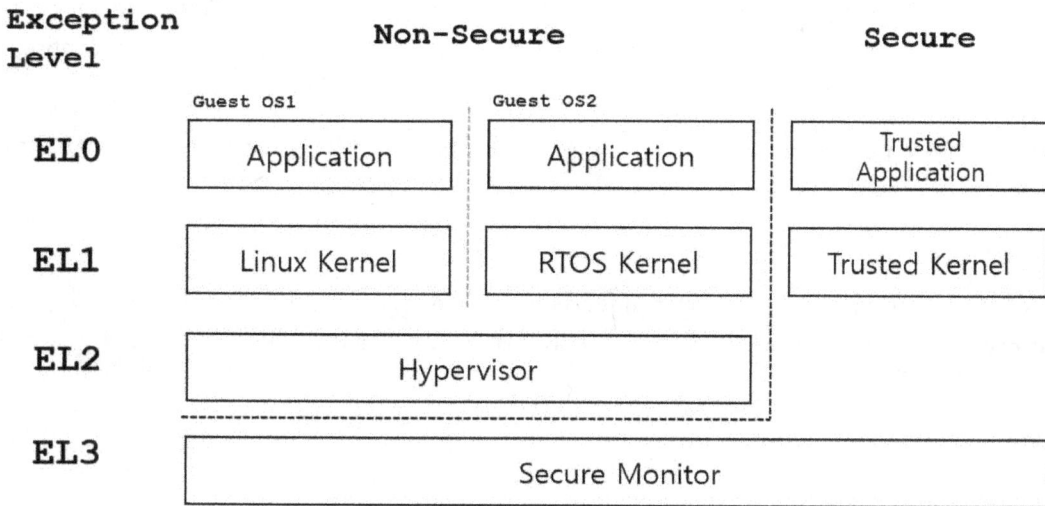

Figure 1.10: System architecture based on exception level

Let's look at how software is running at each exception level:

- **EL0—User application:** User applications run at EL0 to ensure system stability and security by restricting access to hardware configurations such as interrupts, MMU, and cache. If a user application attempts to access hardware resources, it is designed to request service by running the SVC instruction. After the SVC instruction is executed, the exception level switches from EL0 to EL1. When the SVC instruction is executed in EL0, it causes a synchronous exception. The operating system kernel handles the system calls to perform the necessary operations. Then, it returns control to the user-level application in EL0 once the system call has been serviced.

- **EL1—Linux or RTOS kernel:** Since the core job of the Linux kernel is to manage hardware resources such as MMU, interrupt, cache, and peripherals, the Linux kernel or RTOS kernel can run at EL1, where EL1 corresponds to PL1.

- **EL2—Hypervisor:** The hypervisor runs at EL2, where the hypervisor is designed to control two or more guest operating systems by managing the resources (VCPUs, virtual interrupts, etc.). The hypervisor can handle requests from a guest operating system. When a guest operating system attempts to request service, the HVC instruction is executed.

- **EL3—Secure monitor:** EL3 runs with the highest privilege level. This allows the software at EL3 to configure important features of the system, such as registers, memory, and cache. The first bootloader, which usually runs during the boot process, runs at EL3 to configure important features of the system, as previously mentioned.

In practice, as modern operating systems follow this usage model, it is necessary to learn how software is running at EL0~EL3.

Instructions to switch exception levels

To understand the nature of exception levels, it is more important to know how the exception level is changed by running specific instructions such as SVC, HVC, and SMC:

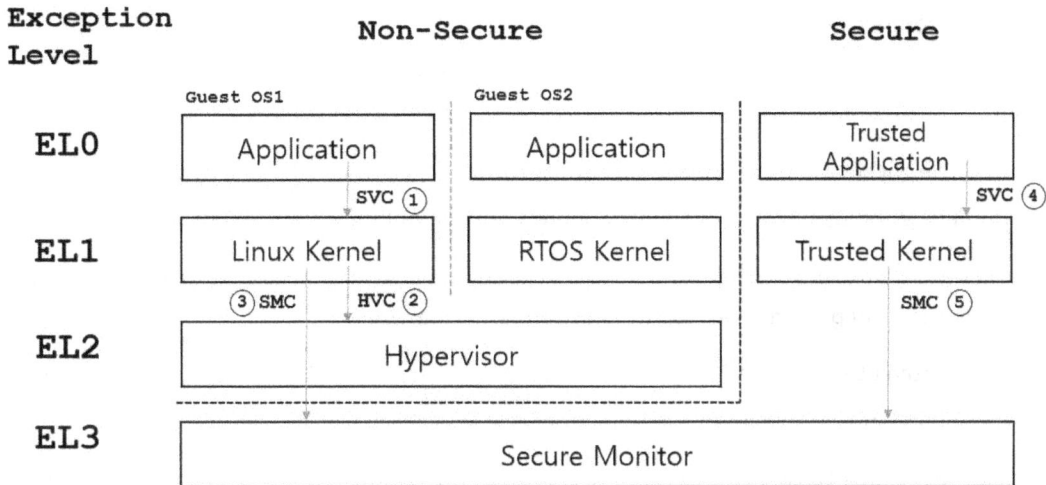

Figure 1.11: How the exception level is switched

Let's dive more into how exception levels can be switched by running instructions.

SVC instruction

A user application at EL0 runs at an unprivileged level, which means it is impossible to access hardware resources. For example, it needs an ID for the particular file, named the file descriptor. Also, it needs to find information on the **process ID (PID)**. When software at EL0 attempts to access hardware resources, it can use a system call by calling standard APIs, such as write, read, open, and close. Running the SVC instruction triggers a system call, which is the interface between EL0 and EL1.

Before the SVC instruction is executed, the system call number is stored in the X8 register. After the SVC instruction is executed, the Arm core generates a synchronous exception by branching into the exception vector address. What happens next? The exception handler located at the exception vector address will perform the following tasks;

- Read the value of the X8 register, which holds the system call number.
- Call the corresponding system call handler using the system call number.

The Linux kernel supports more than 400 system call handlers for various types of system calls.

HVC instruction

In the virtualization environment, the guest operating system can request service to the hypervisor in the following cases:

- The guest operating system may notify the current workload of the hypervisor.
- The guest operating system may request critical system information.

For this operation, the HVC instruction needs to be executed. What happens when HVC is executed? The Arm core will perform the following actions simultaneously:

- Switch EL2 from EL1.
- Branch into the exception vector address at EL2.

HVC is used as an interface between EL1 (guest operating system) and EL2 (hypervisor). It is necessary to configure the HCR_EL2 register for this operation.

SMC instruction

Another assembly instruction used to switch exception levels is SMC. When the SMC instruction is executed at EL1, the exception level can be switched.

SMC stands for *secure monitor call*, which is usually used in security extensions. For more details about the SMC instruction, please refer to *Chapter 14* of this book.

How to determine the current exception level

How does software identify the current exception level? You can access the CurrentEL system register using **Move to Register from System (MRS)** instructions. As the name implies, CurrentEL tells you about the current exception level:

```
MRS <Xt>, CurrentEL
```

When the preceding instruction is executed, the value of the CurrentEL register is loaded into a general-purpose register, denoted as <Xt>. The CurrentEL register holds the bit encoding representing the current exception level, as follows:

- EL0: 0b0000
- EL1: 0b0100
- EL2: 0b1000
- EL3: 0b1100

Note that the 0b prefix indicates that the output is in binary format. For example, 0b0100 is 4 in decimal format.

Example routine to read CurrentEL

Attackers often attempt to run malicious code to escalate higher privilege levels. What happens if the hypervisor is running at EL3 rather than EL2? Note that the hypervisor is designed to run at EL2. The attacker can gain unauthorized access to the resources of the system because EL3 has the highest privilege level. The startup code of the Xen hypervisor checks whether the current exception level is EL2, as follows:

```
arch/arm/arm64/head.S
01 check_cpu_mode:
02     PRINT("- Current EL ")
03     mrs     x5, CurrentEL
04     print_reg x5
05     PRINT(" -\r\n")
06
07     /* Are we in EL2 */
08     cmp     x5, #PSR_MODE_EL2t
09     ccmp    x5, #PSR_MODE_EL2h, #0x4, ne
10     b.ne    1f /* No */
11     ret
12 1:
13     /* OK, we're boned. */
14     PRINT("- Xen must be entered in NS EL2 mode -\r\n")
15     PRINT("- Please update the bootloader -\r\n")
16     b       fail
17 ENDPROC(check_cpu_mode)
```

If it is identified that the Xen hypervisor is not running at EL2, it will crash by printing debug information by branching to the fail label.

In this section, you understood the primary concept of exception levels and their usage model. As mentioned, exception levels can be changed by exceptions. Now, let's explore exceptions in the next section.

Exceptions

In general, CPU architecture supports exceptions. For example, intel x86, MIPS, Armv7, and RISC-V define exceptions.

Key principles of exceptions

When the Arm core generates an exception, it will pause the execution of the software and perform the following actions:

- The program counter (PC) is branched into an exception vector address.
- The exception level can be changed.

We can find assembly instructions at the exception vector address. In practice, these instructions are called exception handlers. At the software level, we can say that when an exception occurs, PC jumps to the exception vector address, and the exception handler runs.

Types of exception

Like other CPU architectures, Armv8-A defines exceptions, including synchronous, IRQ, FIQ, and SError exceptions. These four exceptions can be categorized into two types: synchronous exceptions and asynchronous exceptions. A synchronous exception can be generated while the Arm core is running an instruction. A synchronous exception can occur in the following cases:

- When the Arm core is executing an illegal instruction.
- When the Arm core is attempting to access an invalid address.
- When the Arm core is running exception-generating instructions (SVC, HVC, or SMC).

In the case of asynchronous exceptions, IRQ, FIQ, and SError exceptions can be generated by external events. A typical external event is an interrupt triggered by peripheral devices. For example, if you touch the screen of your smartphone, the touch interrupt is triggered from the touch panel.

After the interrupt controller in the system detects a touch interrupt signal, it sends this to the Arm processor. Then, the processor generates an IRQ exception to handle the interrupt.

Types	Exception	Cause of exception
Synchronous	Synchronous	Illegal instruction
		Accessing invalid address
		Exception-generating instruction
		Misaligned stack access
		Unknown reason
Asynchronous	IRQ interrupt	Interrupt (non-secure)
	FIQ interrupt	Interrupt (secure)
	SError	External memory abort

Table 1.3: Types of exception in Armv8-A

Table 1.3 lists the types of exceptions with their causes. Now that you know about the types, let's explore the exception vector table.

Exception vector table

What happens when an exception occurs in the system? The Arm core generates exceptions by performing two tasks, as already mentioned:

- PC is branched into an exception vector address.
- Exception level can be switched (if necessary).

How can we identify the exception vector address? For this, it is necessary to review the exception vector table, which specifies the rules to branch the exception vector address.

Exception taken from	Offset for exception type			
	Synchronous	IRQ or vIRQ	FIQ or vFIQ	SError or vSError
Current exception level with SP_EL0	0x000	0x080	0x100	0x180
Current exception level with SP_ELx, x>0	0x200	0x280	0x300	0x380
Lower exception level, where the implemented level immediately below the target level is using AArch64	0x400	0x480	0x500	0x580
Lower exception level, where the implemented level immediately below the target level is using AArch32	0x600	0x680	0x700	0x780

Table 1.4: Exception vector table in Armv8-A

You can refer to the following link to find the documentation: *Arm Architecture Reference Manual Armv8-A, for A-profile architecture, Table D1-5 Vector offsets from vector table base address*: https://developer.arm.com/documentation/ddi0487/gb.

The preceding table is an exception vector table, which consists of the type of exception and offset. Columns on the right show exceptions defined in Armv8-A, including Synchronous, IRQ, FIQ, and SError exceptions. Each column contains an offset for each exception. Rows on the left indicates information about the exception level where the exception takes place.

Before going into the details of the exception vector table, there is one thing you should know: the exception vector base address. Each exception type has an offset. This offset is added to the base address to calculate the exception vector address.

> Note
>
> In general, the exception vector base address is stored in VBAR_ELx, which the system boots up in the startup code. VBAR_ELx is thought of as an exception vector base address.

How can we find the software routine associated with the exception vector table? If you follow these rules, it is easy to understand the software routine:

- Base address of exception handler = exception vector base address
- Exception handler = instruction at exception vector address

Now that we have explored the basic principle of the exception vector table, let's look at the details of the exception vector table.

Details of exception vector table

In each column, there is a *current exception level*. The current exception level in the exception vector table ranges from EL1 to EL3. This means we can have three different exception vector tables for three exception levels: EL1, EL2, and EL3. If the current exception level is EL1, then we can see the exception vector table as follows:

Exception taken from	Offset for exception type			
	Synchronous	**IRQ**	**FIQ**	**SError**
EL1 with SP_EL0	0x000	0x080	0x100	0x180
EL1	0x200	0x280	0x300	0x380
EL0 (AArch64)	0x400	0x480	0x500	0x580
EL0 (AArch32)	0x600	0x680	0x700	0x780

Table 1.5: Exception vector table when the current exception level is EL1

Now, let's understand the exception vector table, considering that the current exception level is EL1.

EL1 with SP_EL0

The original term of this column is *current exception level with SP_EL0*, which indicates that the stack pointer register (SP_EL0) is shared across all exception levels. Offsets based on this configuration are 0x000, 0x080, 0x100, and 0x180. In this case, PC is branched into an exception vector address based on the following rules:

- synchronous: VBAR_EL1 + 0x000
- IRQ: VBAR_EL1 + 0x080
- FIQ: VBAR_EL1 + 0x100
- SError: VBAR_EL1 + 0x180

Note that modern operating systems such as the Linux kernel or the Xen hypervisor do not support this configuration, where SP_EL0 is shared across exception levels, as the software at each exception level must have its own stack pointer to ensure that it runs in its own execution environment.

EL1 (current EL with SPx)

If the exception can be triggered at EL1, the 0x200, 0x280, 0x300, and 0x380 offsets can be applied. PC is branched into an exception vector address based on the following rules:

- synchronous: VBAR_EL1 + 0x200
- IRQ: VBAR_EL1 + 0x280
- FIQ: VBAR_EL1 + 0x300
- SError: VBAR_EL1 + 0x380

As you may know, the Linux kernel runs at EL1. For example, if a synchronous exception occurs in the Linux kernel, a 0x200 offset can be added to VBAR_EL1. If an interrupt is triggered when the Linux kernel is running, a 0x280 offset is applied.

EL0 (AArch64)

The original term is *lower exception levels*, which can be determined by the current exceptional level. If the current exception level is EL1, a lower exception level could be EL0 based on a 64-bit environment. A branch to an exception vector address is made based on the following rules:

- Synchronous: VBAR_EL1 + 0x400
- IRQ: VBAR_EL1 + 0x480
- FIQ: VBAR_EL1 + 0x500
- SError: VBAR_EL1 + 0x580

For example, if a synchronous exception occurs at EL0(AArch64) where the user application runs, the core branches into the exception vector address based on VBAR_EL1 + 0x400.

> **Note**
>
> Another important point to remember is that when an exception is triggered at EL0, the exception level switches from EL0 to EL1.

EL0 (AArch32)

This configuration offers compatibility for user applications running in a 32-bit environment at EL0. If an exception occurs when the user application runs at EL0 in a 32-bit environment, PC is branched into the following exception vector address:

- Synchronous: VBAR_EL1 + 0x600
- IRQ: VBAR_EL1 + 0x680
- FIQ: VBAR_EL1 + 0x700
- SError: VBAR_EL1 + 0x780

> **Note**
>
> Part of this section covered the exception vector table based on the assumption that the current exception level is EL1. If you specify the current exception level as EL2 or EL3, then you can have another separate exception vector table. Covering this topic is beyond the scope of this book since it requires additional background knowledge such as virtualization and security extensions.

How an exception is generated with the big picture

Figure 1.12 shows each component when an exception is generated with the big picture:

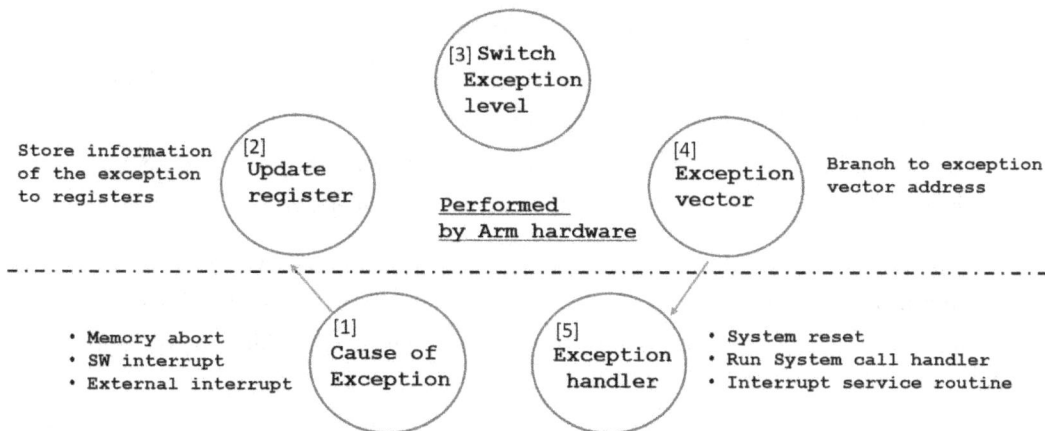

Figure 1.12: How an exception is generated with the big picture

As seen in *Figure 1.12*, there are five steps when generating exceptions, which can be divided into two parts:

- **Lower part (first and fifth steps):** Step 1 shows the cause of the exception, such as a memory abort or an external interrupt. Step 5 explains how the exception is handled.

- **Upper part (second to fourth steps):** These steps indicate how the exception is generated by the Arm core at the hardware level.

Let's look at each component step by step.

Step 1: Indicating the cause of exception

Let's take a look at the first step indicating the cause of the exception. Exceptions can be generated for several reasons, listed as follows:

- **Memory aborts:** The Arm core accesses an invalid address (e.g., instruction abort and data abort)

- **Software interrupt:** An SVC or HVC instruction execution

- **External event:** Interrupt request or SError generation

As discussed in the previous section, a synchronous exception is generated while the Arm core is executing an instruction, whereas IRQ, FIQ, and SError exceptions can be triggered by external events such as interrupts or SError generation.

Step 2: Updating registers

In this step, several registers are updated, including SPSR_ELx, ELR_ELx, and ESR_ELx, as follows:

- Store the value of PSTATE in the SPSR_ELx register.
- Update the ELR_ELx register to return after exception handling is complete.
- Update the FAR_ELx register with the address causing the exception.
- Update [31:26] ESR_ELx (*exception syndrome register*) with the bit-encoding representing the exception class, which indicates the cause of the exception.

Note that these registers are only accessible at a specific exception level (ELn). When performing reverse engineering or debugging over kernel binary, it is important to examine registers that are updated during the generation of exceptions. These registers provide valuable information, as follows:

- Exception level at the moment of the exception
- Detailed cause of the exception
- Address when generating the exception

Generally, an exception handler is designed to read the preceding registers to perform exception handling.

Step 3: Switching the exception level

The exception level can switch depending on where the exception occurs:

- If an exception occurs at EL0, it switches to EL1.
- If an exception occurs at EL1, the exception level does not switch.

> **Note**
>
> If an exception occurs at EL1, EL1 is switched to EL2 in the virtualization system. For this, it is necessary to configure HCR_EL2 to support virtualization.

Step 4: Branching to exception vector address

In this step, PC is branched to the exception vector address for the corresponding exception. This address is calculated using the formula VBAR_EL1 + offset, where VBAR_EL1 represents the exception vector base address. As explained in this section, the exception vector table includes both the offsets and types of exceptions.

Note that the second through fourth steps are performed by Arm hardware. The fifth step is performed from a software perspective.

Step 5: Exception handling

When PC is branched to the exception vector address, it fetches and executes the assembly instruction located at that address. This is the behavior that the exception handler is performing from a software point of view. In other words, we can say that the *exception handler is invoked*. Exception handlers can be implemented depending on the type of exception, as follows:

- Synchronous: System reset or terminate process; execute a system call.
- IRQ: Execute an interrupt service routine to handle the interrupt request.
- SError: System reset.

In this section, we explored how exceptions are generated step by step. Let's take a closer look at how the exception handler behaves for each type of exception.

How an exception handler works

After an exception is generated, the corresponding exception handler is called depending on the type of exception. This means that each exception is implemented in different ways. To fully understand how the Arm core generates exceptions, it is important to learn the scenarios in the exception handler for each type. Let's start with a synchronous exception.

Synchronous exception handler

The cause of a synchronous exception can be categorized into two reasons: memory abort and system call via an SVC instruction. If a memory abort occurs, the corresponding exception handler is designed to execute differently, depending on the exception level:

- If memory abort occurs at EL0, it only terminates the user process because it is considered that the software is in a fatal condition.
- If memory abort occurs at EL1, it causes kernel panic because there's no recovery routine from a fatal condition.

In the case of a system call via an SVC instruction, the scenario of an exception handler for a system call is different from memory abort:

1. Read the system call number from the X8 register.
2. Find the corresponding system call handler using the system call number.
3. The system call handler is called.

As discussed in this section, if the system call is invoked, the Arm core generates a synchronous exception. In the case of memory abort, the Arm core also generates a synchronous exception. To identify the cause of the synchronous exception, the exception handler will read the bit-encoding value of `ESR_ELx`.

If you refer to the exception handler in the Linux kernel or Xen hypervisor, you will notice the exception handler routine, which reads the value of `ESR_ELx` to find the cause of the exception.

IRQ and FIQ exception handler

When a peripheral device signals an interrupt, an `IRQ` exception is generated. The exception handler for `IRQ` will execute routines to manage interrupt handling for the corresponding interrupt. The interrupt is used as the interface between the peripheral device and the Arm core. The Arm core will perform an interrupt service routine to react to the interrupt request.

As for `FIQ`, it is used as a fast `IRQ`, which has a higher priority than `IRQ` in Armv7-A. However, in Armv8-A, `FIQ` is used as a secure interrupt rather than a fast `IRQ`. Normally, `FIQ` is under the control of a secure operating system.

SError exception handler

In the case of `SError` generation, an exception handler is designed to reset the entire system because `SError` is generated when the external memory unit detects memory abort, which is considered fatal from the software's perspective. The cause of the `SError` exception is `SError` generation, which is implementation-defined.

> Note
>
> *Implementation-defined* means some of the specifications or features can be implemented by chipset makers in different ways.

Understanding the exception handler for each exception type is important because this routine is an important checkpoint to start debugging or reverse engineering.

Summary

In this chapter, we learned about the basic concepts of the Armv8-A architecture.

First, we studied Arm architecture and the different types of Arm processors. It is important to understand the Arm processor family and the architecture version when selecting the correct debugging tool.

Next, we learned about registers, including general-purpose registers, special registers, and system registers. We also looked at AAPCS, which is a rule that explains how function calls work. Both the registers and AAPCS are important when you do reverse engineering with binary files.

Then, we covered exception levels and exception handling. These help you understand how software architecture works and give you a better overall picture of the system. This chapter has given you the basic background knowledge you need to start reverse engineering.

In the next chapter, we will learn about ELF, which is important when analyzing various binaries in reverse engineering.

Join our community on Discord

Join our community's Discord space for discussions with the authors and other readers: https://packt.link/embeddedsystems

2

Understanding the ELF Binary Format

When you start reverse engineering, you will need to find the appropriate binary files depending on the mission. All binary files, including object files, executable files, and core dump files, are generated in ELF format once the build is complete, so it is necessary to learn about the ELF format. If you are familiar with ELF, you can find binary files that are relevant to the level of reverse engineering. The most important skill set for reverse engineering is to understand how ELF is organized. This chapter covers the format of ELF as follows:

- ELF header
- Section headers
- Sections
- Program headers

First, let's begin with the introduction to ELF with key features.

Technical requirements

All the code examples and binary files for this chapter are available on GitHub at https://github. com/PacktPublishing/Reverse-Engineering-Armv8-A-Systems.

Introduction to ELF

Before introducing the ELF format, it is necessary to discuss the reason why we need to learn about it.

Why do we need to learn about ELF?

If you are a software developer or interested in programming, you can write a piece of code. After writing the code, you compile it. Once the compilation is complete, an ELF file is generated.

When you build your source code using the GCC or Clang compilers, what you get is usually an object file (*.o) and it is in ELF format. ELF files aren't limited to object files. During development, we can have the following ELF files:

- Shared library files and executable files
- Core dump files when a program crashes

When you build software or check a core dump file, you will often see ELF files.

The common question is: why should we learn about the ELF layout? There are three reasons, as follows:

- Understanding the layout of ELF files gives you a strong debugging ability for reverse engineering. This will allow you to analyze and manipulate object files more effectively, as the binary files you will examine for reverse engineering are in the ELF format.

- Learning about ELF will help you understand low-level code better. If you look at the initialization routines in RTOS and the Linux kernel, you will easily notice that they access code blocks in specific sections.

- Understanding the layout and structure of ELF files can be very useful for recovering or repairing corrupted ELF files. When a crash occurs, we can obtain a core dump file or vmcore file from the sample device. But sometimes, these files can become corrupted or damaged. This can be serious, especially when it is hard to reproduce the symptom. By recovering the data in the corrupted ELF file, you can get important information about the executable or object code.

If you are familiar with the ELF format, you will understand how code and data are organized within an object file. You can gain a deeper understanding of how programs are stored and run on a computer system.

Now that we have discussed the motivation for learning about ELF, let's learn about ELF.

What is ELF?

ELF stands for **Executable and Linkable Format**. ELF is simply a file format. It gives a structured way to organize and store executable code, data, and other important information. ELF is a common standard file format that describes the following types of object files:

- Executable files
- Object files
- Shared libraries
- Core dumps

Remember that executable files, object files, and shared libraries are generated once the compilation is complete, and core dumps are generated when a crash occurs.

Let's examine the layout of the ELF file.

Layout of an ELF file

Let's take a look at *Figure 2.1* to learn about the layout of the ELF file.

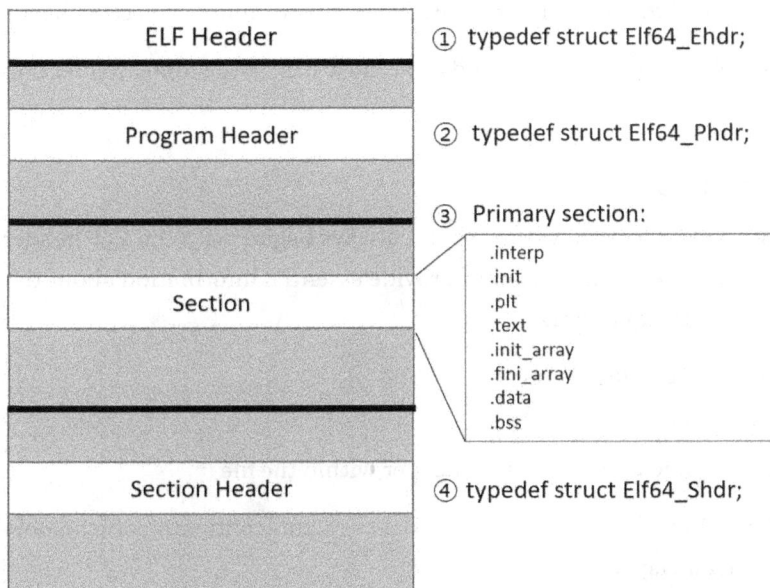

Figure 2.1: Layout of a 64-bit ELF binary

As seen in *Figure 2.1*, an ELF file consists of an ELF header, program header, section, and section header. There are three headers in ELF, which can be listed as follows:

- **ELF header:** Contains information about the type of ELF file. It also provides information about where to find the program header table and the section header table within the ELF file.

- **Program header table:** Describes the segments of the file that need to be loaded into memory. It helps the operating system understand how to load the executable. Additionally, it can be used with various debugging tools.

- **Section header table:** Contains properties about the sections in the file. Sections can contain code, data, and other important components of the program.

Figure 2.1 illustrates other important things to keep in mind regarding the location of each component, as follows:

- The ELF header is always at the beginning of the file.
- The program header table and the section header table do not have fixed positions. Their locations are determined by the ELF header.
- The location of the section is indicated by the corresponding section headers.

We have learned about the ELF layout and its key features. In the following section, we will look at the ELF header.

ELF header

When opening an ELF file, you will see that it always begins with the ELF header. This header contains a structured series of bytes that provide essential information about the ELF file. The ELF header includes the following:

- The file is an ELF file
- The type of ELF
- The offset to find another section header within the file

The ELF header in ELF files serves as the initial segment, containing crucial details about the file's organization and layout.

The ELF header is represented as a C struct called `Elf64_Ehdr` for 64-bit ELF files. The format and contents of this header can be found in the `elf.h` file located in `/usr/include/` or in the ELF specification. You can find this header in the Debian system.

How to identify an ELF header

Let's look at *Figure 2.2*, which shows the layout of an ELF file.

```
typedef struct
{
  unsigned char e_ident[EI_NIDENT];
  Elf64_Half   e_type;
  Elf64_Half   e_machine;
  Elf64_Word   e_version;
  Elf64_Addr   e_entry;
  Elf64_Off    e_phoff;
  Elf64_Off    e_shoff;
  Elf64_Word   e_flags;
  Elf64_Half   e_ehsize;
  Elf64_Half   e_phentsize;
  Elf64_Half   e_phnum;
  Elf64_Half   e_shentsize;
  Elf64_Half   e_shnum;
  Elf64_Half   e_shstrndx;
} Elf64_Ehdr;
```

ELF Header

Program Header

Section

Section Header

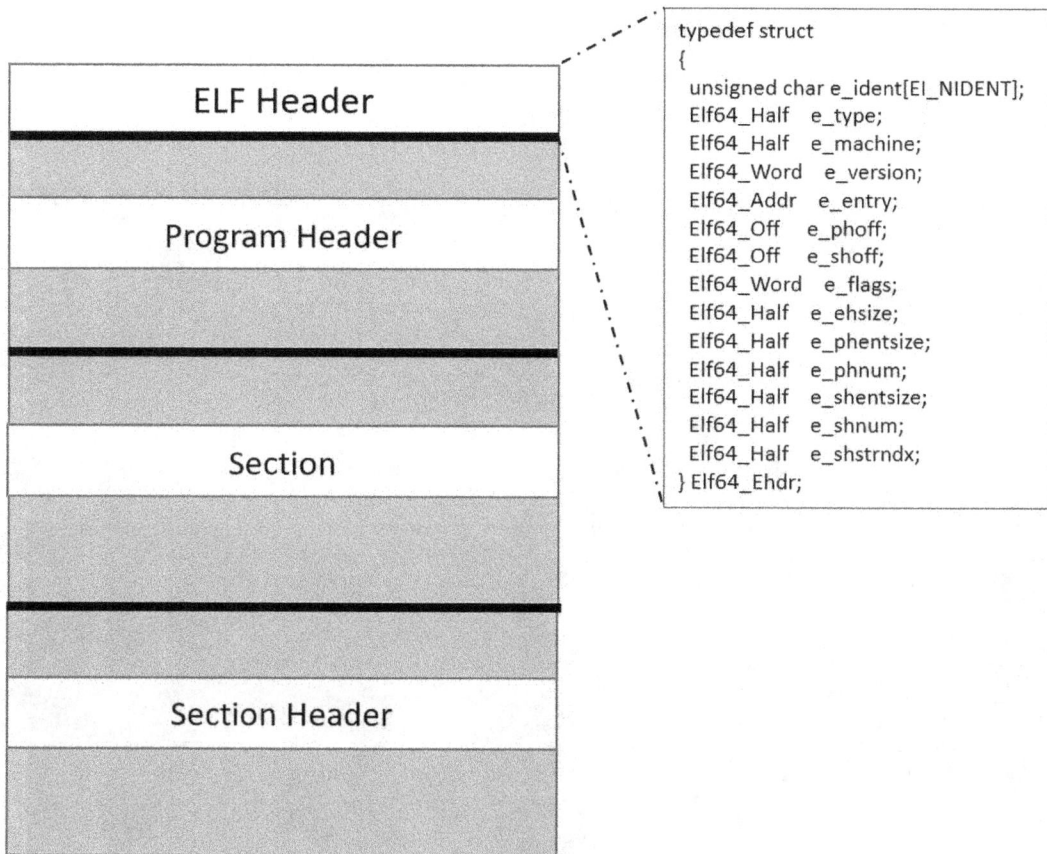

Figure 2.2: Location of the ELF header

As seen in *Figure 2.2*, you can see the position of the ELF header and the data structure that represents the ELF header. *Figure 2.2* provides the following information:

- ELF starts with the ELF header. This is different from the location of the program header and the section header.

- ELF header can be represented by the Elf64_Ehdr structure. The Elf64_Ehdr structure will be explained later in this section.

How to view the ELF header

The easiest way to check the properties of the ELF header is by using the readelf -h <object>
command. Let's run the readelf command with the -h option to find out the type of ELF file,
which is as follows:

```
$ readelf -h trace.so
ELF Header:
  Magic:   7f 45 4c 46 02 01 01 00 00 00 00 00 00 00 00 00
  Class:                             ELF64
  Data:                              2's complement, little endian
  Version:                           1 (current)
  OS/ABI:                            UNIX - System V
  ABI Version:                       0
  Type:                              DYN (Shared object file)
  Machine:                           AArch64
  Version:                           0x1
  Entry point address:               0x0
  Start of program headers:          64 (bytes into file)
  Start of section headers:          129832 (bytes into file)
  Flags:                             0x0
  Size of this header:               64 (bytes)
  Size of program headers:           56 (bytes)
  Number of program headers:         7
  Size of section headers:           64 (bytes)
  Number of section headers:         34
Section header string table index: 33
```

What you can see in the preceding code is human-readable output.

The ELF header is essentially a data structure representing the properties of the ELF file. The
common question is: how can we identify the detailed properties of the ELF header? These details
can be represented using the Elf64_Ehdr structure, which is as follows:

```
typedef struct
{
  unsigned char e_ident[EI_NIDENT];
  Elf64_Half    e_type;
  Elf64_Half    e_machine;
```

```
    Elf64_Word      e_version;
    Elf64_Addr      e_entry;
    Elf64_Off       e_phoff;
    Elf64_Off       e_shoff;
    Elf64_Word      e_flags;
    Elf64_Half      e_ehsize;
    Elf64_Half      e_phentsize;
    Elf64_Half      e_phnum;
    Elf64_Half      e_shentsize;
    Elf64_Half      e_shnum;
    Elf64_Half      e_shstrndx;
} Elf64_Ehdr;
```

Figure 2.3 shows you how the output is displayed via the readelf command.

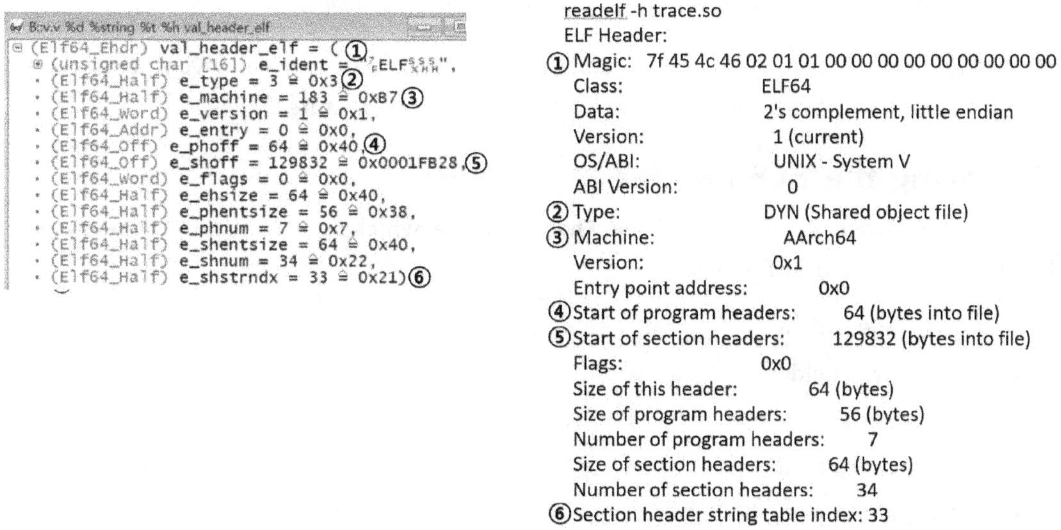

Figure 2.3: The property of the ELF header

The left side of *Figure 2.3* shows the fields of the Elf64_Ehdr structure by the TRACE32 debugger. You can see that each field has its own specific value. The right side of *Figure 2.3* shows the output from the readelf -h trace.so command. There are two important points to note:

- **Left side**: Actual data in the ELF header

- **Right side**: Output via the readelf utility that reads raw data in the section header

The following table outlines the correlation between the output of `readelf` and the element of the `Elf64_Ehdr` structure:

Meaning	The output of readelf	Elf64_Ehdr
Magic value	Magic: 7f 45 4c 46 02 01 01	e_ident = ".ELF..."
Type	DYN (Shared object file)	e_type = 0x3,
Machine	AArch64	e_machine = 0xB7,
Program header offset	64 (bytes into file)	e_phoff = 0x40,
Section header offset	129,832 (bytes into file)	e_shoff = 0x0001FB28,
Section header string table index	33	e_shstrndx = 0x21

Table 2.1: The output of readelf and Elf64_Ehdr

Understanding the meaning of each field in the `Elf64_Ehdr` structure will give you insight into the ELF header. So let's review each field in the `Elf64_Ehdr` structure.

Exploring the ELF header

Now that we have introduced the `Elf64_Ehdr` structure, which represents the ELF header, let's learn about each field, as follows:

- The e_ident field
- The e_type field
- The e_machine field
- The e_entry field
- The e_phoff or e_shoff field
- The e_shstrndx field

First, let's check the e_ident field.

The e_ident field

The e_ident field is an array made of 16 bytes and is the first field in the ELF header. This field shows the overall format of the ELF file. Each byte in the e_ident array has a specific meaning, as follows:

- **Magic number (bytes 1 to 3)**: The first three bytes of the e_ident array contain the magic number, which is considered the ELF file identifier. These bytes are usually set to the values of 0x7F, 0x45, and 0x4C. This means that 0x7F, 0x45, and 0x4C, which are 'E', 'L', and 'F' in ASCII code, respectively, indicate that the file is an ELF file.

- **File class (byte 4)**: Byte 4 of the e_ident array determines the class or architecture of the ELF file. It specifies whether the file is 32-bit (ELFCLASS32) or 64-bit (ELFCLASS64).

> Note
>
> Bytes 5 through 9 to 15 in the e_ident array can hold more information about the properties of ELF, such as little-endian and ABI version. Please understand that this information is out of the scope of this book.

Now that we have looked at the e_ident field that determines the type of ELF file, let's learn about another important field — the e_type field.

The e_type field

The e_type field is used to store the type of ELF. Any ELF file could be one of the following types:

- ET_NONE: Sometimes, the e_type field can be unknown. If the ELF file is corrupted, this field may contain the value of 0x0.

- ET_REL: This indicates a relocatable file. The relocatable file itself is not directly executable: it only contains code and data that can be linked with other relocatable to create an executable or shared object. In general, relocatable object files are examples of **position-independent code (PIC)**. This means they use relative addresses and dynamic relocations to access data and functions.

- ET_EXEC: This denotes an *executable* file type, indicating that it is directly executable by the operating system. In general, these types of files are also considered programs containing binary specific to CPU architecture.

- ET_DYN: This represents a *dynamic type*, indicating the file is either a shared object or a dynamically linked executable. These files can be loaded and linked into a program's process image during program execution. As the name implies, these files contain PIC and data, which allows for dynamic loading during runtime. Unlike standalone executables (ET_EXEC), ET_DYN files are loaded into memory at various addresses each time they run and are shared among multiple processes.

- **ET_CORE**: This indicates a core file type, which represents a core dump. A core dump contains the memory contents at the moment of a crash, such as a segmentation fault. Using the core dump, software developers can debug the issue using tools such as GDB or TRACE32. They can check the memory layout, register values, and stack trace.

The e_type field is used to hold the following values defined as macro:

```
// include/uapi/linux/elf.h
#define ET_NONE    0
#define ET_REL     1
#define ET_EXEC    2
#define ET_DYN     3
#define ET_CORE    4
```

This include/uapi/linux/elf.h header is available in the Linux kernel source tree.

During compilation, we can see that an object file is created. Its ELF type is shown as ET_DYN. Next, let's learn about the e_machine field.

The e_machine field

The e_machine field shows the target architecture that the binary was built for. The operating system runs the binary on the correct hardware using this information. The e_machine field can use different macros to show the architecture type, such as the following:

- **EM_NONE**: Indicates that the machine type is unspecified or unknown
- **EM_X86_64**: Represents the AMD64 (Intel 64) architecture, a 64-bit extension of the x86 architecture
- **EM_ARM**: Specifies the 32-bit Arm architecture
- **EM_AARCH64**: Denotes the Armv8 architecture for 64-bit execution
- **EM_POWERPC**: Represents the PowerPC architecture
- **EM_MIPS**: This indicates the MIPS architecture

The common fields associated with an e_machine field are listed as follows:

```
// /usr/include/linux/elf-em.h
#define EM_ARM          40      /* ARM 32 bit */
#define EM_X86_64       62      /* AMD x86-64 */
#define EM_AARCH64      183     /* ARM 64 bit */
#define EM_RISCV        243     /* RISC-V */
```

There are more macros defined in the header file. If you would like to find more information about machine types, please refer to the /usr/include/linux/elf-em.h header file. This file is available in Debian systems.

The e_entry field

The e_entry field specifies the entry point for program execution, detailing where the program's code begins. Depending on the type of ELF, the e_entry field may have the following entry address:

- ET_EXEC: Indicates the entry point of the starting instruction of the program
- ET_DYN: Specifies the entry point to a function that initializes the library

The e_entry field is important since it tells the operating system where to begin executing the program.

The e_phoff and e_shoff fields

The e_phoff and e_shoff fields indicate the file offsets in bytes to the beginning of the following section headers:

- e_phoff: Offset of the program header table
- e_shoff: Offset of the section header table

While the header of ELF always starts at the beginning of the file, the positions of these tables (section header table and program header table) can vary. An example of these fields is listed as follows:

```
    (unsigned char [16]) e_ident = ".ELF...",
[...]
    (Elf64_Off) e_phoff = 0x40,
    (Elf64_Off) e_shoff = 0x0001FB28,
```

The preceding signature shows that the offset for the program header table is 0x40, and the offset for the section header table is 0x0001FB28. With this information, we can find where the program headers and section headers begin in the file.

Now, let's look at another field: the e_shstrndx field.

The e_shstrndx field

The e_shstrndx field of the Elf64_Ehdr structure tells you about the section header index of the section name. If the e_shstrndx field includes 21, the 21st section header represents the .shstrtab section, which contains the name of the section. When you run the readelf -h <object file> command, the section information is output with the section name by accessing the .shstrtab section.

Another important component in the ELF is the section headers because they provide information about sections that contain the code and data you are analyzing. The section headers and the primary sections will be discussed in the next section.

Section headers

Section headers contain valuable information, especially when performing reverse engineering without access to the source code. By analyzing instructions, you can find function calls and understand routines inside functions. In addition, you can check the values of global variables. All this information is stored in one of the section headers. In this section, we will cover the key elements of section headers, including the layout and primary sections such as the .text, .bss, and .data sections.

Layout of section headers

Before delving into the key elements of section headers, we need to check where the section headers are located in the ELF file. *Figure 2.4* illustrates the position of section headers within the file:

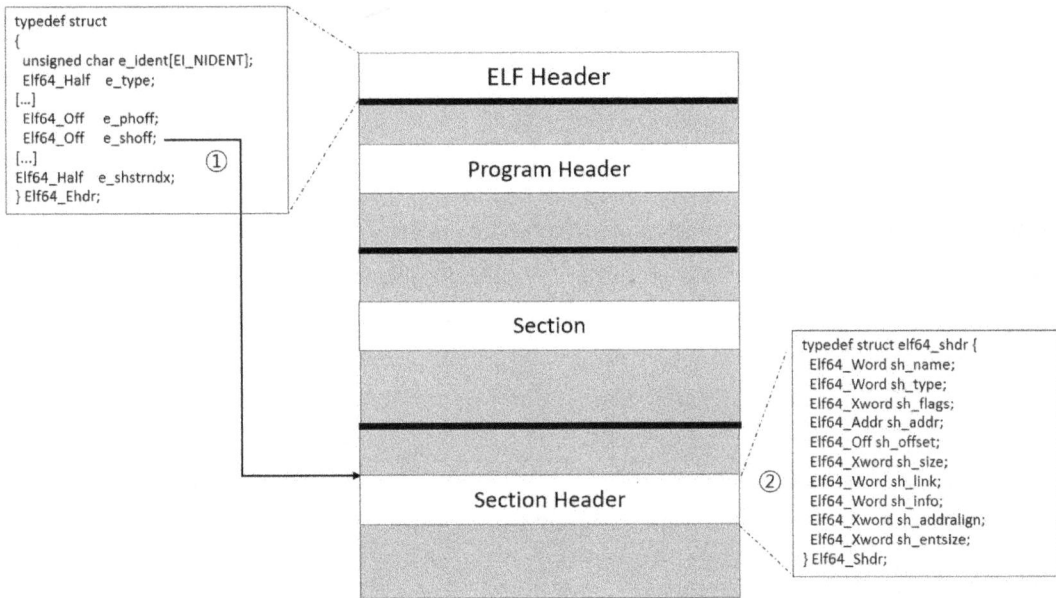

Figure 2.4: Position of section headers in ELF

Figure 2.4 illustrates the position of the section header within ELF. Let's focus on 1 in the figure. The e_shoff field of the Elf64_Ehdr structure contains the offset location of the section header in the ELF. In other words, the arrow in 1 indicates the location of the section header as specified by the e_shoff field of the Elf64_Ehdr structure.

The location of the section header differs in every ELF file, unlike the ELF header. If you would like to know where the section header begins, it is necessary to inspect the e_shoff field in the Elf64_Ehdr structure located in the ELF header.

Each section header represents the properties of the corresponding section using the Elf64_Shdr structure, as follows:

```
// include/uapi/linux/elf.h
typedef struct elf64_shdr {
    Elf64_Word sh_name; /* Section name
    Elf64_Word sh_type; /* Type of section */
    Elf64_Xword sh_flags; // Miscellaneous section attributes
```

```
    Elf64_Addr sh_addr; // Section virtual addr at execution
    Elf64_Off sh_offset; // Section file offset
[...]
    Elf64_Xword sh_entsize; // Entry size
} Elf64_Shdr;
```

Now that we understand the position of section headers, let's identify them. Using the readelf
--wide --sections trace.so command, we can obtain details of the section headers in *Figure 2.5*:

```
There are 34 section headers, starting at offset 0x1fb28:

Section Headers:
  [Nr] Name              Type         Address           Off    Size   ES Flg Lk Inf Al
  [ 0]                   NULL         0000000000000000  000000 000000 00        0   0  0
  [ 1] .note.gnu.build-id NOTE        00000000000001c8  0001c8 000024 00     A  0   0  4
  [ 2] .gnu.hash         GNU_HASH     00000000000001f0  0001f0 000028 00     A  3   0  8
  [ 3] .dynsym           DYNSYM       0000000000000218  000218 000678 18     A  4   3  8
  [...]
  [ 9] .init             PROGBITS     0000000000001490  001490 000018 00     AX 0   0  4
  [10] .plt              PROGBITS     00000000000014b0  0014b0 000360 00     AX 0   0 16
  [11] .text             PROGBITS     0000000000001810  001810 00a3fc 00     AX 0   0 16
  [12] .fini             PROGBITS     000000000000bc0c  00bc0c 000014 00     AX 0   0  4
  [13] .rodata           PROGBITS     000000000000bc20  00bc20 002033 00     A  0   0  8
  [...]
  [16] .init_array       INIT_ARRAY   000000000001fd90  00fd90 000010 08     WA 0   0  8
  [17] .fini_array       FINI_ARRAY   000000000001fda0  00fda0 000010 08     WA 0   0  8
  [18] .dynamic          DYNAMIC      000000000001fdb0  00fdb0 0001c0 10     WA 4   0  8
  [19] .got              PROGBITS     000000000001ff70  00ff70 000078 08     WA 0   0  8
  [20] .got.plt          PROGBITS     000000000001ffe8  00ffe8 0001b8 08     WA 0   0  8
  [21] .data             PROGBITS     00000000000201a0  0101a0 0000f8 00     WA 0   0  8
  [22] .bss              NOBITS       0000000000020298  010298 000ae8 00     WA 0   0  8
  [...]
  [31] .symtab           SYMTAB       0000000000000000  01ccf0 001b90 18        32 228  8
  [32] .strtab           STRTAB       0000000000000000  01e880 001156 00        0   0  1
  [33] .shstrtab         STRTAB       0000000000000000  01f9d6 00014d 00        0   0  1
Key to Flags:
  W (write), A (alloc), X (execute), M (merge), S (strings), I (info),
  L (link order), O (extra OS processing required), G (group), T (TLS),
  C (compressed), x (unknown), o (OS specific), E (exclude),
  D (mbind), p (processor specific)
```

Figure 2.5: Output of the readelf

The output provides the following information about the section headers:

- There are 34 section headers.

- Each section has a unique name. For example, the 11th section is the .text section and
  the 21st section is the .data section. Section names usually start with a dot (.) because
  this is a common convention that comes from Unix assemblers.

- The properties of each section include the type, address, and flags

If you use the readelf --sections <object name> command, it prints the human-readable output. How is this information printed via the readelf --sections <object name> command? *Figure 2.6* illustrates this information.

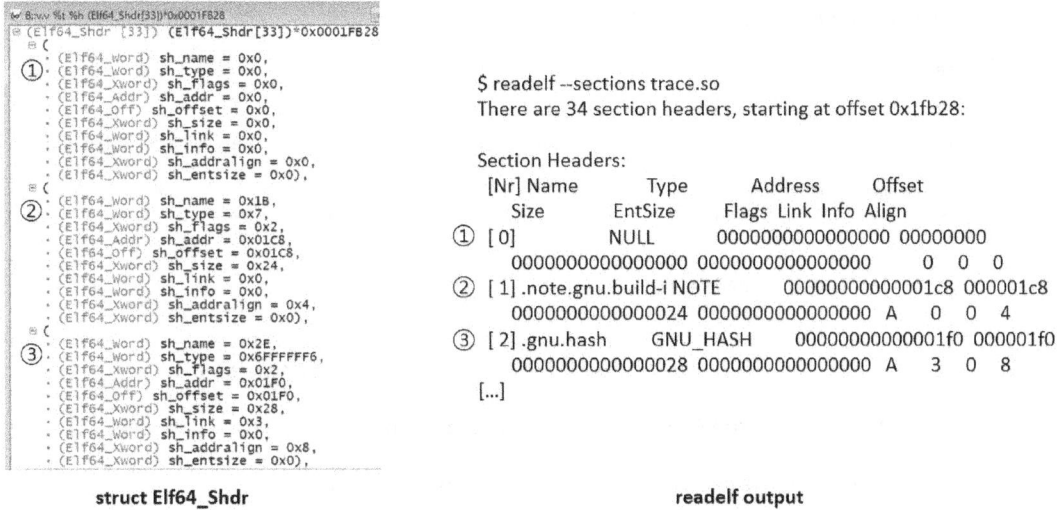

```
$ readelf --sections trace.so
There are 34 section headers, starting at offset 0x1fb28:

Section Headers:
 [Nr] Name           Type          Address          Offset
      Size           EntSize       Flags Link Info Align
① [ 0]               NULL          0000000000000000 00000000
      0000000000000000 0000000000000000     0   0   0
② [ 1] .note.gnu.build-i NOTE         00000000000001c8 000001c8
      0000000000000024 0000000000000000  A   0   0   4
③ [ 2] .gnu.hash      GNU_HASH      00000000000001f0 000001f0
      0000000000000028 0000000000000000  A   3   0   8
      [...]
```

struct Elf64_Shdr   **readelf output**

Figure 2.6: The property of section headers

The left side of *Figure 2.6* shows the fields of the Elf64_Shdr structure, displayed by the TRACE32 debugger. Each field has a specific value. The right side of the figure shows the output of the readelf --sections trace.so command. There are two important points to highlight:

- **Left side**: Actual data in the section header
- **Right side**: Parsed output after the readelf utility reads data in the section header

Understanding the Elf64_Shdr structure will give insight into the program header so that we can review each field in the structure.

Let's explore the details of section headers describing the section information.

Exploring section headers

Among the many fields in the Elf64_Shdr structure, we will focus on the following key fields:

- The sh_name field
- The sh_type field
- The sh_flags field

Let's begin this section with the sh_name field.

The sh_name field

The sh_name field is used to store an index in the string table, which is located in the .shstrtab section. When using readelf --wide --sections trace.so, it will print section header information with section names, as follows:

```
There are 34 section headers, starting at offset 0x1fb28:

Section Headers:
  [Nr] Name              Type      Address            Off    Size   ES Flg Lk Inf Al
  [ 0]                   NULL      0000000000000000   000000 000000 00        0   0  0
  [ 1] .note.gnu.build-id NOTE      00000000000001c8   0001c8 000024 00  A    0   0  4
  [ 2] .gnu.hash         GNU_HASH  00000000000001f0   0001f0 000028 00  A    3   0  8
  [...]
  [ 9] .init             PROGBITS  0000000000001490   001490 000018 00  AX   0   0  4
  [10] .plt              PROGBITS  00000000000014b0   0014b0 000360 00  AX   0   0 16
  [11] .text             PROGBITS  0000000000001810   001810 00a3fc 00  AX   0   0 16
```

Figure 2.7: Output of the readelf --wide --sections trace.so command

As you can see, the name of the 9th section is .init and the name of the 10th section is .plt.

How does readelf show the section names? Here is how it works:

1. It finds the .shstrtab section by accessing the e_shstrndx field of the ELF header.

2. It indexes it with the sh_name field of every section header based on the location of the .shstrtab section.

> **Note**
>
> The .shstrtab section contains the names of sections within the ELF file. The sh_name field specifies the offset of the section's name within this string table.

In summary, the sh_name field indicates the position within this string table where the name of the section described by the section header can be found.

The sh_type field

The sh_type field indicates the type of the section. It also provides the purpose and contents of each section in the ELF file. The sh_type field can have several values, as follows:

- SHT_NULL: If a section header is inactive or has no associated section, the sh_type field is set to this type.

- `SHT_PROGBITS`: This indicates the section that contains program instructions or data, such as code or initialized data. For example, the .text section and the .bss section are of this type.

- `SHT_SYMTAB`: This represents sections containing symbol table entries, which map symbols to their corresponding addresses in the executable.

- `SHT_STRTAB`: Sections of this type are used to store string table data, which is utilized by other parts of the ELF file, such as section names and symbol names.

- `SHT_DYNAMIC`: This specifies sections with dynamic linking information, including the dynamic symbol table and the relocation table.

- `SHT_REL` and `SHT_RELA`: These denote relocation entries for sections that can be modified by the linker or loader in the operating system during runtime.

The most common values for the sh_type field are listed in the related header file:

```
// include/uapi/linux/elf.h
#define DT_NULL      0
#define DT_NEEDED    1
#define DT_PLTRELSZ  2
#define DT_PLTGOT    3
#define DT_HASH      4
#define DT_STRTAB    5
#define DT_SYMTAB    6
#define DT_RELA      7
#define DT_RELASZ    8
```

In *Figure 2.8*, you can see the section headers via the readelf --wide --sections trace.so command:

```
There are 34 section headers, starting at offset 0x1fb28:

Section Headers:
  [Nr] Name              Type            Address          Off    Size   ES Flg Lk Inf Al
  [ 0]                   NULL            0000000000000000 000000 000000 00        0   0  0
  [...]
  [ 9] .init             PROGBITS        0000000000001490 001490 000018 00  AX    0   0  4
  [10] .plt              PROGBITS        00000000000014b0 0014b0 000360 00  AX    0   0 16
  [11] .text             PROGBITS        0000000000001810 001810 00a3fc 00  AX    0   0 16
  [12] .fini             PROGBITS        000000000000bc0c 00bc0c 000014 00  AX    0   0  4
  [13] .rodata           PROGBITS        000000000000bc20 00bc20 002033 00  A     0   0  8
  [14] .eh_frame_hdr     PROGBITS        000000000000dc54 00dc54 000244 00  A     0   0  4
```

Figure 2.8: The properties of the .init, .plt, and .text sections

As seen in *Figure 2.8*, the type of these sections is SHT_PROGBITS. This is because the .init, .plt, and .text sections contain instructions and data needed for program execution.

Next, let's examine the sh_flags field.

The sh_flags field

The sh_flags field is used to store additional information about each section in an ELF file, including various attributes or flags. Common flags in the sh_flags field are SHF_WRITE, SHF_ALLOC, and SHF_EXECINSTR, as follows:

- SHF_WRITE: Specifies whether a section is writable at runtime. It helps tell the difference between static data and variables.
- SHF_ALLOC: Indicates that the section's contents should be loaded into virtual memory when the program executes. This flag is typically set for sections containing executable code or initialized data.
- SHF_EXECINSTR: Specifies that the section contains executable instructions. This flag is set for sections that contain executable code. It is useful in reverse engineering and disassembling.

The most commonly used values stored in the sh_flags field are as follows:

```
// include/uapi/linux/elf.h
/* sh_flags */
#define SHF_WRITE      0x1
#define SHF_ALLOC      0x2
#define SHF_EXECINSTR  0x4
```

These flags can be used together, such as SHF_ALLOC | SHF_EXECINSTR. Understanding these flags provides insight into how sections should be handled during program execution.

The sh_addr field

The sh_addr field is used to hold the virtual address for a section, indicating where the section's data should be loaded. When an ELF file is loaded into memory by the loader, the loader accesses the sh_addr field to determine where each section should be placed. This field is particularly important for sections that are part of required data or the executable code, including the .data (initialized data), .bss (uninitialized data), and .text (code) sections.

> **Note**
>
> When you start reverse engineering, you may check the .text section to see the instructions inside a function. In this case, the sh_addr field in the .text section shows where the code starts in memory.

The sh_offset and sh_size fields

The sh_offset and sh_size fields provide information about when the section's data is loaded by debugging tools and loader in the operating system. The details of each field are as follows:

- The sh_offset field is used to provide the offset value in bytes, which points to where to place the section's data within the file. Debugging tools and loaders read this field in the ELF file to locate the contents of the section.

- The sh_size field has the amount of data in the section, which is accessed by the loader. The loader uses the sh_size field to determine how much memory to allocate for each section and how much data to copy from the file into memory.

To find the position of each section, it is a good idea to check these two fields: sh_offset and sh_addr.

In this section, you have learned about section headers, which represent the properties of sections. There are several sections that contain the code and data of your program, which will be covered in the next section.

Sections

ELF files contain many sections created during the compilation process. Among them, we need to learn about the primary sections that are mainly analyzed for reverse engineering. Let's learn about the following sections:

- The .text section
- The .bss, .data, and .rodata sections
- The dynamic section
- The .init section
- The PLT section
- The GOT section

First, let's learn about the .text section.

The .text section

When adding a piece of code, you will build your code using a compiler. During compilation, the compiler places the machine-specific code in the .text section, which is specific to the CPU architecture. The .text section consists of the compiled and assembled code that the processor will run, so instructions in the function or label are found in the .text section.

The .text section is usually marked as read-only, meaning that the instructions stored in this section cannot be modified during runtime. Additionally, the .text section typically belongs to a segment with the PT_LOAD type, whose flags include PF_X (executable) and PF_R (readable). This specifies that the segment containing the .text section can be executable and read by the program.

The .bss, .data, and .rodata sections

During compilation, global variables and static local variables are placed into the .bss, .data, and .rodata sections. How are global and static local variables placed in these sections? It depends on how these variables are initialized. Let's take a look at each section, as follows:

- .bss: This stands for *Block Started by Symbol* and is a part of the data segment. This section holds uninitialized global data and occupies minimal space on the disk. Unlike the .data section, the .bss section does not store actual data on disk other than a small amount of space to represent the section itself. This data is initialized to zero when the program loads and values can be assigned to it during program execution. Since this section is marked as SHT_NOBITS, the .bss section contains no actual data.

- .data: The .data section stores initialized global and static variables. It is typically read/write protected, allowing programs to read from and modify the data stored within this section during execution. Global variables, whether explicitly declared as global or as static function-local variables, are allocated space in the .data section.

  When the program loads, the initial values of variables in the .data section are set according to their definitions in the source code. This section may include various initialized data used by the program during execution.

- .rodata (**read-only data**): The .rodata section is used to store read-only data. It contains data that should not be modified during program execution, such as constant variables and string literals. Utilities such as objdump can display the contents of the .rodata section, showing the stored string literals in the final binary output.

These sections (.text, .data, .rodata, and .bss) contain code and global variables that are important when performing reverse engineering.

The dynamic section

The dynamic section provides information to the dynamic linker on how to load and configure the ELF file. The dynamic section is made up of several entries, and each entry is represented by the following data structure:

```
// include/uapi/linux/elf.h
typedef struct {
    Elf64_Sxword d_tag;
    union {
        Elf64_Xword d_val;
        Elf64_Addr  d_ptr;
    } d_un;
} Elf64_Dyn;
```

Each element in the Elf64_Dyn structure represents the following properties:

- d_tag: Type of the entry
- d_val or d_ptr: The value or starting address corresponding to the type

Now, let's check the dynamic section information using readelf:

```
$ readelf --dynamic trace.so
Dynamic section at offset 0xfdb0 contains 24 entries:
  Tag        Type                         Name/Value
 0x0000000000000001 (NEEDED)             Shared library: [libc.so.6]
 0x000000000000000c (INIT)               0x1490
 0x000000000000000d (FINI)               0xbc0c
 0x0000000000000019 (INIT_ARRAY)         0x1fd90
 0x000000000000001b (INIT_ARRAYSZ)       16 (bytes)
 0x000000000000001a (FINI_ARRAY)         0x1fda0
 0x000000000000001c (FINI_ARRAYSZ)       16 (bytes)
 0x000000006ffffef5 (GNU_HASH)           0x1f0
...

 0x0000000000000009 (RELAENT)            24 (bytes)
 0x000000006ffffffe (VERNEED)            0xb88
 0x000000006fffffff (VERNEEDNUM)         1
 0x000000006ffffff0 (VERSYM)             0xafe
 0x000000006ffffff9 (RELACOUNT)          27
 0x0000000000000000 (NULL)               0x0
```

When should you check the dynamic section? If you use the address sanitizer feature, you might want to understand how the ELF file is loaded. In this case, you can analyze each entry in the dynamic section to see the loading process.

The .init section

The .init section is a special section that contains initialization code or routines that are executed when the program starts.

The initialization code that runs before the main program starts is placed in the .init section. In general, the code in the .init section is executed by the operating system's loader as part of the process startup procedure. Initialization routines in the .init section may set up runtime environments, initialize global variables, establish data structures, or perform other necessary setup tasks.

The GOT section

In dynamic relocations, the address of an imported symbol must be set. These symbols usually come from shared libraries, and they are often included in the **global offset table (GOT)**. Symbols in the GOT are usually external functions or variables, such as memcpy, strlen, or lseek. For example, if a program uses the memcpy function from the libc library, it needs to know the address of that function at runtime.

However, sometimes, a program might utilize a function such as malloc more than 200 times. Instead of searching for malloc every time it's needed, the program uses a special table called the GOT. This table keeps track of important addresses, such as malloc.

Instead of searching for the function every time, the program stores its address in the GOT. Then, when it needs to call malloc, it checks the GOT. This makes the malloc function call faster and saves time.

The PLT section

Another way to speed up this process is by utilizing the **procedure linkage table (PLT)**, which helps with lazy symbol binding. **Lazy binding** means that symbols (such as functions) in a library are only sought when they are actually needed. This can save time because a program might import numerous symbols, but only utilize a few of them. Hence, instead of looking for all the symbols right away, we wait until we actually need them.

The PLT serves as a small helper for this purpose. It comprises a table of tiny functions, known as stubs, that facilitate lazy binding. When the program wants to use a function such as malloc, it actually calls a PLT stub. This stub works like a placeholder. The first time the program calls malloc, the PLT stub performs some tasks to locate the actual malloc function, stores its address, and then calls it. Subsequently, whenever the program requires malloc again, it directly utilizes the saved address, without the need to search for it again. Consequently, each function is only loaded once, right before it is first used.

Let's look at the following instructions to identify the PLT section:

```
ldrsw    x2, [sp, #0x1024]    ; x2, [sp, #4132]
add      x1, sp, #0x20        ; x1, sp, #32
bl       0x14D0               ; memcpy@plt
```

If your code uses the memcpy function, you will see the memcpy@plt instruction, which is the sample code in the PLT section.

Now that you have learned about section headers and the main sections in an ELF file, in the next section, we will discuss the program header.

Program headers

The program header gives information about how to place the ELF binary into memory space efficiently. Before running the program, the operating system's loader reads the program headers to load the program into memory. These headers consist of a series of segments, detailing where and how to load the ELF file's data into memory.

In this section, the program header will be covered. First, we will look at where the program header is located in the ELF file.

Layout of the program header

Figure 2.9 illustrates the location of the program header in the ELF file.

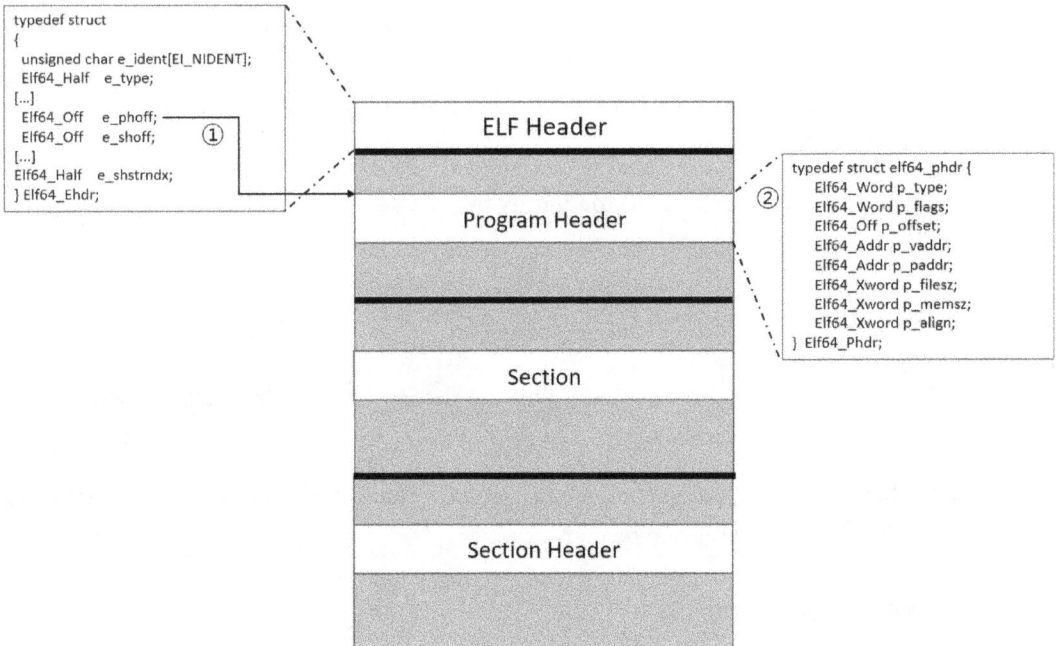

```
typedef struct
{
  unsigned char e_ident[EI_NIDENT];
  Elf64_Half   e_type;
  [...]
  Elf64_Off    e_phoff;      ——
  Elf64_Off    e_shoff;          ①
  [...]
  Elf64_Half   e_shstrndx;
} Elf64_Ehdr;
```

ELF Header

Program Header

Section

Section Header

```
typedef struct elf64_phdr {
    Elf64_Word p_type;
    Elf64_Word p_flags;
    Elf64_Off p_offset;
    Elf64_Addr p_vaddr;
    Elf64_Addr p_paddr;
    Elf64_Xword p_filesz;
    Elf64_Xword p_memsz;
    Elf64_Xword p_align;
} Elf64_Phdr;
```
②

Figure 2.9: Position of program headers in ELF

First, let's take a look at **1** in the figure. The arrow in **1** indicates the location of the program header. The e_phoff field of the Elf64_Ehdr structure indicates the location of the program header in ELF. Here, the Elf64_Ehdr structure represents the ELF header.

The location of the program header is different in each ELF file. If you would like to know where the program header begins, it is necessary to check the e_phoff field of the Elf64_Ehdr structure in the ELF header.

The program header is a data structure that represents the properties of each program header. How can we identify the detailed properties of the program headers? The elf64_phdr structure represents the properties of the program headers. These details are as follows:

```
// include/uapi/linux/elf.h
typedef struct elf64_phdr {
    Elf64_Word    p_type;
    Elf64_Word    p_flags;
```

```
    Elf64_Off    p_offset;   /* Segment file offset */
    Elf64_Addr   p_vaddr;    /* Segment virtual address */
    Elf64_Addr   p_paddr;    /* Segment physical address */
    Elf64_Xword  p_filesz;   /* Segment size in file */
    Elf64_Xword  p_memsz;    /* Segment size in memory */
    Elf64_Xword  p_align;    /* Segment alignment, file & memory */
} Elf64_Phdr;
```

Now that you have learned about the location of the program header, let's look at the details of it.

If you run the readelf --wide trace.so -lw command, you will see the following output:

```
Elf file type is DYN (Shared object file)
Entry point 0x0
There are 7 program headers, starting at offset 64

Program Headers:
  Type           Offset   VirtAddr            PhysAddr            FileSiz  MemSiz   Flg Align
  LOAD           0x000000 0x0000000000000000  0x0000000000000000  0x00e7b4 0x00e7b4 R E 0x10000
  LOAD           0x00fd90 0x000000000001fd90  0x000000000001fd90  0x000508 0x000ff0 RW  0x10000
  DYNAMIC        0x00fdb0 0x000000000001fdb0  0x000000000001fdb0  0x0001c0 0x0001c0 RW  0x8
  NOTE           0x0001c8 0x00000000000001c8  0x00000000000001c8  0x000024 0x000024 R   0x4
  GNU_EH_FRAME   0x00dc54 0x000000000000dc54  0x000000000000dc54  0x000244 0x000244 R   0x4
  GNU_STACK      0x000000 0x0000000000000000  0x0000000000000000  0x000000 0x000000 RW  0x10
  GNU_RELRO      0x00fd90 0x000000000001fd90  0x000000000001fd90  0x000270 0x000270 R   0x1

 Section to Segment mapping:
  Segment Sections...
   00     .note.gnu.build-id .gnu.hash .dynsym .dynstr .gnu.version .gnu.version_r
          .rela.dyn .rela.plt .init .plt .text .fini .rodata .eh_frame_hdr .eh_frame
   01     .init_array .fini_array .dynamic .got .got.plt .data .bss
   02     .dynamic
   03     .note.gnu.build-id
   04     .eh_frame_hdr
   05
   06     .init_array .fini_array .dynamic .got
```

Figure 2.10: The program header using the readelf –wide trace.so –lw command

The preceding output provides readable information about program headers, which can be summarized as follows:

- There are six program headers: LOAD (twice), DYNAMIC, NOTE, GNU_EH_FRAME, GNU_STACK, and GNU_RELRO.

- Section to Segment mapping indicates how sections are mapped into segments. For example, the second LOAD header consists of .init_array, fini_array, .dynamic, .got, .got.plt, .data, and .bss sections.

Remember that the unit of the program header is a segment that consists of sections.

Here, you may have a question: How can the `readelf trace.so -lw` command show the preceding output? *Figure 2.11* shows the property of the program header from the output of the `readelf trace.so -lw` command.

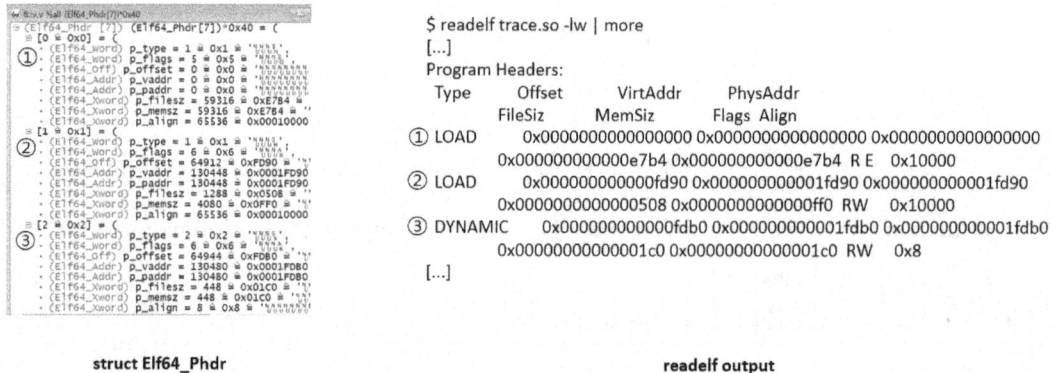

struct Elf64_Phdr   readelf output

Figure 2.11: The properties of the program header

The left side of *Figure 2.11* shows the fields of the `Elf64_Phdr` structure, as seen using the `TRACE32` debugger. Each field has a specific value. The right side of the figure shows the output after running the `readelf trace.so -lw` command. There are two important points to note:

- **Left side**: This shows the actual data inside the program header, based on the `Elf64_Phdr` structure

- **Right side**: This is the parsed result that the `readelf` provides after reading the program header

Understanding the meaning of each field in the `Elf64_Phdr` structure will give you insight into the program header if it is necessary to review the field in the `Elf64_Phdr` structure.

Let's learn about the element of program headers.

Exploring program headers

Now, let's look at important elements of the program header:

- The `p_type` field

- The `p_flags` field

- The `p_offset`, `p_vaddr`, and `p_paddr` fields

First, let's learn about the `p_type` field.

The p_type field

The p_type field holds the type of program header. The program header defines three types, as follows:

- PT_LOAD: This type tells the loader in the operating system how to load the segment. The segment in the program section consists of sections, providing information on where and how to load the data of ELF into memory space. These segments define the size of the loadable chunk and the address at which it should be loaded. Typically, there are at least two PT_LOAD segments — one for non-writable sections and one for writable data sections.

- PT_INTERP: This provides information to the loader on how to bring the ELF binary into memory space. A segment with the PT_INTERP type contains the .interp section, specifying the name of the interpreter responsible for loading the binary. On Linux, you can find the loader located in the /lib/ld-linux-aarch64.so.1. When the program is about to execute, the operating system finds the appropriate loader by accessing information from the INTERP header.

- PT_DYNAMIC: This specifies dynamic linking information for the segment. This segment contains the .dynamic section, informing the interpreter how to parse and prepare the binary for execution.

- PT_NOTE: This denotes auxiliary information or notes about the program. Auxiliary information can be structured metadata that is used by the operating system or loader, such as build IDs and ABI tags.

Understanding the p_type field is crucial for interpreting the purpose and behavior of each program header within the ELF file.

The names of the first and second program headers are LOAD, which is represented in the Elf64_ Phdr structure. On the left side of *Figure 2.11*, we can see the p_type field. As for **1** and **2**, the value of p_type is 1, which means LOAD. As for **3**, the p-type value is 2, which means DYNAMIC.

As you can see, the readelf reads the program header and shows human-readable output based on the values in the Elf64_Phdr structure.

The p_flags field

The p_flags field is used to specify the runtime access permissions for the segment and the behavior of each segment within the file. Three important types of flags are commonly used, as follows:

- PF_X: Denotes that the segment is executable, typically set for code segments.
- PF_W: Specifies that the segment is writable, commonly set for writable data segments. This flag allows programs to modify the contents of the segment during execution.

- PF_R: Indicates that the segment is readable, usually set for both code and data segments. It enables programs to read data from the segment during execution.

The p_flags field helps determine the access permissions and other properties associated with each segment, contributing to the program's proper operation and optimization.

The p_offset, p_vaddr, and p_paddr fields

The p_offset, p_vaddr, and p_paddr fields are used to specify the file offset at which the segment starts, and the virtual address at which it is to be loaded. The descriptions of these fields are as follows:

- p_offset: Specifies the offset from the beginning of the file to the start of the segment. This means it points to where the segment begins within the ELF file.

- p_vaddr: Indicates the starting address in the virtual memory space where to load segment during program execution. This field instructs the operating system's loader to determine where to place each segment in the address space of the process.

- p_paddr: Represents the physical address of a segment within the system's memory. This field is particularly important for systems operating in a physical addressing environment.

When the loader in the operating system is about to load each segment in the program header, the preceding information is accessed.

Summary

In this chapter, you learned about the ELF file format, including the file header, section header, and program header. First, you learned about the ELF file header, which provides detailed information via the readelf command. When you start reverse engineering, you will find yourself searching for relevant binary files. The output of readelf with options will give you the right information in such cases. You also learned about the section header. All of the code is placed into the section header.

After you find an appropriate binary file, it may be corrupted for various reasons. A thorough understanding of the ELF format will help you recover the corrupted binary, making you better perform reverse engineering under any circumstances.

All the code is placed in sections, and these sections are described by the section header. The program header is also important because it tells you how the program is loaded into memory.

In the next chapter, you will learn about data processing instructions. These are also useful for reverse engineering.

3

Manipulating Data with Arm Data Processing Instructions

Arm® assembly instructions are designed to interact directly with Arm processors at a low level. Understanding these instructions is essential for software engineers to analyze and control the activities performed by the Arm processor. This chapter covers the following data processing instructions:

- Move operations
- Arithmetic operations
- Bit-shift operations
- Logical operations
- Practicing data processing instructions

Note that the assembly instructions covered in this chapter are based on AArch64 in Armv8-A. This aligns with the focus of subsequent chapters, which will continue exploring instructions relevant to this architecture.

Let's begin this chapter with the instructions associated with move operations.

Technical requirements

All the code examples and binary files for this chapter can be found on GitHub at https://github. com/PacktPublishing/Reverse-Engineering-Armv8-A-Systems.

To learn more about Armv8-A, you can check the following materials:

- Armv8-A Reference Manual: `https://developer.arm.com/documentation/ddi0487/gb`
- Programmer's Guide for ARMv8-A: `https://developer.arm.com/documentation/den0024/latest/`

Move operations

Let's explore the instruction that is easiest to learn: the move instruction. Armv8-A provides assembly instructions for move operations, which are as follows:

- MOV
- MVN

First, let's explore the syntax of the MOV instruction.

The MOV instruction

The MOV instruction is used to copy the value of an operand into the destination register. *Figure 3.1* shows the syntax of the MOV instruction:

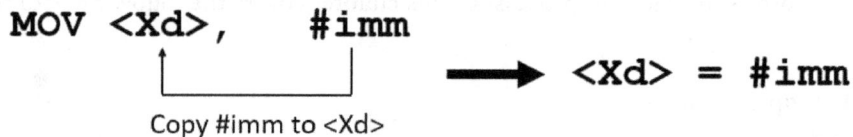

```
MOV <Xd>,      #imm          ➡  <Xd> = #imm
         Copy #imm to <Xd>
```

Figure 3.1: The MOV instruction syntax

Figure 3.1 illustrates the syntax of the MOV instruction, where the operand's value is copied to the destination register denoted as <Xd>. The operand can be either an immediate value or a register.

The syntax of the MOV instruction is easy to learn because it is a simple copy operation. To understand the MOV instruction efficiently, it is important to figure out how MOV is used.

Examples of the MOV instruction

How is the MOV instruction used? It is used to set the destination register, which can correspond to a local variable.

In C programming, when a variable is initialized, the compiler translates this into assembly instructions, using the MOV instruction. For example, let's assume that you add the following code:

```
int x = 7;
```

The compiler will translate this into the following assembly instructions:

```
MOV W0, #7
```

When executing the preceding instruction, it moves the immediate value of 7 into the W0 register (which may represent the x variable). You can find W0 in the preceding example instruction. Any general-purpose register, such as W1 or W2, can also be used. When you encounter the MOV instruction during reverse engineering, consider that this instruction is used to set a local variable.

Now that we have explored the MOV instruction, let's delve into another type of move operation: MVN.

The MVN instruction

The MVN instruction is a bitwise NOT operation on its operand, usually used to initialize a negative integer. Let's take a look at *Figure 3.2*, which shows the syntax of the MVN instruction:

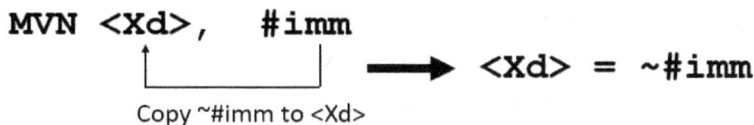

Figure 3.2: The MVN instruction syntax

The MVN instruction performs the two activities simultaneously:

- Performs a bitwise NOT operation on the operand
- Moves this result to the destination register

When a C variable is initialized with a negative value, the compiler may use MVN in the generated assembly code to represent that value.

Examples of the MVN instruction

To understand how the MVN instruction works, we need to analyze instructions in different scenarios. Let's assume the compiler examines the following C code:

```
int X = -1;
```

If W0 corresponds to the local variable, X, the compiler will generate the following instruction:

```
MVN W0,W1 ; W1 holds 0x0
```

The bitwise NOT of 0 results in 0xFFFFFFFF, which represents -1 in two's complement form for a 32-bit integer. This operation can be efficiently performed using the MVN instruction.

Let's consider another example:

```
int Y = -6;
```

-6 is represented as *~6 + 1*, where *~6* is the bitwise NOT operation on 6. The compiler translates this into the following instruction:

```
MOV W1, #5
MVN W0, W1
```

We can read the preceding instruction in the following ways:

1. Move 5 into the W1 register.
2. Take the bitwise NOT of W1, which results in *~5 = -6* in two's complement.

Although move instructions may look simple, it is better to analyze them from a different perspective. When you see a MOV or MVN instruction, ask yourself what the assembly routine is trying to do with the MOV or MVN instruction. By thinking this way, you can better understand the purpose of the instruction during reverse engineering.

Having completed the instructions associated with move operations, let's explore the instructions involved in arithmetic operations.

Arithmetic operations

When you examine assembly instructions, you will encounter arithmetic instructions. These are fundamental for understanding assembly routines. In this section, you will learn about the following arithmetic instructions:

*   ADD
*   ADC
*   SUB
*   SBC

The arithmetic instructions in this chapter are based on the A64 instruction set in Armv8-A. Let's start with the ADD instruction. First, we will look at its syntax.

The ADD instruction

The ADD instruction performs an addition operation. Let's look at *Figure 3.3* to learn about how the ADD instruction is organized.

```
ADD  <Xd>,  <Xn>,  <Xm>              ➔  <Xd>  =  <Xn>  +  <Xm>
```

Add the value of the operand

Store it to <Xd>

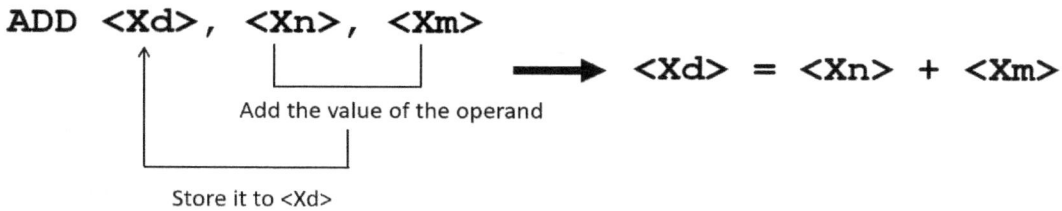

Figure 3.3: The ADD instruction syntax

The ADD instruction adds data between registers. In *Figure 3.3*, the addition operation is performed between <Xn> and <Xm>, and the result is stored in <Xd>. Here, <Xn> is the first operand, <Xm> is the second operand, and <Xd> is the destination register. The second operand can be either a general-purpose register or an immediate value.

The ADD instruction can be structured in various forms, as follows:

```
01 ADD X0, X1, #16  ; X0 = X1 + 16;
02 ADD X1, X1, X2   ;  X1 = X1 + X2 // where X2 is 20;
```

In the case of the instruction on the first line, the second operand is 16, which is an immediate value. This means 16 is added to the value of the X1 register, and the result is stored in the X0 register. If X1 contains 0x1000, then X0 is updated to 0x1010 based on the following equation:

```
X0 = X1 + 16 (0x10);
0x1010 = 0x1000 + 0x10;
```

The second line adds 20 to the value in the X1 register and stores the result back in X1. If the initial value in X1 is 1, then after this operation, X1 will be updated to 21 (0x15) as shown in the following formula:

```
X1 = X1 + 20 (0x14);
0x15 = 0x1 + 20 (0x14);
```

As explained, the ADD instruction performs the addition operation on the value of the operand. Although the ADD instruction is typically used for addition, it can also be utilized in different ways.

Examples of the ADD instruction

Another usage of the ADD instruction is to calculate the offset of an element in a structure in C code. In C programming, when dealing with structures and arrays, it's common to compute offsets to access specific elements. The ADD instruction is often used for this purpose.

Let's analyze the following example code:

```
struct Task {
    int x;
    int y;
};

struct Task p;
int *py = &(p.y);
```

To access the address of the y field given a pointer to a Task structure, it is necessary to calculate the offset of the y field. In assembly, you can use the ADD instruction to calculate an address. You can observe how the ADD instruction is used by looking at the corresponding assembly routine:

```
01 MOV X0, #offset_of_y
02 ADD X1, X2, X0
```

The breakdown analysis of the preceding example code is as follows:

- **The first line**: #offset_of_y has the offset of the y field in the Task struct. In a 64-bit environment, #offset_of_y is 8. After the MOV instruction runs, X0 contains 0x8, which is the offset of the y field.
- **The second line**: The address of p.y is calculated by adding the offset in X0 to the base address in X2. The result is stored in X1.

Armv8-A architecture offers the ADC instruction, which has a similar functionality to ADD. Let's understand the ADC instruction.

The ADC instruction

The ADC instruction stands for **Add with Carry**. Let's take a look at *Figure 3.4*, which shows the operation of the ADC instruction:

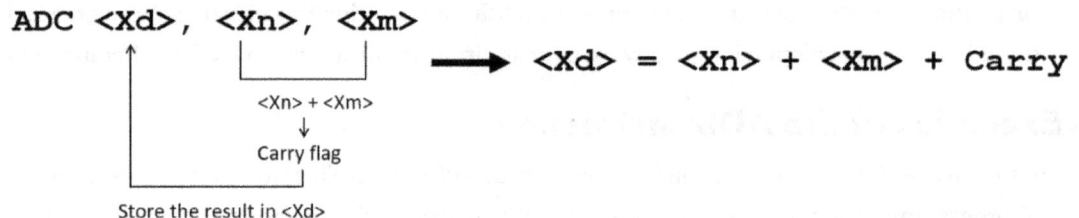

Figure 3.4: The ADC instruction syntax

The ADC instruction essentially supports addition operations and is quite similar to the ADD instruction but with one key difference: the carry flag is applied when executing the addition operation. The result of adding the value of the <Xm> register to the value of the <Xn> register also includes the carry flag. The result is stored in the <Xd> register.

> **Note**
>
> The carry flag is part of the conditional flags in PSTATE. It is used to indicate an overflow out of the most significant bit in unsigned arithmetic operations. It's crucial for multi-word arithmetic where carry propagation between words is necessary.

Now that we've looked at the syntax of the ADC instruction, let's understand how it works by looking at the example code.

Example of the ADC instruction

Let's analyze the following code with the ADC instruction. Note that the carry flag is set before executing the ADC instruction.

```
ADC X0, X1, #8
ADC X0, X1, SP
```

The precondition before executing the instructions is that X1 is 0x2000 and SP is 0x1000.

First, line 01 can be represented in pseudocode as follows:

```
X0 = 0x2000 + 0x8 + carry
0x2009 = 0x2000 + 0x8 + 1
```

Since the ADC instruction adds 1 (representing the carry) in the addition operation, X0 will store 0x2009.

Next, let's analyze line 02. Similar to line 01, the ADC instruction performs the addition operation by applying the carry flag. This can be represented as follows:

```
X0 = 0x2000 + 0x1000 + carry
0x3001 = 0x2000 + 0x1000 + 1
```

Since the ADC instruction performs the addition operation including the carry value of 1, 0x3001 is stored in X0.

Now that have you learned about the ADD and ADC instructions, let's learn about another instruction: SUB.

The SUB instruction

The SUB instruction is used to perform subtraction operations. Let's look at *Figure 3.5* to understand how the SUB instruction works:

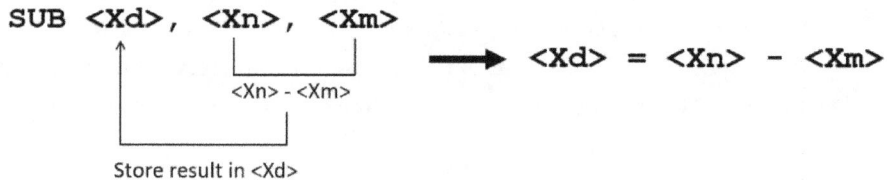

Figure 3.5: The SUB instruction syntax

The SUB instruction subtracts two operands. For example, it takes <Xn> and <Xm>, subtracts them, and stores the result in <Xd>. Here, <Xn> is the first operand, <Xm> is the second operand, and <Xd> is the destination register. The second operand can be either any of the general-purpose registers or an immediate value.

SUB is used as another form, as follows:

```
SUB Xd, Xn, #imm   ; Xd = Xn - imm (immediate value)
```

Let's understand the SUB instruction in the various forms.

Examples of the SUB instruction

Let's understand the SUB instruction by reviewing the example code:

```
01 SUB X0, X1, #8
02 SUB X0, SP, X1
```

Preconditions before running the example code are that X1 is 0x2000 and SP is 0x10000.

First, let's analyze the instruction on line 01. It performs the operation of subtracting 8 from the value of the X1 register, which is 0x2000. The result is stored in X0, which is the destination register. This operation can be represented in pseudocode as follows:

```
X0 = X1 - 8;
```

Next, let's examine line 02. This instruction subtracts the value in the X1 register from the stack pointer, SP, and stores the result in the X0 register.

Now that you understand the SUB instruction, let's look at the SBC instruction, which works in a similar way but also uses the carry flag.

SBC instruction

The SBC instruction stands for **Subtract with Carry**, which is shown in *Figure 3.6*:

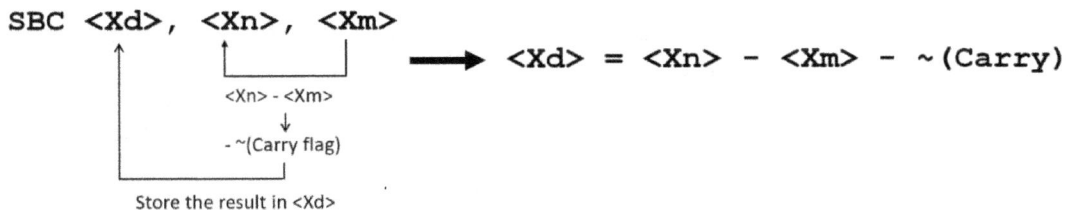

```
SBC <Xd>, <Xn>, <Xm>    ➡    <Xd> = <Xn> - <Xm> - ~(Carry)

        <Xn> - <Xm>
            ↓
        - ~(Carry flag)

    Store the result in <Xd>
```

Figure 3.6: The SBC instruction syntax

The SBC instruction supports subtraction operations and is similar to the SUB instruction. The difference from the SUB instruction is that the carry flag is applied during the subtraction operation. The result of subtracting the value of the <Xm> register from the value of the <Xn> register also subtracts the carry value. Depending on the carry flag, we can calculate it in the following ways:

- If the carry value is 1, the result of the operation is 0
- If the carry value is 0, the result is 1

Now that we understand the syntax of the SBC instruction, let's examine how it is used in the example code.

Examples of the SBC instruction

Let's take a look at the following example code in two forms:

```
SBC X0, X1, #8
SBC X0, X1, SP
```

Consider the following example with initial conditions where X1 is 0x2000, SP is 0x1000, and the carry flag is set before executing the instructions. First, let's represent line 01 in pseudocode:

```
X0 = 0x2000 - 0x8 - ~carry
0x1FF8 = 0x2000 - 0x8 - 0
```

If you perform a NOT operation on the carry (which is 1), the result is 0. So, subtracting 0 does not change the result.

Next, let's analyze line 02. Similar to line 01, the SBC instruction performs subtraction with consideration of the carry. This can be represented as follows:

```
X0 = 0x2000 - 0x1000 - ~carry
0x1000 = 0x2000 - 0x1000 - 0
```

In the calculation process involving the SBC instruction, performing a NOT operation on the carry value, which is 1, results in 0. This value has no impact on the subtraction operation.

Having completed the instructions involved with the move and arithmetic operations, let's analyze the instructions associated with bit-shifting operations.

Bit-shift operations

Bit-shift instructions are common in assembly, especially when working with low-level tasks such as bit manipulation, data packing, or unpacking. This section will explain the main bit-shift instructions:

- LSL
- LSR
- ASR
- ROR

Let's begin this section with the LSL instruction.

The LSL instruction

The LSL instruction stands for **Logical Shift Left**, which shifts the value in a register to the left by a specified number of bits. Let's take a look at *Figure 3.7* to learn how the LSL instruction works:

```
LSL <Xd>, <Xn>, <Xm>
```

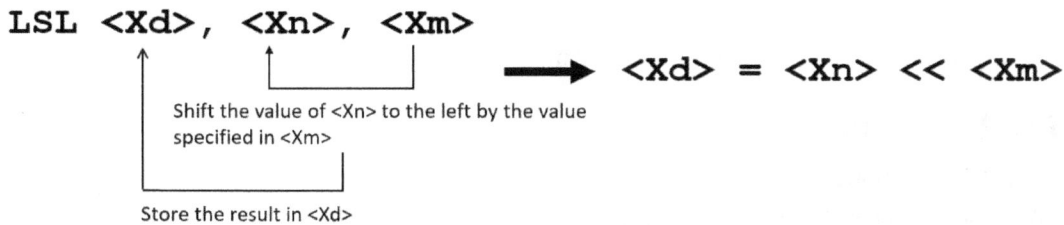

$$<Xd> = <Xn> << <Xm>$$

Shift the value of <Xn> to the left by the value
specified in <Xm>

Store the result in <Xd>

Figure 3.7: The LSL instruction syntax

As illustrated in *Figure 3.7*, the LSL instruction performs a left-bit shift operation. When analyzing the LSL instruction, you first examine the register that will be shifted to the left. *In Figure 3.7*, the value in the <Xn> register is the one that will be shifted.

Next, you need to determine the number of positions to shift to the left by examining the value in the <Xm> register. With the value in the <Xm> register, a left bit-shift operation is performed on the value in the <Xn> register.

The LSL instruction has several forms. Its basic syntax looks like this:

```
01 LSL <Xd>, <Xn>, <Xm>
02 LSL <Xd>, <Xn>, #<shift>
```

The second operand can be either a general-purpose register or an immediate value. Similar to other instructions, the result of the left bit-shift operation performed by the LSL instruction is stored in the destination register, <Xd>.

Examples of the LSL instruction

The following example code shows the LSL instruction in two forms:

```
01 LSL X0, X1, #2
02 LSL X0, X1, X2
```

The first line shifts the bits of the X1 register two places to the left. It can be represented as follows:

```
X0 = X1 << 2;
```

Remember that the second operand is an immediate value.

In the second line, the second operand is the X2 register. This means the bits in the X1 register will be shifted to the left by the value in X2. This can be represented as follows:

```
X0 = X1 << X2;
```

Together with the LSR instruction, the LSL instruction is one of the most commonly used bit shift instructions. Let's delve deeper into the LSR instruction.

The LSR instruction

The LSR instruction stands for **Logical Shift Right**. It shifts the bits in a register to the right. Let's take a look at *Figure 3.8* to understand how the LSR instruction works:

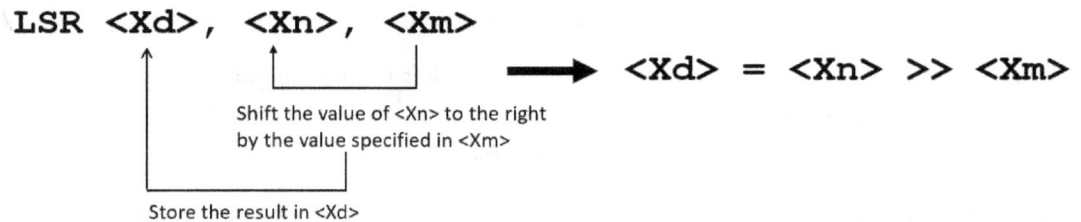

```
LSR <Xd>, <Xn>, <Xm>                 <Xd> = <Xn> >> <Xm>
```

Shift the value of <Xn> to the right
by the value specified in <Xm>

Store the result in <Xd>

Figure 3.8: The LSR instruction syntax

Similar to the LSL instruction, the LSR instruction shifts the bits of the value in the <Xn> register to the right, as seen in *Figure 3.8*. The <Xm> register specifies the number of positions to shift to the right, and the value in the <Xn> register is shifted accordingly. The result of this instruction is stored in the destination register, <Xd>.

In general, the syntax of the LSR instruction with various forms can be listed as follows:

```
LSR <Xd>, <Xn>, <Xm>
LSR <Xd>, <Xn>, #<shift>
```

Note that the second operand can be either a general-purpose register or an immediate value. Similar to other instructions, the result of the right bit-shift operation performed by the LSR instruction is stored in the destination register, <Xd>.

Examples of the LSR instruction

The best way to learn about the LSR instruction is to analyze many assembly routines in various forms. Let's examine the following example code that includes the LSR instruction:

```
01 LSR X0, X1, #2
02 LSR X0, X1, X2
```

The first line shifts the bits of the X1 register two places to the right, which can be represented as follows:

```
X0 = X1 >> 2;
```

Next, the second line shifts the bits of the X1 register to the right by the value specified in the X2 register. This can be represented as follows:

```
X0 = X1 >> X2;
```

Now that we have explored the LSL and LSR instructions, let's learn another bit-shift instruction.

The ASR instruction

The ASR instruction stands for **Arithmetic Shift Right**, which shifts the bits of a value to the right by a specified number of positions. Let's look at *Figure 3.9* to understand how the ASR instruction is organized:

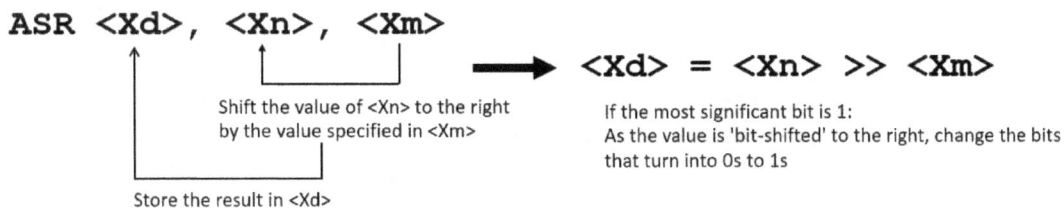

Figure 3.9: The ASR instruction syntax

The syntax of the ASR instruction is broadly similar to LSR but with one key difference: if the **most significant bit** (MSB) is 1, the bits that are shifted to the right are replaced with 1s instead of 0s.

Figure 3.10 shows the details of the bit-shift operation of the ASR instruction:

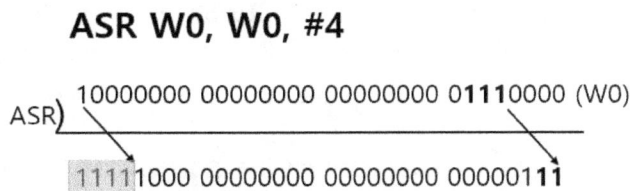

Figure 3.10: The execution of the ASR instruction

First, let's examine the value of W0 in binary format. The 0b10000000 00000000 00000000 01110000 value in the W0 register is shifted to the right by 4 bits. However, because the MSB of the value stored in the W0 register is 1, the 4 bits that are shifted out to the right are replaced with 1s instead of 0s. You can observe this operation in the box located at the bottom left. This bit operation is a key difference between the ASR and LSR instructions.

The ROR instruction

The ROR instruction stands for **Rotate Right**, which shifts bits to the right by a specified number of positions while the bits that are shifted out from the right are updated to the leftmost significant bit. Let's look at *Figure 3.11* to understand how the ROR instruction works:

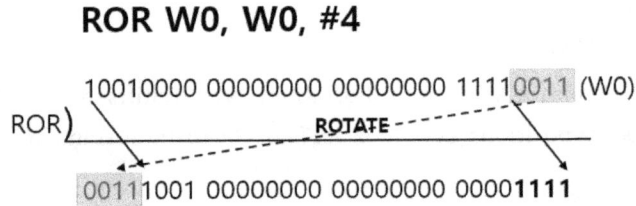

Figure 3.11: The execution of the ROR instruction

Figure 3.11 illustrates the syntax of executing the ROR instruction on the value in the W0 register in detail. The ROR instruction operates similarly to the LSR instruction, but with one key difference: as the bits are shifted to the right, the bits that are shifted out move directly to the leftmost significant bit position. This results in an output that appears as if the bits are both rotated and shifted simultaneously.

In *Figure 3.11*, the 0b10010000 00000000 00000000 11110011 value in the W0 register is first shifted to the right by 4 bits. As the bits are shifted, the 4 bits (0b0011) that are shifted out appear at the leftmost part of the result. You can observe this operation in the box located at the bottom left.

Until now, you have learned about instructions related to bit-shift operations. As you may already know, bit-shift operations are commonly used in low-level programming. Next, let's explore how bit-shift operations are utilized by examining the Linux kernel source code.

Case study — bit-shift operations in assembly code

Bit-shift operations are used a lot in programming. They are typically used to read or write specific bits in a register. Let's look at an example code in the Linux kernel that uses bit-shift operations:

```
asmlinkage void noinstr el1_sync_handler(struct pt_regs *regs)
{
    unsigned long esr = read_sysreg(esr_el1);

    switch (ESR_ELx_EC(esr)) {
    case ESR_ELx_EC_DABT_CUR:
    case ESR_ELx_EC_IABT_CUR:
```

```
        el1_abort(regs, esr);
        break;
    }
[…]
}
```

Please refer to the location of the preceding code in the Linux kernel: `https://elixir.bootlin.com/linux/v6.14/source/arch/arm64/kernel/entry-common.c`.

In this code, the `switch` statement checks the value from `ESR_ELx_EC(esr)`. The `ESR_ELx_EC()` function reads specific bits of the `ESR_EL1` register:

```
#define ESR_ELx_EC(esr) (((esr) & ESR_ELx_EC_MASK) >> ESR_ELx_EC_SHIFT)
```

Please refer to the location of the preceding code in the Linux kernel: `https://elixir.bootlin.com/linux/v6.14/source/arch/arm64/include/asm/esr.h`.

The bits from 31 to 26 in the `ESR_EL1` register tell us the cause of the exception. So, `ESR_ELx_EC()` is implemented based on this specification.

Using a disassembler, we can see how `el1_sync_handler()` looks in the assembly language:

```
01 ffffffc010acbf90 <el1_sync_handler>:
02      ffffffc010acbf90:   paciasp
03      ffffffc010acbf94:   stp     x29, x30, [sp, #-16]!
04      ffffffc010acbf98:   mov     x29, sp
05      ffffffc010acbf9c:   mrs     x1, esr_el1
06      ffffffc010acbfa0:   lsr     w2, w1, #26
07      ffffffc010acbfa4:   cmp     x2, #0x22
08      ffffffc010acbfa8:   b.eq    ffffffc010acc064
```

Here's a simple explanation of what each line does:

- **Line 5:** Reads the value from the `ESR_EL1` register and stores it in the X1 register.
- **Line 6:** Uses the LSR instruction to shift bits to the right by 26 positions. This way, we can read bits 31 to 26 from the `ESR_EL1` register.
- **Line 7:** The CMP instruction compares the value in X2 with 0x22.
- **Line 8:** Depending on the comparison result, it decides where to branch next.

This is how bit-shift operations are used to read specific bits and make decisions based on their values.

This section covered bit-shift instructions. By mastering bit-shift operations, you can gain precise control over data manipulation at the bit level. These shift operations are important for improving performance and reducing memory usage.

Now, let's move on to logical instructions in assembly.

Logical operations

All CPU architecture supports assembly instructions associated with logic bitwise operations such as AND, OR, and XOR. The Armv8-A architecture provides the following instructions related to bitwise operations. This section will cover instructions associated with the logical operation, as follows:

- AND
- ORR
- ORN
- BIC
- EOR

Let's begin this section with the AND instruction.

The AND instruction

The AND instruction performs a **bitwise AND** operation on operand values. Since the AND instruction operates on a bitwise level, it is important to understand the truth table for AND operations. *Table 3.1* shows the truth table for the AND operation:

X	Y	X AND Y
0	0	0
0	1	0
1	0	0
1	1	1

Table 3.1: Truth table for AND operations

In software development, a bitwise AND operation is often used to clear specific bits. This is useful in state machines or other control systems where each bit represents a different state or flag.

Let's examine *Figure 3.12* to understand how the `AND` instruction is executed:

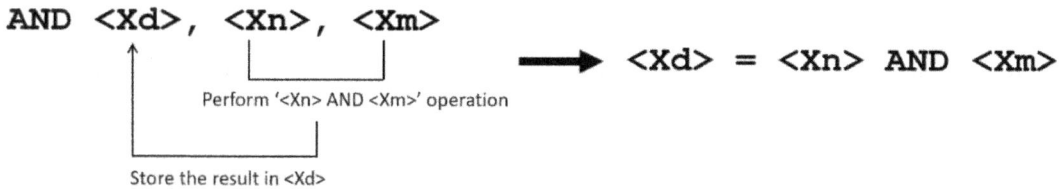

Figure 3.12: The AND instruction syntax

As shown in *Figure 3.12*, the result of performing a bitwise `AND` operation on the values in the `<Xn>` and `<Xm>` registers is stored in `<Xd>`. In C language syntax, this can be expressed as `<Xn> & <Xm>`.

Example of the AND instruction

Let's analyze the following example that uses the `AND` instruction:

```
AND W0, W0, #0x123
```

Note that the `W0` register has a value of `0x3023` before the instruction is performed. Since the `AND` instruction involves a bitwise operation, you need to analyze this instruction from another perspective, as illustrated in *Figure 3.13*:

```
   00000000 00000000 00110000 00100011   (W0: 0x3023)
&) 00000000 00000000 00000001 00100011        (0x123)
   -----------------------------------
   00000000 00000000 00000000 00100011         (0x23)
```

Figure 3.13: The bitwise AND operation

The bitwise `AND` operator results in a 1 only if both corresponding bits of the operands are 1. If either bit is 0, the result is 0. Therefore, the `AND` instruction in the example shown in *Figure 3.13* can be expressed using a bitwise `AND` operation as follows:

```
W0 = W0 & #0x123
```

This means the value of `W0` will be the result of performing a bitwise `AND` operation between the current value of `W0` and `0x123`.

Let's explore another bitwise instruction: the `ORR` instruction.

The ORR instruction

As the ORR instruction performs a **bitwise OR** operation, the truth table for the OR operation is introduced before explaining the ORR instruction. *Table 3.2* shows the truth table for the OR operation.

X	Y	X OR Y
0	0	0
0	1	1
1	0	1
1	1	1

Table 3.2: Truth table for OR operations

In software development, a bitwise OR operation is often used to set specific bits to 1 while leaving the remaining bits unchanged. This technique is particularly useful when configuring the bit fields of specific system registers in Armv8-A.

The ORR instruction performs a **bitwise OR** operation on operand values. Let's refer to *Figure 3.14* to understand how the ORR instruction works:

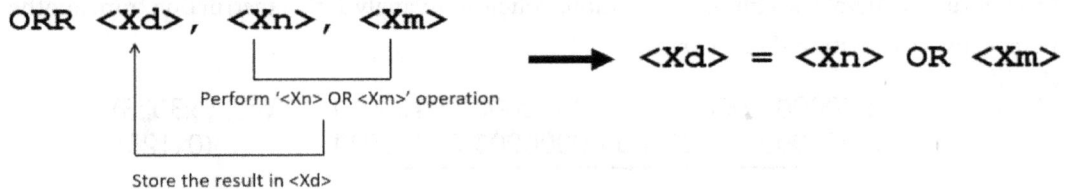

Figure 3.14: The ORR instruction syntax

As illustrated in *Figure 3.14*, the result of performing a bitwise OR operation on the values in the <Xn> and <Xm> registers is stored in <Xd>. This can be expressed in C language syntax as <Xn> | <Xm>.

Example of the ORR instruction

Let's now look at an example to better understand the ORR instruction:

```
ORR W0, W0, #0x103
```

Before the instruction runs, the W0 register contains 0x3023. The instruction performs a bitwise OR operation with the value of 0x103, as shown in *Figure 3.15*:

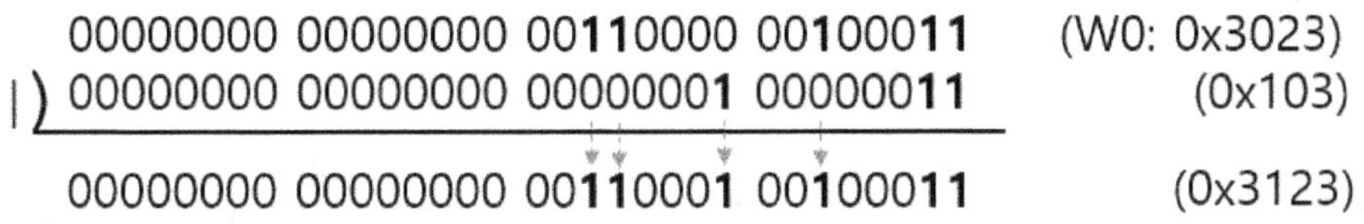
00000000 00000000 00110000 00100011 (W0: 0x3023)
|) 00000000 00000000 00000001 00000011 (0x103)
00000000 00000000 00110001 00100011 (0x3123)

Figure 3.15: The bitwise OR operation

The bitwise `OR` operator results in `1` if at least one of the corresponding bits in the operands has a value of `1`. As demonstrated in *Figure 3.15*, the `ORR` instruction performs a bitwise `OR` operation between the value of `0x3023` in the `W0` register and `0x103`. The result of this operation is then stored back into the `W0` register.

Therefore, the `ORR` instruction can be expressed using the bitwise `OR` operator as follows:

```
W0 = W0 | #0x103
```

After execution, the `W0` register will contain the result of `0x3023` `OR` `0x103`.

The ORN instruction

The `ORN` instruction stands for **bitwise OR NOT**. Let's learn about the `ORN` instruction by looking at *Figure 3.16*:

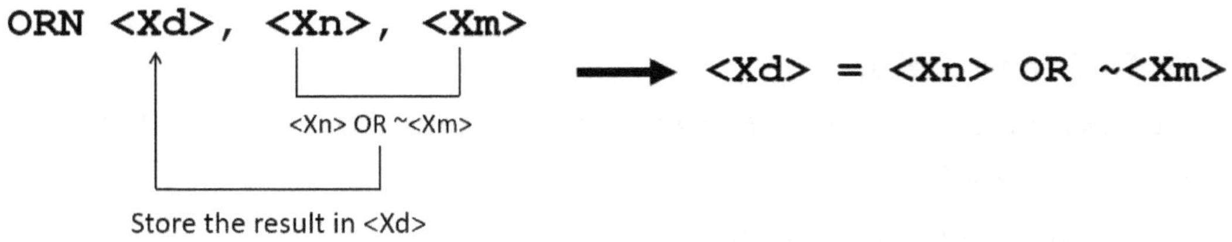
ORN <Xd>, <Xn>, <Xm>
<Xd> = <Xn> OR ~<Xm>
<Xn> OR ~<Xm>
Store the result in <Xd>

Figure 3.16: The ORN instruction syntax

As shown in *Figure 3.16*, the `ORN` instruction performs a bitwise `OR` operation on the value in the `<Xn>` register and the bitwise `NOT` of the value in the `<Xm>` register, and then stores the result in the destination register, `<Xd>`. This can be expressed in C language syntax as `<Xn> | ~<Xm>`.

Example of the ORN instruction

The following is an example code using the `ORN` instruction:

```
ORN W0, W0, #0x123
```

The W0 register contains 0x23 before the ORN instruction is executed. Since the example instruction involves bitwise operations, its detailed operation is illustrated in *Figure 3.17*:

```
      00000000 00000000 00000000 00100011     (W0: 0x23)
 ② |) 11111111 11111111 11111110 11011100     0xFFFF_FEDC = ~(0x123)

      11111111 11111111 11111110 11111111     0xFFFF_FEFF

  (WHERE)

 ① ~) 00000000 00000000 00000001 00100011     (0x123)

      11111111 11111111 11111110 11011100     (0xFFFF_FEDC =~0x123)
```

Figure 3.17: The detailed operation: the ORN instruction

When executing the ORN W0, W0, #0x123 instruction, the detailed bitwise operations can be analyzed in two steps:

1. Perform a bitwise NOT operation on #0x123, denoted as (~0x123). The result is 0xFFFF_FEDC.

2. Perform a bitwise OR operation between the value in the W0 register and 0xFFFF_FEDC.

In summary, the ORN instruction performs a bitwise NOT operation on its second operand and then performs a bitwise OR operation with the first operand (W0), similar to the ORR instruction.

The BIC instruction

The BIC instruction stands for **Bitwise Bit Clear**. Let's take a look at *Figure 3.18*, which illustrates the syntax of the BIC instruction:

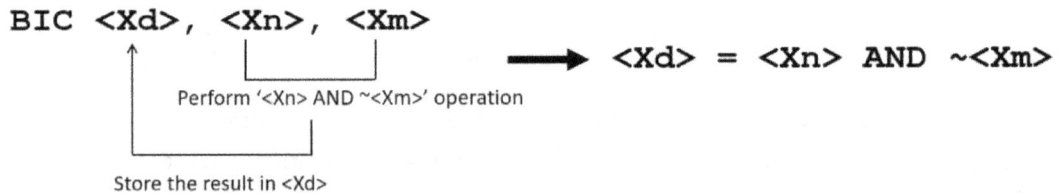

```
BIC  <Xd>,  <Xn>,  <Xm>                    ➡    <Xd>  =  <Xn>  AND  ~<Xm>

              Perform '<Xn> AND ~<Xm>' operation

     Store the result in <Xd>
```

Figure 3.18: The BIC instruction syntax

At first, the instructions in *Figure 3.18* may look a bit complicated. To understand the BIC instruction, we should break it into two simple steps:

1. Perform a bitwise inversion operation on the value of <Xm>.

2. Perform a bitwise AND operation on <Xn> and the result from *Step 1* (~<Xm>).

Broadly speaking, the BIC instruction works similarly to the AND instruction because both involve a bitwise AND operation. However, there is a key difference: the BIC instruction operates on the bitwise inverted result of the second operand (~<Xm>) with the first operand (<Xn>), while the ORN instruction performs a bitwise OR NOT operation between the operands.

Examples of the BIC instruction

Let's analyze the example code to understand how the BIC instruction works:

```
BIC W0, W1, W2
```

Before running the instruction, the W1 register has 0xFF, and the W2 register contains 0xF. *Figure 3.19* illustrates the detailed operation of the instruction in the example code:

```
         00000000 00000000 00000000 11111111      (W1: 0xFF)
 ②&)     11111111 11111111 11111111 11110000      0xFFFF_FFF0 = ~(W2: 0xF)
         00000000 00000000 00000000 11110000      0xF0

    (WHERE)

 ① ~)    00000000 00000000 00000000 00001111      (0xF)
         11111111 11111111 11111111 11110000      (0xFFFF_FFF0 = ~0xF)
```

Figure 3.19: The detailed operation: the BIC instruction

We can analyze the BIC W0, W1, W2 instruction in *Figure 3.19* in two steps:

1. Perform a bitwise inversion operation on the value in the W2 register. This result is indicated by ~0xF.

2. Perform a bitwise AND operation between the value of 0xFF in the W1 register and the result of ~0xF (0xFFFF_FFF0).

The BIC instruction clears specific bits in the first operand. In the preceding example, the value in the W1 register is the target for this operation. The bits set to 1 in the second operand determine which bits in the first operand will be cleared, turning those bits to 0.

The EOR instruction

The EOR instruction performs a bitwise XOR (**Exclusive OR**) operation. To understand this, we can look at the truth table for XOR in *Table 3.3*:

X	Y	X XOR Y
0	0	0
0	1	1
1	0	1
1	1	0

Table 3.3: Truth table for EOR operations

In low-level programming and systems programming, the EOR operation is used as a way to manipulate individual bits. EOR is particularly useful for toggling bits, meaning it can switch a bit from 0 to 1 or from 1 to 0.

The EOR instruction performs a **bitwise XOR** operation between registers. Let's look at *Figure 3.20* to learn about the EOR instruction:

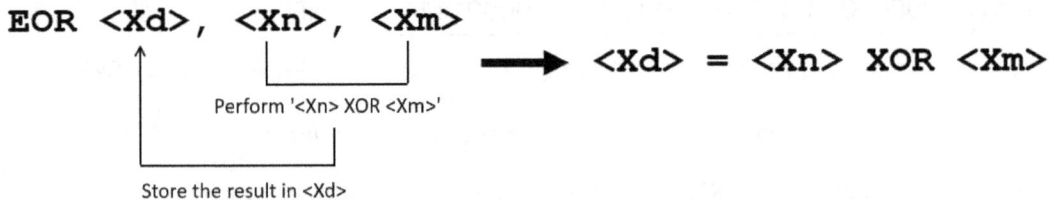

Figure 3.20: The EOR instruction syntax

As shown in *Figure 3.20*, the result of performing a bitwise XOR operation on the values in the <Xn> and <Xm> registers is stored in <Xd>. This can be expressed in C language syntax as <Xn> ^ <Xm>.

Examples of the EOR instruction

Let's analyze the example code with the EOR instruction to understand how it works:

```
EOR W0, W1, W2
```

Before executing the preceding instruction, the precondition is that the W1 register holds 0xC0F, and the value of the W2 register is 0xCF0.

The operation of the example instruction can be represented in the following figure:

```
  00000000 00000000 00001100 00001111     (W1: 0xC0F)
^) 00000000 00000000 00001100 11110000     (W2: 0xCF0)
   ─────────────────────────────────────
  00000000 00000000 00000000 11111111           (0xFF)
```

Figure 3.21: The detailed operation: the EOR instruction

Figure 3.21 shows how the XOR operation works between the values stored in the W1 (0xC0F) and W2 (0xCF0) registers. XOR gives a result of 1 only when exactly one of the compared bits is 1.

After executing this instruction, the W0 register is updated to 0xFF, as shown in the lower part of *Figure 3.21*.

In this section, we have learned about instructions for logical operations. Now, let's practice using them in code examples.

Practicing logical operations

First, here is simple C code that uses logical operations:

```c
#include <stdio.h>
void logical_operation(void)
{
    unsigned int x = 0x23, y = 0x123, z = 0x103;
    unsigned int a = 0xf, b = 0xf0;
    unsigned int result1, result2, result3;

    result1 = x & y;
    result2 = x | z;
    result3 = a ^ b;

    printf("result1: 0x%x result2: 0x%x result3: 0x%x \n",
            result1, result2, result3);
}

int main()
{
    logical_operation();
    return 0;
}
```

Here's what the code does related to logical operations:

- `result1 = x & y`; uses AND to compare x and y
- `result2 = x | z`; uses OR to compare x and z
- `result3 = a ^ b`; uses XOR to compare a and b
- The `printf` function then prints the results

After we compile the C code, we can use a tool called a disassembler to see the assembly code. Let's look at what the compiler generates for each part of our code.

The AND operation

First, let's examine the AND instruction:

```
result1 = x & y;
```

In assembly, it looks like this:

```
784:    b9402fe1    ldr    w1, [sp, #44]
788:    b9402be0    ldr    w0, [sp, #40]
78c:    0a000020    and    w0, w1, w0
```

Here's how the code works:

- The AND instruction performs a bitwise AND operation on the values in W1 and W0
- The result is stored in W0

The OR operation

Next, we are going to analyze the ORR instruction, as follows:

```
result2 = x | z;
```

In assembly, we can see the following code:

```
794:    b9402fe1    ldr    w1, [sp, #44]
798:    b94027e0    ldr    w0, [sp, #36]
79c:    2a000020    orr    w0, w1, w0
```

Here's what the code does:

- The ORR instruction performs a bitwise OR operation on the values in W1 and W0
- The result is stored in W0

The XOR operation

Let's look at the following C code associated with the XOR operation:

```
result3 = a ^ b;
```

In assembly, the preceding code looks like this:

```
7a4:    b94023e1    ldr    w1, [sp, #32]
7a8:    b9401fe0    ldr    w0, [sp, #28]
7ac:    4a000020    eor    w0, w1, w0
```

Here's what the code performs:

- The EOR instruction performs a bitwise XOR operation on the values in W1 and W0
- The result is stored in W0

In this section, we have learned about the fundamental instructions involved in logical operations. These instructions are used to perform bit manipulation, which is crucial when dealing with state machines in software routines. Note that bit manipulation is especially important in low-level software development, particularly under memory constraints. Additionally, when reading or writing a specific bit in a variable, instructions related to logical operations are commonly used.

Now that we have finished the logical operation instructions, let's learn how to reconstruct assembly instructions based on C code in the next section.

Practicing data processing instructions

After understanding the syntax of each instruction, the next step is to practice by examining as many assembly instructions as possible. In this section, you will learn how instructions related to data-processing operations are executed to perform specific tasks.

Here is a C code that uses logical operations and a comparison statement:

```
#include <stdio.h>
#include <unistd.h>
#include <sys/types.h>

#define TASK_RUNNING            0x0000
#define TASK_INTERRUPTIBLE      0x0001
#define TASK_UNINTERRUPTIBLE    0x0002
#define __TASK_STOPPED          0x0004
```

```
void compare_operation(void)
{
    unsigned int state = TASK_UNINTERRUPTIBLE | TASK_INTERRUPTIBLE;
    unsigned int count = 1;

    if (state & TASK_UNINTERRUPTIBLE) {
        count++;
        state &= ~TASK_UNINTERRUPTIBLE;
    }
    else {
        count--;
        state |= __TASK_STOPPED;
    }
    check_curr_state(state);
}

int main()
{
    compare_operation();
    return 0;
}
```

When we compile this C code, we can use a tool called a disassembler to see the assembly code. Let's examine the assembly code that the compiler generates for each part of our code.

Initializing variables

First, let's review the routine for setting local variables. The compare_operation function contains C code along with its corresponding assembly instructions:

```
01 void compare_operation(void)
02 {
03 788: a9be7bfd    stp x29, x30, [sp, #-32]!
04 78c: 910003fd    mov x29, sp
05 unsigned int state = TASK_UNINTERRUPTIBLE | TASK_INTERRUPTIBLE;
06 790: 52800060    mov w0, #0x3              // #3
07 794: b9001fe0    str w0, [sp, #28]
08 unsigned int count = 1;
09 798: 52800020    mov w0, #0x1              // #1
```

Here, the assembly code is setting up the local variables. The MOV instruction is used to set state to 0x3 and count to 0x1, and then it stores these values in the stack.

Checking the state

Now, let's check the assembly instruction for the state & TASK_UNINTERRUPTIBLE expression inside the if statement:

```
01 void compare_operation(void)
02 {
[...]
03 if (state & TASK_UNINTERRUPTIBLE) {
04 7a0: b9401fe0    ldr w0, [sp, #28]
05 7a4: 121f0000    and w0, w0, #0x2
06 7a8: 7100001f    cmp w0, #0x0
07 7ac: 54000100    b.eq 7cc <compare_operation+0x44>  // b.none
08 count++;
09 7b0: b9401be0    ldr w0, [sp, #24]
10 7b4: 11000400    add w0, w0, #0x1
```

Here, the code checks whether state has the TASK_UNINTERRUPTIBLE bit set. The AND instruction checks this by comparing the state with 0x2. If a state has this bit set, the code increments the count.

Clearing a bit

Inside the if block, there is the state &= ~TASK_UNINTERRUPTIBLE statement. Let's analyze how this statement is implemented in assembly language:

```
01 void compare_operation(void)
02 {
[...]
03 state &= ~TASK_UNINTERRUPTIBLE;
04 7bc: b9401fe0    ldr w0, [sp, #28]
05 7c0: 121e7800    and w0, w0, #0xfffffffd
06 7c4: b9001fe0    str w0, [sp, #28]
07 7c8: 14000007    b 7e4 <compare_operation+0x5c>
```

This part of the code clears the TASK_UNINTERRUPTIBLE bit in state. The AND instruction keeps all bits the same except for the one that needs to be cleared—that is, 0b10.

Handling the else part

Inside the else block, there is the state |= __TASK_STOPPED statement. Let's find out how this statement is implemented in assembly language:

```
01 void compare_operation(void)
02 {
[...]
03 else {
04 count--;
05 7cc: b9401be0    ldr w0, [sp, #24]
06 7d0: 51000400    sub w0, w0, #0x1
07 7d4: b9001be0    str w0, [sp, #24]
08 state |= __TASK_STOPPED;
09 7d8: b9401fe0    ldr w0, [sp, #28]
10 7dc: 321e0000    orr w0, w0, #0x4
11 7e0: b9001fe0    str w0, [sp, #28]
```

Here, the code decreases the count if the TASK_UNINTERRUPTIBLE bit is not set. It then sets the __TASK_STOPPED bit in state using the ORR instruction.

In this section, you learned how instructions are used to complete specific tasks. Instructions such as MOV, AND, and ORR are common in many programs. After understanding the content in this section, you will be able to convert assembly instructions into C code.

Summary

In this chapter, you learned about important instructions for arithmetic, logic, and bit-shift operations. These instructions are very useful in reverse engineering because you will often see them in many assembly programs. They also help you understand how data is processed in both software and hardware.

Next, we analyzed assembly instructions together with C code. This helps us convert assembly instructions back into C code. This type of work is very common in reverse engineering.

The next chapter will focus on assembly instructions for memory access. These instructions are important for storing, loading, and changing data in software programs.

Join our community on Discord

Join our community's Discord space for discussions with the authors and other readers: `https://packt.link/embeddedsystems`

4

Reading and Writing with Memory Access Instructions

The Arm® architecture does not work directly with data in memory. Instead, it first accesses a memory address, loads the data into a register, performs the operation using the register, and then stores the result back in memory through the register. This method helps ensure efficient and accurate data processing.

To support this process, the Arm architecture provides several instructions for memory access. The most common ones are LDR and STR.

In this chapter, we will focus on the LDR and STR instructions and cover the following main topics:

- The LDR instruction
- The STR instruction
- Extension: Memory access operation
- Practicing memory access instructions

Note that you will likely encounter the LDR and STR instructions in any assembly routine, as they are essential operations in Arm assembly programming. Additionally, these instructions are crucial for reverse engineering.

Now, let's begin this chapter by looking at the LDR instruction.

Technical requirements

All the code examples and binary files for this chapter can be found on GitHub at `https://github.com/PacktPublishing/Reverse-Engineering-Armv8-A-Systems`.

To learn more about Armv8-A, you can check the following materials:

- Armv8-A Reference Manual: `https://developer.arm.com/documentation/ddi0487/gb`
- Programmer's Guide for ARMv8-A: `https://developer.arm.com/documentation/den0024/latest/`

The LDR instruction

The `LDR` instruction stands for *load register*, which is used to load a **word** of data from memory into a register. Here, a word is a unit of data that the CPU handles at once, and it usually matches the register size. For example, in AArch64 Armv8-A, the word size is 64 bits.

First, let's review the syntax of the `LDR` instruction in its basic form. Then, we will examine the `LDR` instruction with the offset addressing mode.

Syntax: LDR instruction in basic form

Let's take a look at *Figure 4.1*, which illustrates the syntax of the `LDR` instruction.

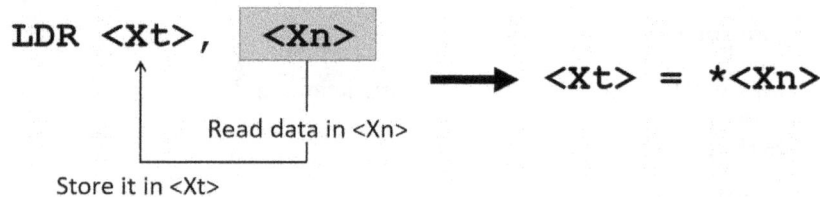

Figure 4.1: The syntax of the LDR instruction

Here, `<Xn>` is the base register, which holds the memory address to access, while `<Xt>` is the destination register. In other words, we can say that it reads the data from `<Xt>` and stores it in `<Xn>`. When running the `LDR` instruction illustrated in *Figure 4.1*, it performs the following actions simultaneously:

- It accesses the memory address indicated by the base register, `<Xn>`.
- The data at the memory address is loaded in the destination register, `<Xt>`.

Considering the memory access operation, the base register is a memory address to access. So, the LDR instruction corresponds to the following equation:

```
<Xt> = *<Xn>;
```

Since the LDR instruction is associated with memory access, you need to visualize the memory layout. Let's look at *Figure 4.2*, which illustrates how the LDR instruction operates.

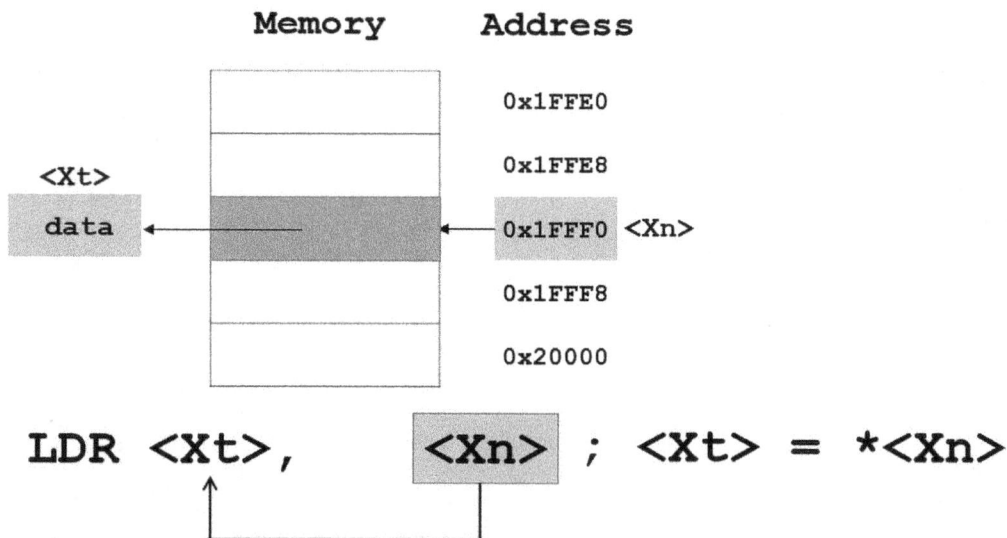

Figure 4.2: The LDR instruction with memory layout

As seen in *Figure 4.2*, there is a memory layout starting from 0x1FFE0 to 0x2000. If <Xn> holds the value 0x1FFF0, the LDR instruction stores the data at address 0x1FFF0 into <Xt>. Here, <Xt> and <Xn> can be specified by any of the general-purpose registers. The following are example instructions related to the basic LDR instruction:

```
01 LDR X1, [X2] ; X1 = *X2
02 LDR X3, [X7] ; X3 = *X7
```

Let's analyze the instruction on line 01 as an example. If X2 holds the value 0x1FFF0, the data at the 0x1FFF0 memory address is loaded into X1. Similarly, considering the instruction on line 02, if X7 holds the value 0x1FFF0, the data at the 0x1FFF0 address is loaded into the X3 register.

When examining an assembly routine, you will encounter other forms of LDR instruction that use
offset addressing mode. *Figure 4.3* illustrates how the LDR instruction works with this addressing
mode:

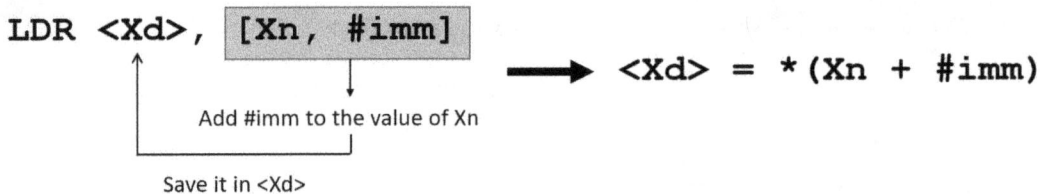

```
LDR <Xd>, [Xn, #imm]            ➞    <Xd> = *(Xn + #imm)
          │         │
          │  Add #imm to the value of Xn
          └─────────┘
       Save it in <Xd>
```

Figure 4.3: The syntax of the LDR instruction with offset addressing mode

As shown in *Figure 4.3*, the <Xn> register holds the base address in memory. Therefore, <Xn> is
referred to as the base register in the LDR instruction. #imm represents an offset, which is an integer
value. This offset is added to the value in the <Xn> register to determine the address from which
to load the data. The data at the <Xn> + #imm address is then loaded into the <Xd> register. This
operation can be represented by the following equation:

```
<Xd> = *<Xn + #imm>;
```

Now that you have learned the basic form of the LDR instruction, let's explore the LDR instruction
using offset addressing mode with memory layout.

LDR instruction with offset addressing mode

Let's explore how the LDR instruction works with offset addressing mode. *Figure 4.4* visualizes
this operation in detail.

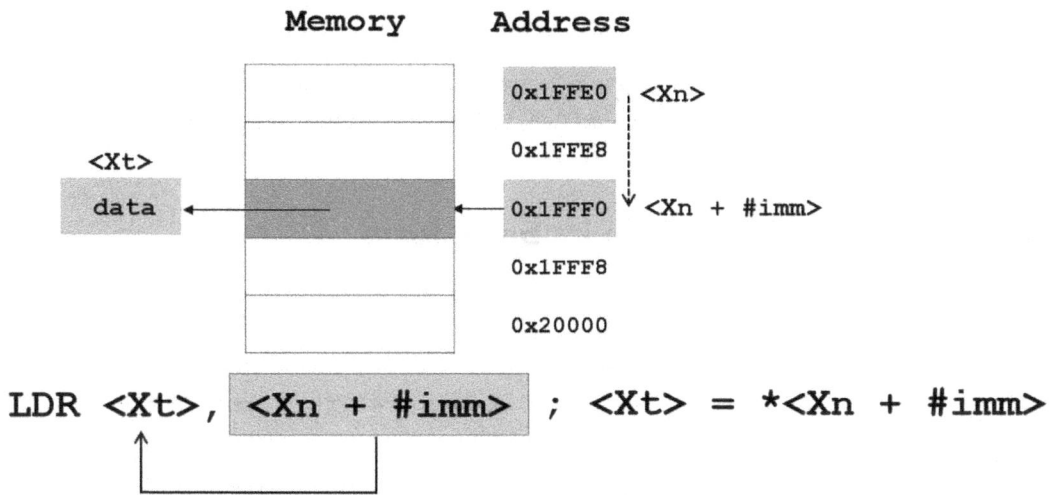

Figure 4.4: The LDR instruction with memory layout

As seen in *Figure 4.4*, there is a memory layout ranging from 0x1FFE0 to 0x2000. If <Xn> has the value 0x1FFE0, the #imm offset is added to 0x1FFE0. The address to access can be calculated as follows:

```
0x1FFF0 = 0x1FFE0 + 0x10;
```

This LDR instruction loads the data from the 0x1FFF0 address into <Xt>. The <Xt> and <Xn> can be any of the general-purpose registers. The following are example instructions relevant to the basic LDR instruction:

```
01 LDR X1, [X2, #0x10] ; X1 = *(X2 + 0x10)
02 LDR X3, [X7, #0x10] ; X3 = *(X7 + 0x10)
```

Let's analyze the instruction on line 01 as an example. If X2 holds the value 0x1FFE0, the address to access is calculated as 0x1FFE0 + 0x10. Therefore, the data at address 0x1FFF0 is loaded into X1.

Similarly, for the instruction on line 02, if X7 holds the value 0x1FFE0, the data at address 0x1FFF0 (i.e., 0x1FFE0 + 0x10) is loaded into X3.

In this section, we have explored the LDR instruction, which is used to load data from memory. You will likely encounter the LDR instruction when analyzing any assembly routines, so it's important to understand it well. Next, we will examine the STR instruction, which is responsible for storing data in memory.

The STR instruction

The STR instruction stands for *store register*, which is another memory access instruction. First, let's analyze the syntax of the STR instruction in its basic form. Then, we will investigate the STR instruction with the offset addressing mode.

Syntax: STR instruction in its basic form

Let's look at *Figure 4.5* to learn about the STR instruction in its basic form.

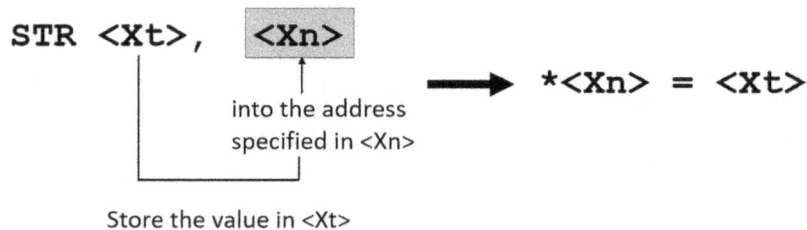

Figure 4.5: The syntax of the STR instruction

When we analyze the STR instruction, the first step is to check the value of the operand used in the instruction. One special feature of the STR instruction is that it does not have a destination register like other instructions. Instead, the STR instruction takes the value from the <Xt> and stores it in the memory address given by the <Xn>.

In terms of memory access, the <Xn> register holds the memory address. Thus, the STR instruction can be represented by the following equation:

```
*<Xn> = <Xt>;
```

Here, <Xn> is the base register that indicates the memory address where the data from <Xt> is stored.

Similar to the LDR instruction, it is important to visualize the memory layout when learning the STR instruction, as it is associated with memory access. *Figure 4.6* illustrates how the STR instruction works.

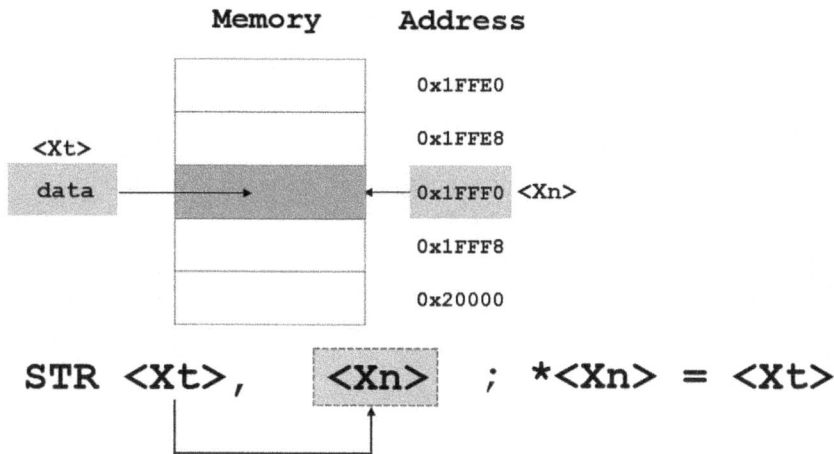

Figure 4.6: The STR instruction with memory layout

In *Figure 4.6*, you can see a memory layout from address 0x1FFE0 to 0x2000. This layout shows how the STR instruction works. If <Xn> had the value 0x1FFF0, the STR instruction would store the value in <Xt> at the 0x1FFF0 memory address. Both <Xt> and <Xn> can be any of the general-purpose registers. The following are example instructions that use the basic STR instruction:

```
01 STR X1, [X2] ; *X2 = X1
02 STR X3, [X7] ; *X7 = X3
```

Let's look at the instruction on line 01 as an example. If X2 has the value 0x1FFF0, the value in X1 is stored at memory address 0x1FFF0. The instruction on line 02 also does a store operation. If X7 has the value 0x1FFF0, then the value in X3 is stored at the memory address given by X7, which is 0x1FFF0.

STR instruction with offset addressing mode

Now that you have learned how the STR instruction works, you are ready to explore the STR instruction with offset addressing mode, as seen in *Figure 4.7*:

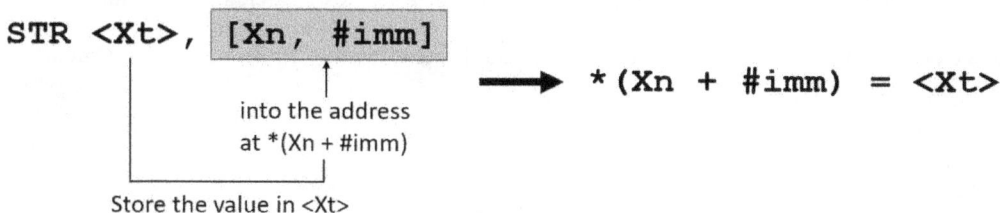

Figure 4.7: The syntax of the STR instruction with offset addressing mode

As shown in *Figure 4.7*, the <Xn> register holds a memory address as the base address, so <Xn> is considered the base register in the STR instruction. #imm represents an offset, which is an integer value. This offset is added to the value in the <Xn> register to determine the final address where the data will be stored. The value of <Xt> is then stored in the memory location at <Xn> + #imm. The STR instruction with offset addressing mode can be represented as follows:

```
*<Xn + #imm> = <Xt>;
```

At this point, let's look at *Figure 4.8* to explore how the STR instruction works with offset addressing mode in more detail.

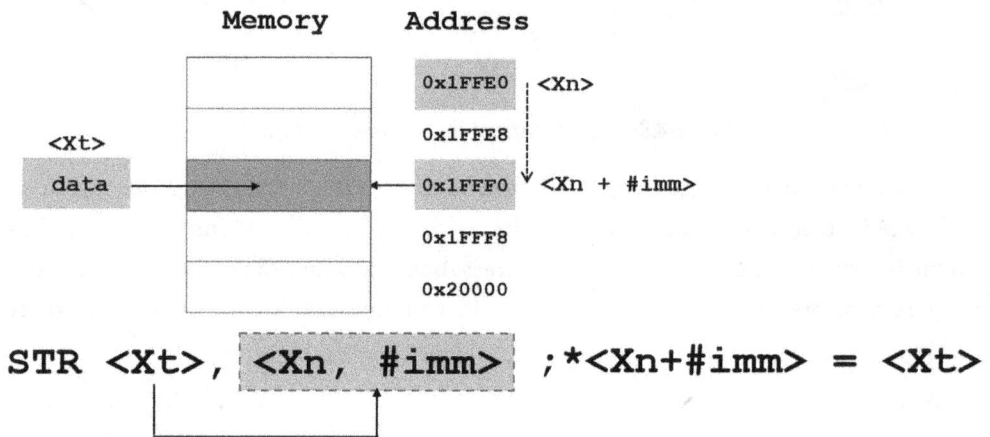

Figure 4.8: The STR instruction with memory layout

As seen in *Figure 4.8*, the memory layout ranges from 0x1FFE0 to 0x2000. If <Xn> has the value 0x1FFE0 and the #imm offset is 0x10, the address to store the value from <Xt> can be represented in the following way:

```
0x1FFF0 = 0x1FFE0 + 0x10;
```

This STR instruction stores the value in <Xt> into the memory location at 0x1FFF0. Note that <Xt> and <Xn> can be specified by any of the general-purpose registers, such as X0 to X30.

To better understand the STR instruction, it is helpful to analyze various examples. Consider the following instructions:

```
01 STR X1, [X2, #0x10] ; *(X2 + 0x10) = X1;
02 STR X3, [X7, #0x10] ; *(X7 + 0x10) = X3;
```

Let's break it down, line by line:

- Line 01: If X2 has the value 0x1FFE0, the target address is calculated as 0x1FFE0 + 0x10. So, the value in X1 is stored at address 0x1FFF0.

- Line 02: If X7 has the value 0x1FFE0, then the value in X3 is stored at address 0x1FFF0 (which is 0x1FFE0 + 0x10).

In this section, we looked at the basic syntax of the STR instruction and how it works in storing data. Since you will also need to analyze the STR instruction alongside the LDR instruction during reverse engineering, it's important to learn it thoroughly. Additionally, the Arm architecture provides extended instructions for both LDR and STR. In the next section, we will explore these extended instructions.

Extension: Memory access operation

Up to this point, we have explored the LDR and STR instructions. Now, let's explore the variations of these instructions that support different data sizes during load operations.

Various load operations

Armv8-A offers more instructions associated with load operations, as follows:

- LDRH (load register halfword): Loads 16-bit (zero-extended) data from memory into a register

- LDRSH (load register signed halfword): Loads 16-bit (sign-extended) data from memory into a register

- LDRB (load register byte): Loads 8-bit (zero-extended) data from memory into a register

- LDRSB (load register signed byte): Loads 8-bit (sign-extended) data from memory into a register

The zero extension and sign extension mentioned in the preceding instructions have the following features:

- **Zero-extended:** Typically used for processing unsigned numbers. When a smaller value (e.g., 16-bit or 8-bit) is loaded into a larger register (e.g., 64-bit), the upper bits (from the size of the original value up to the full register width) are filled with 0s. This happens in instructions such as LDRH (load halfword, 16 bits) or LDRB (load byte, 8 bits).

- **Sign-extended:** Usually used for processing signed numbers, which can represent both positive and negative values. If the data is negative, the remaining bit positions up to the most significant bits are filled with 1s. If the data is positive, the upper bits will be filled with 0s.

The LDR instruction works similarly to these other instructions, with the primary difference being the size of the data that is loaded.

Various store operations

Similar to instructions that support load operations, there are more instructions associated with store operations, which are as follows:

- STRB (store register byte): Stores the least significant byte (8 bits) of a register into memory
- STRH (store register halfword): Stores the least significant 16 bits (halfword) of a register into memory

The STR instruction works similarly to the previously listed instruction; the only difference is the size of the data being stored, which can be either 1 byte or 2 bytes. For example, the STRB instruction stores data of 1-byte size from memory, while the STRH instruction stores data of 2-byte size.

The secret behind load operations

As explained, the LDRH instruction reads 16-bit data from memory, and the LDRB instruction reads 8-bit data. Some engineers use these instructions to optimize operations because reading smaller data sizes can be useful in certain situations.

However, using LDRH or LDRB does not always make data reading faster. This is because the Arm core usually reads data from the cache, not directly from the main memory (like DRAM). In Arm processors such as the Cortex®-A53, the cache line size is often 64 bytes. No matter whether you use LDR, LDRH, or LDRB, the data is normally already in the cache.

Note

The cache is a smaller, faster memory located closer to the CPU, designed to reduce the time needed to access frequently used data. When the required data is already in the cache, the access time is significantly reduced compared to accessing it from the main memory.

So, choosing between LDR, LDRH, and LDRB is mainly about the size of the data you want to access, not about making the operation faster. The actual performance benefit of using these instructions comes from the efficient use of memory bandwidth and a reduced memory footprint, not from the smaller size of the load operation. This is because no matter which instruction you use, the Arm core still gets data from the cache.

In summary, while LDRH and LDRB can be useful for handling smaller data sizes, they do not inherently improve read speed due to the Arm core's reliance on cache memory.

Understanding this helps in making informed decisions about which instruction to use based on the data size requirements, rather than expecting performance improvements in terms of access speed.

In this section, you have learned about the extended LDR and STR instructions for memory access. In the following section, we will analyze example code that utilizes the LDR and STR instructions.

Practicing memory access instructions

After understanding the syntax of each instruction, it is highly recommended to examine how each instruction is used to perform specific tasks. This allows you to figure out how memory access instructions such as LDR and STR are employed at the assembly level.

Introducing example code

In this section, you will learn how instructions related to memory access are executed to accomplish specific operations. Here is an example C snippet for practice.

```c
#include <stdio.h>
#include <stdint.h>
#include <stdlib.h>

struct task_struct {
    int flags;
    int state;
    char task_name[15];
};

void init_task_state(void)
{
    struct task_struct *ptr;
```

```
    ptr = (struct task_struct *)malloc(sizeof(*ptr));
    ptr->state = 1;

    printf("state:%d \n", ptr->state);
    free(ptr);
}

int main(void)
{
    init_task_state();

    return 0;
}
```

Using the example code here, you can see how high-level code translates into assembly instructions, particularly focusing on memory access operations. We can highlight what the example code does:

- Defines a structure
- Allocates memory for it
- Assigns a value to one of its fields
- Prints the result

Let's examine the assembly routine in the init_task_state function after disassembling this function. You will learn how the LDR and STR instructions are used to handle memory allocation with malloc, assign values to structure members, and manage function calls:

```
01 init_task_state:  // @init_task_state
02   sub      sp, sp, #32
03   stp      x29, x30, [sp, #16]  // 16-byte Folded Spill
04   add      x29, sp, #16
05   mov      x0, #24
06   bl       malloc
07   str      x0, [sp, #8]
08   ldr      x9, [sp, #8]
09   mov      w8, #1
10   str      w8, [x9, #4]
11   ldr      x8, [sp, #8]
12   ldr      w1, [x8, #4]
```

```
13    adrp    x0, .L.str
14    add     x0, x0, :lo12:.L.str
15    bl      printf
16    ldp     x29, x30, [sp, #16] // 16-byte Folded Reload
17    add     sp, sp, #32
18    ret
```

Let's focus on the behavior of the STR and LDR instructions in the example code.

Analyzing assembly routine: STR and LDR

The following is the first part of the routine:

```
06    bl      malloc
07    str     x0, [sp, #8]
08    ldr     x9, [sp, #8]
09    mov     w8, #1
10    str     w8, [x9, #4]
```

Note that the above code corresponds to the following C code snippet:

```
ptr = (struct task_struct *)malloc(sizeof(*ptr));
ptr->state = 1;
```

First, let's analyze line 07, which contains the STR instruction. When the instruction on line 07 is executed, the value in register x0 is stored in a memory location, represented as [sp, #8]. The x0 register holds the address returned by the malloc function, which corresponds to the ptr local variable. The detailed operation in line 07 can be described as follows:

- The base register is sp, which is the stack pointer for the process.
- The address to store the data is calculated as sp + 8. For example, if sp is 0x10000, then sp + 8 would be 0x10008.
- The data in x0 is stored in the memory address at sp + 8.

> **Note**
>
> Since the base register for the STR instruction is sp, where sp stands for stack pointer register, we can refer to this operation as a stack push. This is because the instruction effectively saves the current value of x0 onto the stack, ensuring it can be retrieved later.

Let's look at the second part of the assembly routine:

```
08   ldr    x9, [sp, #8]
09   mov    w8, #1
10   str    w8, [x9, #4]
```

As you can see, the assembly instruction in line 08 is LDR, which loads data from memory. The base register for this operation is sp, and the immediate value is 8. As the LDR instruction performs the load operation, it accesses the address at sp + 8. The data at sp + 8 is then stored in x9. Note that x9 now holds the start address of struct task_struct, because this address was stored at sp + 8 in the previous instruction.

Remember that the base register for this case is sp. What this instruction does can be thought of as a stack pop, retrieving the stored address from the stack.

Next, let's examine line 09. The value 1 is moved into the w8 register. This instruction corresponds to the following C code:

```
ptr->state = 1;
```

Finally, let's examine the code in line 10. The STR instruction stores the value in w8 to the memory location denoted as [x9, #4]. Here, it is important to understand why the immediate value is #4. The reason is that 4 is the offset for the state field in struct task_struct, which is declared as follows:

```
struct task_struct {
    int flags;
    int state;
    char task_name[15];
};
```

When analyzing this routine from a reverse engineering point of view, you will see that line 10 performs the operation to store the value 1 into ptr->state, which is located at [x9, #4].

This step-by-step analysis shows how high-level C code translates into assembly instructions. By understanding each instruction, you can see how memory is allocated, accessed, and manipulated at a low level.

Summary

A key principle in the Armv8-A architecture is that all data in memory must first be loaded into a register before any arithmetic or logical operations can be performed. Once an operation is completed, the result held in the register is then saved back into the memory space. This process ensures efficient data manipulation.

In this chapter, you learned about assembly instructions that support memory access operations. First, we reviewed the syntax of the LDR and STR instructions and analyzed example code using these instructions.

You studied how LDR and STR instructions perform specific tasks in a routine. These instructions are used to move data between registers and memory, which makes them very important for debugging. Next, we looked at a snippet of C source code and saw how it is converted into assembly instructions during disassembly. Then, you learned how LDR and STR are used to assign values to specific fields in a structure.

When you read any assembly code, you will often see LDR and STR instructions. So, understanding how they work is important for effective debugging.

In the next chapter, we will learn about assembly instructions used for flow control. You will also learn how specific instructions are used to control the execution flow.

5

Controlling Execution with Flow Control Instructions

When analyzing source code, software developers focus on the execution flow. In C code, this often involves if/else statements and conditional expressions that handle return values from functions. When you disassemble this code, you'll see that it uses conditional branch instructions to perform these tasks.

This chapter covers the following operations and their associated assembly instructions:

- Branch operations
- Comparison operations
- Conditional branch operations
- System control operations

Understanding these assembly instructions helps us analyze the execution flow of an assembly routine. Like in other chapters, the flow control instructions covered in this chapter are based on AArch64 (64-bit) in the Armv8-A.

Technical requirements

All the code examples and binary files for this chapter can be found on GitHub at https://github.com/PacktPublishing/Reverse-Engineering-Armv8-A-Systems.

To learn more about Armv8-A, you can check the following materials:

- Armv8-A Reference Manual: `https://developer.arm.com/documentation/ddi0487/gb`
- Programmer's Guide for ARMv8-A: `https://developer.arm.com/documentation/den0024/latest/`

Branch instructions

`Armv8-A` supports the following instructions associated with branch operations:

- `B, BR`
- `BL, BLR`

The branch instruction changes the execution flow. How does it change? The branch instruction updates the PC with the target address specified in the branch instruction. The target address in the branch instruction can be either the start address of a label or function or an address to the branch inside a label or function. In addition, the branch instruction is used for conditional logic, loops (`for` or `while`), and subroutines.

Let's begin this section with the `B` instruction.

The B instruction

The `B` instruction stands for *Branch* and performs a basic branch operation. Let's review *Figure 5.1*, which shows the syntax of the `B` instruction:

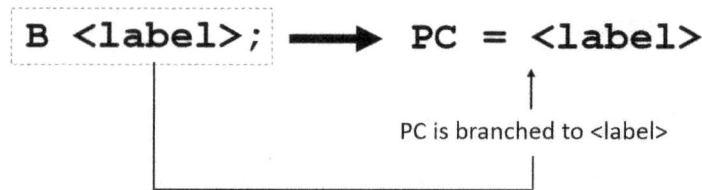

Figure 5.1: The syntax of the B instruction

The `B` instruction performs an unconditional branch to a target address or label. When the `B` instruction runs, it updates the PC with the target address. This address can be given directly or written as a label in the code. The target address tells the Arm core where to go next. `<label>` is a name for the target location in the code.

> **Note**
>
> It's common to see the destination register in many assembly instructions. However, for branch operations, there is no destination register. Instead of modifying a destination register, the Arm core updates the PC while executing the branch instruction.

This type of B <label> instruction is often used in startup code or routines that initialize the resources of the system.

The BL instruction

Let's learn about the BL instruction. BL stands for *Branch with Link*. To understand how the BL instruction works, let's examine *Figure 5.2*:

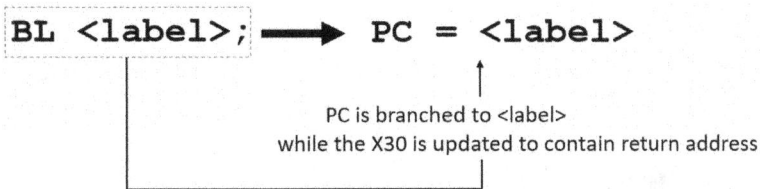

BL <label>; ⟶ PC = <label>

PC is branched to <label>
while the X30 is updated to contain return address

Figure 5.2: The syntax of the BL instruction

As shown in *Figure 5.2*, when the BL instruction is executed, the Arm core performs the following actions simultaneously:

- Branches to the address specified by <label>.
- Updates the X30 register to hold the return address.

The key difference from the B instruction is that X30 is updated to store the return address. A common question is how the BL instruction is used in real projects. The answer is: in practice, statements related to calling a function in C code are translated into the BL instruction.

The BR instruction

BR stands for *Branch to Register*. This instruction branches to the address specified in a register. Let's take a look at *Figure 5.3*, which describes the format of the BR instruction:

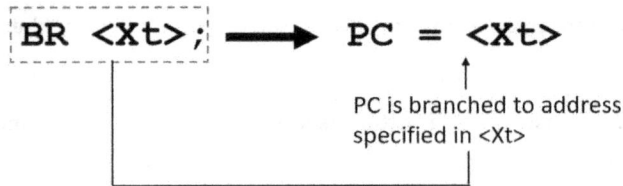

$$BR\ \text{<Xt>;} \longrightarrow PC\ =\ \text{<Xt>}$$

PC is branched to address specified in <Xt>

Figure 5.3: The syntax of the BR instruction

As shown in *Figure 5.3*, the BR instruction uses <Xt>, which can be any of the general-purpose registers, such as X0, X1, X2, ..., or X30. How is <Xt> used? The BR instruction updates the value in <Xt> to the PC. In other words, the PC is updated to the address held in <Xt>.

The behavior of the BR instruction is almost identical to that of the B instruction; the difference is that the BR instruction performs an unconditional branch operation specified by a register.

The BLR instruction

BLR stands for *Branch with Link and Register*. When the BLR instruction is executed, it branches to the address specified in a register and updates the link register with the return address. Let's review *Figure 5.4* to understand the format of the BLR instruction:

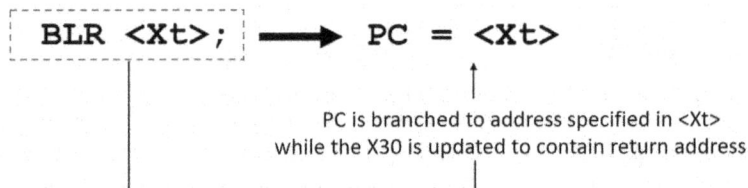

$$BLR\ \text{<Xt>;} \longrightarrow PC\ =\ \text{<Xt>}$$

PC is branched to address specified in <Xt>
while the X30 is updated to contain return address

Figure 5.4: The syntax of the BLR instruction

When the BLR <Xt> instruction runs, the Arm core updates the return address in the link register, which is the X30 register. In the C language, when code calls a function using a function pointer, the compiler creates a BLR <Xt> instruction to do the function call.

Analyzing an example routine

Let's examine *Figure 5.5* to learn about the differences between the B and BL instructions together:

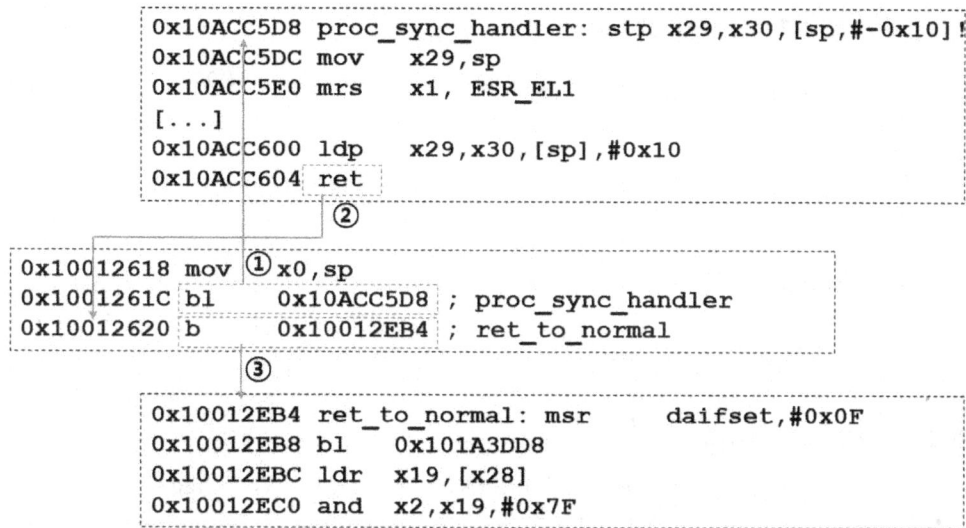

```
0x10ACC5D8 proc_sync_handler: stp x29,x30,[sp,#-0x10]!
0x10ACC5DC mov    x29,sp
0x10ACC5E0 mrs    x1, ESR_EL1
[...]
0x10ACC600 ldp    x29,x30,[sp],#0x10
0x10ACC604 ret
                  ②


0x10012618 mov  ① x0,sp
0x1001261C bl     0x10ACC5D8 ; proc_sync_handler
0x10012620 b      0x10012EB4 ; ret_to_normal
                  ③


0x10012EB4 ret_to_normal: msr      daifset,#0x0F
0x10012EB8 bl     0x101A3DD8
0x10012EBC ldr    x19,[x28]
0x10012EC0 and    x2,x19,#0x7F
```

Figure 5.5: The workflow of the B and BL instructions

First, let's look at the part marked as **1** in the assembly instructions in the middle of the figure:

```
0x1001261C bl     0x10ACC5D8 ; proc_sync_handler
0x10012620 b      0x10012EB4 ; ret_to_normal
```

When the bl 0x10ACC5D8 instruction is executed, the following actions occur simultaneously:

- The PC is branched to the address 0x10ACC5D8.
- The x30 register is updated to the return address 0x10012620, which is the next address after the proc_sync_handler symbol.

Next, look at the part marked as **2** in the figure. This shows the execution of the RET instruction, which completes the proc_sync_handler. When the RET instruction is executed, the PC is updated to the address 0x10012620, which is the return address.

Finally, look at the part marked as **3** in the figure. This shows the branch to the address 0x10012EB4, where the ret_to_normal label is located. One important point to note: when branching to the address 0x10012EB4, the return address is not updated in the x30 register.

When analyzing an assembly routine, you will encounter the B and BL instructions in any code. It is good to remember the difference between these two instructions.

Now that you have learned about unconditional branch operation, let's learn about the instructions associated with comparison operation.

Comparison operations

The Armv8-A architecture provides the following comparison instructions:

- CMP
- CMN
- TST

When these instructions are executed, the Arm core checks the operands' data and updates the *NZCV* flags. In this section, we will explain the PSTATE related to the *NZCV* flags, followed by explanations of the CMP, CMN, and TST instructions.

The condition flags in PSTATE

Before we explore the comparison instruction, let's understand the *NZCV* flags in PSTATE, as these flags can affect the instructions related to comparison operation. As discussed in *Chapter 1*, the PSTATE provides an abstraction that contains the process state. *Figure 5.6* indicates the condition flags of the PSTATE:

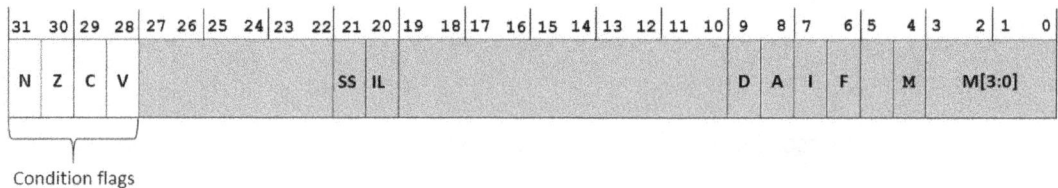

Figure 5.6: Condition flags in PSTATE

As you can see in *Figure 5.6*, the condition flags are located in bits [31:28] of the PSTATE. The following are descriptions of how these flags are updated:

- N (Negative): Indicates that an operation yielded a negative value.
- Z (Zero): Indicates that an operation results in zero.
- C (Carry): Specifies that an operation yielded carry.
- V (oVerflow): Indicates that the arithmetic operation yielded a signed overflow.

When a comparison instruction is executed, the result is updated in the condition flags. The value of these conditional flags may affect the execution of the next conditional branch instruction. It is essential to check the condition flags because they are associated with the control flow of the assembly routine.

> **Note**
>
> Not all of the instructions update the NZCV flags in the PSTATE. If the CMP, CMN, and TST instructions are performed, the NZCV flags can be updated.
>
> A common question is: How are the conditional instructions organized? To answer this question, we need to figure out the condition code in *Table 5.1*.

From now on, we will use PSTATE.{N,Z,C,V} to represent the NZCV flags for better understanding.

The CMP instruction

The CMP instruction stands for *Compare*. As the name implies, the CMP instruction supports the compare operation between two operands. *Figure 5.7* shows the basic format of the CMP instruction:

Figure 5.7: The syntax of the CMP instruction

As shown in *Figure 5.7*, the CMP instruction updates NZCV flags, which are condition flag bits PSTATE.{N,Z,C,V} with the result of the Xn - Op2 operation. Let's break down how the CMP instruction performs:

- It performs a subtraction operation between the two operands.
- The result updates PSTATE.{N,Z,C,V}.
- The CMP instruction does not show a destination register.
- The result of the CMP instruction affects the conditional branch instructions that follow it

> **Note**
>
> After running the CMP instruction, there is no way to check the result in a destination register.

Now that you have learned about the syntax of CMP, let's analyze an example routine using the CMP instruction.

CMP instruction example

Let's examine the following example assembly routine together:

```
01 0x10013BC4    cmp     x0,x1
02 0x10013BC8    b.eq    0x10013C14
03 0x10013BCC    mov     x1,x0
```

On line 01, x0 - x1 is executed, only to update PSTATE.{N,Z,C,V}. If x0 is equal to x1, the *Z(Zero)* bit is setup 1 in PSTATE.{N,Z,C,V}. Let's analyze line 02. Based on PSTATE.{N,Z,C,V}, b.eq works differently:

- If *Z(Zero)* bit is 1: PC is branched to 0x10013C14
- If *Z(Zero)* bit is 0: PC is branched to the next address, 0x10013BCC.

From a reverse engineering point of view, you can generate C code based on the preceding example assembly routine:

```
void compare_and_branch(int x0, int x1) {
    if (x0 == x1) {
        // Routine if x0 == x1
        // ...
    } else {
        // Routine if x0 != x1
        // ...
    }
}
```

When analyzing assembly code, it is good practice to think about how this code would be implemented in C.

The CMN instruction

The CMN instruction stands for *Compare Negative*. It compares <Xn> with an operand. You can see the basic format of the CMN instruction in *Figure 5.8*:

Figure 5.8: The syntax of the CMN instruction

As shown in *Figure 5.8*, the CMN instruction updates PSTATE.{N,Z,C,V} with the result of the Xn + Op2 operation. CMN performs an addition operation between the two operands in the following manners:

- The result updates PSTATE.{N,Z,C,V}.
- The CMN instruction does not show a destination register.
- The result of the CMN instruction affects the conditional branch instructions that follow it.

Similar to the CMP instruction, it is impossible to see the result in a destination register.

CMN instruction example

Let's understand the CMN instruction by examining the following assembly routine:

```
01 0x10015914    cmn      w0,#0x1
02 0x10015918    b.eq     0x10015964
03 0x1001591C    tst      w0,#0x0F
```

On line 01, w0 + 0x1 is performed because the CMN instruction involves the addition operation between values in two operands. When running the CMN instruction, it updates PSTATE.{N,Z,C,V} based on the result. If w0 is -1, the *Z(Zero)* bit is setup 1 in PSTATE.{N,Z,C,V}. Let's analyze line 02. Based on PSTATE.{N,Z,C,V}, b.eq works in a different way:

- If *Z(Zero)* bit is 1: PC is branched to 0x10015964.
- If *Z(Zero)* bit is 0: PC is branched to the next address, 0x1001591C.

It is good practice to review and write the corresponding C code based on the preceding assembly instruction. The following is one example:

```
void compare_negative_branch(int w0)
{
    if (w0 == -1) {
        printf("w0 is equal to -1\n");
    }
    return;
}
```

Having completed the CMP and CMN instructions, let's learn about the TST instruction.

The TST instruction

The TST instruction stands for *Test*. It performs a bitwise AND operation between <Xn> and an operand. Let's take a look at *Figure 5.9* to understand the TST instruction:

Figure 5.9: The syntax of the TST instruction

As shown in *Figure 5.9*, the TST instruction updates the Z and N flags in PSTATE.{N,Z,C,V}. with the result of the Xn & Op2 operation.

The TST instruction performs an AND bit-wise operation between the two operands in the following manners:

- The result updates the Z and N flags in PSTATE.{N,Z,C,V}.
- The result of the AND bit-wise operation is discarded.

The updated PSTATE.{N,Z,C,V} affects the conditional branch instructions that follow it. It is a good idea to monitor PSTATE.{N,Z,C,V} to check the result.

TST instruction example

Let's learn about the TST instruction by examining the following assembly routine:

```
0x1001E764    tst     x0,#0x0F
0x1001E768    b.eq    0x1001E834
0x1001E76C    mov     x19,x1
```

On line 1, a bitwise AND operation is performed between the value in x0 and 0x0F. When executing the TST instruction, Z or N in PSTATE.{N,Z,C,V} is updated based on the result. If x0 is 0, the *Z(Zero)* flag is set to 1 because 0x0 & 0xF yields 0x0.

As for line 2, the b.eq instruction works in a different way depending on the state of the Z flag:

- If the *Z(Zero)* flag is 1, the PC branches to 0x1001E834.
- If the *Z(Zero)* flag is 0, the PC branches to the next address, 0x1001E76C.

Now, let's reconstruct the C code from the preceding assembly instructions, which is as follows:

```
void tst_operation(unsigned int x0) {
    if (x0 & 0xF)
        return;
    printf("x0: %x\n", x0);
    return;
}
```

When you encounter the TST instruction, remember what you've learned in this section. Now that we understand the comparison instruction, let's move on to the next topic: conditional codes.

Conditional codes

Conditional codes are a list of instructions that specify conditions for execution based on the values of PSTATE.{N,Z,C,V}. Most instructions containing conditional codes are executed after instructions such as CMP or TST.

Introducing conditional codes

Let's look at the conditional codes in *Table 5.1*:

Name	Meaning	Condition flags
EQ	Equal	Z==1
NE	Not equal	Z==0
CS	Carry set (identical to HS)	C==1
HS	Greater than, equal to (unsigned) (identical to CS)	C==1
CC	Carry clear (identical to LO)	C==0
LO	Unsigned lower (identical to CC)	C==0
MI	Minus or negative result	N==1
PL	Positive or zero result	N==0
VS	Overflow	V==1
VC	No overflow	V==0
HI	Unsigned higher	C==1 AND Z == 0
LS	Unsigned lower or same	C==0 OR Z == 1
GE	Signed greater than or equal	N==V
LT	Signed less than	N!=V

GT	Signed greater than	Z==0 AND N==V
LE	Signed less than or equal	Z==1 OR N!= V
AL	Always. This is the default.	Any

Table 5.1: The conditional codes

The conditional codes listed in *Table 5.1* are commonly used with branch instructions such as B. Let's find out how the conditional codes are used by analyzing example assembly instructions. In addition, let's figure out how to interpret the conditional codes in *Table 5.1*.

Analyzing an example routine with conditional codes

Let's analyze the following example routine with conditional codes:

```
01 0x1010530    cmp     x0, 0x1
02 0x1010534    b.eq    0x1010570
03 0x1010538    mov     x19, x1
```

In the b.eq instruction, you can see that b is suffixed with eq. What does eq mean? eq is a condition code that is valid when the Z flag is 1 in PSTATE.{N,Z,C,V}. In other words, you can say that the branch instruction will only be executed if the Z flag is 1.

In line 02, the code branches to the address 0x1010570 if the Z flag is 1. If not, the program moves to the address 0x1010538 on line 03 and executes the mov instruction.

Now let's analyze the instruction from a different perspective. In line 01, when the value in the x0 register is 1, the Z flag is set to 1. So, if x0 contains 0x1, the code will branch to the address 0x1010570.

Now let's look at another example routine:

```
01 0x1010530    cmp     x1, 0x1
02 0x1010534    b.ne    0x1010570
03 0x1010538    mov     x19, x1
```

In line 02, you can see the suffix ne in the b.ne instruction. ne is a condition code that is valid when the Z flag is 0 in PSTATE.{N,Z,C,V}. The PC is branched to the address 0x1010570 if the Z flag is 0. If not, the PC moves to the address 0x1010538 on line 03 and executes the mov instruction.

Here, we need to examine the comparison instruction from another viewpoint. What happens if the x1 register is not equal to 1? In this case, the Z flag is set to 0, so it will branch to the address at 0x1010570.

Instructions such as CMP, CMN, and TST can be used together with conditional branch instructions, such as B.EQ and B.NE. Instead of analyzing each comparison instruction, we recommend you analyze the entire assembly routine to properly understand how compare instructions and conditional branch instructions work together.

> Note
>
> As seen in *Table 5.1*, there are many conditional codes available. So, it is hard to explain each conditional code that is defined depending on PSTATE.{N,Z,C,V}. When you encounter an instruction with conditional code, please refer to *Table 5.1* to check the meaning of it accordingly.

In this section, we learned about example instructions that are processed conditionally based on the values of PSTATE.{N,Z,C,V}. Next, let's explore other types of conditional instructions.

Conditional branch operations

In the previous section, you learned about the instructions associated with conditional operations that are affected by PSTATE.{N,Z,C,V}. Armv8-A supports the following instructions, which perform conditional operations without using the NZCV flags:

Instruction	Meaning
CBZ <Xt>,<label>	Branches to <label> if the <Xt> register is zero (0). Otherwise, moves to the next address (PC+0x4).
CBNZ <Xt>,<label>	Branches to <label> if the <Xt> register is non-zero (not 0). Otherwise, moves to the next address (PC+0x4).
TBZ <Xt>,bit,<label>	If the specified bit in the <Xt> register is 0. Otherwise, move to the next address (PC+0x4).
TBNZ <Xt>,bit,<label>	Branches to <label> if the specified bit in the <Xt> register is not 0. Otherwise, moves to the next address (PC+0x4).

Table 5.2: The list of the conditional branch instructions

There is a difference between the conditional branch instructions in *Table 5.2* and the comparison instructions discussed in the previous section. That is, the execution of the conditional branch instructions is not affected by PSTATE.{N,Z,C,V}.

Let's start this section with the CBZ instruction.

The CBZ instruction

CBZ stands for *Compare and Branch if Zero*. The following is the format of the CBZ instruction:

```
CBZ <Xt>, <label>
```

When analyzing the CBZ instruction, you need to first examine the value in the <Xt> register. If the value in the <Xt> register is 0, it branches to the specified address or label. <Xt> can be any of the general-purpose registers, such as X0, X1, and X2.

The following is the pseudocode that represents how CBZ works:

```
if (Xt == 0)
    b <label>
else
    execute the next instruction
```

As indicated in the preceding pseudocode, the CBZ instruction works depending on whether the <Xt> register is zero or not. If <Xt> is equal to 0, the PC will branch to <label>.

Let's look at the following example code for a better understanding of the CBZ instruction:

```
01 0x10019C74:  cbz  w26, 0x10019E5C
02 0x10019C78:  mov  w0, w26
```

In line 01, if w26 is 0, it branches to the address 0x10019E5C. If w26 is not 0, the PC is branched to the address in line 02. This can be represented using the following pseudocode:

```
if (w26 == 0)
    b 0x10019E5C
else
    execute the instruction at the next address (0x10019C78)
```

Let's move on to the CBNZ instruction.

The CBNZ instruction

The CBNZ instruction stands for *Compare and Branch if Non-Zero*. The following is the format of CBNZ:

```
CBNZ <Xt>, <label>
```

Similar to the CBZ instruction, the value in <Xt> affects the execution of the CBNZ instruction. If the value in the <Xt> register is not zero, it branches to the specified address or label.

Let's take a look at the following pseudocode, which shows how the CBNZ instruction performs:

```
if (Xt != 0)
    b <label>
else
    execute the next instruction
```

Based on the condition of the Xt value, the CBNZ instruction executes a branch operation.

For a better understanding, let's look at the following example code:

```
01 0x10019C74:  cbnz w26, 0x10019E5C
02 0x10019C78:  cmp  w19, w26
```

In line 01, if w26 has a non-zero value, it branches to the address 0x10019E5C. If w26 is zero, the PC moves to the address in line 02. This can be represented in pseudocode as follows:

```
if (w26 != 0)
    b 0x10019E5C
else
    execute the instruction at the next address (0x10019C78)
```

The pseudocode indicates that CBNZ branches the address or label if w26 is non-zero.

The TBZ instruction

The TBZ instruction stands for *Test Bit and Branch if Zero*. Let's review the format of the TBZ instruction, which is as follows:

```
TBZ <Xt>, #imm, <label>
```

The preceding format consists of the following components:

- <Xt>: This can be any of the general-purpose registers.
- #imm: This represents a specific bit position to be checked in <Xt>.
- <label>: This is the target address to be branched if the condition is met.

If a specific bit in the <Xt> register is zero, it branches to the specified label. Otherwise, it moves to the next address.

Now that you have learned about the format of the TBZ instruction, let's look at the following example code with the TBZ instruction:

```
01 0x10019C74:  tbz  w26, #11, 0x10019E5C
02 0x10019C78:  cmp  w19, w26
```

In line 01, w26 is the name of the register and #11 is the bit position. If the 11th bit in the w26 register is zero, it branches to the address 0x10019E5C. If the 11th bit in the w26 register is not zero, it executes the instruction at the address in line 02.

For a better understanding, the preceding example code can be represented using the following pseudocode:

```
if !(w26 & 0x800)
    b 0x10019E5C
else
    execute the instruction at the next address (0x10019C78)
```

Narrowing down the !(w26 & 0x800) statement, you can derive the following analysis:

- 0x800 can be viewed as 0b1000 0000 0000 in the binary format, where the 11th bit of 0b1000 0000 0000 is 1.
- It performs a bit-wise AND operation between w26 and 0x800.
- If the 11th bit of w26 is zero, the PC is branched to the address 0x10019E5C. If not, it goes to the next address after 0x10019C78.

There is another instruction that is similar to TBZ, which we will explore next—the TBNZ instruction.

The TBNZ instruction

The TBNZ instruction stands for *Test Bit and Branch if Non-Zero*. Let's review the format of the instruction, which is as follows:

```
TBNZ <Xt>, #imm, <label>
```

The preceding format consists of the following components:

- <Xt>: This can be any of the general-purpose registers.
- #imm: This represents a specific bit position to be checked in <Xt>.
- <label>: The target address to be branched if the condition is met.

As the name of the TBNZ instruction implies, it performs a branch operation by updating the PC with the specified label if a specific bit in the <Xt> register is non-zero. Otherwise, the PC moves to the next address after the TBNZ instruction.

For a better understanding, we need to examine the following example code:

```
01 0x10019C74:   tbnz   w26, #11, 0x10019E5C
02 0x10019C78:   cmp    w19, w26
```

In line 01, w26 is the name of the register and #11 is the bit position. If the 11th bit in the w26 register is not zero, the PC branches to the address 0x10019E5C. If not, it moves to the address in line 02.

Let's look at the following pseudocode, which corresponds to the example assembly instruction that has been analyzed so far:

```
if (w26 & 0x800)
    b 0x10019E5C
else
    execute the instruction at the next address (0x10019C78)
```

The preceding pseudocode can be analyzed in the following ways:

- It performs the AND bit-wise operation between w26 and 0x800.
- 0x800 can be viewed as 0b1000 0000 0000 in the binary format, where the 11th bit of 0b1000 0000 0000 is 1.
- If the 11th bit of w26 is non-zero, it branches to the address 0x10019E5C. Otherwise, the PC is branched to the next instruction.

We have learned about conditional branch instructions. Now, let's analyze various assembly routines that include conditional branch instructions and restore the assembly routines to C code.

Analyzing assembly routines for reverse engineering

In this section, you have learned about the syntax and functionality of the CBZ and CBNZ instructions. Using these instructions, assembly routines can be organized to handle the following scenarios:

- **Loop implementation:** The program can repeatedly execute a block of code until a certain condition is met. This can be done by using CBNZ to continue looping as long as a specific register value is non-zero.
- **Exceptional routine handling:** The program can branch to a specific section of code if an error or exceptional condition is detected after the function call is made. This routine is implemented using CBZ. For example, if the value in a register is zero, it indicates an error or exceptional cases.

By analyzing the example assembly routines in this section, you will better understand how assembly code translates into higher-level logic and control structures.

Let's start this section with the assembly routine, which consists of the CBZ instruction.

The CBZ instruction

We will analyze an assembly routine that includes the CBZ instruction. First, we will examine the assembly routine, and then we will construct C code based on an assembly routine.

Analyzing an assembly routine

Let's look at the following example code, which contains an exception-handling routine that checks the value returned by a function using the CBZ instruction:

```
01 0x100135EC    mov     w0, w19
02 0x100135F0    bl      0x101B2DA0 ; trace_buf_alloc
03 0x100135F4    mov     x20, x0
04 0x100135F8    cbz     x0, 0x10013664
05 ...
06 0x10013664    ldp     x29, x30, [sp], #0x10
07 0x10013668    ret
```

In the preceding assembly routine, the cbz instruction is used to perform flow control based on the value in a register. The following is a detailed analysis of the example assembly routine:

- Line 02: The bl instruction is used to call the trace_buf_alloc function. When this instruction is executed, X30 is updated to contain the return address 0x100135F4, which is the address of the next instruction after the bl instruction.

- Line 03: The value in x0 is copied into x20. After trace_buf_alloc executes, its return value (or result) is stored in x0 and then copied to x20 for further use. Here, x0 typically holds the return value of a function.

- Line 04: The cbz instruction checks whether the value in x0 is zero. If x0 is zero, it branches to the address 0x10013664. In practice, if the trace_buf_alloc function returns a null or zero result, it indicates that there is an error or exceptional condition.

- Line 06: If the branch operation is performed (i.e., if x0 is zero), the process proceeds to load the values from the stack into x29 and x30. At this point, x30 has the address to return to.

- Line 07: When the ret instruction is executed, it updates the PC with the value in x30. This allows the subroutine to return to the exact address where the function call was made.

Now that you understand the assembly routine, let's construct C code based on the preceding routines.

Constructing the corresponding C code

Based on the assembly instructions that we analyzed, we can construct the following C code:

```c
void* trace_buf_alloc(unsigned int size);

void some_function() {
    unsigned int w19 = /* some value */;
    void* result;

    // Move w19 into w0 and call trace_buf_alloc
    result = trace_buf_alloc(w19);
    void* x20 = result;

    if (result == NULL) {
        // Equivalent to the branch to 0x10013664
        goto function_end;
    }

function_end:
    return;
}
```

Let's analyze each statement of the C code along with the corresponding assembly instructions:

- trace_buf_alloc(w19) corresponds to the bl trace_buf_alloc assembly instruction, where w0 (the first argument register) receives the value of w19.
- The result (which corresponds to x0) is then checked using if (result == NULL), which corresponds to cbz x0.
- The goto function_end; is used to simulate the branch to 0x10013664, effectively skipping the remaining function body if the result is NULL.
- Finally, the function returns, just as the ret instruction in assembly performs.

Usually, when a function is called, the return value is checked, and then the exception-handling routine is implemented. When the compiler sees C code like this, it generates assembly instructions using the cbz instruction.

The CBNZ instruction

The compiler can construct loops in different ways using the cbnz instruction. Let's analyze an assembly routine that uses the cbnz instruction. Then, we will convert the assembly instructions into C language. First, let's introduce the example assembly code.

Analyzing an assembly routine

Let's analyze the following assembly routine, which contains a loop using the cbnz instruction:

```
01 0x10013C1C           mov     w0, #0x0A        ; w0 = 10
02 0x10013C20 loop_run: sub     w0, w0, #0x1   ; w0 = w0 - 1
03 0x10013C24           cbnz    w0, 0x10013C20
04 0x10013C28           ldp     x29, x30, [sp, #0x10]
05 0x10013C2C           ret
```

You can analyze the preceding routine in detail, line by line, as follows:

- Line 01: The mov instruction initializes the register w0 with the value 10 (#0x0A). We can deduce that w0 corresponds to a local variable. This is often used as a counter in loops.

- Line 02: A label named loop_run is located at the address 0x10013C20. The subtraction operation (sub) subtracts 1 from the current value of w0. When this instruction is executed for the first time, w0 is updated to 9. This indicates that the loop will continue decrementing w0 with each iteration.

- Line 03: The cbnz instruction checks if w0 is not zero. If w0 is non-zero, the program branches back to the address 0x10013C20, where the loop_run label is located.

    Since w0 is 9 after the first subtraction, the PC goes back to loop_run, repeating the loop. This loop will continue executing until w0 becomes zero.

- Line 04: Once w0 reaches zero, the loop exits, and the program moves to address 0x10013C28. Here, the ldp instruction loads the values of x29 and x30 from the stack, where x30 contains the address to return.

- Line 05: The ret instruction returns control to the address that originally called this subroutine. This address is stored in x30, which is also known as the link register. This marks the end of the subroutine execution.

What we analyzed is a simple loop mechanism where a counter (w0) is decremented from 10 to 0. The cbnz instruction ensures that the loop continues to execute as long as w0 is non-zero. Once w0 reaches zero, the loop terminates and the function restores the previous state by loading values from the stack, and then returns control to the calling function.

Constructing the corresponding C code

Now that you have analyzed the assembly instructions, it is time to construct the following routine in C code:

```c
void some_function() {
    int w0 = 10;  // Corresponds to mov w0, #0x0A

    // loop_run:
    while (w0 != 0) {  // Corresponds to cbnz w0, loop_run
        w0--;          // Corresponds to sub w0, w0, #0x1
    }

    // Equivalent to restoring registers (ldp x19, x20, [sp, #0x10])
    return;  // Corresponds to ret
}
```

Here is the analysis that shows how each assembly instruction corresponds to the C code:

- `int w0 = 10;` corresponds to `mov w0, #0x0A`, where `w0` is initialized with the value 10.
- The `while (w0 != 0)` loop corresponds to the `cbnz` instruction, which checks if `w0` is not zero and branches back to the `loop_run` label.
- `w0--;` corresponds to `sub w0, w0, #0x1`, decrementing the value of `w0` by 1 on each loop iteration.
- The `return;` statement at the end corresponds to the `ret` instruction in assembly, indicating the end of the function and the return to the caller.

What we see is a simple loop that decrements a counter from 10 to 0. Once the counter reaches 0, the function ends and returns control to the caller.

The TBZ instruction

The TBZ instruction allows us to perform branch operations by checking the specific bit in the register. Let's analyze an assembly routine with the TBZ instruction and convert the assembly instructions into C language.

Analyzing an assembly routine

Here is an example assembly routine with the TBZ instruction that you are going to analyze:

```
01 0x10010534    mrs     x1, DAIF
02 0x10010538    tbz     x1, #0x7, 0x100105d4
```

```
03 0x1001053c    mov     w0, 0x0
04 0x100105d0    ret
...
05 0x100105d4    mov     w0, 0x1
06 0x100105d8    ret
```

Here is the breakdown of the preceding assembly routine, which is as follows:

- Line 01: The MRS instruction stores the value of the DAIF system register in x1. The DAIF register contains status flags related to interrupts and other conditions. Note that the DAIF system register contains bit flags in PSTATE.DAIF.

- Line 02: The TBZ instruction branches to the address 0x100105d4 if the 7th bit (0x7) in x1 is zero.

- Lines 03-04: If the 7th bit in x1 is non-zero, the PC branches to the address at 0x1001053c. The mov instruction sets the w0 register to 0, which is the return value from the subroutine. In line 4, the RET instruction then returns control to the calling address.

- Lines 05-06: If the branch operation is performed (i.e. if bit 7 is zero), the instruction sets the w0 register to 1. In line 6, the RET instruction returns from the subroutine, using the value in w0 as the return value.

What you have analyzed can be seen in a number of routines in low-level software, such as boot-loaders and the Linux kernel.

Constructing the corresponding C code

Based on the assembly routine with the TBZ instruction, we can generate the corresponding C code as follows:

```
unsigned int check_and_set_daif_bit7() {
    unsigned long daif;
    unsigned int result;

    // Read the DAIF register into a variable
    asm volatile ("mrs %0, DAIF" : "=r" (daif));

    // Check if bit 7 of DAIF is zero
    if ((daif & (1 << 7)) == 0) {
        result = 1;   // Corresponds to mov w0, 0x1
    } else {
```

```
        result = 0;  // Corresponds to mov w0, 0x0
    }


    // Return the result
    return result;  // Corresponds to ret
}
```

Let's analyze the C code with the assembly routine. The following explanation shows how the assembly instructions match the C language statements:

- Reading the DAIF register: The mrs instruction reads the DAIF register into the daif variable using inline assembly.

- Checking the 7th bit: The if statement checks if the 7th bit of the daif variable is zero: ((daif & (1 << 7)) == 0). This corresponds to the tbz instruction.

- Setting the result based on the condition:

    - If the 7th bit is zero, the result variable is set to 1 (mov w0, 0x1), which corresponds to the branch target 0x100105d4.

    - If the 7th bit is not zero, the result variable is set to 0 (mov w0, 0x0), which corresponds to the non-branching path.

- Returning the result: The function returns the value of the result, which corresponds to the ret instructions in the assembly code.

This C code behaves like the assembly instructions. The function checks a specific bit in the DAIF register and returns either 0 or 1 based on the result.

So far, we have looked at routines related to conditional branch operations, which affect flow control. In the next section, we will learn about instructions that change the execution flow by causing exceptions.

System control operations

In this chapter, we have analyzed the assembly instructions line by line to see how the program's flow changes. The flow can change due to exceptions, and Armv8-A provides the following instructions that can trigger exceptions:

- SVC (*supervisor call*): User application switches to kernel space.

- HVC (*hypervisor call*): Switches from the guest OS to the hypervisor.

- SMC (*secure monitor call*): Switches from Non-secure world to Secure world or vice versa.

First, let's understand the SVC instruction.

The SVC instruction

In `Armv8-A`, there are different *exception levels* (`EL`s) that determine the level of access and privileges of the executing code, as follows:

- `EL0` is the lowest privilege level, typically used for user applications.
- `EL1` is a higher privilege level used for the kernel.

When a user application wants to perform an operation that requires higher privileges (such as accessing hardware resources), it executes the SVC instruction. This instruction triggers a change in the exception level from `EL0` to `EL1`.

Let's take a look at *Figure 5.10* to figure out how the SVC works:

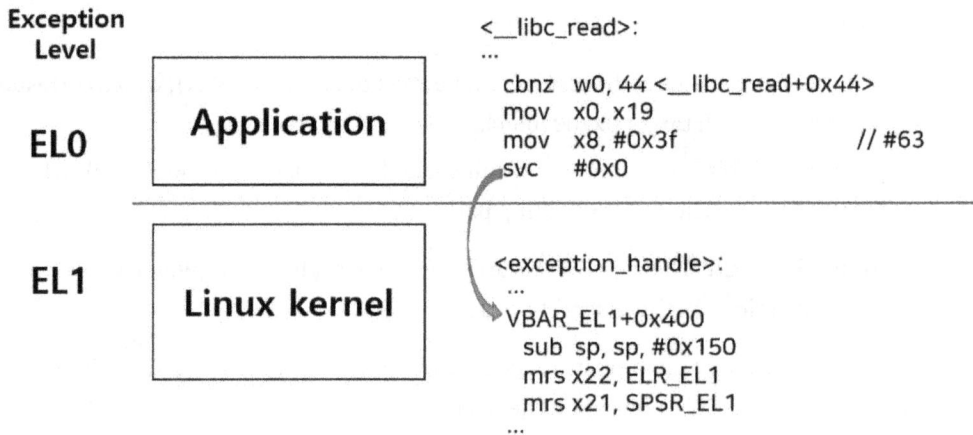

Figure 5.10: Workflow when the SVC is executed

In *Figure 5.10*, the upper part shows that the user application runs at `EL0` with the following instructions:

```
<__libc_read>:
...
01 cbnz w0, 44 <__libc_read+0x44>
02 mov x0, x19
03 mov x8, #0x3f // #63
04 svc #0x0
```

Let's analyze lines 03 and 04 together.

In line 03, the value 0x3F (63) is copied to x8, where x8 holds the system call number. The system call number is used to find the corresponding system call handler.

In line 04, you can see the svc instruction. In the svc #0x0 instruction, #0x0 is the immediate field that is passed to the exception handler. When svc #0x0 is performed, the Arm core simultaneously does two tasks:

- It switches the exception level from EL0 to EL1.
- It branches to the exception vector address based on VBAR_EL1 + 0x400.

> Note
>
> How the exception vector address is organized is specified in the exception vector table in Armv8-A. The execution of the SVC instruction triggers a synchronous exception.

Next, let's take a look at the lower part of *Figure 5.10*. The PC branches to the exception vector address for the synchronous exception. The base address for the exception handler is stored in VBAR_EL1, which is usually initialized at boot.

The execution of the SVC instruction effectively generates a *system call*. A system call is a way for user applications to request services from the kernel, such as file operations, network communication, or memory management.

The HVC instruction

HVC stands for *Hypervisor Call*, and it is an instruction that is used to transition from the kernel of an operating system to the hypervisor.

When the kernel needs to perform a task that requires hypervisor privileges (for example, managing virtual machines), it executes the HVC instruction. This instruction causes a transition from EL1 to EL2, allowing the kernel to enter hypervisor mode.

Let's look at *Figure 5.11* to understand what happens when the HVC instruction is executed.

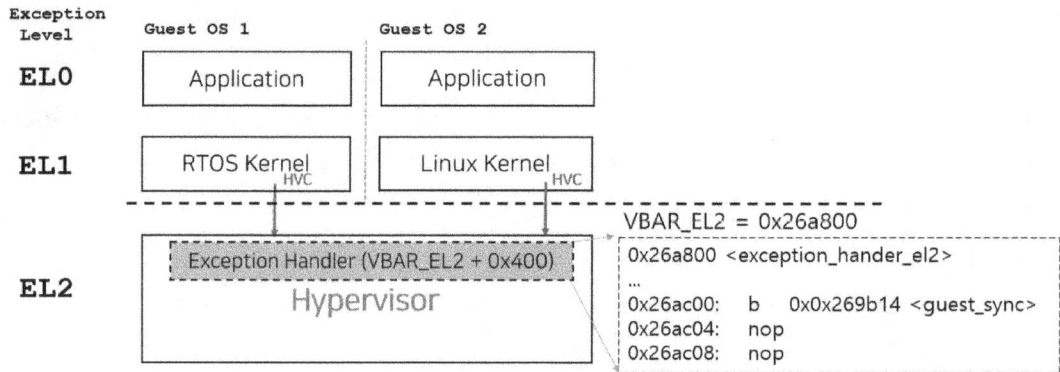

Figure 5.11: Workflow when HVC is executed

In *Figure 5.11*, let's first check two parts:

- **Guest OS**: In a virtualization system, it is possible to run more than one operating system. These multiple operating systems are considered guest OSes. In *Figure 5.11*, there are two guest Oses—an RTOS and the Linux kernel.

- **Hypervisor**: Beneath the guest OSes is the hypervisor. The hypervisor manages the resources of the guest OSes, such as the virtual CPU and virtual interrupts.

When the HVC instruction is executed, the following tasks are performed simultaneously:

- It switches the exception level from EL1 to EL2.
- It branches to the exception vector address based on VBAR_EL2 + 0x400.

In *Figure 5.11*, when the HVC instruction is executed, the PC branches to the address 0x26ac00. In this example, VBAR_EL2 is 0x26a800. When the guest OS executes the HVC instruction, the PC branches to the address 0x26ac00, according to the VBAR_EL2 + 0x400 rule.

The SMC instruction

SMC stands for *secure monitor call*. It is an important instruction, which is supported by *TrustZone*. TrustZone is a hardware-based security extension that creates a secure environment (Secure world) alongside the regular operating environment (Non-secure world).

Let's look at *Figure 5.12* to understand the workflow related to the execution of the SMC instruction:

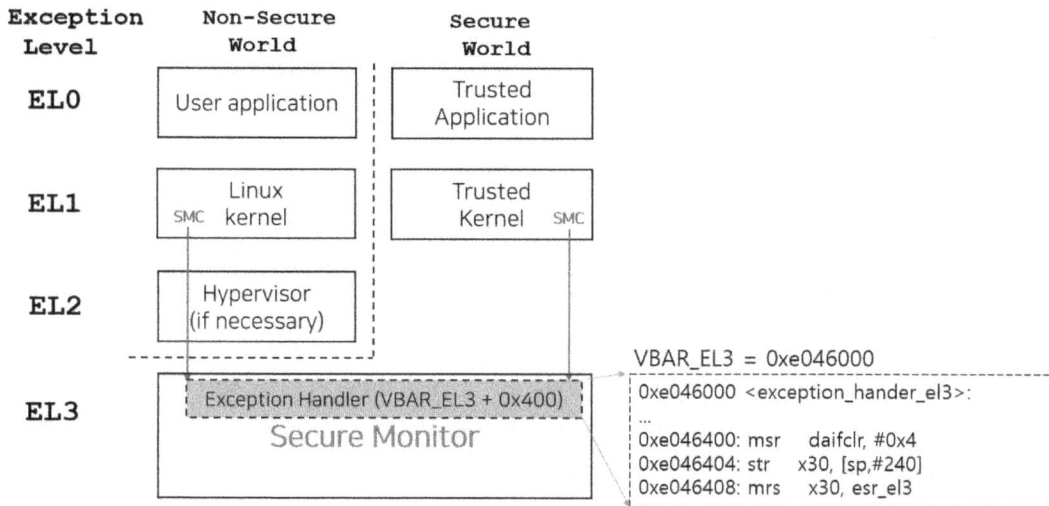

Figure 5.12: Workflow when SMC is executed

In *Figure 5.12*, we need to figure out two things:

- **Non-secure world:** This is the execution environment where regular software runs. Operating systems such as Linux run in Non-secure world.

- **Secure world**: This is the execution environment where high-security enhanced software operates. For example, applications such as internet banking or fingerprint recognition run in the secure world.

How do you switch from Non-secure world to Secure world? The answer is by running the SMC instruction. When the SMC instruction is executed in Non-secure world, the following tasks are performed simultaneously:

- It switches the exception level from EL1 to EL3.
- It branches to the exception vector address based on VBAR_EL3 + 0x400.

In *Figure 5.12*, the PC branches to the address 0xe046400 after the SMC instruction is executed. How does this happen? In this example, VBAR_EL3 is set to 0xe046000, so that the PC branches to the address 0xe046400 according to the VBAR_EL3 + 0x400 rule.

The SMC instruction is used to switch execution flow between Non-secure world and Secure world. This mechanism allows for secure operations to be performed, such as accessing sensitive data or executing trusted applications.

Summary

In this chapter, we explored assembly instructions related to flow control, which manages the execution flow of a program. Flow control is important because it determines how a program responds to different conditions and inputs.

First, we learned about comparison instructions. These instructions affect the control flow of the next instruction by updating the condition flags in PSTATE. We also analyzed conditional branch instructions such as CBZ, CBNZ, TBZ, and TBNZ. These instructions are important for controlling how the program runs. When analyzing example assembly code, understanding the execution flow is essential.

Additionally, you learned how to convert assembly instructions into C code. This is a key skill when debugging or analyzing firmware binaries. As you continue to practice, your ability to debug and understand how assembly maps to C code will improve.

The next chapter will introduce reverse engineering and explain how to perform it using methods such as static analysis and dynamic analysis.

Join our community on Discord

Join our community's Discord space for discussions with the authors and other readers: https://packt.link/embeddedsystems

Part 2

Background Knowledge for Binary Analysis

In this part, we will review important background knowledge needed to start binary analysis and reverse engineering. We will introduce reverse engineering, explain how to set up an Arm board, and cover basic concepts of the Linux kernel. These topics will help you understand how binaries work and how to analyze them effectively.

This part includes the following chapters:

- *Chapter 6, Introducing Reverse Engineering*
- *Chapter 7, Setting Up a Practice Environment with an Arm Device*
- *Chapter 8, Unpacking the Kernel with Linux Fundamentals*

6

Introducing Reverse Engineering

Reverse engineering is the process of analyzing binaries to understand the flow of a program without needing the original source code. The source code could be written in languages such as C, C++, Rust, or Go. To examine the binary in more detail, we need to understand assembly instructions, as the binary is directly mapped to them. We also use binary utilities to check the binary format supported by Linux. These topics were all covered in the previous chapter.

In this chapter, we will explore the following topics:

- Why reverse engineering is necessary
- Methods of reverse engineering
- Compilation process
- Assembly instructions and machine code
- Essential background knowledge of reverse engineering

By reading this chapter, you'll learn why it is important to check binaries on Arm devices. Let's start this chapter by discussing why learning about reverse engineering is necessary.

Technical requirements

All the code examples for this chapter can be found on GitHub at `https://github.com/PacktPublishing/Reverse-Engineering-Armv8-A-Systems`.

Why reverse engineering is necessary

Why do we need to learn about reverse engineering? What is the skill set for reversing used in real projects? These are important questions to consider as you begin learning about reverse engineering.

Library and firmware debugging

To address the necessity of reverse engineering, we need to discuss the development process of a project from a software perspective. If your project doesn't require complex features, all of the requirements might be implemented by your company alone.

However, in a real-world project, software development often involves collaboration with other companies. For example, your company might develop certain features, while another company develops drivers or applications. In many cases, the deliverables from other companies are provided in the following binary form:

- Application package
- Library
- Firmware
- Module-type device driver

Many software products are developed by integrating these binary files. This means you might install an application, library, firmware, or module-type device driver from another company to build the complete software package.

But why do other companies provide files in binary format? They do this to develop efficiently and for an important reason—many software companies provide libraries to avoid sharing the source code for the purpose of protecting their valuable algorithms and proprietary information.

However, during development, you might encounter issues with the library or firmware provided by another company. Here are some common cases:

- **High stack usage:** After running the library or firmware code, you might notice that a lot of stack is being used. You could find issues such as stack corruption or stack overflow.
- **Memory leaks:** After running the library or firmware code, you might find that the system has memory leaks. This is a common issue in many projects.
- **Crash or segmentation fault:** In specific cases, a crash or segmentation fault occurs inside the library or firmware.

To understand whether these problems are caused by the library or the firmware, you need reverse engineering skills. If you find bugs in the library or firmware, you will need to investigate the corresponding library to debug it. In this case, the ability to analyze the binary code without looking at the C source code is necessary.

Legacy systems

When you work on a project, you often need to do maintenance on products that have already been released. Sometimes, problems such as crashes or performance issues can happen in products that were released 5 or 10 years ago. To debug these issues, you usually need the source code. If you go through the following situations, what will you do to follow up on this issue?

- There is no C source code available for the problem
- There is no engineer who wrote the code and knows how to fix these issues

In this situation, we have no choice but to examine the binary file to understand what is being executed. This section introduces a typical scenario where software developers need to maintain or update software without having access to the original source code.

In such cases, reverse engineering is the only way to figure out how the software works and make the necessary changes. It's important to note that in industries such as aerospace, automotive, and industrial control systems, hardware and software have been used for a long time.

Now, let's discuss another reason why we need to learn about reverse engineering.

Improving debugging skills

If you improve your reverse engineering abilities, your debugging skills will also be enhanced. Debugging and reverse engineering are closely related disciplines that share many techniques and require similar skill sets. For example, during a project, software engineers need to resolve issues or fix bugs. In practice, fixing bugs can involve the following activities:

- Analyzing logs or symptoms
- Examining the code related to the bug
- Modifying the code

These tasks are very similar to what you do in reverse engineering. By learning about reverse engineering, you will improve your debugging skills and learn how to resolve more difficult problems. You will also do well in situations where you do not have the source code or need to analyze optimized binaries.

So, learning about reverse engineering is a good choice for developers who want to improve their skills in software development and debugging.

Case study – how reverse engineering skills enhance debugging abilities

Let's explore how the skill set gained from reverse engineering can significantly impact your debugging capabilities. When you're involved in a project, the project manager may assign you various bugs or issues to resolve. Some of these issues might be related to performance degradation.

The skills you acquire from reverse engineering are incredibly valuable for addressing performance-related bugs. This is because reverse engineering teaches you how to understand code optimizations and see how the code transforms from its original high-level form to low-level assembly. This understanding is crucial when debugging performance issues or working to maximize system efficiency. Here are some typical examples of performance-related issues:

- **Compiler optimization**: Modern compilers often optimize code to enhance system performance, either by increasing speed or reducing memory usage. By understanding and configuring compiler options, you can fine-tune these optimizations to improve overall system performance.

- **Inlining functions**: While analyzing assembly instructions, you might identify frequently called functions that consist of only two or three lines of code. By declaring these functions as **inline**, you can eliminate the overhead of pushing arguments onto the stack, which occurs during regular function calls. This small change can lead to significant performance improvements.

- **Trap handling optimization**: Unnecessary traps can cause performance degradation. By optimizing the routines that handle these traps, you can reduce the performance impact, resulting in a more efficient system.

In summary, learning about reverse engineering equips you with essential skills that are highly valuable for software development. Developers who excel in reverse engineering often become exceptional debuggers, as the two disciplines are closely related.

Now that you understand why learning reverse engineering is important, let's talk about the methods used for reverse engineering.

Methods of reverse engineering

The methods of reverse engineering are mainly divided into the following categories:

- Static analysis
- Dynamic analysis

Static analysis and dynamic analysis are similar in the reverse engineering process. Both methods involve analyzing assembly instructions and checking the execution flow. The background knowledge needed for both is also similar. Both require a good understanding of Arm architecture or the Linux system.

Static analysis

Static analysis is a method used to predict how a system will behave by examining its binary code without actually running it on the target hardware. Using static analysis, you can understand the software's structure and identify potential issues. In addition, it allows you to gain insights into its functionality without executing the code.

> Note
>
> If you cannot perform static analysis, you will likely struggle with dynamic analysis, which requires a deeper understanding of the system's runtime behavior.

Static analysis involves reading and understanding binary code. This includes the following activities:

- Examining assembly instructions
- Understanding object file formats
- Recognizing patterns in the code
- Identifying specific functions

To do static analysis well, you need to be familiar with different debugging tools. Here are some of the most commonly used tools for static analysis:

- **Ghidra**: Ghidra is a powerful tool for reverse engineers and is available as an open source project. This tool provides a complete set of features for analyzing binaries, including disassembly, decompilation, and graphical code representations. It supports various CPU architectures, such as Armv8-A, x86, and others.
- **GNU Debugger (GDB)**: GDB is another popular debugging tool used in Linux that allows you to analyze binaries. GDB is also essential for dynamic analysis, as it provides insights into how binaries operate during execution.

- **Binary Utilities (binutils)**: The GNU Binary Utilities are a collection of command-line tools for inspecting binary files in Linux. The following are popular utilities:

  - **objdump**: Disassembles binaries to display their assembly code
  - **readelf**: Extracts and displays information about **Executable and Linkable Format (ELF)** files
  - **nm**: Displays the symbol table of a binary, showing function names and their addresses

  Using these tools, we can do static analysis to view the structure of binary files and their assembly instructions. These tools help reverse engineers disassemble and analyze the code.

In summary, static analysis is a basic skill in reverse engineering. It helps you look into binary code, understand how it is built, and guess what it will do—all without running the code. This skill is important before learning about more advanced methods such as dynamic analysis.

Dynamic analysis

Another method used in reverse engineering is dynamic analysis. **Dynamic analysis** involves running the software on the actual target board or system to observe its behavior in real time. This method helps you understand how the software interacts with the system while it is running.

There are a couple of ways to perform dynamic analysis, as follows:

- **Using debuggers**: Tools such as GDB or TRACE32 allow you to run the program and inspect its execution. With these debuggers, you can identify the following signatures:

  - **Call stack**: This shows the sequence of function calls that led to the current point in the program
  - **Memory dump**: This provides a snapshot of the memory contents at a specific moment
  - **Local variables**: You can inspect the values of variables in the current function

- **Logging and tracing**: Sometimes, you cannot use a debugger to monitor the program. In such cases, you can extract logs or trace information. The following are the most used logs:

  - **uftrace logs**: These logs show tracing information in the user space
  - **Kernel logs**: These logs provide information from the operating system's kernel about the execution of the process
  - **ftrace logs**: These logs offer detailed tracing of function calls and other system events in the kernel space

Usually, developers begin with static analysis before doing dynamic analysis. This is because dynamic analysis needs access to the target device and requires knowledge of how to use debugging tools correctly.

In the next section, we will introduce dump analysis with a practical example.

Dump analysis

Traditionally, reverse engineering methods are divided into two main categories: static analysis and dynamic analysis. However, this book introduces a method that isn't often covered in other books—**dump analysis**.

Static analysis and dynamic analysis each offer distinct advantages and limitations. Static analysis allows you to reverse engineer by examining the code without running it on the actual device. This means you can only work with limited information, mostly just analyzing the assembly instructions. You can't see the call stack, which shows the sequence of executed processes.

On the other hand, dynamic analysis provides more debugging information compared to static analysis. With dynamic analysis, you can view the following:

- Call stacks
- Memory dumps
- Local and global variables

However, dynamic analysis has some limits. It is sometimes difficult to connect a debugger to the system and check detailed information. This is why dump analysis is discussed in *Chapter 12*, which could be the main focus of this book. Dump analysis can address some of the limitations associated with dynamic analysis.

Introducing binary for dump analysis

Now, let's consider how this method is applied in real projects. In actual software development, it's becoming more common to extract memory dumps from a target system or device while the software is running. What types of memory dumps might you analyze? In Linux systems, the following dump files can be extracted from the target device:

- **core dump**: This is a memory dump from a user application, usually generated when a segmentation fault occurs. By loading the core dump file into GDB along with the corresponding ELF file, you can view the call stack, local variables, and detailed process information, just as you would during dynamic analysis.

- **vmcore**: When a kernel crash occurs, a vmcore file can be extracted from the device. The vmcore file contains memory from the kernel space, allowing you to examine the call stack of kernel processes and explore memory contents in the kernel.

Another point to remember is that both core dump and vmcore files use the ELF format.

Advantage of dump analysis

Using memory dumps for analysis is a common practice in many projects. Let's look at the background to understand it better.

When a bug occurs during development, it's usually assigned to the appropriate developer, who will try to reproduce the issue. For example, if there's a display problem in a certain scenario, the developer will attempt to reproduce the bug. But some bugs only happen under specific conditions. Imagine a bug in a car navigation system that only appears after driving for 10 hours. Should the developer spend all that time just to reproduce the issue? Reproducing such issues can be very time-consuming and inefficient.

This is why dump analysis proves invaluable. If a qualification team extracts a core dump or vmcore file after a bug occurs, software developers can analyze the memory dump instead of attempting to reproduce the issue. This approach is commonly used by chipset developers and offers a significant advantage—it saves time. This method allows developers to focus on analyzing the binary without needing to reproduce the issue.

In this section, we saw the methods of reverse engineering. Detailed techniques for reverse engineering will be covered in *Chapters 9 to 12*.

In the next section, we will explore the compilation process, which is essential background knowledge for reverse engineering.

Compilation process

As stated many times, reverse engineering involves examining binary files to determine what a program does. A common question is: Who generates these binary files? The answer is the compiler. When you add or modify code, you run the compiler to ensure that your code is syntactically correct and free of errors. During this process, an object file is produced.

What the compiler does

From a different perspective, analyzing binary files in reverse engineering essentially reverses the compilation process. To fully understand this, it's important to grasp how compilation works.

What is the compiler's main role? Its primary mission is to produce a binary image, which is a structured collection of native code, also known as machine code. Native code consists of low-level instructions directly executed by the processor, allowing the software to operate on a specific CPU.

To generate a binary image, the compilation process uses various types of source files, including *.c, *.h, and *.s files:

- **C source files** (*.c): These contain the main logic and routines written in C.
- **Header files** (*.h): These define macros, constants, data types, and function declarations. Header files can be shared across multiple source files and are included in C source files.
- **Assembly files** (*.s): These include low-level instructions specific to the CPU architecture. These files are often used to optimize performance-critical routines.

With a clear understanding of the compiler's role, let's delve deeper into the breakdown of the compilation process.

The breakdown of compilation

Figure 6.1 illustrates the breakdown of the **compilation** process:

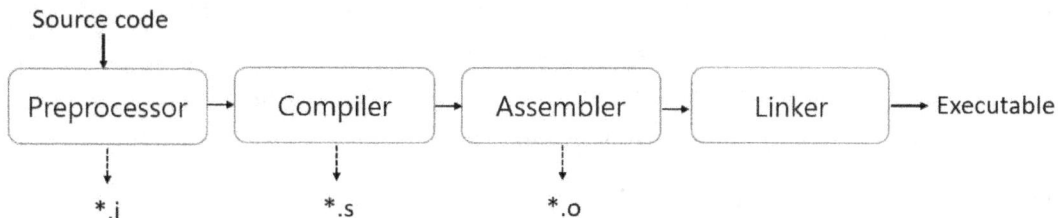

Figure 6.1: Compilation process

The compilation process can start with these source files. Here is the breakdown of the compilation:

- **Preprocessor:** In C source files, you can find macros (indicated by #define) and #include directives. The #include directives are used to include header files (with the .h extension) that the source file depends on. The preprocessor performs the following tasks:
    - Parses #define, #include, #ifdef, and #error directives.
    - Generates preprocessed code that is then passed to the compiler. A preprocessed file is needed to expand macros and include different header files before the actual compilation begins.

- **Compiler**: As the next step, the compiler takes this code processed by the preprocessor. The main job of the compiler is to convert these files into assembly code. The C compiler is specifically designed to translate preprocessed code into assembly code.

- **Assembler**: An assembler converts assembly code into object code. The name of the object file generated by the assembler is generally derived from the source filename but has a different extension. For example, if the source file is named `main.c`, the corresponding object file will be named `main.o`. This object file contains machine code that is specific to the CPU architecture.

- **Linker**: The linking phase is the final step of the compilation process. As the name suggests, the linker's role is to link together all the object files, along with any necessary library files, into a single executable binary. The linker's primary task is to resolve references between different object files and libraries, combining them into a single program. The output of the linker is the executable file, which shares the base name of the source file. These executable files are ready to be run on the target machine.

The compilation process is not only crucial for effective reverse engineering but also fundamental knowledge for software developers.

The compiler option — optimization level

Additionally, the compiler provides different options that can change how the machine code is generated. One of these options is the optimization level.

Let's look at the example code:

```
int add_func(int x, int y)
{
    int result;
    result = x + y;

    printf("result: %d \n", result);
    return result;
}
```

If you compile the preceding code, the assembly instructions may look different depending on the compiler options. Let's look at *Figure 6.2*:

```
        gcc -o main main.c -O2                              gcc -o main main.c
00000000000007a0 <add_func>:                      0000000000000754 <add_func>:
  7a0:  a9be7bfd      stp   x29, x30, [sp, #-32]!    754:  a9bd7bfd      stp   x29, x30, [sp, #-48]!
  7a4:  910003fd      mov   x29, sp                  758:  910003fd      mov   x29, sp
  7a8:  f9000bf3      str   x19, [sp, #16]           75c:  b9001fe0      str   w0, [sp, #28]
  7ac:  0b010013      add   w19, w0, w1              760:  b9001be1      str   w1, [sp, #24]
  7b0:  2a1303e1      mov   w1, w19                  764:  b9401fe1      ldr   w1, [sp, #28]
  7b4:  90000000      adrp  x0, 0 <__abi_tag-0x278>  768:  b9401be0      ldr   w0, [sp, #24]
  7b8:  911fc000      add   x0, x0, #0x7f0           76c:  0b000020      add   w0, w1, w0
  7bc:  97ffff9d      bl    630 <printf@plt>         770:  b9002fe0      str   w0, [sp, #44]
  7c0:  2a1303e0      mov   w0, w19                  774:  b9402fe1      ldr   w1, [sp, #44]
  7c4:  f9400bf3      ldr   x19, [sp, #16]           778:  90000000      adrp  x0, 0 <__abi_tag-0x278>
  7c8:  a8c27bfd      ldp   x29, x30, [sp], #32      77c:  911f4000      add   x0, x0, #0x7d0
  7cc:  d65f03c0      ret                            780:  97ffffac      bl    630 <printf@plt>
                                                     784:  b9402fe0      ldr   w0, [sp, #44]
                                                     788:  a8c37bfd      ldp   x29, x30, [sp], #48
                                                     78c:  d65f03c0      ret
```

Figure 6.2: The assembly instructions with different optimization levels

Figure 6.2 shows two examples of assembly code:

- The left side shows the assembly code for add_func with the -O2 optimization level
- The right side shows the assembly code for add_func without optimization

Knowing that different compiler options can generate different assembly code is helpful when analyzing instructions.

The following section will cover the relationship between machine code and instructions, as discussed in the compilation process.

Assembly instructions and machine code

To start reverse engineering, it's essential to understand the relationship between machine code and instructions. Machine code can be viewed in its raw format, and we will examine it directly. Additionally, we will review the corresponding opcodes and mnemonics related to the machine code.

Opcode and instruction

Let's examine the following data in hexadecimal format:

```
0000750 ffd8 97ff 0020 5280 e260 3900 0bf3 f940
0000760 7bfd a8c2 03c0 d65f 201f d503 201f d503
0000770 ffdc 17ff 7bfd a9bd 03fd 9100 1fe0 b900
0000780 1be1 b900 1fe1 b940 1be0 b940 0020 0b00
0000790 2fe0 b900 1be2 b940 1fe1 b940 0000 9000
00007a0 0000 9122 ffab 97ff 2fe0 b940 7bfd a8c3
00007b0 03c0 d65f 7bfd a9bf 03fd 9100 0061 5280
00007c0 0040 5280 ffec 97ff 0000 5280 7bfd a8c1
```

Figure 6.3: The example machine code

At first glance, this may look like a random stream of hexadecimal numbers. It's difficult to interpret this data directly because it's not human-readable in this form. However, this data represents machine code, which is directly executed by the processor. **Machine code** is the most basic level of code, instructing the processor on exactly what operations to perform.

Next, we'll look at the corresponding assembly instructions in *Figure 6.4*:

```
0000000000000774 <add_func>:
 774:   a9bd7bfd            stp     x29, x30, [sp, #-48]!
 778:   910003fd            mov     x29, sp
 77c:   b9001fe0            str     w0, [sp, #28]
 780:   b9001be1            str     w1, [sp, #24]
 784:   b9401fe1            ldr     w1, [sp, #28]
 788:   b9401be0            ldr     w0, [sp, #24]
 78c:   0b000020            add     w0, w1, w0
 790:   b9002fe0            str     w0, [sp, #44]
 794:   b9401be2            ldr     w2, [sp, #24]
 798:   b9401fe1            ldr     w1, [sp, #28]
 79c:   90000000            adrp    x0, 0 <_init-0x5d0>
 7a0:   91220000            add     x0, x0, #0x880
 7a4:   97ffffab            bl      650 <printf@plt>
 7a8:   b9402fe0            ldr     w0, [sp, #44]
 7ac:   a8c37bfd            ldp     x29, x30, [sp], #48
 7b0:   d65f03c0            ret
```

Figure 6.4: Assembly instruction for machine code

The data represented in *Figure 6.4* is easier to understand because it's shown as assembly instructions. Assembly language translates machine code into a format that's more readable for humans, allowing developers to better understand low-level operations.

Let's take a closer look at one of these instructions:

```
 778:   910003fd            mov     x29, sp
```

What exactly does the mov x29, sp instruction do? This instruction is derived from parsing the 910003fd machine code into a human-readable assembly format. So, what does 910003fd represent?

To understand how the Arm processor interprets this machine code, we need to convert it into its binary form:

```
910003fd in binary: 1001 0001 0000 0000 0000 0011 1111 1101
```

In this binary form, the bits from positions `[28:23]` (which are `0b100010`) specify the `MOV` instruction. `0b100010` is an opcode that corresponds to the `MOV` mnemonic. A mnemonic is a shorthand for the assembly instruction, such as `ADD` or `SUB`. Using this approach, any machine code can be translated into an assembly instruction with its respective mnemonic.

What we've covered so far is a fundamental step in reverse engineering. By decoding the hexadecimal `910003fd`, we identified the `mov x29, sp` instruction. *Figure 6.5* shows the machine code and its assembly instructions:

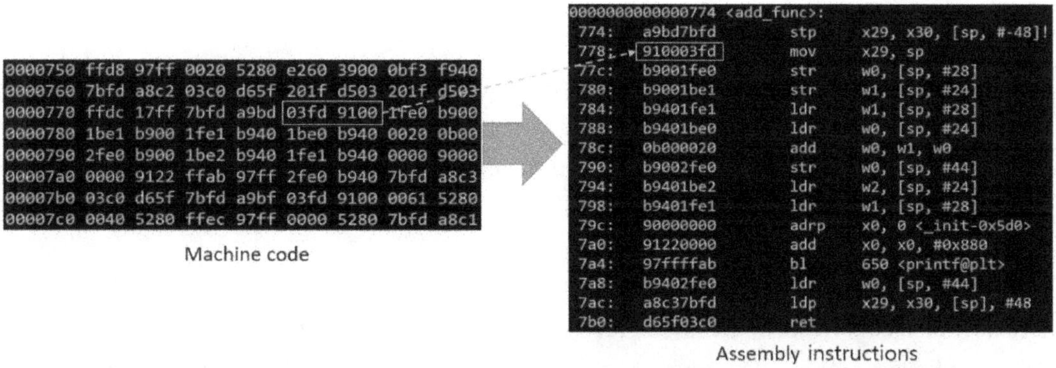
0000750 ffd8 97ff 0020 5280 e260 3900 0bf3 f940
0000760 7bfd a8c2 03c0 d65f 201f d503 201f d503
0000770 ffdc 17ff 7bfd a9bd 03fd 9100 1fe0 b900
0000780 1be1 b900 1fe1 b940 1be0 b940 0020 0b00
0000790 2fe0 b900 1be2 b940 1fe1 b940 0000 9000
00007a0 0000 9122 ffab 97ff 2fe0 b940 7bfd a8c3
00007b0 03c0 d65f 7bfd a9bf 03fd 9100 0061 5280
00007c0 0040 5280 ffec 97ff 0000 5280 7bfd a8c1
Machine code
0000000000000774 <add_func>:
774: a9bd7bfd stp x29, x30, [sp, #-48]!
778: 910003fd mov x29, sp
77c: b9001fe0 str w0, [sp, #28]
780: b9001be1 str w1, [sp, #24]
784: b9401fe1 ldr w1, [sp, #28]
788: b9401be0 ldr w0, [sp, #24]
78c: 0b000020 add w0, w1, w0
790: b9002fe0 str w0, [sp, #44]
794: b9401be2 ldr w2, [sp, #24]
798: b9401fe1 ldr w1, [sp, #28]
79c: 90000000 adrp x0, 0 <_init-0x5d0>
7a0: 91220000 add x0, x0, #0x880
7a4: 97ffffab bl 650 <printf@plt>
7a8: b9402fe0 ldr w0, [sp, #44]
7ac: a8c37bfd ldp x29, x30, [sp], #48
7b0: d65f03c0 ret
Assembly instructions

Figure 6.5: Machine code with assembly instructions

This decoding process is crucial for understanding how low-level software interacts with hardware. Knowing this relationship is essential, particularly for debugging or reverse engineering, as it helps you understand and manipulate the basic operations of a system. Additionally, the ability to read and interpret both hexadecimal machine code and assembly instructions is vital for debugging, optimizing performance, and ensuring application security.

Background knowledge of reverse engineering

In this chapter, we explore the importance of reverse engineering and outline the fundamental methods involved. If you're new to reverse engineering, you might wonder which topics to study as foundational knowledge. There are several areas to understand, but the following three are primary areas that will enhance your understanding of reverse engineering:

- Assembly instructions
- The Linux kernel (or RTOS kernel)
- The ELF format

First, let's delve into the first topic—assembly instructions

Assembly instructions

The core element of a binary is machine code, which maps directly to assembly instructions. Reading and interpreting these assembly instructions from machine code is the crucial first step in reverse engineering.

Understanding how assembly instructions are organized is essential for effective reverse engineering. This process involves analyzing the control flow of a program by examining its binaries. Essentially, reverse engineering aims to reconstruct high-level code in C, C++, Rust, or Go language from its assembly routines.

From a security perspective, a solid grasp of assembly instructions is vital for tasks such as vulnerability assessment, malware analysis, and software optimization. It allows you to understand the underlying operations of a program, identify potential security flaws, and enhance software performance.

Linux kernel

Assembly instructions are at the lowest level of the software stack. In terms of software languages, C is considered a higher-level language compared to assembly. This leads to another question: Which software, written in C, interacts with the Arm processor? The answer is the operating system. These kernels control the execution of the Arm processor.

From a software perspective, processes are responsible for executing each assembly instruction. During a function call, arguments or values in the link register are stored in the process's stack. Therefore, *Chapter 8* delves into the Linux kernel fundamentals necessary for reverse engineering.

Understanding how the Linux kernel or RTOS kernel manages low-level operations is important. It helps you see how the processor runs instructions, manages memory, and handles processes. This knowledge is essential for analyzing system behavior, debugging, and finding vulnerabilities.

ELF format

Another important topic to learn about is the ELF format. Before you start reverse engineering, you need to decide which binary file you will open and analyze. For this reason, understanding the layout of the ELF format is crucial when analyzing instructions in a binary file.

As mentioned earlier, compilers generate binaries in the ELF format, producing object files and executable files at various stages of compilation.

When you work on a real project, you will likely see different software releases during development. You will come across various binaries, including object files, executable files, and more.

In general, you will use tools such as objdump or other debugging tools. These tools help you disassemble binaries and examine their structure. In some cases, the tools cannot disassemble the target binary because the binary file might be damaged or corrupted. In such cases, you might need to open the binary in its raw format to find important data or signatures. Knowing the ELF format well is crucial in these special situations.

In all these scenarios, a deep understanding of the ELF format is crucial for effectively analyzing and reverse engineering binaries. Mastering reverse engineering not only helps you navigate complex binary files but also enhances your overall development skills, making it a vital area to focus on.

Summary

This chapter introduced reverse engineering, a vital skill for understanding software when the source code is unavailable. It highlighted the importance of reverse engineering in debugging, especially for proprietary or old systems, and discussed the challenges of interpreting binary files.

You learned about two primary approaches to reverse engineering:

- **Static analysis**: This method involves examining binary files without executing them, allowing you to analyze their structure and content
- **Dynamic analysis**: This involves running the software on the target hardware to observe its runtime behavior and interactions

Additionally, we explored memory dump analysis as an alternative method for gaining insights into the software's operation. You also learned about the compilation process and how machine code is converted into assembly instructions. Understanding this conversion process reinforces the importance of these skills for effective debugging and system analysis. Finally, you were introduced to three key areas to enhance your reverse engineering abilities.

In the next chapter, you will learn how to configure QEMU and Arm devices for further analysis.

7

Setting Up a Practice Environment with an Arm Device

Many years ago, it was hard to get an Arm board. Even if you could buy one, they were expensive and difficult to set up. These days, there are many affordable Arm boards available for practice. Among them, Raspberry Pi is the most widely used. Another popular option is using QEMU for emulation without an Arm board.

In this chapter, we will discuss the Arm boards you can use for hands-on practice:

- Raspberry Pi
- QEMU

Both options are good for learning and practicing binary analysis. If you already have an Arm board or know how to use the Arm development environment, you can skip this chapter.

Let's start with the Raspberry Pi, which is the most popular Arm board.

Technical requirements

All the code examples for this chapter can be found on GitHub at https://github.com/PacktPublishing/Reverse-Engineering-Armv8-A-Systems.

Raspberry Pi

In the market, you will find a number of Arm-based boards such as BeagleBoard, ODROID, and others. Among them, the most widely used is the Raspberry Pi.

Introducing Raspberry Pi

The **Raspberry Pi** is everywhere. It is a useful Arm board and is used not only for educational purposes in schools but also extensively in IT companies. The following are reasons why the use of Raspberry Pi is recommended:

- **Strong community**: One of Raspberry Pi's biggest strengths is its user and developer community. You can easily find various resources on Raspberry Pi, including blogs and books that cover it in detail. The strong community offers support, making it easier to troubleshoot issues and explore new projects.

- **Stable board**: Raspberry Pi boards are known for their stability in both software and hardware, having been tested in various environments. Software updates are regularly provided to maintain reliability. This is a key reason why Raspberry Pi is popular for demo projects and prototypes.

- **Support for various software distributions**: Raspberry Pi boards allow you to run various software distributions, such as Raspberry Pi OS (formerly Raspbian), Ubuntu, and Debian. Having the chance to run multiple Linux distributions is a great advantage. Additionally, software such as machine learning frameworks can run on Raspberry Pi's supported distributions.

The Raspberry Pi community provides a lot of practical material. If you visit `https://www.raspberrypi.com`, you can find useful information, which is outlined as follows:

- **General information**: You can find detailed information about Raspberry Pi features. You will understand what the Raspberry Pi can do depending on your needs.

- **Installation guide**: The installation guide provides step-by-step instructions that are easy to follow. It includes setting up Raspberry Pi by installing the operating system and connecting peripherals. Even if it's your first time setting up a Raspberry Pi, the guide will make it easy to get started.

- **Q&A**: In the Q&A section, you'll find frequently asked questions and common issues discussed by users. There are plenty of solutions and troubleshooting tips to help you resolve problems you might encounter while using Raspberry Pi.

Now that the Raspberry Pi has been introduced, let's explore more features and capabilities of the Raspberry Pi.

Arm processor profile in each Raspberry Pi

There are several versions of Raspberry Pi, and the specifications of the most commonly used boards are as follows:

- **Raspberry Pi 3B**: Cortex®-A53
- **Raspberry Pi 4B**: Cortex®-A72
- **Raspberry Pi 5**: Cortex®-A76

Since this book focuses on reverse engineering with binaries built for the Armv8-A architecture, it is recommended that you install **Raspbian** (Linux), which supports AArch64 (64-bit Armv8-A). This operating system will ensure compatibility with the 64-bit processor architecture.

When installing a software image on your Raspberry Pi, you might want to check which Arm processor is currently being used. To do this, you can use the following command:

```
$ cat /proc/cpuinfo
processor        : 0
BogoMIPS         : 108.00
Features         : fp asimd evtstrm aes pmull sha1 sha2 crc32 atomics fphp
asimdhp cpuid asimdrdm lrcpc dcpop asimddp
CPU implementer : 0x41
CPU architecture: 8
CPU variant      : 0x4
CPU part         : 0xd0b
CPU revision     : 1
```

The output is displayed on a Raspberry Pi 5 and shows details about the Arm processor. This indicates that the Cortex-A76 processor is embedded in the Raspberry Pi 5.

Which software prints the preceding output with the `cat /proc/cpuinfo` command? The answer is the Linux kernel. This output is generated by a specific part of the Linux kernel code. You can find the relevant information in the source file, `arch/arm64/kernel/cpuinfo.c`, particularly in the `c_show` function.

Here is a snippet of how the output of the `cat /proc/cpuinfo` command is printed in the Linux kernel code:

```
static int c_show(struct seq_file *m, void *v)
{
    ...
    seq_puts(m, "\n");
    seq_printf(m, "CPU implementer\t: 0x%02x\n", MIDR_IMPLEMENTOR(midr));
    seq_printf(m, "CPU architecture: 8\n");
    seq_printf(m, "CPU variant\t: 0x%x\n", MIDR_VARIANT(midr));
    seq_printf(m, "CPU part\t: 0x%03x\n", MIDR_PARTNUM(midr));
    seq_printf(m, "CPU revision\t: %d\n\n", MIDR_REVISION(midr));
}
```

So far, we've introduced the Raspberry Pi, which is the most commonly used Arm board. You can find detailed information on configuring the Raspberry Pi and helpful tips in many blogs and online communities. For more information, please check the links provided in this section.

Now that we've covered this popular Arm board, let's move on to our next topic: QEMU. QEMU is a powerful tool for emulating different hardware architectures. It allows you to run and test software as if it were on various hardware platforms.

QEMU

Although Raspberry Pi communities provide practical resources, you still need to do some setup to run a Raspberry Pi board. For example, you will need a charger and a microSD card to power and boot the Raspberry Pi.

Another good option is to use **QEMU**. QEMU is a virtualization program that allows you to run Arm devices without needing the actual hardware. Using QEMU can save time and resources by allowing you to work with Arm software without needing physical Arm hardware. This flexibility makes it a valuable tool for developers and testers.

QEMU supports various CPU architectures and software distributions on an x86 desktop environment. In this section, we will explain how to use QEMU to simulate an Arm device environment with a Linux system. QEMU generally offers the following modes:

- User-mode emulation
- Full system emulation

Let's start by exploring the user-mode emulation.

User-mode emulation

Before running QEMU, some configurations are needed. However, if you're using an x86_64 machine with **Ubuntu** or **Debian**, testing AArch64 binaries is simple by running QEMU in user-mode emulation. Using QEMU in this mode doesn't require much effort.

In this section, you will learn how to set up QEMU in user-mode emulation and perform basic debugging. The steps that will be covered are outlined as follows:

1. Install the necessary utilities for user-mode emulation in QEMU.
2. Set up the tools required for cross-compiling.
3. Compile your code for AArch64 using a cross-compiler.
4. Run the compiled Arm binary using QEMU in user-mode emulation.

Additionally, we will use basic binary utilities to check the AArch64 binary.

> **Note**
>
> In this chapter, the Linux system is based on Ubuntu, and the version used is 22.04.1-Ubuntu with x86_64 GNU. Please use a version of Ubuntu that is newer than 22.04.1-Ubuntu.

First, install the QEMU user-mode package by running the following command:

```
$ sudo apt install qemu-user qemu-user-static
```

Next, you need to install the necessary tools for compiling code for AArch64 via the following command:

```
$ sudo apt install gcc-aarch64-linux-gnu make libncurses5-dev libssl-dev
bc bison flex
```

Now that you've installed the necessary utilities, you're ready to run QEMU in user-mode emulation and start debugging your Arm binaries.

Let's look at a simple code example. The following example code is the simplest Hello World program in Linux system programming:

```
#include <stdio.h>

int main(void)
```

```
{
    printf("Hello, I am an Aarch64 executable binary. \n");
    return 0;
}
```

You can save the preceding code as aarch64_hello.c. As the next step, you need to compile the source file using the Arm cross-compiler with the following command:

```
$ aarch64-linux-gnu-gcc -static -o aarch64_hello aarch64_hello.c
```

You can run this command on Ubuntu or Debian systems running on x86_64 architecture. After the compilation completes without errors, you'll find the aarch64_hello binary file in the same directory. This aarch64_hello file is an executable binary.

You might wonder what type of binary file it is. In this case, you can check the header information of aarch64_hello by running the readelf binary utility with the following command:

```
$ aarch64-linux-gnu-readelf -h aarch64_hello
```

Here is a part of the output:

```
ELF Header:
  Magic:   7f 45 4c 46 02 01 01 03 00 00 00 00 00 00 00 00
  Class:                             ELF64
  Data:                              2's complement, little endian
  Version:                           1 (current)
  OS/ABI:                            UNIX - GNU
  ABI Version:                       0
  Type:                              EXEC (Executable file)
  Machine:                           AArch64
  Version:                           0x1
```

The readelf utility is used to display header information from binary files in ELF format. At the end of the output, you'll see Machine: AArch64, confirming that the binary is built for an Armv8-A-based 64-bit system and this file is compiled for the AArch64 architecture.

Next, let's run the objdump binary utility with the -x option to inspect more details:

```
$ aarch64-linux-gnu-objdump -x aarch64_hello | more
aarch64_hello:     file format elf64-littleaarch64
aarch64_hello
architecture: aarch64, flags 0x00000112:
```

```
EXEC_P, HAS_SYMS, D_PAGED
start address 0x00000000004002b4
```

Again, you can see `architecture: aarch64`, indicating that this binary is built on a 64-bit Armv8 architecture.

So far, we've used binary utilities to analyze the `aarch64_hello` file. Now, let's run the `aarch64_hello` binary directly using QEMU. To do this, run the following command:

```
$ qemu-aarch64 ./aarch64_hello
Hello, I am an Aarch64 executable binary
```

Even though your Linux system is x86-based, you are running an AArch64 binary using the `qemu-aarch64` command. By following this method, you can easily run simple binary or source files on any machine.

Many system software developers use QEMU's user-mode emulation to directly execute binaries from different architectures.

Full system emulation

Another way to use QEMU is through full system emulation. With this method, you can emulate the experience of running an actual Arm device. Since there are many books and blogs that explain how to run QEMU in detail, this section will focus on the basic steps. QEMU supports various Linux distributions and architectures, including x86 and RISC-V.

There are two main ways to run AArch64 using QEMU:

- Using a Windows 10 desktop with x86_64 architecture
- Running QEMU on an Arm64 platform

In this section, we will focus on how to run QEMU in a Windows 10 desktop environment. We will also explain how to use QEMU to run an Ubuntu distribution.

> **Note**
>
> Running QEMU on an Arm64 platform can be done using KVM on a Raspberry Pi to run Arm64 Linux or using UTM on an Apple MacBook. Since Arm64 binaries can already run directly in these environments, we won't cover those methods here.

Before installing QEMU in full system emulation, you need to download an Ubuntu Linux image from the following links:

- **Ubuntu Jammy release**: `https://cloud-images.ubuntu.com/releases/jammy/release`
- **Ubuntu 22.04 Arm64 cloud image**: `https://cloud-images.ubuntu.com/releases/jammy/release/ubuntu-22.04-server-cloudimg-arm64.img`

The following is a screenshot of the web page at `https://cloud-images.ubuntu.com/releases/jammy/release`:

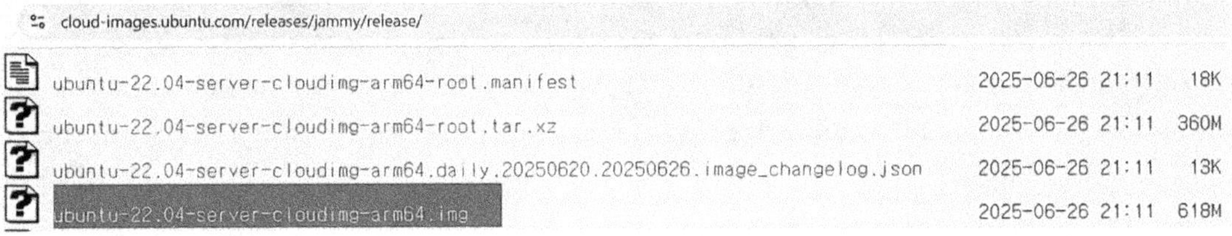
cloud-images.ubuntu.com/releases/jammy/release/
ubuntu-22.04-server-cloudimg-arm64-root.manifest 2025-06-26 21:11 18K
ubuntu-22.04-server-cloudimg-arm64-root.tar.xz 2025-06-26 21:11 360M
ubuntu-22.04-server-cloudimg-arm64.daily.20250620.20250626.image_changelog.json 2025-06-26 21:11 13K
ubuntu-22.04-server-cloudimg-arm64.img 2025-06-26 21:11 618M

Figure 7.1: A screenshot of the Ubuntu 22.04 Arm64 Cloud Image web page

Let's assume you've downloaded the `ubuntu-22.04-server-cloudimg-arm64.img` file from the preceding link.

> Note
>
> If you are using a Windows desktop PC, you can run a 64-bit Linux environment using programs such as VirtualBox or VMware Workstation Player. Many guides and books are available that explain how to do this. To keep it simple, we will skip the steps for setting up Linux in VirtualBox.

On a Windows 10 desktop, you can use **Chocolatey** to easily install QEMU. First, install Chocolatey by following the instructions from these links:

- **Installation guide**: `https://chocolatey.org/install`
- **QEMU package for Chocolatey**: `https://community.chocolatey.org/packages/Qemu`

The following is the screenshot of the web page at `https://chocolatey.org/install`:

Install Chocolatey for Individual Use:

1. First, ensure that you are using an *administrative shell* - you can also install as a non-admin, check out Non-Administrative Installation.

2. Install with powershell.exe

> ℹ **NOTE**
>
> Please inspect https://community.chocolatey.org/install.ps1 prior to running any of these scripts to ensure safety. We already know it's safe, but you should verify the security and contents of *any* script from the internet you are not familiar with. All of these scripts download a remote PowerShell script and execute it on your machine. We take security very seriously. Learn more about our security protocols.

With PowerShell, you must ensure Get-ExecutionPolicy is not Restricted. We suggest using Bypass to bypass the policy to get things installed or AllSigned for quite a bit more security.

  ○ Run Get-ExecutionPolicy. If it returns Restricted, then run Set-ExecutionPolicy AllSigned or Set-ExecutionPolicy Bypass -Scope Process.

Now run the following command:

> Set-ExecutionPolicy Bypass -Scope Process -Force; [System.Net.ServicePointManager]::SecurityProtocol = [System.Net.ServicePointManager]::SecurityProtocol -bor 3072; iex ((New-Object System.Net.Web ▯

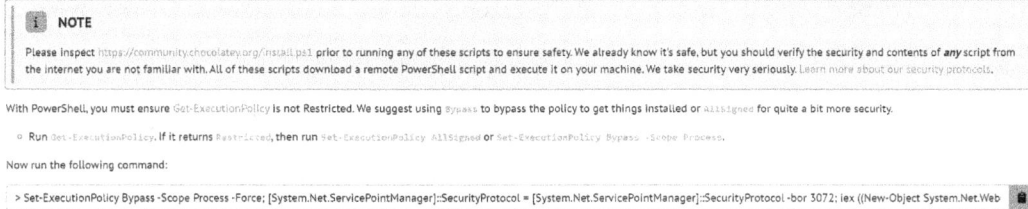

Figure 7.2: A screenshot of the Chocolatey application web page

After following the installation guide, you can easily install QEMU. Depending on your desktop PC's capabilities, you might need to adjust the disk size for the virtual machine according to the space needed for your environment.

To increase the disk size, you need to run the following command:

```
$ qemu-img resize ubuntu-22.04-server-cloudimg-arm64.img +10G
```

Next, to run QEMU and specify the Ubuntu image you downloaded, use this command:

```
$ qemu-system-aarch64 -m 4096 -cpu cortex-a72 -smp 4 -M virt -M gic_
version=3 -nographic -bios QEMU_EFI.fd -drive if=none,file=ubuntu-22.04-
server-cloudimg-arm64.img,id=hd0 -device virtio-blk-device,drive=hd0
-drive file=user-data.img,format=raw -device virtio-net-device,netdev=net0
-netdev user,hostfwd=tcp:127.0.0.1:2222-:22,id=net0
```

If you follow these steps carefully, you will be able to run QEMU successfully using Chocolatey. After running the command, you will have an emulated Arm environment in which you can test and explore. If you have any issues during installation, make sure your settings match your desktop's specifications. Try it out and see how QEMU works for you.

Summary

In this chapter, we learned about Arm boards. To analyze various binaries built with the Arm compiler, you first need to set up a development environment. We looked at the Raspberry Pi, one of the most popular boards used in schools and IT industries. Setting up the right environment is very important for development. Raspberry Pi boards can help you better understand how real-world hardware works.

We also discussed QEMU. QEMU is a tool that allows you to reverse engineer Arm binaries without needing a physical Arm board. If you don't have a Raspberry Pi or a similar Arm board, QEMU can help you work more efficiently on reverse engineering.

In the next chapter, we will cover the important topics about the Linux system that you need to know for reverse engineering.

Join our community on Discord

Join our community's Discord space for discussions with the authors and other readers: https://packt.link/embeddedsystems

8

Unpacking the Kernel with Linux Fundamentals

The earlier chapters covered the fundamental features of Arm architecture, including exception levels and assembly instructions. However, analyzing assembly instructions solely from the perspective of Arm architecture can make it challenging to fully understand their behavior. This is because the process is the key component responsible for executing these instructions.

For this, understanding the Linux operating system is considered essential background knowledge. In this chapter, we will focus on the following key topics:

- Architecture overview
- Process management
- Memory management
- Key security hardening features

Let's start this chapter by reviewing the architecture of the Linux operating system, which is one of the most widely used operating systems.

Technical requirements

If you like to explore more about key features of Linux Kernel, you will find the practical resources at https://docs.kernel.org.

Architecture overview

When you perform reverse engineering, you examine a binary file without having access to the source code. To develop the skill of interpreting a binary, it's important to become familiar with how to identify the basic characteristics of the binary itself. A binary file contains machine code, which is translated into assembly instructions, so it's essential to understand these instructions.

As a background, having a strong understanding of operating system fundamentals is crucial. This is because knowing the basic rules and patterns of how software operates helps you understand who is executing the assembly instructions. Additionally, learning about memory management, process execution, and system calls can give you better insight into how programs work at a low level.

What is the Linux kernel?

Let's examine the key features and functions of the Linux kernel, as shown in *Figure 8.1*:

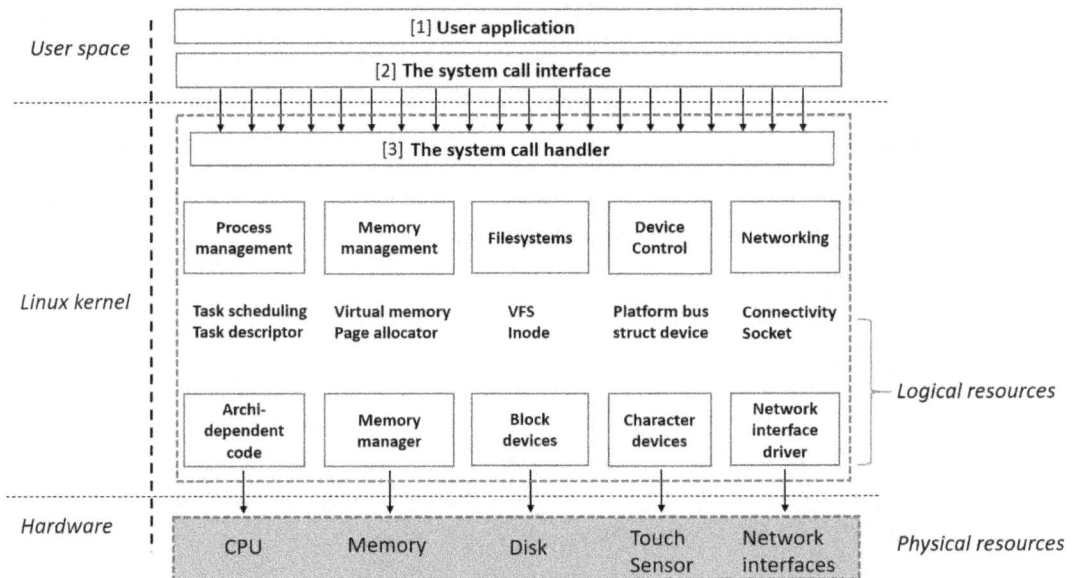

Figure 8.1: The overall structure of the Linux system

Figure 8.1 looks complicated, but we can view it narrowly to understand the Linux kernel from two main perspectives:

- Resource manager
- Supporting execution environment

Resource manager

From the first perspective, we can think of the Linux kernel as a resource manager where resources are divided into physical resources and logical resources. At the bottom of *Figure 8.1*, you can see elements such as the CPU, memory, disk, touchscreens, sensors, and other hardware devices. These are considered physical resources because they physically exist as hardware components.

Now, what are logical resources? In *Figure 8.1*, you can find logical resources are above the physical resources.

In the software world, the term logical has a broad meaning. In this context, logical refers to the implementation of something at the software level. From this perspective, logical resources are the software-level implementation of physical resources. In other words, logical resources represent physical resources in a way that the software can interact with and use effectively.

For example, a CPU core can be represented in terms of process, and physical memory can be represented in terms of pages. This helps the operating system manage and allocate resources effectively.

Here are some examples of how physical resources are represented as logical resources:

- **CPU**: Process (`struct task_struct`)
- **Memory**: Page (`struct page`)
- **Disk**: Filesystem (`struct super_block`)
- **Network Interface**: Socket (`struct socket`)
- **Sensors, Touch Peripherals**: Device drivers (`struct device`)

Let's explain memory in more detail, among the logical resources mentioned above, as it is one of the most common concepts in system software development. Memory, as a physical resource, can be managed as a logical resource in the Linux kernel using **pages** . This is represented by a structure called `struct  page`. In addition, the disk, which is another physical resource, is managed by the Linux kernel through the filesystem. This is represented by a structure called `struct super_block`.

The role of the Linux kernel is to manage physical resources by representing them as logical resources. The Linux kernel supports many subsystems that implement these logical resources and their APIs.

Supporting the execution environment

Applications running in user space may need to use these resources. For example, a user application might want to control a physical resource by accessing its corresponding logical resource. To do this, the Linux kernel should support the necessary execution environment, which is the second perspective of the Linux kernel. The Linux kernel supports an execution environment where user applications can run.

Let's go back to **[3]** in *Figure 8.1* to see how this works. When a user space program wants to interact with logical resources, it uses system calls. System calls are APIs that can be accessed from user space. The following are key examples of system calls:

- fork: Creates a process
- open: Opens a specific file
- read: Reads a file
- brk: Requests more heap memory
- mmap: Accesses a specific memory space

The system call interface provides an API for higher layers to access the main functions of the Linux kernel.

So far, we have looked at both perspectives of the Linux kernel, including the resource manager and supporting the execution environment. To properly understand the structure of a Linux system, it is important to know how system calls work and are processed. Next, let's learn more about the system call.

Understanding system calls

The **system call** is the operation where user mode switches into kernel mode. In addition, a system call acts as the interface between user space and kernel space.

User space and kernel space

To understand how system calls work, we need to discuss the layers of user space and kernel space. What are user space and kernel space? In the Linux operating system, the execution mode and space are classified into user space and kernel space based on privilege levels.

A common question is: What are privilege levels? Privilege levels determine access to running instructions, configuring registers, and using memory addresses to control hardware resources. Software running with lower privilege levels is restricted from using certain instructions, registers, or memory addresses.

Let's look at *Figure 8.2*, which shows the user space and kernel space:

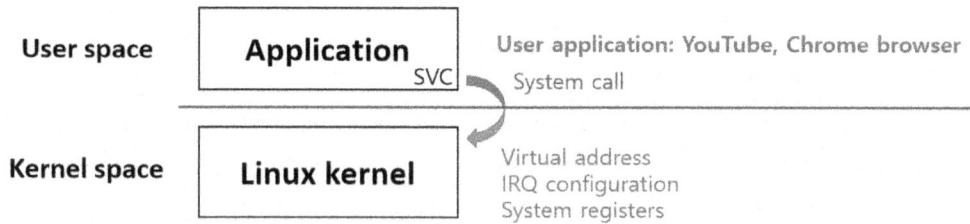

Figure 8.2: The workflow of the system call

At the top of *Figure 8.2*, you can see the user space, which has the following characteristics:

- User applications run in user space
- Less privileged access to hardware resources
- Running certain instructions is restricted
- Access to specific system registers is not allowed

Applications running in user space have restrictions on accessing resources. What happens if software running in user space tries to directly access hardware resources in kernel space? For example, if user space attempts to access a system register that is only allowed in kernel space, an exception occurs. Additionally, if user space accesses a memory address that is restricted to kernel space, a segmentation fault will be generated. A segmentation fault happens when a program tries to access an invalid address, such as a null pointer, causing it to crash.

At the bottom of *Figure 8.2*, you will find the kernel space. The main characteristics of kernel space are as follows:

- Can run any kernel API supported by the Linux kernel
- Can execute any instructions to control hardware peripherals
- Can read and write data to system registers
- Can have privileged access to the memory in the kernel space

The key characteristics of user space and kernel space can be summarized as follows:

- **User space**: Software runs with the lowest privilege level and cannot directly access hardware resources
- **Kernel space**: Software runs with higher privileges, allowing it to directly control hardware resources

Now that we have explored user space and kernel space, let's look at the key operations of system calls in more detail.

How the system call works

A system call refers to the operation where user space transitions into kernel space. When does user space need to enter kernel space? The answer is when user space requests a service from the kernel. Here are some typical examples where user space needs to enter kernel space:

- When it needs to read or write a file from the filesystem
- When it wants to obtain process information such as the PID
- When it requests system information, such as the attributes of the filesystem

In such scenarios, the application invokes a system call, transferring control from user space to kernel space.

The concepts we discussed are illustrated in *Figure 8.3*.

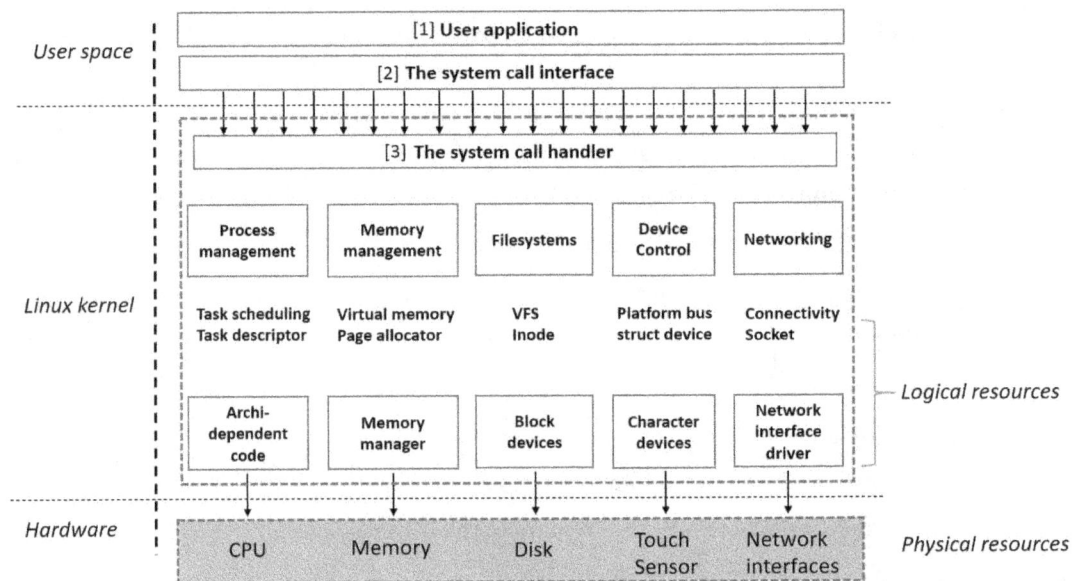

Figure 8.3: The Linux system layout: system call

[1] in *Figure 8.3* shows that standard input/output functions such as open, read, and write are called in a Linux system program. [2] indicates a library in user space that triggers a system call by using the svc instruction. [3] represents the system handler that runs in kernel space.

Now, let's take a closer look at *Figure 8.3* to understand how system calls work in more detail. First, we need to look at section **[1]**. In user applications, you can use APIs such as open, write, read, and close. After these APIs are called, the following assembly instructions can be executed inside the libraries that correspond to **[2]**:

```
0x0d9a50 <__write@@GLIBC_2.17>:
...
01   mov      x0, x19
02   mov      x8, #0x40   // #64
03   svc      #0x0
04   mov      x19, x0
05   cmn      x0, #0x1, lsl #12
```

In line 02, the value 64 is moved into the x8 register. This number, 64, represents the system call number for the write operation. When line 03 is executed, it triggers a synchronous exception from the viewpoint of Armv8-A.

From a reverse engineering perspective, executing the svc instruction causes a switch to kernel space. When the software's execution flow enters kernel space, the Linux kernel performs the following task:

- It reads the value in the x8 register and accesses the system call handler in kernel space
- The system call handler corresponding to the system call number is called, and the sub-routine is processed

In this example, 64 is the write system call number. If a write system call is executed, the write system call handler function is called. Then, the write system call handler function writes a value to the file. What happens if a fork system call is triggered? The system call handler function for fork is called, and the subroutine is executed to create the process.

The system calls we have discussed so far serve as the interface between user space and kernel space in a Linux system. From another perspective, system calls ensure secure communication between user space and kernel space. To understand the detailed implementation of system calls, it is necessary to learn about the system call numbers and the system call handlers that make up the system call.

System call number and system call handler

As shown in *Figure 8.3*, switching from user space to kernel space is done through a system call. A system call consists of two main components:

- System call number
- System call handler

If you look at the code in any Arm-based device such as a Raspberry Pi running Linux, you will find the system call numbers:

```
/usr/include/asm-generic/unistd.h
#define __NR_read      63
__SYSCALL(__NR_read, sys_read)
#define __NR_write     64
__SYSCALL(__NR_write, sys_write)
#define __NR_readv     65
__SC_COMP(__NR_readv, sys_readv, sys_readv)
#define __NR_writev    66
__SC_COMP(__NR_writev, sys_writev, sys_writev)
```

In the first line, you see __NR_read and 63. In this case, 63 is the system call number for the read operation. The third line shows __NR_write and 64, where 64 is the system call number for the write operation. In addition, you can find out another system call number by looking at __NR_readv 65 and __NR_writev 66.

Many believe that the system call numbers are the same in any Arm architecture. But it is not true. Note that the system call numbers are different between the 32-bit Armv7 architecture and the 64-bit Armv8 architecture.

Monitoring system call operations

Let's perform an experiment to see how system calls work. To do that, run the following command in the Linux terminal:

```
$ sudo strace -c -p 1
strace: Process 1 attached
% time     seconds  usecs/call     calls    errors syscall
------ ----------- ----------- --------- --------- ----------------
100.00    0.000861         287         3           waitid
  0.00    0.000000           0         1         1 lgetxattr
```

```
  0.00    0.000000         0         7               epoll_ctl
  0.00    0.000000         0        12               epoll_pwait
  0.00    0.000000         0         3        3 ioctl
  0.00    0.000000         0         4        1 openat
  0.00    0.000000         0         4          close
  0.00    0.000000         0         7          read
  0.00    0.000000         0         3          newfstatat
  0.00    0.000000         0        13          gettid
  0.00    0.000000         0         1          sendto
  0.00    0.000000         0         3        1 recvfrom
  0.00    0.000000         0         1          getsockopt
  0.00    0.000000         0         1          accept4
------ ------------ ---------- --------- --------- ----------------
100.00    0.000861        13        63        6 total
```

In the rightmost column, ioctl, close, and read are all examples of system calls.

By using this command, you can monitor which system calls are being made and how long each system call takes. This kind of observation is useful for understanding how system calls are performed and how system calls handle user requests.

In this section, we explored how the Linux system is structured by reviewing the key features of the Linux kernel and system calls. In the next section, we will discuss the characteristics of processes, which is one of the most important features of the Linux system.

Process management

A **process** is one of the most important features of a Linux system. There are two effective ways to learn about processes. The first is to analyze the source code that implements the process's behavior or properties. The second method is to debug processes using several commands.

In this section, we'll explain the basic concept of processes and explore their properties through various commands.

Introducing processes

What is a process? A process is generally considered a running program. Some software engineers also use the term task to refer to a process in real projects. When you refer to technical documentation during a project, you might come across terms such as process scheduling or multi-processing.

Let's dive deeper into the concept of a process from a developer's point of view. What does a process do? The main job of a process is to execute the instructions or code that you are working with. For a better understanding, consider the following simple sample code:

```
#include <stdio.h>
int main(void)
{
    printf("hello Aarch64 reversing\n");
    return 0;
}
```

Now, imagine you compile and run the preceding code. Who is responsible for executing this code? The process is in charge of running the instructions inside the main function. This applies to any other code you are working on as well.

Let's take another example from the Linux kernel:

```
kernel/sched/core.c
asmlinkage __visible void __sched schedule(void)
{
    struct task_struct *tsk = current;

    sched_submit_work(tsk);
    do {
        preempt_disable();
        __schedule(SM_NONE);
        sched_preempt_enable_no_resched();
    } while (need_resched());
    sched_update_worker(tsk);
}
EXPORT_SYMBOL(schedule);
```

Please note that the schedule function is a crucial kernel API responsible for task scheduling, and it may be called more than 100 times per second. Another question to ask is: who runs the schedule function? The answer is the process.

Every piece of code you analyze in a Linux system is executed by a process. A process also performs other important tasks for the Linux system. Here are the key features of a process:

- Executing applications
- Managing system resources
- Interacting with user space and kernel space

Understanding processes helps broaden your perspective as a system software engineer. It will give you insight into how other features of the Linux system are designed.

The data structure of the process

The Linux kernel is developed as an open source project. Any software engineer can contribute to the Linux kernel community. Since the Linux kernel source code is publicly available on GitHub, you can analyze its features by analyzing the source code.

If you want to explore how processes are implemented in the Linux kernel, you need to focus on the data structures or APIs related to processes. First, let's examine the data structure that represents the properties of a process in the Linux kernel. This is called the task descriptor, which is represented by the task_struct structure.

You can view the structure of task_struct by checking the Linux kernel source code. Additionally, you can examine it by opening the kernel binary using a tool such as the crash utility. The following is an example of the output from the struct task_struct command using the crash utility:

```
crash> struct task_struct
struct task_struct {
    struct thread_info thread_info;
    unsigned int __state;
    void *stack;
    refcount_t usage;
    ...
    pid_t pid;
    ...
    char comm[16];
    ...
    struct thread_struct thread;
}
```

As you can see, the task_struct structure consists of many elements. This structure contains important information required for process management in the Linux kernel. Here are some key elements in the structure:

- thread_info: It stores information specific to the process, depending on the CPU architecture
- __state: It shows the current state of the process, such as running, sleeping, or stopped
- *stack: It points to the process's stack, which is important for handling function calls and execution
- usage: It keeps track of how many times the process is being referenced
- pid: It stores the **process ID (PID)**
- comm: It stores the command name or the name of the process
- thread: It holds architecture-specific details, such as CPU registers, used during context switching

The task_struct structure is similar to an ID card or social security number assigned to a person when they are born. Every process in the Linux system is represented by this task_struct data structure. It holds various details about the process, including its state and behavior.

You may be wondering how the task_struct structure is used in a Linux system. If you run commands such as ps or top, the output shows process information. During this operation, it accesses specific parts of the task_struct structure. You will notice many fields in the task_struct structure, but we won't cover all of them here as it is beyond the scope of this book.

Understanding the call stack of the process

So far, you have learned that the properties of a process are managed by the task_struct structure. Another important aspect of processes to understand is the call stack. When a process is created, the kernel allocates stack space for the process. Every process has its own stack area to run the program, saving temporary data such as local variables or return addresses to manage the control flow.

From a software perspective, the flow of a process's execution can be represented by the call stack. Why do software engineers often look into the call stack whenever there is a bug to fix? The main reason is that the call stack shows how functions are called. Using this information, the software developer can identify which module is being executed, which helps trace the execution flow. This activity will make it easier to identify where an issue might have occurred.

Let's take a closer look at how the call stack works. Here's an example of function calls in the Linux kernel using a crash-utility program:

```
crash> bt 1
PID: 1           TASK: ffffff8041018040  CPU: 0     COMMAND: "systemd"
 #0 [ffffffc00802bb10] __switch_to at ffffffd129e0ee94
 #1 [ffffffc00802bb30] __schedule at ffffffd129e0f258
 #2 [ffffffc00802bbb0] schedule at ffffffd129e0f910
 #3 [ffffffc00802bbd0] schedule_hrtimeout_range_clock at ffffffd129e16f58
 #4 [ffffffc00802bc60] schedule_hrtimeout_range at ffffffd129e16f8c
 #5 [ffffffc00802bc70] do_epoll_wait at ffffffd1295845e0
 #6 [ffffffc00802bd70] do_epoll_pwait at ffffffd1295846e8
 #7 [ffffffc00802bd90] __arm64_sys_epoll_pwait at ffffffd129585b44
 #8 [ffffffc00802be00] invoke_syscall at ffffffd12922952c
 #9 [ffffffc00802be30] el0_svc_common.constprop.0 at ffffffd129229664
#10 [ffffffc00802be70] do_el0_svc at ffffffd129229758
#11 [ffffffc00802be80] el0_svc at ffffffd129e0c4cc
#12 [ffffffc00802bea0] el0t_64_sync_handler at ffffffd129e0c8ec
#13 [ffffffc00802bfe0] el0t_64_sync at ffffffd129211544
```

The preceding output represents the call stack of systemd. The function call flow is from the bottom to the top.

How does the crash utility display the call stack of a process? It reads data from the process's stack area, such as return addresses and previous stack addresses. Using this information, the crash utility reconstructs and displays the call stack of a specific process.

From a reverse engineering perspective, checking the call stack is a critical task. Developers often analyze raw data from the stack to trace the execution flow of a process. This is similar to how they examine memory dumps in real-world projects when analyzing or debugging issues.

So far, we have explored what a process is and the structure that stores its properties. We've also introduced the concept of the process call stack. Next, we will look at processes from another perspective—how to manage and control multiple processes within a system.

Multiprocess management

It's important to remember how processes run on a computer: a CPU core can only run one process at a time. You might think that an operating system has only one process ready for execution, but that's not true. In fact, there are usually more than 100 processes available in the system. So, how does the operating system manage all these processes?

There is a special part of the Linux kernel called the task scheduler that does this job. The task scheduler decides which process to run based on its priority and lets that process run for a short amount of time. Here's what the task scheduler does:

1. It selects a process from the available ones in the system based on its priority.
2. The selected process runs on the CPU core for a specific period of time.

This switching happens more than 100 times per second. We call this multitasking or multiprocessing. For example, when you use your smartphone, you can make a call while browsing the web or using other apps. This is possible because of multitasking.

Now that we understand there are many processes in the system, let's check the list of processes on a Linux system.

Figure 8.4 shows the output of the ps -el command.

```
root@raspberrypi:/home/austin# ps -el
F S   UID    PID   PPID  C PRI  NI ADDR SZ WCHAN  TTY          TIME CMD
4 S     0      1      0  0  80   0 - 10575 do_epo ?        00:00:00 systemd
1 S     0      2      0  0  80   0 -     0 kthrea ?        00:00:00 kthreadd
1 S     0      3      2  0  80   0 -     0 kthrea ?        00:00:00 pool_workqueue_release
1 I     0      4      2  0  60 -20 -     0 rescue ?        00:00:00 kworker/R-rcu_g
1 I     0      5      2  0  60 -20 -     0 rescue ?        00:00:00 kworker/R-rcu_p
1 I     0      6      2  0  60 -20 -     0 rescue ?        00:00:00 kworker/R-slub_
1 I     0      7      2  0  60 -20 -     0 rescue ?        00:00:00 kworker/R-netns
1 I     0     11      2  0  80   0 -     0 worker ?        00:00:00 kworker/u8:0-netns
1 I     0     12      2  0  60 -20 -     0 rescue ?        00:00:00 kworker/R-mm_pe
1 I     0     13      2  0  80   0 -     0 rcu_ta ?        00:00:00 rcu_tasks_kthread
1 I     0     14      2  0  80   0 -     0 rcu_ta ?        00:00:00 rcu_tasks_rude_kthread
1 I     0     15      2  0  80   0 -     0 rcu_ta ?        00:00:00 rcu_tasks_trace_kthread
1 S     0     16      2  0  80   0 -     0 smpboo ?        00:00:00 ksoftirqd/0
```

Figure 8.4: Output of the ps –el command

By using the ps -el command, you can see a list of processes running in the system. Generally, the number of processes exceeds 100 in the system. The output shows the properties of each process. Let's look at the first line, which is seen as follows:

```
F S   UID    PID   PPID  C PRI  NI ADDR SZ WCHAN  TTY       TIME       CMD
4 S     0      1            0   0  80   0 - 10575 do_epo ?
00:00:00 systemd
```

From the first line, you can find the following information about the process:

- The PID is 1
- The **Parent PID (PPID)** is 0
- The process name is systemd

You might wonder how this information is printed. Internally, the Linux kernel stores and manages process information using a structure called `task_struct`. The `ps` command reads these fields from the kernel and displays them in a clear format. This command is often used when you want to check the state of the system and see the list of processes that are ready to run.

Now, let's explore the `top` command. This command shows more detailed information about how much CPU and memory each process is using. It provides real-time updates, so you can see how system resources are being utilized.

Let's review *Figure 8.5*, which displays the output of the top command.

```
top - 07:47:09 up 33 min,  4 users,  load average: 0.00, 0.00, 0.00
Tasks: 194 total,   1 running, 193 sleeping,   0 stopped,   0 zombie
%Cpu(s):  0.0 us,  0.1 sy,  0.0 ni, 99.9 id,  0.0 wa,  0.0 hi,  0.0 si,  0.0 st
MiB Mem :   8052.3 total,   6952.1 free,    476.7 used,    730.0 buff/cache
MiB Swap:    200.0 total,    200.0 free,      0.0 used.   7575.6 avail Mem

  PID USER      PR  NI    VIRT    RES    SHR S  %CPU  %MEM     TIME+ COMMAND
    1 root      20   0  169200  11184   8192 S   0.0   0.1   0:00.66 systemd
    2 root      20   0       0      0      0 S   0.0   0.0   0:00.00 kthreadd
    3 root      20   0       0      0      0 S   0.0   0.0   0:00.00 pool_workqueue_release
    4 root       0 -20       0      0      0 I   0.0   0.0   0:00.00 kworker/R-rcu_g
    5 root       0 -20       0      0      0 I   0.0   0.0   0:00.00 kworker/R-rcu_p
    6 root       0 -20       0      0      0 I   0.0   0.0   0:00.00 kworker/R-slub_
```

Figure 8.5: The output of the top command

The output of the top command is similar to that of the `ps` command. However, `top` provides more details about process resource usage. To better understand this, let's analyze the `systemd` process using the top command:

```
  PID USER      PR  NI    VIRT    RES      SHR  S  %CPU  %MEM       TIME+
COMMAND
    1 root      20   0  169200  11184     8192 S    0.0          0.1   0:00.66
systemd
    2 root      20   0       0                0            0 S   0.0
0.0   0:00.00      kthreadd
```

In the output, we see that the PID is 1 and the process name is `systemd`. The PID and process name are common identifiers for a process. This information can be helpful when debugging logs or other data.

Every process has a parent process, sibling processes, and child processes. This means that all processes belong to a process family, and each process is grouped into this family. A process is part of a family, so it's important to understand the relationships between processes when managing them.

Let's look at this with another command:

```
$ ps -ejH
      PID    PGID     SID TTY           TIME CMD
        2       0       0 ?         00:00:00 kthreadd
        3       0       0 ?         00:00:00   pool_workqueue_release
        4       0       0 ?         00:00:00   kworker/R-rcu_g
        5       0       0 ?         00:00:00   kworker/R-rcu_p
        6       0       0 ?         00:00:00   kworker/R-slub_
        7       0       0 ?         00:00:00   kworker/R-netns
```

The ps -ejH command shows the parent-child relationships of processes. From the output, we can see the following:

- pool_workqueue_release, kworker/R-rcu_g, kworker/R-rcu_p, kworker/R-slub_, and kworker/R-netns are sibling processes
- Their parent process is kthreadd

Just like humans are created by their parents, processes are also created by their parent processes. A process cannot create itself; it must be created by a parent process.

Note that kthreadd is an important process because it is responsible for creating kernel threads, which are processes that run only in kernel space.

Now, let's look at another output from the ps -ejH command:

```
$ ps -ejH
...
        1       1       1 ?         00:00:00   systemd
      297     297     297 ?         00:00:00     systemd-journal
      333     333     333 ?         00:00:00     systemd-udevd
      629     629     629 ?         00:00:00     systemd-timesyn
      664     664     664 ?         00:00:00     accounts-daemon
     1122     962     962 ?         00:00:00     systemd-inhibit
     1145     962     962 ?         00:00:00     gtk-nop
```

We can see that systemd-journal, systemd-udevd, systemd-timesyn, accounts-daemon, and systemd-inhibit are sibling processes. Their parent is the systemd process (PID 1). The systemd process is the parent process of all user processes.

Introducing threads

Let's explore an important concept in the Linux operating system: **threads**. Before diving into threads, it's helpful to understand what happens when the Linux kernel creates and runs a process. The kernel, which is the core part of Linux, manages everything that happens in the system. When it creates a process, there are several tasks it must handle to ensure the process runs smoothly and safely.

When the kernel creates a user process, it first sets up a separate virtual memory space for that process. But what is virtual memory? Imagine it as a private workspace where the process can run its tasks without interfering with other processes. This separation ensures that one process cannot access another process's memory.

For example, imagine you are running two programs on your computer at the same time: a web browser and a text editor. These programs are separate processes, and the virtual memory provided by the kernel keeps them isolated from each other. This isolation means that if your web browser crashes, it will not affect your text editor, and you won't lose any unsaved work.

In addition to virtual memory, the kernel also sets up a file descriptor table for each process. This table helps processes manage files. For instance, when a process opens a file to read or write data, the file descriptor table keeps track of which files are open, making it easier for the process to perform tasks such as reading from or writing to files.

It's important to note that creating a process requires a lot of resources. These resources, such as virtual memory and file descriptors, can be considered heavy. In software development, when we say heavy, we mean that these resources take up a lot of memory. These heavy resources are continuously managed by various subsystems within the Linux kernel. That's why developers sometimes need a more efficient way to run smaller tasks without creating new processes every time.

This brings us to the concept of threads. When developers need to run tasks that don't require as many resources, they can use threads instead of processes. So, what exactly is a thread?

A thread is a lightweight task that runs within a process. It shares the resources of the process it belongs to. This means the thread can access the same virtual memory and file descriptors as the process. However, a thread is much lighter than a process, meaning it uses fewer resources and is faster to create.

Let's look at a real-world example: web browsers. When you use a web browser such as Chrome, it performs a lot of tasks in the background. For instance, it may be handling multiple tabs at the same time, loading different web pages, or playing videos. If the browser used a single process for everything, it would be slow, especially if one task performs multiple operations. Instead, web browsers use multiple threads to handle different tasks simultaneously. So, even if one thread is busy loading a web page, another thread can handle user input, such as clicking buttons or scrolling the page.

In this section, we've discussed processes. A process is the main entity responsible for all tasks in Linux. Whether you're doing reverse engineering or development, it's crucial to figure out how a process works and what patterns it follows.

The next section will focus on memory management in the Linux system.

Memory management

As discussed in *Chapter 7*, reverse engineering is the process of understanding a program's execution flow by analyzing its binaries without access to the source code. When examining binaries, you will encounter the following patterns:

- Values of global or local variables
- Machine code that maps to specific instructions
- Addresses, including stack addresses and function addresses

To become familiar with these binary patterns, it's also important to understand how the operating system organizes and manages memory addresses. This knowledge will help us analyze binaries more effectively and trace the program's flow more easily.

Memory management is a vast topic, so we'll focus only on the essential parts needed for reverse engineering. Virtual addresses can be viewed differently depending on whether you are looking from the perspective of the Arm architecture or the Linux kernel. In this section, we will introduce key memory features in the Linux kernel. Next, we will discuss how the virtual address is organized from the perspectives of Arm architecture and reverse engineering.

Key memory features in the Linux system

The Linux kernel supports various types of addresses. Let's first explore how addresses are interpreted in a Linux system. You'll find that different types of addresses are used for different purposes, and each type has its own characteristics and limitations:

- **User virtual address**: This is the virtual address used in user space, handled separately from kernel space. We call this the user virtual address. The way it's managed depends on the type of CPU architecture.

- **Kernel virtual address**: This is the address used in the Linux kernel. A kernel virtual address can be mapped to physical addresses depending on the situation. Additionally, a kernel logical address is linearly mapped to physical memory during runtime. In Armv8-A, the virtual addresses used by the Linux kernel are translated using a page table, which is managed by the TTBR1_EL1 register.

- **Physical address**: A physical address refers to an actual location in the main memory. In the Linux kernel, physical memory is managed in 4K pages. Each page is represented by a structure called struct page.

Understanding how virtual addresses are managed in the Linux kernel is essential. By learning about each component, you can see how paging operates with physical addresses.

Rich operating systems such as Linux use paging as a key technique for managing memory. Paging divides memory into small units called pages, with typical sizes being 4 KB or 8 KB, depending on the architecture.

In short, physical memory is divided into 0x1000 units, and each 0x1000 block of memory is called a page frame. The Linux kernel manages physical memory based on these pages. You can refer to *Figure 8.6*, which shows how virtual addresses are managed:

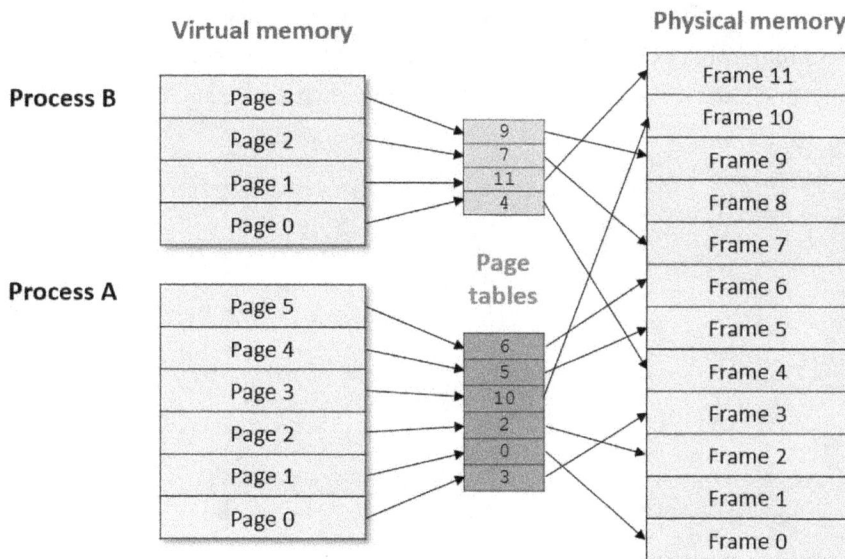

Figure 8.6: The overall workflow of the paging

The leftmost box represents a process. Each process has its own separate virtual address space. Each process has its own page table that converts virtual addresses into physical addresses. The page table manages physical addresses as page frames and links them to virtual addresses.

To understand the paging mechanism, you need to first learn about how virtual addresses are divided. They are categorized into the following:

- **Page Frame Number (PFN)**: This represents the page's number
- **Offset within the page**: This is the offset inside the page

For example, in a 32-bit architecture with a 4 KB page size (`PAGE_SIZE = 4KB`), the upper 20 bits are used for the PFN, while the lower 12 bits are used for the offset. It's a complex concept with many features you need to understand. For more information, please refer to the Linux kernel documentation at this link: `https://www.kernel.org/doc/html/v4.9/kernel-documentation.html`.

Next, let's talk about **Virtual Memory Area (VMA)**. In the Linux kernel, user processes run in both user space and kernel space. Kernel threads and other kernel processes, however, run exclusively in kernel space. To execute a user process in user space, a separate address space needs to be created, allowing the process to run safely in user space.

User process memory can be divided into areas such as text, data, heap, and stack, based on their characteristics. These memory areas are grouped into what we call VMAs. The following figure illustrates VMA in user space.

Here, VMA represents the virtual address space of the user process. You can view VMAs through procfs by running `/proc/<pid>/maps`. If you type the `cat /proc/self/maps` command in the Linux terminal, it will show the VMA for the current process (such as `cat`). The format looks like this:

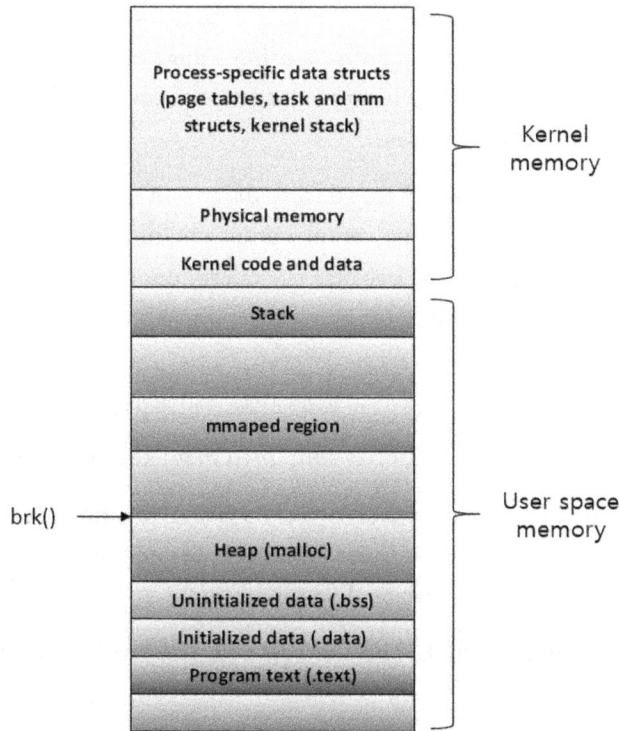

Figure 8.7: The layout of the virtual memory area

In this section, we have summarized how virtual addresses are managed in the Linux kernel. Let's understand the basic concept of the virtual memory system by looking at *Figure 8.8*.

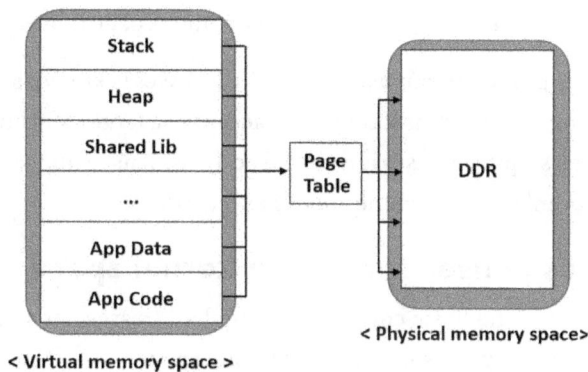

Figure 8.8: The workflow of virtual memory translation

When reading data from a virtual address or writing data to a virtual address, the system translates the virtual address into a physical address using a page table. The right box in *Figure 8.8* represents the virtual memory space, while the middle box shows the page table that translates virtual addresses into physical addresses.

The page table contains the necessary translation data to map virtual addresses to their corresponding physical addresses. However, you won't be able to observe this process even if you analyze assembly instructions. This is because the operation is handled by the **Memory Management Unit (MMU)** hardware inside the Arm processor.

In *Figure 8.8*, the page table is shown as a single table for simplicity. In reality, the virtual address is divided into specific patterns, and the translation from virtual to physical addresses is done on multiple levels. However, this explanation is simplified to make it easier to understand.

Actually, there are more elements to learn about in the virtual memory system, such as the MMU and relevant system registers. Note that these topics are beyond the scope of this book. For more information, refer to the Arm specification documentation.

In the following section, let's first look at how virtual addresses are handled from the perspective of the Arm architecture.

Introducing the virtual memory system

These days, most operating systems, such as Linux, are built on a virtual memory system. A common question is: how does the operating system manage virtual addresses? To answer this, there are a few key concepts you need to understand. The first is the idea of a virtual address. To figure out what a virtual address is, you'll need to learn about page tables and physical addresses.

The environment where programs run using virtual addresses is known as a virtual memory system. In this system, programs work as if they have access to a large, continuous block of memory. Simply put, every address a process uses is a virtual address. This includes addresses for the stack, global variables, and even where machine code is executed.

Virtual addresses in user space and kernel space

Now that we have covered the basic concept of virtual addresses, let's discuss how virtual addresses are handled separately in user space and kernel space.

Let's examine *Figure 8.9* to see how the virtual address is handled from the Armv8-A perspective.

Exception Level		First page lookup	Virtual address range
EL0	**Application**	**TTBR0_EL1**	start: 0x00000000_00000000 end: 0x0000FFFF_00000000
EL1	**Linux kernel**	**TTBR1_EL1**	start: 0xFFFF0000_00000000 end: 0xFFFFFFFF_FFFFFFFF

Figure 8.9: Virtual address management (VA_48)

Let's start with how the virtual address space is handled in user space. You can see **EL0** in the upper part of *Figure 8.9*. In Armv8-A, user space corresponds to **EL0**, where user applications run. When virtual addresses are translated into physical addresses at **EL0**, a separate page table is used, controlled by the **TTBR0_EL1** register. The virtual addresses in user space range from 0x0 to 0x0000FFFF_FFFFFFFF in hexadecimal.

Now, let's explore how the virtual address space is managed in kernel space. In Arm architecture, kernel space corresponds to **EL1**, where the Linux kernel operates. The virtual addresses accessed in **EL1** are translated using the page table linked to the **TTBR1_EL1** register. Kernel space virtual addresses range from **0xFFFF0000_00000000** to **0xFFFFFFFF_FFFFFFFF**.

Figure 8.10 provides a detailed view of what we've discussed so far.

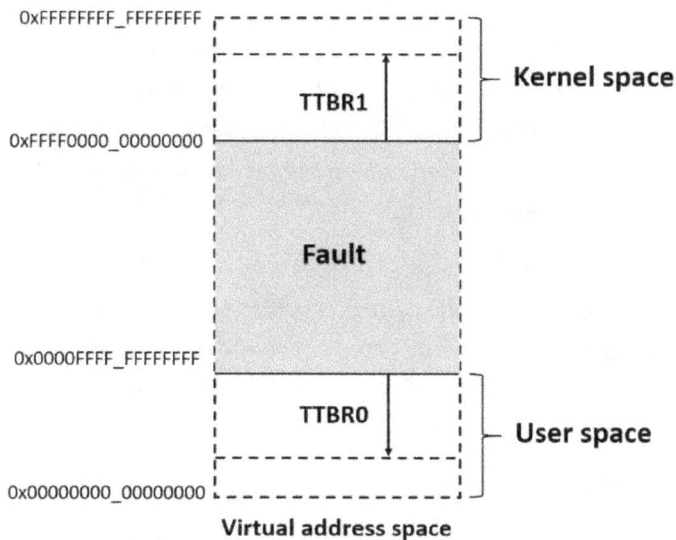

Figure 8.10: How user space and kernel space memory are handled

Figure 8.10 shows the layout of the virtual address space. As you can see, the virtual addresses for kernel space and user space are used separately.

When you inspect a memory dump, recognizing address patterns can be very helpful, especially for reverse engineering. What software components might you identify in virtual addresses?

- Function addresses
- Stack addresses and local variables
- Addresses used for dynamic memory

In this section, the virtual addresses in user space and kernel space apply to these scenarios. Make sure to become familiar with these details.

Let's look at the following example assembly instruction to better understand what a virtual address is:

```
01  ffffffc008c0f8bc <schedule>:
02  ffffffc008c0f8bc: stp     x29, x30, [sp, #-32]!
03  ffffffc008c0f8c0: mov     x29, sp
04  ffffffc008c0f8c4: stp     x19, x20, [sp, #16]
05  ffffffc008c0f8c8: mrs     x20, sp_el0
06  ffffffc008c0f8cc: ldr     w0, [x20, #24]
07  ffffffc008c0f8d0: cbz     w0, ffffffc008c0f8fc
08  ffffffc008c0f8d4: ldr     w0, [x20, #44]
```

Let's assume the process is running the first line of instruction. In this case, the **program counter** (**PC**) of the Arm core will contain the address 0xffffffc008c0f8bc. Internally, the Arm core will fetch the instruction at this memory location, 0xffffffc008c0f8bc. What you are seeing here is a virtual address. In brief, the address shown on the far-left side is the virtual address, and this is the address the process is working with.

Now, let's look at how another operation accesses a virtual address by analyzing an example instruction. When the PC moves to the address 0xffffffc008c0f8cc at line 6, what will it perform? It will execute the instruction ldr w0, [x20, #24]. If the x20 register holds the value 0xffffff804bb04140, it will access the address 0xffffff804bb04158 using the following calculation:

$$*0xffffff804bb04158 = *(0xffffff804bb04140 + 0x18)$$

The instruction will then read the data at the address 0xffffff804bb04158 and load it into the w0 register. Here, 0xffffff804bb04158 is also a virtual address.

Through this example assembly instruction, we have directly observed virtual addresses in kernel space. Now, let's take a broader look at the execution flow and understand how virtual addresses are translated into physical addresses.

Understanding the virtual memory area

Let's learn about the virtual address space of a user process. A user process, after being created, runs in both user space and kernel space. The user process operates in an independent memory space called **virtual memory area (VMA)**. In Linux, the VMA information is represented by the vm_area_struct structure, which is part of the task_struct.mm.mmap field. The Linux kernel assigns each user process its own page table to ensure that it runs in an independent virtual memory space. This information is managed in the task_struct.mm.pgd field.

Now, let's briefly explain virtual and physical addresses. A virtual address does not physically exist; it is mapped to a physical address through a page table. When discussing virtual addresses, we must also consider physical addresses, which are mapped to the corresponding virtual addresses. To handle this, the system needs a table that translates virtual addresses to physical ones. This table is called a page table, and it is actually managed through a **Translation Lookaside Buffer (TLB)** in the MMU.

One important feature of user process memory management is on-demand paging. On-demand paging ensures that when a user process writes data to memory or reads data from memory, it maps the virtual address to the actual physical address. If you run the top command, you can check the amount of memory a process is using. However, you may notice that the size of the physical address space used by the process differs from the virtual address space. This is because the process uses on-demand paging.

Next, let's check the virtual address space accessed in user space on Linux.

```
$ cat /proc/1/maps
5555ea5f0000-5555ea604000 r-xp 00000000 b3:02 6783 /usr/lib/systemd/
systemd
5555ea61c000-5555ea620000 r--p 0001c000 b3:02 6783 /usr/lib/systemd/
systemd
5555ea620000-5555ea624000 rw-p 00020000 b3:02 6783 /usr/lib/systemd/
systemd
5555f18f0000-5555f1b2c000 rw-p 00000000 00:00 0      [heap]
7fff24000000-7fff24024000 rw-p 00000000 00:00 0
7fff24024000-7fff28000000 ---p 00000000 00:00 0
7fff2c000000-7fff2c024000 rw-p 00000000 00:00 0
```

```
7fff2c024000-7fff30000000 ---p 00000000 00:00 0
7fff30270000-7fff30280000 ---p 00000000 00:00 0
7fff30280000-7fff30a80000 rw-p 00000000 00:00 0
7fff30a80000-7fff30a90000 ---p 00000000 00:00 0
7fff30a90000-7fff31290000 rw-p 00000000 00:00 0
7fff31290000-7fff312b4000 r-xp 00000000 b3:02 8073 /usr/lib/aarch64-linux-
gnu/libgpg-error.so.0.33.1
```

When reading /proc/[pid]/maps using the terminal, it displays the virtual memory space for the process with the corresponding PID. The first line of the output shows the range 5555ea5f0000-5555ea604000, which indicates that the code for /usr/lib/systemd/systemd is mapped to the address range 5555ea5f0000-5555ea604000. In this case, 5555ea5f0000 is an example of a virtual address in the user space. Additionally, you may see addresses such as 7fff24000000, which is another example of a virtual address in the user space.

When you encounter address patterns such as 7fff24000000 or 5555ea5f0000 in memory, you can safely assume that these are virtual addresses being accessed in user space.

In this section, we explored the key features of virtual memory in the Linux kernel. Next, we will examine the primary security hardening features in Linux.

Key security hardening features

The Linux kernel is made up of various subsystems, and one of its essential features is security. Let's take a closer look at two key security mechanisms in the Linux kernel: **Linux Security Modules (LSM)** and the **Address Sanitization** feature.

LSM

One of the most commonly used security features in Linux is **LSM**. Many Linux systems run with LSM enabled because it allows the kernel to implement additional security measures, such as controlling access to system resources. With LSM, the Linux environment is generally divided into two levels of execution privileges—general user privileges and root privilege:

- **General privileges**: On a Linux system, most users typically have general privileges. This means they can perform basic tasks, such as reading and writing files within their own directories. If you log in to a server as a normal user, you will operate with general privileges.

- **Root privileges**: The root user has full access to the system. System administrators usually work with root privileges. The root user can modify any file, change system configurations, install software, and even shut down the entire system. Because root has such extensive privileges, attackers often try to gain root access. This attempt is referred to as privilege escalation in the context of security.

In the field of security, it is well-known that attackers often attempt to escalate their privileges to root. This is because, once they gain root access, they can take full control of the system. In the worst-case scenario, they could access sensitive information or modify critical system files.

For this reason, monitoring and controlling who has root privileges is essential for maintaining system security. Even when the system operates with root privileges, unrestricted access to all system resources can lead to serious issues. This is the primary reason why LSM was introduced—to provide better control and enhance system security.

Currently, there are more than five LSMs available in Linux. Among them, two of the most widely used LSMs are **Security-Enhanced Linux (SELinux)** and **Simplified Mandatory Access Control Kernel (SMACK)**. These modules help ensure that even if an attacker gains root access, their actions are restricted:

- **SELinux**: SELinux is one of the most advanced LSMs, commonly used in Android smartphones. It allows system administrators to define strict policies about who can access specific resources, such as files and key objects in the Linux kernel. For example, SELinux can block an operation that tries to read certain files, even if the process is running with root privileges.

- **SMACK**: SMACK is another LSM widely used in the automotive sector. It is simpler to configure than SELinux and provides basic security policies to control which processes can access files or other critical objects.

Some developers argue that using LSMs such as SELinux may cause performance degradation. This happens because LSM adds extra security checks through several hooks whenever a process accesses a resource, which can make the system run slightly slower. However, since security is a critical factor, most developers are willing to accept minor performance trade-offs to ensure the system remains secure.

Address sanitizer

Another important security feature in Linux is **Address Sanitizer (ASan)**, which is supported by the recent compiler. This technique helps protect the system by randomizing the memory address locations of processes when they are loaded into memory.

Why the Address Sanitizer was introduced

To understand its importance, let's first explore how attackers exploit memory addresses. During runtime, every process executes within a specific memory space. For example, when a function is executed, its starting address can be determined within the process's memory space.

A process also has memory addresses for its variables, functions, and other critical information. If a process is executed repeatedly, it becomes possible to observe that a specific function always runs at the same memory address.

Attackers can take advantage of this predictable pattern. If they identify the memory address of a particular symbol (such as a function or variable), they can use this information to target the system. Techniques such as **return-oriented programming (ROP)** often rely on such predictable memory addresses.

Since Linux is an open source operating system, its source code is accessible to everyone, including attackers. They can analyze the kernel, libraries, and other system components to predict the locations of symbols in memory. By identifying these patterns, attackers can plan their attacks to target specific parts of the system.

To minimize the attack surface, you can use Address Sanitizer, which is supported by recent versions of major compilers such as GCC and Clang. With Address Sanitizer enabled, every time a process starts to execute, its memory addresses are different. Even if an attacker knows the address of a specific symbol during one execution, that information becomes useless the next time the process runs with a different memory layout.

Understanding the KASLR feature

In addition to address sanitizer, the Linux kernel also supports **Kernel Address Space Layout Randomization (KASLR)**. KASLR enhances security by randomizing the addresses of kernel symbols during system boot.

When the system starts, KASLR randomizes the locations of kernel symbols, such as functions, variables, and other critical data used by the kernel. Without KASLR, if an attacker discovers the memory location of one kernel function, they can estimate the positions of other functions by analyzing their relative locations in memory.

KASLR disrupts this pattern by assigning new, random addresses to kernel symbols every time the system boots. Even if an attacker identifies a kernel function's address during one boot, that information will not be valid after the next reboot.

KASLR is part of a broader security approach known as hardening. Hardening includes techniques and methods designed to make a system more resistant to attacks. While hardening does not guarantee complete protection, it significantly increases the complexity of potential attacks.

With KASLR, attackers must spend much more time and effort locating the symbols they want to target. This additional complexity can discourage attackers from attempting to exploit the system.

In this section, we explored two key security features in Linux:

- **LSM**: Tools such as SELinux and SMACK help control access to system resources, even for users with root privileges
- **Address sanitizer and KASLR**: These features protect the memory addresses of processes and the kernel by introducing randomness, making it much harder for attackers to exploit predictable patterns

While no system can be made completely secure, these features play a critical role in reducing vulnerabilities. By making attacks more difficult and time-consuming, they provide an essential layer of protection for modern Linux systems.

Summary

In this chapter, we covered the Linux system, one of the most widely used systems in the IT industry, along with its key features.

First, we examined the overall structure of the Linux system. It consists of two main parts: user space and kernel space. System calls act as the interface between these two, enabling access to kernel space from user space.

We also explored the process in Linux. In the Linux kernel, process properties are represented by task_struct. Additionally, the process execution flow can be traced through the call stack.

Next, we discussed memory management in the Linux kernel. We reviewed the general features of memory management and analyzed the differences between user space and kernel space addresses from an Arm architecture perspective.

We also explored two key security features provided by the Linux kernel: **Linux Security Module (LSM)** and **Kernel Address Space Layout Randomization (KASLR)**. Many Linux systems, including those in various distributions, use these features to harden the system against potential attacks.

All the topics covered in this chapter will be valuable when working on reverse engineering tasks. The next chapter will focus on static analysis, which is considered a fundamental skill for reverse engineering.

Part 3

Unlocking Key Binary Analysis Skills for Reverse Engineering

This part focuses on important skills for binary analysis, including static analysis and dynamic analysis. You will learn how to analyze binaries without running them on a device. You will also learn how to analyze binaries from real devices. The techniques in this part are practical and can be used directly in real-world reverse engineering tasks.

This part includes the following chapters:

- *Chapter 9, Understanding Basic Static Analysis*
- *Chapter 10, Going Deeper with Advanced Static Analysis*
- *Chapter 11, Analyzing Program Behavior with Basic Dynamic Analysis*
- *Chapter 12, Expert Techniques in Advanced Dynamic Analysis*
- *Chapter 13, Tracing Execution with uftrace*

9

Understanding Basic Static Analysis

In general, reverse engineering can be divided into two main methods: static analysis and dynamic analysis. In many cases, static analysis is performed first, followed by dynamic analysis. In this chapter, we will focus on static analysis and explore several important topics:

- Introducing static analysis
- Identifying binaries
- Analyzing the control flow with if statements
- Analyzing the control flow with for loops
- Identifying log output patterns

By developing skills in static analysis, you will understand how to change different assembly instructions into C code, which will improve your debugging skills as a software engineer. Let's begin this chapter with an introduction to static analysis.

Technical requirements

All the code examples and binary files for this chapter can be found on GitHub at https://github.com/PacktPublishing/Reverse-Engineering-Armv8-A-Systems.

Introducing static analysis

In this section, we will discuss static analysis in the context of reverse engineering. First, we will introduce the concept of static analysis and outline the steps involved in this process. Then, we will explore the tools and techniques that can help you effectively analyze binary files.

What is static analysis?

Static analysis involves examining binary code before executing it on a real device. Analyzing assembly instructions in an **Executable and Linkable Format (ELF)** binary file is a type of static analysis. Another method in reverse engineering is dynamic analysis, which observes the software's behavior by running it on the real target device.

Let's look at some key characteristics of static analysis:

1. **Safety**: Static analysis checks how the software works without running the binary file. This is safer, especially when the file might be harmful, such as malware.

2. **First step**: Static analysis is usually the first step in reverse engineering. Since it does not involve executing the software, you cannot fully predict its behavior.

3. **Foundational process**: Before starting dynamic analysis, it's helpful to create a plan during static analysis. For example, you can decide which debugging tools you'll need later. This makes the static analysis more effective. On the other hand, if you don't perform a thorough static analysis, it may be challenging to proceed with dynamic analysis.

Now, what background knowledge is necessary for conducting static analysis effectively? It is recommended to understand the following topics before you begin:

-   **ELF**: The first step in reverse engineering is to select the correct binary file. It's essential to understand the basic structure of the binary file. Make sure to check the type of the binary file and extract assembly instructions from it. Sometimes, ELF files can be corrupted, or some information may not appear correctly in reverse engineering tools. In these situations, knowing the structure of the ELF format is necessary.

-   **Assembly instructions**: Understanding the basics of the assembly instruction format and syntax is crucial for analyzing them and predicting how the program will run. If you are not familiar with the basics of assembly instructions, refer to *Chapters 3* to *5*.

-   **C language**: Understanding how C code is used in programs is important because it helps you identify common coding patterns. This knowledge will make it easier for you to understand the code you are analyzing.

-   **Debugging tools**: Familiarity with the available debugging tools will help you choose the right ones for your reverse engineering tasks. Understanding these tools can improve your efficiency and effectiveness in the reverse engineering process. Many debugging tools, such as IDA and Ghidra, offer a feature that allows you to decompile binary into C.

Now that we have figured out the basic knowledge we need, let's start looking at the debugging tools that are important for doing static analysis well.

Programs used for static analysis

When performing reverse engineering, choosing the right debugging program is important. Many tools are available, each with unique features for examining binaries. Let's look at some popular programs that are commonly used for this purpose:

- **IDA Pro**: IDA Pro is one of the most popular tools among reverse engineers. When you load a binary file in IDA Pro, it displays the function flow and other statistics in a graphical format. This visual representation makes it easier to understand how the program works. IDA Pro has a strong community and extensive documentation, making it easier to find useful material. However, this software requires a license, which means it is not free. You can try a free trial, but some features might be limited.

- **Binary Ninja**: Binary Ninja is another widely used tool for reverse engineering. Similar to IDA Pro, it provides information on binary files, including function flows presented in various layouts. This makes it easier to analyze complex binaries. Like IDA Pro, Binary Ninja is also a paid program.

- **Ghidra**: Ghidra is another popular tool for reverse engineering, especially in hacking competitions. Originally developed by the **National Security Agency** (**NSA**), it was made available to the public in 2019. A major benefit of Ghidra is that it is free and open source. With Ghidra, you can analyze assembly instruction flows and examine ELF file information.

- **Binary utilities**: Binary utilities are also widely used and available to anyone. If you are using a Linux distribution, such as **Ubuntu** or **Debian**, you will find that binary utilities come installed by default. These tools operate from the command line, meaning you need to enter specific commands or options. Since they are command-line-based, the output is in text format. This might be challenging if you prefer **graphical user interface** (**GUI**) programs. However, binary utilities cover many basics that are helpful for static analysis, and this chapter will explain static analysis using these utilities.

> Note
>
> Many reverse engineering programs offer GUIs that make it easier to follow and understand the function flows of data. However, it is important not to rely too much on the outputs of these debugging tools. While these tools help visualize how a binary works, they may not always be completely accurate. Additionally, a developer who depends only on reverse engineering tools without understanding assembly instructions and the ELF structure may miss out on important skills.

Now that we've reviewed what static analysis is and the main tools for reverse engineering, we'll move on to exploring how to identify binary file types in the next section.

Identifying binaries

When you start reverse engineering, the first step is often to determine the type of file you are dealing with. Whether you're a reverse engineer or a software developer, you'll encounter a variety of file types, such as executables, text files, and object files. Recognizing the file type is essential for effective reverse engineering, as different formats may require specific analysis approaches. For static analysis, it's essential to start by understanding the binary file you plan to work with.

Imagine you've been assigned a binary file to analyze. Will your project manager or teammates always provide you with the exact file you need? Not necessarily. This is why it's crucial to know how to select the right binary file for your analysis.

In this section, we'll introduce some useful tools for identifying binary file types. Let's start by learning how to check the format of a binary file.

Introducing binary utilities to check binary files

When you first encounter a binary file, what's the first thing you look at? Often, it's the file extension, which can give a general idea of what kind of file it is. Most people recognize common file extensions because they indicate which type of application will open the file. The following are some typical examples:

- Opening a .exe file on Windows launches a program
- A .png file opens in an image viewer
- A .pdf file opens in a PDF reader
- Opening a .txt file might open a text editor such as Notepad

For most users, checking the file extension is a normal first step. However, for reverse engineers, relying only on file extensions is not recommended. File extensions can sometimes be misleading or even incorrect. Therefore, many reverse engineers use commands such as file or readelf in Linux to correctly identify file types, regardless of the extension.

So, what tools are available to check a binary file's format? You can find some of the most commonly used ones here:

- file: This is one of the most frequently used tools in Linux for checking file types. The file utility identifies the type of a file without depending on the extension, making it reliable for analyzing binaries.

- readelf: This tool reads the header information of ELF files. readelf provides detailed information about a binary's structure and properties. To understand the output fully, it's helpful to know a bit about ELF.

- xxd: This tool displays the exact byte stream of a file in hexadecimal or decimal format. xxd is important for reverse engineering because it shows the raw data inside the binary, allowing you to see the actual bytes that make up the file.

By using these tools, you can identify a file's type in more detail and explore its contents.

The file utility

The file utility is used to identify the type of a file, especially when there is no extension to provide a hint. Now, let's use this utility to identify the type of the libc.so.6 file:

```
$ file libc.so.6
libc.so.6: ELF 64-bit LSB shared object, ARM aarch64, version 1 (GNU/
Linux), dynamically linked, interpreter /lib/ld-linux-aarch64.so.1,
BuildID[sha1]=2574e252ac817144887801e115daccfcddef3a91, for GNU/Linux
3.7.0, stripped
```

This output provides important information about the library file named libc.so.6. You can figure out some key properties that the output reveals:

- The file is an ELF file
- It's a 64-bit shared library

Now, let's consider another example where you run the file command with the same name, libc.so.6. This time, it gives a different result:

```
$ file libc.so.6
libc.so.6: ELF 32-bit LSB shared object, ARM, EABI5 version 1
(SYSV), dynamically linked, interpreter /lib/ld-linux-armhf.so.3,
BuildID[sha1]=7933f4662114c8fbdd2577c7dc1f9fdbd97d4528, for GNU/Linux
3.2.0, stripped
```

In this case, we see that the libc.so.6 file is still in ELF format, but it is a 32-bit shared library.

On an Arm-based system, binaries can be compiled for either 32-bit or 64-bit architecture. This means you cannot know whether the binary is built for a 32-bit or 64-bit system just by looking at the filename. Because of this, it is a good practice to regularly check binary files using the file command.

> **Note**
>
> When a `libc.so.6` library file is built for a 64-bit system, it won't execute correctly on a 32-bit system, and similarly, a 32-bit version may not run properly on a 64-bit system. This is why determining the correct format is crucial.

So, how does the file utility display the format of a binary file? It does this by reading and interpreting the header information in ELF files. We will explore this further when examining the xxd utility later in this section.

The readelf utility

If you need to check more detailed information about a binary file, the readelf utility is a good choice. It shows how the binary is structured and indicates the offsets of the section headers. Let's examine more information about `libc.so.6` using the `readelf -h` command:

```
$ readelf -h libc.so.6
ELF Header:
  Magic:   7f 45 4c 46 02 01 01 03 00 00 00 00 00 00 00 00
  Class:                             ELF64
[...]
  Machine:                           AArch64
  Version:                           0x1
  Entry point address:               0x27970
[...]
  Size of section headers:           64 (bytes)
  Number of section headers:         63
  Section header string table index: 62
```

The output from `readelf -h` gives us valuable details about the binary file. The following are some important points to note:

- The machine architecture, in this case, is listed as AArch64
- The ELF class indicates that it is in ELF64 format

Additionally, the output provides other useful information, such as the entry point address and the size of the program header.

When you analyze ELF binaries, it's a good idea to use readelf regularly, because this tool helps you understand the binary file's structure in greater detail.

The xxd utility

The file and readelf utilities are used to identify the types of binary files by reading and interpreting the header information found in those files. They parse this information and provide clear, readable output in text format. However, sometimes the header information in a binary file can become corrupted. Additionally, some types of malware are designed with modified headers to avoid detection.

Identifying the raw data of binary file

To examine the raw data of a binary file, you can use the xxd utility. This tool displays binary data in hexadecimal format, which is very useful for analyzing binary files. Let's see how the xxd utility works by analyzing the libc.so.6 binary file, as follows:

```
$ xxd libc.so.6 | head -10
00000000: 7f45 4c46 0201 0103 0000 0000 0000 0000  .ELF............
00000010: 0300 b700 0100 0000 7079 0200 0000 0000  ........py......
00000020: 4000 0000 0000 0000 5023 1900 0000 0000  @.......P#......
00000030: 0000 0000 4000 3800 0a00 4000 3f00 3e00  ....@.8...@.?.>.
```

Before diving into the details of the output, it's useful to understand its overall structure:

- The far-left column shows the offset of each hex dump in the binary file. For example, at offset 0x10, the data stored is 0x0300, and at offset 0x20, the data stored is 0x0400.
- The eight columns in the center contain the binary data in hexadecimal format.
- The columns on the right represents ASCII characters, providing a readable form of each byte.

Now, let's analyze the key signature within the raw data generated by the xxd utility. You may recall that an ELF binary file begins with the ASCII character ELF. In hexadecimal, this corresponds to 7f45 4c46, which you will find in the first line of the xxd output.

By default, xxd shows data in hexadecimal format. This format is common for developers because hexadecimal is easier to read and understand. Sometimes, you may want to view raw data in binary format instead of hexadecimal. The xxd command allows you to see binary data in various formats. With the -b option, it shows each byte as binary.

Here's an example of the information provided by the xxd -b command:

```
$ xxd -b libc.so.6 | head -5
00000000: 01111111 01000101 01001100 01000110 00000010 00000001   .ELF..
00000006: 00000001 00000011 00000000 00000000 00000000 00000000   ......
0000000c: 00000000 00000000 00000000 00000000 00000011 00000000   ......
```

There may also be times when you are working with raw **RGB** data or want to embed binary data directly into your code for better performance. In these situations, the -i option of xxd outputs the data in an array format, making it ready for use in your code:

```
$ xxd -i libc.so.6 | head -5
unsigned char libc_so_6[] = {
  0x7f, 0x45, 0x4c, 0x46, 0x02, 0x01, 0x01, 0x03, 0x00, 0x00, 0x00, 0x00,
  0x00, 0x00, 0x00, 0x00, 0x03, 0x00, 0xb7, 0x00, 0x01, 0x00, 0x00, 0x00,
  0x70, 0x79, 0x02, 0x00, 0x00, 0x00, 0x00, 0x00, 0x40, 0x00, 0x00, 0x00,
```

This feature is useful when you need raw data inside binary.

Identifying the raw data of a text file

So far, we have examined the libc.so.6 binary file using the xxd command. Now, let's see how the file command can show the type of a text file. The following is the body of the hello.c file:

```c
#include <stdio.h>
int main()
{
    printf("Hello, World!\n");
    return 0;
}
```

If you open hello.c with xxd, you can also see its contents in binary format. First, let's check hello.c in text format using the file utility:

```
$ file hello.c
hello.c: ASCII text
```

Here, the file command shows that hello.c is an ASCII text file. This means that the file contains readable text instead of binary data. Now, let's open hello.c using the xxd utility to see its contents in binary format:

```
$ xxd hello.c
00000000: 6865 6c6c 6f0a                          hello.
```

In the data output from xxd, we can see the ASCII codes for the text hello in the hello.c file. Each pair of hexadecimal digits corresponds to a character in the string. For example, 68 represents the letter h, 65 represents e, 6c represents l, and so on.

One important observation is that this file does not begin with the typical hexadecimal signature found in ELF files, which usually starts with the ASCII characters ELF. This further confirms that hello.c is a text file rather than a binary file. If you inspect a file with xxd and do not see the ELF string or similar indicators, you can conclude that it is likely a text file.

So far, you have learned about how to identify different types of files using various utilities. In the next section, we will analyze a corrupted binary file using the file, readelf, and xxd utilities. We will see how each tool shows attributes of the corrupted object file. You will also explore the binary structure by checking the results after running each tool.

Case study of the corrupted binary file

Now, let's perform a practical exercise that you might encounter in reverse engineering. You will identify a corrupted binary file, using the file, readelf, and xxd utilities.

> **Note**
>
> There are several ways to edit data in binary files, but one of the simplest is to use the Vim editor along with the xxd utility. Here's how: open the binary file in Vim, and then enter the :%!xxd command to switch into hex mode. In this hex mode, you can directly edit any data in the binary file. After you make changes, you can convert it back to binary format by typing :%!xxd -r. Finally, save it with the :w command.

For example, let's look at a binary file where the data does not start with the usual ELF file signature in hexadecimal, such as 0x7f 45 4c 46. Instead, it starts with 0x00, which indicates that this binary file may not be in the standard ELF format.

The following is the output when running xxd with a corrupted libc.so.6 file where the starting byte is altered:

```
$ xxd libc.so.6 | head -5
00000000: 0000 0000 0000 0000 0000 0000 0000 0000  ................
00000010: 0300 b700 0100 0000 7079 0200 0000 0000  ........py......
00000020: 4000 0000 0000 0000 5023 1900 0000 0000  @.......P#......
```

As you can see, this binary file does not start with the usual hexadecimal values found in standard ELF files, such as `0x7f 45 4c 46`. Instead, it starts with `0x00`, indicating this binary might not be in the expected ELF format.

Let's see what happens when we try to check this file using the `file` utility. This exercise is a good way to review some of the key points from earlier sections:

```
$ file libc.so.6
libc.so.6: data
```

As shown in the output, `libc.so.6` is recognized as just data rather than an ELF file. If `libc.so.6` were not corrupted, xxd would show that it's an ELF file. This shows us that the `file` utility reads and interprets the initial bytes at the start of a binary file to determine its format.

Now, let's try using the `readelf` command on this corrupted `libc.so.6` file:

```
$ readelf -h libc.so.6
readelf: Error: Not an ELF file - it has the wrong magic bytes at the
start
```

Here, `readelf` also fails to recognize `libc.so.6` as an ELF file, pointing out that the *magic bytes* (the identifying signature at the start of the file) are incorrect.

In this example, we purposefully changed the hexadecimal stream where the ELF signature normally appears. From this, we can see that the `file` and `readelf` utilities read the bit patterns at the beginning of a binary file to understand its format.

So, what can you do if `file` or `readelf` can't correctly identify a binary file? In this case, we can use the xxd utility to directly see the data stream. This can help us understand important details about the binary file.

Now that we learned about how to identify a binary format, we're ready to move on to the next topic—constructing C code from assembly instructions, focusing on control flow.

Analyzing the control flow with if statements

In this section, we will explore how different statements in C code are converted into assembly instructions. We'll start by examining how statements that control the flow of software routines—such as `if`, `if-else`, `break`, and `return` statements—are transformed into assembly instructions. After that, we'll also learn about analyzing strings in assembly.

To start, let's examine how conditional expressions in C influence the pattern of the resulting assembly instructions.

Basic **if** statement

Let's look at the following sample C code with an `if` condition:

```c
if (x > 0x100)
{
    puts("x > 0x100");
}
```

When this code is disassembled, it translates into the following assembly instructions:

```
82c:    cmp     w0, #0x100
830:    b.le    840 <func+0x2c>
834:    adrp    x0, 0 <__abi_tag-0x278>
838:    add     x0, x0, #0x920
83c:    bl      6c0 <puts@plt>
840:    nop
844:    ldp     x29, x30, [sp], #48
848:    ret
```

In this assembly code, the key point to note is that if the `if (x > 0x100)` condition is not satisfied, the program branches (or jumps) to address 840. Specifically, the instruction at 830 (`b.le`) checks the value in the `w0` register. If `w0` contains a value less than or equal to 0x100, the program branches to the specified address 840.

> **Note**
>
> It is important to note that `w0` corresponds to a local variable, x, in the example assembly block.

This means the `puts("x > 0x100");` statement is skipped, and the program moves to address 840 to execute the `nop`, `ldp`, and `ret` instructions, which end the routine.

Now, let's modify the condition to `if (x == 0x0)` to observe how the assembly code changes:

```c
if (x == 0x0)
{
    puts("x == 0x0");
}
```

When this code is disassembled, you will see the following assembly instructions:

```
82c:    cmp     w0, #0x0
830:    b.ne    840 <func+0x2c>
834:    adrp    x0, 0 <__abi_tag-0x278>
838:    add     x0, x0, #0x928
83c:    bl      6c0 <puts@plt>
840:    nop
844:    ldp     x29, x30, [sp], #48
848:    ret
```

You can see that changing the if condition also changes the branch instruction from b.le to b.ne. This modification means that the assembly instruction is updated to match the new condition in the if statement. From this, we can understand that branch instructions such as b.le and b.ne change depending on the condition in the if statement.

Now, if we further change the condition to if (x < 0x100), we expect the branch instruction to adjust accordingly. For this new condition, the assembly instruction changes as follows:

```
82c:    cmp     w0, #0x100
830:    b.gt    840
```

As you can see, the b.le instruction is now replaced with b.gt, because the condition has changed to check whether x is less than 0x100. This demonstrates that the branch instruction following the cmp instruction changes depending on the if condition, showing how conditional expressions impact the pattern of assembly instructions.

In the following subsection, we will look at how if-else statements are converted into assembly instructions.

The if-else statement

Let's examine conditional statements with multiple layers by adding an else statement to our previous example. This will help us understand how additional conditions impact the assembly code.

Let's modify the previous code example to include an else statement:

```
if (x > 0x100)
    puts("x > 0x100");
else
    puts("x is else ");
```

When this code is disassembled, what kind of assembly instructions can we expect? Let's look at the assembly routine with a different pattern:

```
82c:    cmp     w0, #0x100
830:    b.le    844 <func+0x30>
834:    adrp    x0, 0 <__abi_tag-0x278>
838:    add     x0, x0, #0x938
83c:    bl      6c0 <puts@plt>
840:    b       850 <func+0x3c>
844:    adrp    x0, 0 <__abi_tag-0x278>
848:    add     x0, x0, #0x948
84c:    bl      6c0 <puts@plt>
850:    nop
854:    ldp     x29, x30, [sp], #48
858:    ret
```

When you first look at this code, you may notice it's slightly longer than the previous example. However, the main branching instruction hasn't changed. The b.le instruction at address 830 is still there, and it handles the condition check for if (x > 0x100) as before.

What has changed is the addition of assembly instructions that enable the puts statement in the else block. These instructions allow the program to print "x is else " when the if condition isn't met. You can see the additional instructions for the else case here:

```
844:    adrp    x0, 0 <__abi_tag-0x278>
848:    add     x0, x0, #0x948
84c:    bl      6c0 <puts@plt>
```

This set of instructions is responsible for printing the "x is else " message. Then, the following instructions are executed:

```
850     nop
854     ldp     x29, x30, [sp], #48
858     ret
```

As you know, the function begins with the instruction to push the value in x29 and x30. This code pops the values of x29 and x30 from the stack back into those registers. It means that this code is ready to complete this function.

Finally, the ret instruction at address 858 transfers control back to the function, which is called func in this example code.

The else-if statement

When programming, you often use multiple else-if statements to handle various conditions. Let's examine how the following code might look when converted into assembly instructions:

```
if (x > 0x100)
    puts("x > 0x100");
else if (x < 0x300)
    puts("x > 0x100 and x < 0x300");
else
    puts("x is else");
```

The following is the corresponding assembly code:

```
82c:    cmp     w0, #0x100
830:    b.le    844 <func+0x30>
834:    adrp    x0, 0 <__abi_tag-0x278>
838:    add     x0, x0, #0x958
83c:    bl      6c0 <puts@plt>
840:    b       86c <func+0x58>
844:    ldr     w0, [sp, #44]
848:    cmp     w0, #0x2ff
84c:    b.gt    860 <func+0x4c>
850:    adrp    x0, 0 <__abi_tag-0x278>
854:    add     x0, x0, #0x968
858:    bl      6c0 <puts@plt>
85c:    b       86c <func+0x58>
860:    adrp    x0, 0 <__abi_tag-0x278>
864:    add     x0, x0, #0x980
868:    bl      6c0 <puts@plt>
86c:    nop
870:    ldp     x29, x30, [sp], #48
874:    ret
```

In the preceding assembly code, notice that a branch instruction at address 848 along with a condition comparison is added:

```
848:    cmp     w0, #0x2ff
84c:    b.gt    860 <func+0x4c>
```

Let's take a look at *Figure 9.1* to identify the control flow of the instruction:

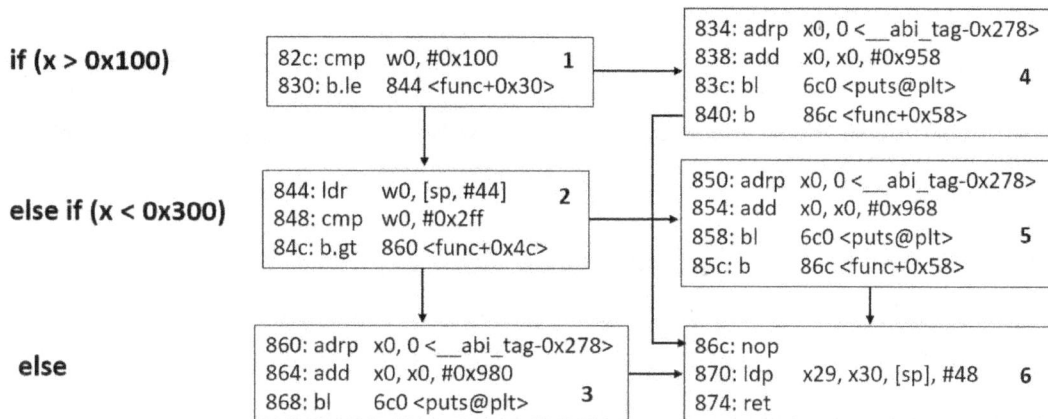

```
if (x > 0x100)      82c: cmp   w0, #0x100    1      834: adrp  x0, 0 <__abi_tag-0x278>
                    830: b.le  844 <func+0x30>       838: add   x0, x0, #0x958
                                                     83c: bl    6c0 <puts@plt>           4
                                                     840: b     86c <func+0x58>

else if (x < 0x300) 844: ldr   w0, [sp, #44]  2      850: adrp  x0, 0 <__abi_tag-0x278>
                    848: cmp   w0, #0x2ff            854: add   x0, x0, #0x968
                    84c: b.gt  860 <func+0x4c>       858: bl    6c0 <puts@plt>           5
                                                     85c: b     86c <func+0x58>

else                860: adrp  x0, 0 <__abi_tag-0x278>   86c: nop
                    864: add   x0, x0, #0x980            870: ldp   x29, x30, [sp], #48   6
                    868: bl    6c0 <puts@plt>   3       874: ret
```

Figure 9.1: Breakdown of the assembly block

In *Figure 9.1*, the full assembly code is divided into six parts, from block **1** to block **6**. Let's go through each part step by step:

- **[1]**: The code first compares x to 0x100. If x is less than or equal to 0x100, the flow moves to block **[2]**. If x is greater than 0x100, it proceeds to output the message "x > 0x100" after moving to block **[4]**. Then, the control is passed to block **6** to terminate the function.

- **[2]**: In this block, x is compared with 0x300. If x is not less than 0x300, the program jumps to block **[3]**. Otherwise, it continues to puts("x > 0x100 and x < 0x300)" after moving to block **[5]**. Then, the control is transferred to block **6** to terminate the function.

- **[3]**: This block represents the else clause, which outputs the message "x is else". Then, the execution moves to block **[6]** to terminate the function.

Once any of these blocks have been executed, the program continues to a common end, block **[6]**, where the function completes.

You can see how the control moves from block **[1]** to block **[6]** based on the conditions in the assembly instructions.

While analyzing routines like this might feel repetitive, it's essential to understand these patterns. Assembly routines like this appear frequently across various projects, and knowing how to interpret them is a valuable skill.

> **Note**
>
> Some debugging tools show the function flow in a simple and easy-to-understand way. However, if you rely too much on these tools, it may limit your capability as a software engineer. It is important to understand the basic patterns in assembly code by yourself.

The if with return statement

Until now, we've explored how the pattern of if-else statements is handled in assembly code. Another common structure you often see with an if statement is the return statement.

The return statement stops the execution of the function and transfers control back to the address of the function that called it. In other words, once a return statement is reached, the current function exits immediately, and the program resumes from the point where this function was originally called. This can be useful when certain conditions are met and there's no need to execute the rest of the function's code.

Now, let's take a look at *Figure 9.2* to see how this return statement is translated into assembly instructions:

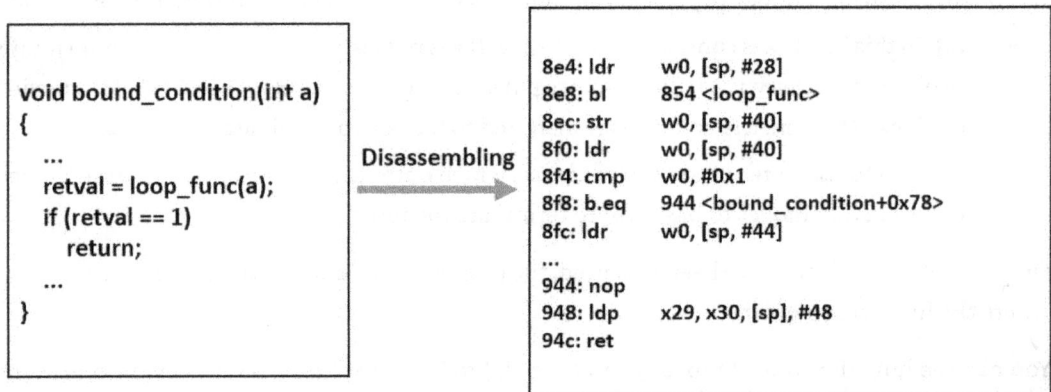

```
void bound_condition(int a)
{
    ...
    retval = loop_func(a);
    if (retval == 1)
        return;
    ...
}
```

Disassembling →

```
8e4: ldr    w0, [sp, #28]
8e8: bl     854 <loop_func>
8ec: str    w0, [sp, #40]
8f0: ldr    w0, [sp, #40]
8f4: cmp    w0, #0x1
8f8: b.eq   944 <bound_condition+0x78>
8fc: ldr    w0, [sp, #44]
...
944: nop
948: ldp    x29, x30, [sp], #48
94c: ret
```

Figure 9.2: C code and assembly block for checking the function's return value

Let's begin by analyzing the first assembly block together:

```
8e4:    ldr    w0, [sp, #28]
8e8:    bl     854 <loop_func>
8ec:    str    w0, [sp, #40]
8f0:    ldr    w0, [sp, #40]
```

```
8f4:    cmp     w0, #0x1
8f8:    b.eq    944 <func+0x78>  // branch if equal
8fc:    ldr     w0, [sp, #44]
```

Breaking down this instruction block, we can observe the following operations:

- At addresses 8e4 to 8e8: The ldr w0, [sp, #28] instruction loads a function argument into the w0 register, and then the bl (branch and link) instruction calls the loop_func function

- At addresses 8ec and 8f0: The str instruction saves the value in w0 to the stack area at [sp, #40] and then reloads it back into w0

> **Note**
>
> Now, an important question arises: why is w0 saved to the stack after calling the function with bl? This is because w0 (or x0 in 64-bit size) contains the function's return value, which we need to use in later steps.

Next, let's look more closely at the instructions at address 8f4:

- The cmp instruction compares the value in the w0 register with 0x1. In many cases, right after a function call, the assembly code checks whether the return value in w0 is zero or some specific value. In this case, w0 corresponds to the retval local variable, which holds the return value from the loop_func function.

- Based on this comparison, the b.eq (branch if equal) instruction will take one of two actions:

    - If the retval variable contains 1, the program jumps to address 944 (corresponding to bound_condition+0x78)

    - If the retval variable is not 1, the code continues to address 8fc

Now, let's examine the instructions starting at address 944:

```
944: d503201f  nop
948: a8c37bfd  ldp x29, x30, [sp], #48
94c: d65f03c0  ret
```

What each of these instructions accomplishes can be explained as follows:

- The nop (no operation) instruction at 944 doesn't perform any action but can act as a placeholder in the code.

- The ldp (load pair) instruction at 948 loads data from the stack. This data is stored in x29 and x30. This step restores data stored from earlier in the function.

- The ret instruction at 94c returns control to the function that initially called this function.

Analyzing these assembly instructions provides some key points to remember:

- **Function arguments**: Before calling a function, its arguments are loaded into specific registers, such as x0. Here, only one argument is used, so we only need x0.

- **Return value check**: After the function call, a routine checks the return value stored in x0. This is a common assembly pattern to validate a function's return value and decide the next steps.

- **Flow control**: The b.eq instruction, following the cmp instruction, controls the flow based on whether the condition is met.

You can often see this pattern in the assembly code when a function is called. It is important because it shows how parameters are passed and how return values are handled at the assembly level.

Until now, you have learned about how the assembly block is organized with if and if-else statements. In the following section, let's explore how to control the flow inside a for loop in more detail.

Analyzing the control flow with for loops

In this section, we'll look at common patterns found in loops written in C. We'll also see how the code adapts when using specific statements such as the following:

- break statements
- continue statements
- return statements

Let's start by looking at a simple example of a for loop. Note that a for loop is commonly used to repeat a set of instructions a specific number of times.

Basic for loop

The C code for this loop, along with the corresponding disassembled assembly instructions, is shown in *Figure 9.3*:

```
0000000000000854 <loop_func>:
854: stp    x29, x30, [sp, #-48]!
858: mov    x29, sp
85c: str    w0, [sp, #28]
860: str    wzr, [sp, #44]
864: str    wzr, [sp, #40]
868: b      894 <loop_func+0x40>
86c: ldr    w1, [sp, #44]
870: adrp   x0, 0 <__abi_tag-0x278>
874: add    x0, x0, #0xa18
878: bl     710 <printf@plt>
87c: ldr    w0, [sp, #44]
880: add    w0, w0, #0x1
884: str    w0, [sp, #44]
888: ldr    w0, [sp, #40]
88c: add    w0, w0, #0x1
890: str    w0, [sp, #40]
894: ldr    w0, [sp, #40]
898: cmp    w0, #0x63
89c: b.le   86c <loop_func+0x18>
8a0: ldr    w1, [sp, #28]
8a4: ldr    w0, [sp, #44]
8a8: add    w0, w1, w0
8ac: ldp    x29, x30, [sp], #48
8b0: ret
```

```
int loop_func(int c)
{
   int a = 0;

    for (int i = 0; i < 100; i++) {
       printf("loop_func count: %d \n", a);
       a++;
    }
    return (c + a);
}
```

Disassembling ━━━➤

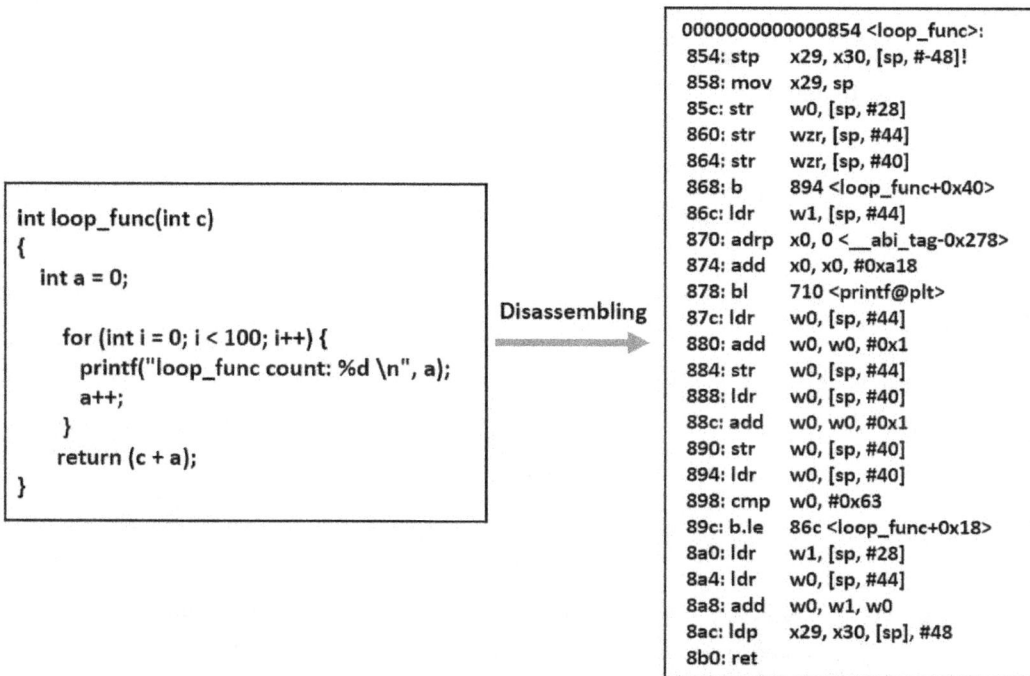

Figure 9.3: Basic for loop: C code and assembly block

Let's go through these instructions step by step by breaking them down into different blocks. We'll start with the initial setup block of the function:

```
0000000000000854 <loop_func>:
    854:      stp    x29, x30, [sp, #-48]!
    858:      mov    x29, sp
    85c:      str    w0, [sp, #28]
    860:      str    wzr, [sp, #44]
    864:      str    wzr, [sp, #40]
    868:      b      894 <loop_func+0x40>
```

The first part of the example code can be broken down into the following actions:

- The x29 and x30 registers are pushed onto the stack
- The first argument, stored in w0, is saved to the stack
- A branch is made to address 894

These instructions set up the function, which is a typical pattern found at the beginning of most function assembly code. Now, let's move to the next block starting at address 894. Let's go over each instruction in detail:

```
894:    ldr     w0, [sp, #40]
898:    cmp     w0, #0x63
89c:    b.le    86c <loop_func+0x18>
8a0:    ldr     w1, [sp, #28]
```

This block performs the following actions:

- It reloads the value of w0 from the stack.
- It compares w0 to 0x63 (decimal 99). If w0 is less than or equal to 0x63, the program jumps to address 86c. If not, it moves on to address 8a0.

> **Note**
>
> In the preceding assembly block, w0 corresponds to the local variable, i, which is incremented by 1 inside the for loop.

Now, let's look at what happens at address 86c:

```
86c:    ldr     w1, [sp, #44]
870:    adrp    x0, 0 <__abi_tag-0x278>
874:    add     x0, x0, #0xa18
878:    bl      710 <printf@plt>
87c:    ldr     w0, [sp, #44]
880:    add     w0, w0, #0x1
884:    str     w0, [sp, #44]
888:    ldr     w0, [sp, #40]
88c:    add     w0, w0, #0x1
890:    str     w0, [sp, #40]
894:    ldr     w0, [sp, #40]
898:    cmp     w0, #0x63
89c:    b.le    86c <loop_func+0x18>
8a0:    ldr     w1, [sp, #28]
```

This section of the code performs the following operations:

- It outputs a log message using printf
- The value in w0 is incremented by 1, where w0 corresponds to the local variable, i
- The updated value of w0 is stored back in the stack and reloaded

From this, we can identify the key parts of the loop routine:

- The value in w0 is compared to 0x63 (99).
- If w0 is less than or equal to 0x63, the code loops back to address 86c. If w0 is greater than 0x63, it moves forward to address 8a0.

Based on this analysis, the loop runs from address 86c to 89c. Now, let's see what happens when the value in w0 exceeds 0x63 (99) and the flow jumps to address 8a0:

```
8a0:    ldr     w1, [sp, #28]
8a4:    ldr     w0, [sp, #44]
8a8:    add     w0, w1, w0
8ac:    ldp     x29, x30, [sp], #48
8b0:    ret
```

What you have seen here can be broken down as follows:

- The final value for w0 is calculated and updated to return
- The values of x29 and x30 registers are loaded from the stack area
- The ret instruction is performed to exit the function

You can see the full control flow of this loop in *Figure 9.4*, which shows the execution flow discussed so far:

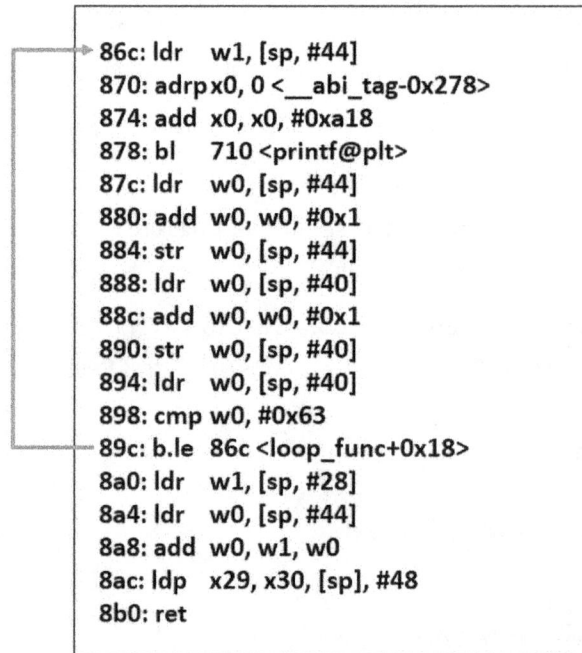

```
86c: ldr    w1, [sp, #44]
870: adrp x0, 0 <__abi_tag-0x278>
874: add    x0, x0, #0xa18
878: bl     710 <printf@plt>
87c: ldr    w0, [sp, #44]
880: add    w0, w0, #0x1
884: str    w0, [sp, #44]
888: ldr    w0, [sp, #40]
88c: add    w0, w0, #0x1
890: str    w0, [sp, #40]
894: ldr    w0, [sp, #40]
898: cmp    w0, #0x63
89c: b.le   86c <loop_func+0x18>
8a0: ldr    w1, [sp, #28]
8a4: ldr    w0, [sp, #44]
8a8: add    w0, w1, w0
8ac: ldp    x29, x30, [sp], #48
8b0: ret
```

Figure 9.4: Execution flow of the for loop

Now that you have learned how a for loop runs using an assembly block, next, let's analyze additional assembly instructions by adding a break statement.

A for loop with a break statement

Next, let's see how the assembly code changes when a break statement is added within a for loop. You can refer to *Figure 9.5*, where the C code and the newly added assembly instructions are displayed side by side:

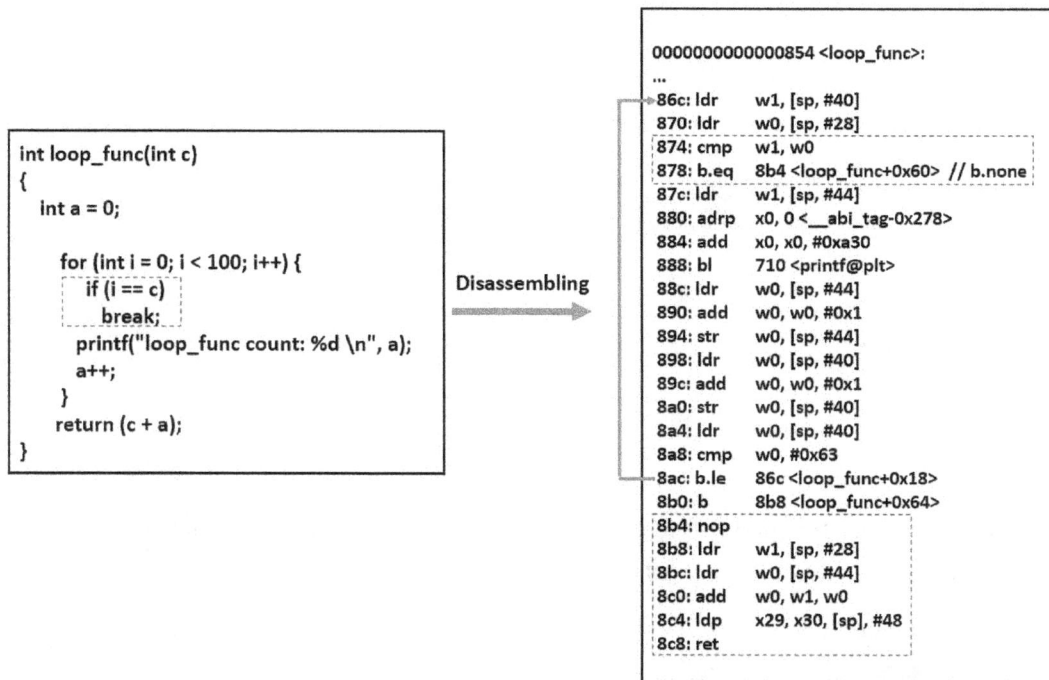

```
0000000000000854 <loop_func>:
...
86c: ldr    w1, [sp, #40]
870: ldr    w0, [sp, #28]
874: cmp    w1, w0
878: b.eq   8b4 <loop_func+0x60> // b.none
87c: ldr    w1, [sp, #44]
880: adrp   x0, 0 <__abi_tag-0x278>
884: add    x0, x0, #0xa30
888: bl     710 <printf@plt>
88c: ldr    w0, [sp, #44]
890: add    w0, w0, #0x1
894: str    w0, [sp, #44]
898: ldr    w0, [sp, #40]
89c: add    w0, w0, #0x1
8a0: str    w0, [sp, #40]
8a4: ldr    w0, [sp, #40]
8a8: cmp    w0, #0x63
8ac: b.le   86c <loop_func+0x18>
8b0: b      8b8 <loop_func+0x64>
8b4: nop
8b8: ldr    w1, [sp, #28]
8bc: ldr    w0, [sp, #44]
8c0: add    w0, w1, w0
8c4: ldp    x29, x30, [sp], #48
8c8: ret
```

```c
int loop_func(int c)
{
  int a = 0;

    for (int i = 0; i < 100; i++) {
      if (i == c)
        break;
      printf("loop_func count: %d \n", a);
      a++;
    }
    return (c + a);
}
```

Disassembling

Figure 9.5: Execution flow of the assembly block with a break statement

In *Figure 9.5*, you will see that a break statement is added with an if statement inside the for loop:

```
if (i == c)
    break;
```

This if condition checks whether the values of i and c are equal. If they are, the break statement stops the loop immediately. Now, let's examine the additional assembly instructions generated by this condition:

```
874:    cmp    w1, w0
878:    b.eq   8b4 <loop_func+0x60>   // branch if equal
87c:    ldr    w1, [sp, #44]
```

In this new assembly code block, it performs the following operations:

- The values in the w1 and w0 registers are compared.
- If w1 and w0 are equal, the program branches to address 8b4. If they are not equal, the program continues to address 87c.

Let's now see what happens at address 8b4, where the loop exits if i equals c:

```
8b4:    nop
8b8:    ldr     w1, [sp, #28]
8bc:    ldr     w0, [sp, #44]
8c0:    add     w0, w1, w0
8c4:    ldp     x29, x30, [sp], #48
8c8:    ret
```

At address 8b4, a nop instruction is found, which essentially acts as a placeholder. Following this, the code performs the final steps of the function:

- The ldp instruction restores the x29 and x30 registers, which were previously stored on the stack
- The ret instruction returns control to the calling function, ending the current function

This finalization routine is similar to what we saw in the previous section, so we will not repeat all the details here. In short, when a certain condition is met, the break statement causes an early exit from the loop.

A for loop with a continue statement

Next, let's explore how the assembly code pattern changes when a continue statement is added within a for loop. You can refer to *Figure 9.6*, where the updated C code and the new assembly instructions are shown:

```
int loop_func(int c)
{
  int a = 0;

    for (int i = 0; i < 100; i++) {
      if (i == c)
        continue;
      printf("loop_func count: %d \n", a);
      a++;
    }
    return (c + a);
}
```

Disassembling →

```
0000000000000854 <loop_func>:
...
86c: ldr    w1, [sp, #40]
870: ldr    w0, [sp, #28]
874: cmp    w1, w0
878: b.eq   89c <loop_func+0x48> // b.none
87c: ldr    w1, [sp, #44]
880: adrp   x0, 0 <__abi_tag-0x278>
884: add    x0, x0, #0xa30
888: bl     710 <printf@plt>
88c: ldr    w0, [sp, #44]
890: add    w0, w0, #0x1
894: str    w0, [sp, #44]
898: b      8a0 <loop_func+0x4c>
89c: nop
8a0: ldr    w0, [sp, #40]
8a4: add    w0, w0, #0x1
8a8: str    w0, [sp, #40]
8ac: ldr    w0, [sp, #40]
8b0: cmp    w0, #0x63
8b4: b.le   86c <loop_func+0x18>
8b8: ldr    w1, [sp, #28]
8bc: ldr    w0, [sp, #44]
8c0: add    w0, w1, w0
8c4: ldp    x29, x30, [sp], #48
8c8: ret
```

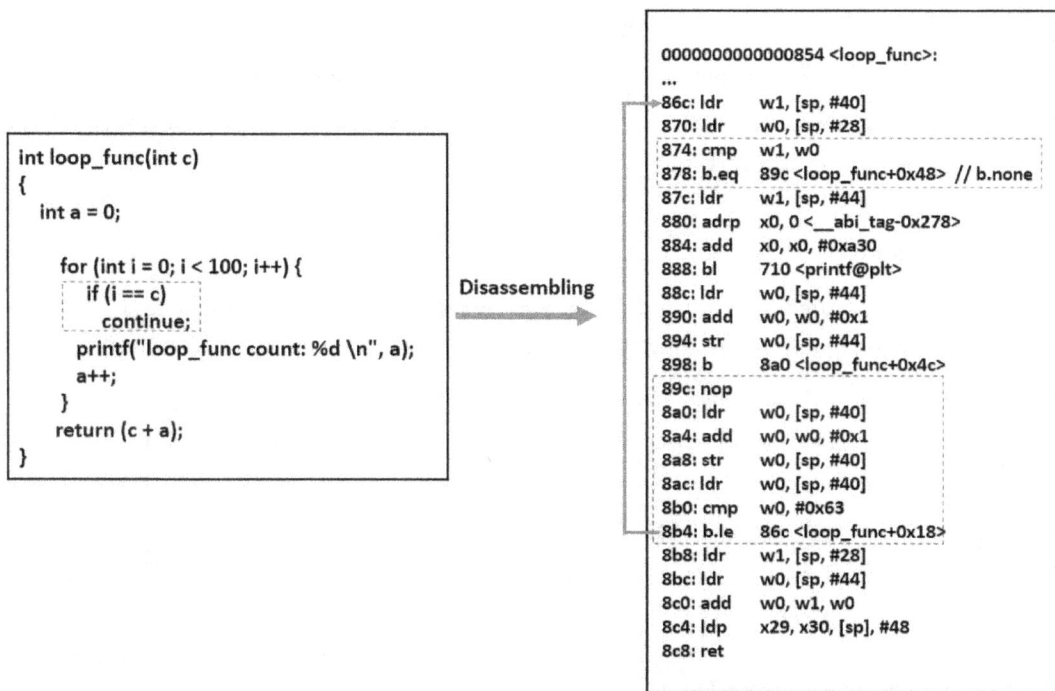

Figure 9.6: Execution flow of the assembly block with a continue statement

In *Figure 9.6*, you will notice that a `continue` statement, along with an `if` statement, is added inside the `for` loop:

```
if (i == c)
    continue;
```

This condition checks whether the values of `i` and `c` are equal. If they are equal, the `continue` statement skips the rest of the current loop iteration and jumps back to the start of the loop. Now, let's examine the new assembly code that is generated by this condition:

```
874:    cmp    w1, w0
878:    b.eq   89c <loop_func+0x48>  // branch if equal
87c:    ldr    w1, [sp, #44]
```

In this assembly block, we can see the following operations:

- A comparison is made between the values in the w1 and w0 registers.
- If these values are equal, the program branches to address 89c. If they are not equal, the program moves to address 87c.

> **Note**
>
> In the preceding assembly block, w0 corresponds to the local variable, i, and w1 corresponds to the argument, c, that is passed to the loop_func function.

Let's find out what is going to happen at address 89c, where the loop continues if i equals c:

```
89c:    nop
8a0:    ldr     w0, [sp, #40]
8a4:    add     w0, w0, #0x1
8a8:    str     w0, [sp, #40]
8ac:    ldr     w0, [sp, #40]
8b0:    cmp     w0, #0x63
8b4:    b.le    86c <loop_func+0x18>
8b8:    ldr     w1, [sp, #28]
```

Looking at this code block, we can summarize the steps as follows:

- The value of i, which is stored in w0, is incremented by 1.
- The program then compares i to 0x63 (which is 99 in decimal).
- If i is less than or equal to 99, the loop continues from address 86c. Otherwise, the program jumps to 8b8.

By examining the assembly instructions, we can see that the code loops back to the beginning of the for loop without calling the printf function, as expected when a continue statement is used. This assembly code effectively implements the continue behavior by jumping back to the start of the loop.

A for loop with a return 0 statement

Next, let's explore how the assembly code pattern changes when a return 0 statement is added within the for loop. In *Figure 9.7*, you can see the updated C code and the new assembly instructions:

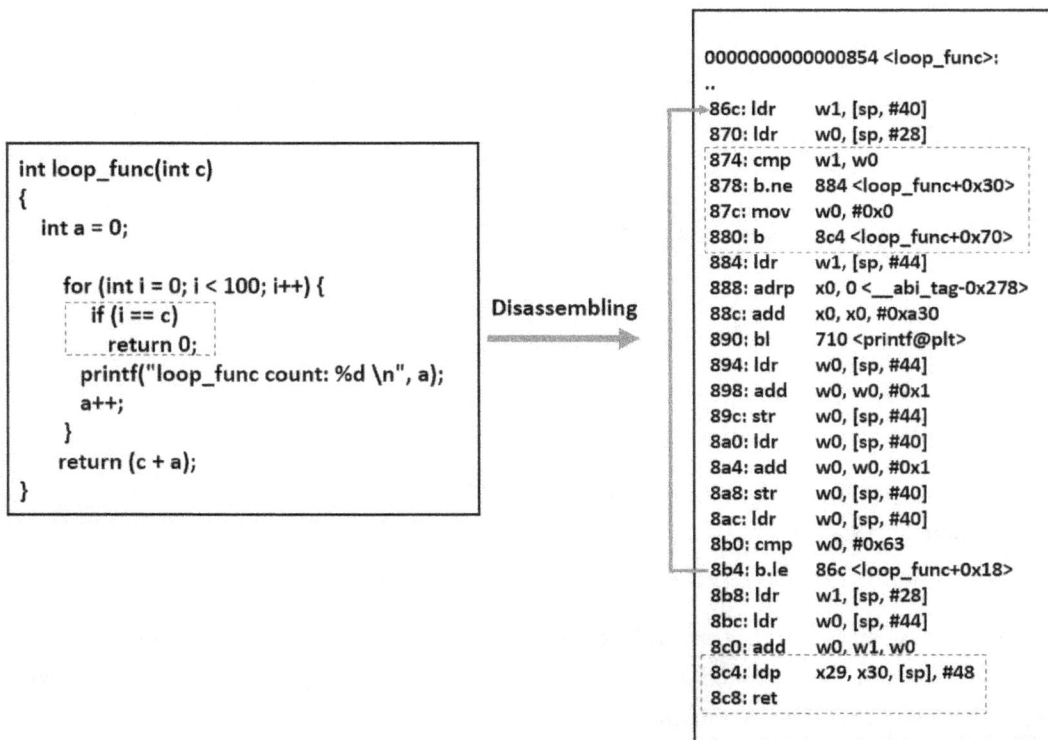

```
0000000000000854 <loop_func>:
..
86c: ldr    w1, [sp, #40]
870: ldr    w0, [sp, #28]
874: cmp    w1, w0
878: b.ne   884 <loop_func+0x30>
87c: mov    w0, #0x0
880: b      8c4 <loop_func+0x70>
884: ldr    w1, [sp, #44]
888: adrp   x0, 0 <__abi_tag-0x278>
88c: add    x0, x0, #0xa30
890: bl     710 <printf@plt>
894: ldr    w0, [sp, #44]
898: add    w0, w0, #0x1
89c: str    w0, [sp, #44]
8a0: ldr    w0, [sp, #40]
8a4: add    w0, w0, #0x1
8a8: str    w0, [sp, #40]
8ac: ldr    w0, [sp, #40]
8b0: cmp    w0, #0x63
8b4: b.le   86c <loop_func+0x18>
8b8: ldr    w1, [sp, #28]
8bc: ldr    w0, [sp, #44]
8c0: add    w0, w1, w0
8c4: ldp    x29, x30, [sp], #48
8c8: ret
```

```
int loop_func(int c)
{
  int a = 0;

    for (int i = 0; i < 100; i++) {
      if (i == c)
        return 0;
      printf("loop_func count: %d \n", a);
      a++;
    }
    return (c + a);
}
```

Disassembling

Figure 9.7: Execution flow of the assembly block with a return 0 statement

In *Figure 9.7*, you can see that the following code block includes the return 0 statement:

```
if (i == c)
    return 0;
```

After adding this block inside the loop, the disassembly generates the following code:

```
874:    cmp    w1, w0
878:    b.ne   884 <loop_func+0x30>
87c:    mov    w0, #0x0
880:    b      8c4 <loop_func+0x70>
884:    ldr    w1, [sp, #44]
```

This new assembly block performs the following actions:

- A comparison is made between the values in the w1 and w0 registers.

- If the values are not equal, the program jumps to address 884. Otherwise, it moves to 8c4.

- The w0 register is updated to the value of 0, which will be the return value when the function exits.

> **Note**
>
> In the preceding assembly block, w0 corresponds to the local variable, i, and w1 corresponds to the argument, c, that is passed to the loop_func function.

At address 8c4, we can see the finalization routine, which is similar to what we saw in previous sections:

```
8c4:    ldp    x29, x30, [sp], #48
8c8:    ret
```

This routine performs the following actions:

- The ldp instruction performs the operation. The registers x29 and x30, which were previously stored on the stack, are restored with the ldp instruction.
- The ret instruction returns control to the calling function.

In summary, when return 0 is executed, the function stops early and exits. This routine is similar to what we saw in previous sections, so we will not explain it again. Remember, this early exit is important to control the program flow and how functions complete their tasks.

In this section, you have learned about different execution flows with if statements in for loops. When you see these patterns in the assembly instructions, remember that the break, continue, and return statements are used with if statements. By analyzing this function at the assembly level, you can understand how common C code structures, such as loops and conditions, work. This understanding is very important for debugging and improving system software performance.

The following section will focus on the patterns of the assembly block related to printing logs.

Identifying log output patterns

In this section, we will look at assembly instructions used for printing logs and examine their structure. When analyzing logs in a real project, you will identify which software routine generates the corresponding logs. This process helps narrow down the issue and provides a deeper understanding of the symptoms.

First, let's understand why recognizing the log pattern is important. Then, we will analyze the assembly instructions that produce printf logs.

Why do we need to understand log output routines?

In software development, engineers often spend a lot of time examining logs and looking for specific log signatures. But why is this necessary? There are two main reasons:

- **Fixing bugs**: One reason is to identify and fix software bugs. Many software engineers rely on logs to understand where issues are happening and then work to fix them. To fix a bug, it's crucial to identify its exact location, and logs often provide signatures about where and why the problem occurs.

- **Understanding the execution flow**: Logs can also show how a module runs within the system. For example, in products such as Android devices, various logs are generated because of the many running modules and features. By examining these logs, engineers can understand the order of execution and behavior of different parts of the system. Logs are not just for errors; they are also generated when key features or functions are enabled.

Analyzing logs is an important part of a developer's daily work. It helps make sure that the system is working correctly.

Analyzing the call to the printf function

In a basic Linux system program, you'll often encounter the `printf` function, which outputs messages to the log. But what does `printf` look like in assembly language? Let's look at the following example code:

```
01 printf("Hello world %d \n", debug);
02 bl    6c0 <printf@plt>
```

The first line is a `printf` statement in C, while the second line is an assembly instruction that calls `printf` using the bl (branch with link) instruction. Note that the second assembly instruction corresponds to the first line of C code.

Here, the `printf` function is responsible for generating log output. To understand how `printf` works in the log, we need to analyze the `printf@plt` assembly instruction.

The `printf` function usually takes one or more arguments:

- **First argument**: Address of the string, which is the message that `printf` will output
- **Second and additional arguments**: Information such as variable values that will be printed along with the string

In addition, the arguments for `printf` are stored in specific registers:

- X0: Contains the address where the string `"Hello world %d \n"` is stored
- X1: Holds the value of the `debug` variable

The address of the string is stored in the `x0` register. By checking the memory contents that `x0` indicates, you can see exactly what ASCII characters are included in the message. This allows you to more easily trace the log messages.

> Note
>
> Many functions use macros instead of directly calling the `printf` function because macros give more flexibility in how logs are printed, depending on the build options. As a result, when looking at C code, it may be harder to immediately know what will be logged, as macros can obscure the exact output. However, by examining the assembly instructions, you can see the precise message that will be logged.

If you are involved in any project, you will likely need to review logs at some point. Understanding the patterns within an assembly routine is crucial, as these patterns are often linked to the tracing logs.

When printf becomes puts

When you add the `printf()` function to your C code, you might expect that the disassembler will show `printf@plt`. However, this is not always true. The compiler can change `printf()` to `puts@plt` in some cases. This happens in the following cases:

- The format string does not include a conversion specifier (such as %d, %s, etc.)
- The format string ends with a newline character (\n)
- There are no extra arguments used in `printf()`

In this situation, the compiler replaces `printf()` with `puts()` to make the code simpler and faster. From another perspective, if you encounter `puts@plt` in the assembly routine, you can think of the three cases mentioned here.

Summary

In this chapter, we learned some basic and important skills for reverse engineering using static analysis.

First, we explained what static analysis is. Then, we looked at some popular tools for reverse engineering, such as IDA Pro, Binary Ninja, Ghidra, and binary utilities.

We also learned how to check the type of a binary file using these tools. After that, we used a corrupted object file to learn how to find information about the file's properties.

Next, we learned how to convert assembly code into C code. For example, we saw how to recognize `if-else` statements by checking special patterns in assembly. We also learned how to understand function calls, and how `break`, `continue`, and `return` statements work inside a `for` loop.

These skills are a basic foundation for binary analysis. In the next chapter, we will learn about more advanced static analysis, with a focus on analyzing kernel binaries.

Join our community on Discord

Join our community's Discord space for discussions with the authors and other readers: https://packt.link/embeddedsystems

10

Going Deeper with Advanced Static Analysis

Reverse engineering involves analyzing binaries. Kernel space binaries share some similarities with user space binaries but also have notable differences. In this chapter, we will focus on analyzing kernel binaries with the following topics:

- Methodology for static analysis
- Introducing advanced static analysis
- How the kernel binary is organized
- Key features of kernel binaries
- Understanding the pattern of struct data structures

We will begin by discussing strategies for effective static analysis. Next, we will guide you through advanced techniques and examine various patterns in kernel binaries. Additionally, we will explore the key features of kernel binaries and analyze several critical patterns commonly found in kernel binaries.

Technical requirements

All the code examples and binary files for this chapter can be found on GitHub at https://github. com/PacktPublishing/Reverse-Engineering-Armv8-A-Systems.

Methodology for static analysis

Before starting the reverse engineering process, it is essential to identify the type of binary file you will be analyzing. Once you have selected a binary file, the next step is to explore the assembly instructions it contains. This involves examining the low-level code to understand the behavior of the program.

An equally important aspect of reverse engineering is to define your goals clearly. When setting goals, it is crucial to be aware of the limitations of static analysis. While it provides a comprehensive view of the binary's structure and logic, static analysis does not reveal runtime behaviors such as memory interactions or dynamic dependencies.

This section will cover how to establish clear goals and navigate the challenges of static analysis to ensure a productive reverse engineering process.

Setting clear and flexible goals

Before you begin static analysis, it is important to set clear goals. Tracing the execution flow in a binary file can feel like searching in the dark. Depending on your objectives in reverse engineering, it is best to create a flexible plan that matches your specific goal. Set these goals, ask yourself questions to help you stay focused during the analysis, and be prepared to adjust your objectives if necessary.

Here are some helpful points to consider:

- Sometimes, you might need to search for specific patterns across multiple binaries. For example, you may want to check if a binary was built with options like Address Sanitizer. You can inspect different binaries to see if they share the same log patterns.

- In some cases, you cannot see certain essential details from the original C code in the binary. This happens especially if the code was compiled with higher optimization levels. Higher optimizations often change the position of code written in C, which can make reverse engineering more challenging.

- Be aware of the limitations of static analysis. In general, reverse engineering relies on both static and dynamic analysis to fully understand how a binary behaves.

Now, let's delve into several methods for analyzing assembly instructions.

Techniques for analyzing instructions

When analyzing assembly code, you can apply different approaches, but they generally fall into two main methods. The first is line-by-line analysis, and the second is control flow analysis based on function calls.

Line-by-line analysis

This approach involves analyzing the source code from top to bottom and examining it line by line. If you find an important routine or a block of assembly instructions, you can use this strategy to gain insights. By looking at each line, you will encounter functions and can understand what each function executes by examining its implementation.

However, this strategy is not commonly used in most cases. Why is that? Because it is very time-consuming. In practice, when reverse engineering, you may need to analyze hundreds of binary files. Unless a binary file holds crucial information, analyzing code line by line is rarely an efficient approach.

Control flow analysis using function calls

The second method is to analyze the assembly code by checking how functions are called. Developers follow the function call flow, just like they would in C code, to understand the control flow of the program.

This method of analyzing assembly instructions is effective for several reasons:

- **Functions as basic units**: Functions are the fundamental building blocks of many programs. By understanding how functions are executed, you can predict how the program works.
- **Ease of modification**: When you need to make changes, you can often add new code within a function. This method is useful for understanding where to apply updates.

By focusing on the control flow, you can gain a clearer picture of how the program operates, which is essential for effective reverse engineering.

> Note
>
> Function names often provide clues about what the function does. Many software engineers name functions based on the specific task they handle, which makes analyzing a binary by following its function flow a useful strategy.

In general, analyzing instructions based on function call flow involves the following steps:

1. Find the entry function that first executes in the binary. The `main` function is generally considered the entry point.

2. Analyze the flow of functions that are called from the main function. Programs such as IDA Pro and Ghidra can assist by giving a graphical view of this function flow, making it easier to understand.

3. Focus on functions called during initialization and shutdown. These functions can often reveal the program's main features or purposes, especially those in the beginning and end stages of execution.

4. Analyze functions to monitor how often they are called. Commonly called functions can be examined in more detail because they're essential to the program's operations. Functions that are rarely called are generally a lower priority for analysis.

When discussing static analysis, many point out its limitations. Let's explore these limitations in more detail.

Understanding the limitations of static analysis

What are the limitations of static analysis? A major challenge is tracking function calls, especially when function pointers are used. When a function is called using a function pointer, it is not easy to know which function is actually called. In this case, the BLR (**Branch with Link and Register**) instruction is used, but it does not clearly show the function name.

The following is the typical example assembly block:

```
01 ldr x2, [x3, 0x8]
02 blr x2
```

In the second line, the program branches to the address stored in the x2 register. But can you tell exactly where it branches? It is not easy. In situations like this, you need to debug the program to find the specific address stored in the x2 register. To know this exact value, you must run the program on the target device, which will show you exactly where it branches.

In short, static analysis alone does not provide the complete picture of how a program will execute. This is why **dynamic analysis** should follow static analysis, because dynamic analysis allows you to observe the program's behavior in real time, tracing any indirect function calls that static analysis may miss.

Comparing static analysis and dynamic analysis

Static analysis is usually performed before dynamic analysis, as it offers an overview of the code without needing to execute it. Let's explore the differences between static and dynamic analysis by examining an example in *Figure 10.1*:

Static analysis	Dynamic analysis
0x814 <bound_condition>:	0x7fa0000814 <bound_condition>:
0x814: stp x29, x30, [sp, #-48]!	0x7fa0000814: stp x29, x30, [sp, #-48]!
0x818: mov x29, sp	0x7fa0000818: mov x29, sp
0x81c: str w0, [sp, #28]	0x7fa000081c: str w0, [sp, #28]
0x820: ldr w0, [sp, #28]	0x7fa0000820: ldr w0, [sp, #28]
0x824: str w0, [sp, #44]	0x7fa0000824: str w0, [sp, #44]
0x828: ldr w0, [sp, #44]	0x7fa0000828: ldr w0, [sp, #44]
0x82c: cmp w0, #0x200	0x7fa000082c: cmp w0, #0x200
0x830: b.le 840	0x7fa0000830: b.le 0x7fa0000840

Figure 10.1: Address view of assembly instructions: static and dynamic analysis

On the left side of *Figure 10.1*, what you can see is the address range is from 814 to 830. These are memory addresses that specify locations where instructions are stored. During runtime, these addresses are updated by the system loader. This static view lets you observe each assembly instruction at its designated address.

Now, let's look at the right side of *Figure 10.1*, which shows the assembly instructions as observed through dynamic analysis, with addresses ranging from 0x7fa0000814 to 0x7fa0000830. When you analyze the bound_condition function using dynamic analysis, you can observe two main differences:

- **Address differences**: In dynamic analysis, the memory address of a function can change at runtime. This is because the loader adjusts the addresses when the program runs. So, the address you see during static analysis may be different from what you see during dynamic analysis.
- **Instruction consistency**: Although the memory addresses differ between static and dynamic analysis, the instructions themselves remain the same. Each instruction performs the same operation.

Figure 10.1 is a good example to compare how memory addresses appear in static and dynamic analysis. One more important point to note: Static analysis helps you look at the instructions and their structure before the program runs. Dynamic analysis gives extra information, such as actual memory addresses, the call stack, and register values during execution.

> Note
>
> Starting with static analysis gives you a solid overview of the assembly instructions. Then, using dynamic analysis helps you confirm how the code behaves in real time. This combined approach gives both basic knowledge and practical insight into how the program works.

Now that we've looked at the basic approach and direction of static analysis, we are ready for the next topic—advanced static analysis.

Introducing advanced static analysis

In traditional reverse engineering, the main focus is on analyzing binaries that run in user space. These include shared libraries and executable binaries that run in user space. In this book, we use basic static analysis to describe the static analysis of user space binary.

In this section, we will introduce a new term—advanced static analysis, which is for analyzing kernel binaries. First, we will compare the key differences between binaries running in kernel space and those in user space. Next, we will explain the main features of kernel binaries. Additionally, you will learn about some widely used tools to analyze kernel binaries.

Key features of kernel binaries

Let's take a look at *Figure 10.2*, which shows the binary in user space and kernel space.

Exception Level	Software	Binary type
EL0	**Application**	**User space binary**
EL1	**Linux kernel**	**Kernel binary**

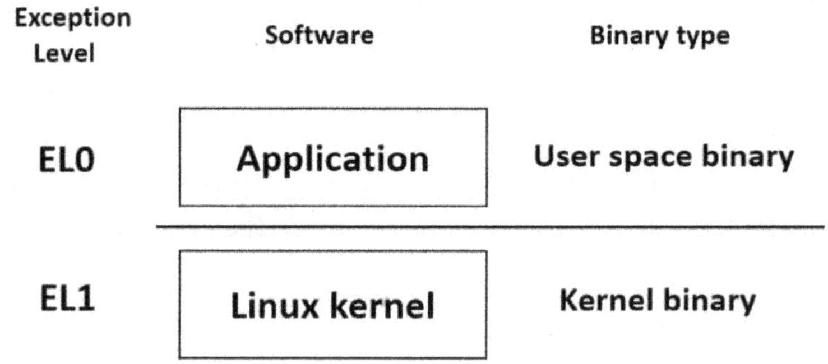

Figure 10.2: Binary in user space and kernel space

When we analyze user space binaries, we can understand how user processes work, including how they use libraries and make system calls. However, analyzing only user space is sometimes not enough to fully understand system behavior. This is because many important operations happen in the kernel. These include the following:

- Hardware interactions
- Low-level system management
- Essential system configurations

Since these operations are managed by the kernel, focusing only on user-space binaries can make it difficult to fully understand the key functionalities of the entire system. To gain a comprehensive view of how a system works, it is essential to also analyze kernel binaries. Additionally, this deeper analysis allows us to see how user-space processes interact with the kernel and how system-level tasks are executed.

Analyzing kernel binaries is **advanced static analysis**, where the goal is to understand the structure and behavior of the kernel. This differs from basic static analysis, which primarily focuses on analyzing user-space binaries.

Having discussed why kernel binary analysis is essential, let's now explore the typical kernel binary that is commonly analyzed.

Selecting kernel binaries for analysis

When starting with reverse engineering, the first step is always to choose the binary file you will analyze. This principle applies when analyzing kernel binaries as well. Among the most commonly used kernel binaries are the *.ko (kernel module driver) and vmlinux files. Each of these has unique characteristics that make them suitable for different types of analysis:

- *.ko files: These files are device drivers in kernel module format. A modular device driver consists of multiple source files, and the *.ko file contains all the functions from these source files. In general, the Linux kernel is made up of core functions (subsystems) and device drivers that handle essential operations. Many embedded software engineers develop module-type device drivers. The result of developing these drivers is a *.ko file.
- vmlinux file: This is a binary file containing key debug information after the Linux kernel is built. When you compile the kernel, the source files are generated as *.o object files, but it's usually best to analyze the vmlinux file directly.

Remember that the ELF file introduced here is not only useful for reverse engineering but is also frequently used during debugging in real development processes.

Debugging program for kernel binaries

Do software engineers use different debugging tools for kernel binaries? Not entirely. While the tools for analyzing and debugging kernel binaries overlap, they serve different purposes and some tasks may require specialized tools for each task. The debugging tools used in kernel binary analysis include those discussed in *Chapter 9*. Now, let's explore the tools available for analyzing kernel binaries:

- **IDA Pro** and **Binary Ninja**: Both tools can parse *.ko files and vmlinux, displaying the results. They also have features to convert assembly instructions into various C code forms, which is helpful for analysis.

- **Ghidra**: Ghidra is also a powerful reverse engineering tool. It can parse *.ko files and vmlinux and display the results. The function graph and function table features are particularly useful for understanding function call flows.

- **TRACE32**: TRACE32 is a hardware debugger that is widely used in the embedded software field. Many software developers use TRACE32 to monitor the different types of binaries.

Now that we have learned about kernel binaries and discussed why examining them is important, let's explore the structure of kernel binaries.

Structure of kernel binaries

The most commonly examined kernel binaries are vmlinux and *.ko files. In this section, we will explore how vmlinux and *.ko files are organized and how they follow the ELF format. First, let's take a closer look at vmlinux.

Exploring vmlinux

When you compile the source code of the Linux kernel, object files (*.o) are generated for each source file. After the compilation process is complete, the vmlinux file is generated by linking these multiple object files together.

How to generate vmlinux

So, what is the simplest way to see how the vmlinux file is generated? When you build the Raspbian kernel source code, you will notice that a vmlinux file is generated once the build process is complete. If you want to try building the Raspbian kernel, you can refer to the Raspberry Pi community resources.

> **Note**
>
> One important point to remember when building the Linux kernel is to enable the
> CONFIG_DEBUG_INFO=y configuration. This ensures that debugging symbols are
> included in the vmlinux file. Without this setting, the symbol table will not be available
> in the generated vmlinux file.

Now that you have learned about the vmlinux file in the Linux kernel, let's move on to explore
the header information in the vmlinux file.

Inspecting header sections in vmlinux

Let's analyze the vmlinux file using the file command:

```
$ file vmlinux
vmlinux: ELF 64-bit LSB shared object, Arm aarch64, version 1 (SYSV),
statically linked, with debug_info, not stripped
```

The output confirms that vmlinux is an ELF file designed for the Arm AArch64 architecture. It also
shows that the file is statically linked and contains debugging information.

The details provided by the file command are extracted from the header information within
the ELF file. To verify this metadata further, we need to examine the raw hexadecimal data of
the vmlinux file using the xxd utility. *Figure 10.3* illustrates the raw header data of the vmlinux
file via the xxd utility:

```
$ xxd vmlinux | head -7
00000000: 7f45 4c46 0201 0100 0000 0000 0000 0000  .ELF............
00000010: 0300 b700 0100 0000 0000 0008 c0ff ffff  ................
00000020: 4000 0000 0000 0000 8814 a90e 0000 0000  @...............
00000030: 0000 0000 4000 3800 0200 4000 2c00 2b00  ....@.8...@.,.+.
00000040: 0100 0000 0700 0000 0000 0100 0000 0000  ................
00000050: 0000 0008 c0ff ffff 0000 0008 c0ff ffff  ................
00000060: 00a2 5101 0000 0000 98ed 6001 0000 0000  ..Q.......`.....
```

Figure 10.3: The raw data in the header of vmlinux using xxd utility

From this output, we can see that the vmlinux file begins with the sequence 7f 45 4c 46 02 01.
This corresponds to the ASCII representation of ELF, which indicates the signature of the ELF
file format.

To gain a more structured view of the ELF header, let's use the readelf -h command:

```
$ readelf -h vmlinux
ELF Header:
  Magic:   7f 45 4c 46 02 01 01 00 00 00 00 00 00 00 00 00
  Class:                             ELF64
  Data:                              2's complement, little endian
  Version:                           1 (current)
  OS/ABI:                            UNIX - System V
  ABI Version:                       0
  Type:                              DYN (Shared object file)
  Machine:                           AArch64
  Version:                           0x1
  Entry point address:               0xffffffc008000000
  Start of program headers:          64 (bytes into file)
  Start of section headers:          245961864 (bytes into file)
  [...]
  Section header string table index: 43
```

Figure 10.4: The output of the readelf –h command

Looking at this output, we can identify key attributes of the ELF file, including the following:

- **DYN**: Indicates that this is a shared object file

- **AArch64**: Specifies that the file is for a 64-bit Arm architecture (Armv8)

- **Entry point address**: 0xffffffc008000000, which marks where execution begins

These details are crucial when preparing to open and analyze the vmlinux file during reverse engineering.

To explore the various sections of vmlinux, you can see the readelf -S command:

```
$ readelf -S vmlinux
There are 44 section headers, starting at offset 0xea91488:
Section Headers:
  [Nr] Name              Type             Address           Offset
       Size              EntSize          Flags  Link  Info  Align
  [ 0]                   NULL             0000000000000000  00000000
       0000000000000000  0000000000000000         0     0     0
  [ 1] .head.text        PROGBITS         ffffffc008000000  00010000
       0000000000010000  0000000000000000  AX     0     0     65536
  [ 2] .text             PROGBITS         ffffffc008010000  00020000
       0000000000b5ff38  0000000000000008  AX     0     0     65536
  ...
  [16] .init.text        PROGBITS         ffffffc008f80000  00f90000
       00000000004d3a4   0000000000000000  AX     0     0     4
  [17] .exit.text        PROGBITS         ffffffc008fcd3a4  00fdd3a4
       00000000000037b0  0000000000000000  AX     0     0     4
```

Figure 10.5: The output of the readelf -S command

Some important sections in vmlinux include the following:

- .head.text: Contains CPU-specific startup code executed during the boot process
- .text: Stores runtime code that runs after system initialization
- .init.text: Holds initialization routines executed during the driver initialization phase
- .exit.text: Contains termination routines executed during the driver shutdown phase

As we learned, the vmlinux file is in ELF format. It is helpful to check the structure and details of the vmlinux file. This is because it allows us to understand which functions are located in specific sections when analyzing assembly instructions.

Understanding *.ko files (kernel modules)

*.ko files are the standard format for module-type device drivers in Linux. For those unfamiliar with Linux device drivers, let's first explore the different types of device drivers in Linux. Afterward, we will discuss why it is important to examine the *.ko file before loading it onto an actual device. Finally, we will investigate the attributes inside the *.ko file by examining the .modinfo section, which contains crucial information about the module.

Types of device drivers

During Linux development, you will notice that there are two types of device drivers in Linux:

- **Built-in driver**: In this approach, the device driver is added directly to the Linux kernel image, meaning the driver's code becomes part of the kernel itself. This method is typically used when only a small number of new drivers are added to keep the kernel manageable. However, if a large amount of driver code is included, the kernel image size will increase. If the size of the kernel image increases, the size of the partition used to store the kernel image may also need to increase accordingly.
- **Module driver**: With this approach, the device driver is compiled separately as a module (*.ko file) and then installed after the Linux kernel has finished booting. Many systems use the modular method because it allows the system to load many device drivers independently.

Nowadays, many device drivers are developed as module types. This approach offers greater flexibility for maintenance and eliminates concerns about increasing the kernel binary size.

Why is it important to analyze *.ko files?

As a product developer or DevOps engineer, you may frequently need to gather and install multiple device driver files (*.ko). These files are often provided by other teams or external companies. In some projects, managing and installing more than 100 different *.ko files is not uncommon. During this process, a couple of questions may arise, as follows:

- What if the *.ko file fails to install as expected?
- If loading a *.ko file triggers a fault, what steps can we take to resolve it?

The primary reason for these questions is that the behavior of device drivers is often unpredictable. This unpredictability makes troubleshooting and managing *.ko files particularly challenging.

One approach to address these issues is to perform static analysis on the *.ko file. By doing so, you can examine its properties and structure without actually executing the file, reducing the risk of faults during installation. Static analysis can help identify potential compatibility issues, dependencies, or configuration mismatches in advance.

In this section, we will explore the structure of *.ko files and discuss how to analyze their properties effectively.

> **Note**
>
> This section does not explain the internal workings of the Linux kernel in detail. Instead, it focuses on analyzing .ko files to understand their file structure.

When analyzing *.ko files, an important aspect to consider is how they differ from standard ELF files. Unlike other ELF files, *.ko files include a unique section called .modinfo. The .modinfo section contains critical metadata, such as licensing details, author information, and other module-specific attributes. If the metadata in the *.ko file does not contain the necessary information, the installation of the module-type device driver will fail.

In the following section, we will explore the .modinfo section in greater detail.

Checking header information in a *.ko file

When we open a *.ko file using the file utility, we can see that it is in ELF format. Now, let's examine the header inside the hello_world.ko file using the file command:

```
$ file hello_world.ko
hello_world.ko: ELF 64-bit LSB relocatable, Arm aarch64, version 1 (SYSV),
BuildID[sha1]=23bba3f1233af4160c7d8001f25fa3adb2943c77, not stripped
```

Note that `hello_world.ko` is generated from the simplest Hello World device driver.

The output reveals attributes similar to those of `vmlinux`, indicating that `hello_world.ko` is an **Executable and Linkable Format (ELF)** file of the relocatable type. A relocatable ELF file can be dynamically loaded into the kernel.

To dive deeper, let's examine the raw data of `hello_world.ko` using the xxd utility:

```
$ xxd hello_world.ko | head -7
00000000: 7f45 4c46 0201 0100 0000 0000 0000 0000  .ELF............
00000010: 0100 b700 0100 0000 0000 0000 0000 0000  ................
00000020: 0000 0000 0000 0000 9810 0000 0000 0000  ................
00000030: 0000 0000 4000 0000 0000 4000 1e00 1d00  ....@.....@.....
00000040: 0400 0000 1400 0000 0300 0000 474e 5500  ............GNU.
00000050: 23bb a3f1 233a f416 0c7d 8001 f25f a3ad  #...#:...}..._..
00000060: b294 3c77 fd7b bfa9 0000 0090 0000 0091  ..<w.{..........
```

Figure 10.6: The raw data in the header of hello_world.ko using xxd utility

As seen in *Figure 10.6*, we can recognize the familiar ELF signature. Specifically, the raw data begins with the ELF magic number (7f45 4c46 0201), just like in `vmlinux`.

Now, let's extract more detailed information about the ELF header. For this, we can use the `readelf -h` command:

```
$ readelf -h hello_world.ko
ELF Header:
  Magic:   7f 45 4c 46 02 01 01 00 00 00 00 00 00 00 00 00
  Class:                             ELF64
  Data:                              2's complement, little endian
  Version:                           1 (current)
  OS/ABI:                            UNIX - System V
  ABI Version:                       0
  Type:                              REL (Relocatable file)
  Machine:                           AArch64
  Version:                           0x1
  Entry point address:               0x0
  [...]
  Number of section headers:         30
  Section header string table index: 29
```

Figure 10.7: The output of the readelf -h command with hello_world.ko

The output of `readelf -h` shows that `hello_world.ko` is intended for Armv8-A (Aarch64).

Next, let's analyze the sections within the hello_world.ko file using the readelf -S command:

```
$ readelf -S hello_world.ko
There are 30 section headers, starting at offset 0x1098:

Section Headers:
  [Nr] Name                Type             Address           Offset
       Size                EntSize          Flags  Link  Info  Align
  [...]
  [ 2] .text               PROGBITS         0000000000000000  00000064
       0000000000000000    0000000000000000  AX     0     0     1
  [ 3] .exit.text          PROGBITS         0000000000000000  00000064
       000000000000001c    0000000000000000  AX     0     0     4
  [ 4] .rela.exit.text     RELA             0000000000000000  00000e68
       0000000000000048    0000000000000018  I      27    3     8
  [ 5] .init.text          PROGBITS         0000000000000000  00000080
       0000000000000028    0000000000000000  AX     0     0     4
  [ 6] .rela.init.text     RELA             0000000000000000  00000eb0
       0000000000000060    0000000000000018  I      27    5     8
  [ 7] .modinfo            PROGBITS         0000000000000000  000000a8
       00000000000000cb    0000000000000000  A      0     0     1
  [...]
```

Figure 10.8: The output of the readelf -S command with hello_world.ko

In *Figure 10.8*, you can see that the output reveals section information similar to what we observe in vmlinux. Among the different sections, it is important to carefully check the .modinfo section. This section contains metadata about the module-type device driver, such as the author's name and license information.

Inspecting metadata in the .modinfo section

Why do we need to inspect the .modinfo section? Because *.ko files contain their own metadata, which includes important details such as the author and licensing properties in the .modinfo section.

During the installation stage, when a module is loaded using the insmod command, this metadata is checked to ensure that the structure and layout of the *.ko file are organized as expected.

Let's examine the .modinfo section using the readelf command, which is as follows:

```
$ readelf -p .modinfo hello_world.ko

String dump of section '.modinfo':
  [     0]  license=GPL
  [     c]  description=Hello world
  [    24]  author=Austin Kim <austindh.kim@gmail.com>
```

```
[      4f]    srcversion=9462A271F3F6146BF91F093
[      72]    depends=
[      7b]    name=hello_world
[      8c]    vermagic=6.6.47+rpt-rpi-2712 SMP preempt mod_unload
modversions aarch64
```

As you can see, the output message shows the details of the .modinfo section.

Now, another question is how can we see the raw data in the .modinfo section? *Figure 10.9* shows this information:

```
$ readelf -S hello_world.ko
There are 30 section headers, starting at offset 0x1060:

Section Headers:
  [Nr] Name              Type             Address           Offset
       Size              EntSize          Flags  Link  Info  Align
  [ 0]                   NULL             0000000000000000  00000000
       0000000000000000  0000000000000000         0     0     0
  [ 1] .text             PROGBITS         0000000000000000  00000040
       0000000000000000  0000000000000000  AX     0     0     1
  [ 2] .exit.text        PROGBITS         0000000000000000  00000040
       0000000000000024  0000000000000000  AX     0     0     8
  [...]
  [19] .modinfo          PROGBITS         0000000000000000  000005a6    [1]
       00000000000000d4  0000000000000000  A      0     0     1

$ xxd hello_world.ko
00000000: 7f45 4c46 0201 0100 0000 0000 0000 0000  .ELF............
00000010: 0100 b700 0100 0000 0000 0000 0000 0000  ................
[...]
000005a0: 726c 642e 0a00 6c69 6365 6e73 653d 4750  rld...license=GP
000005b0: 4c00 6465 7363 7269 7074 696f 6e3d 4865  L.description=He
000005c0: 6c6c 6f20 776f 726c 6400 6175 7468 6f72  llo world.author
000005d0: 3d41 7573 7469 6e20 4b69 6d20 3c61 7573  =Austin Kim <aus
000005e0: 7469 6e64 682e 6b69 6d40 676d 6169 6c2e  tindh.kim@gmail.
000005f0: 636f 6d3e 0073 7263 7665 7273 696f 6e3d  com>.srcversion=
00000600: 3934 3632 4132 3731 4633 4636 3134 3642  9462A271F3F6146B
00000610: 4639 3146 3039 3300 6465 7065 6e64 733d  F91F093.depends=
00000620: 006e 616d 653d 6865 6c6c 6f5f 776f 726c  .name=hello_worl
00000630: 6400 7665 726d 6167 6963 3d36 2e36 2e34  d.vermagic=6.6.4
00000640: 372b 7270 742d 7270 692d 3237 3132 2053  7+rpt-rpi-2712 S
00000650: 4d50 2070 7265 656d 7074 206d 6f64 5f75  MP preempt mod_u
00000660: 6e6c 6f61 6420 6d6f 6476 6572 7369 6f6e  nload modversion
00000670: 7320 6161 7263 6836 3400 0000 0000 0000  s aarch64.......
```

[2]

Figure 10.9: The offset and raw data in the .modinfo section

If we refer to **[1]** in *Figure 10.9*, we can see that the .modinfo section begins at offset 0x5a6. This offset is calculated relative to the start of the hello_world.ko file. In **[2]**, we observe the raw data stored in the .modinfo section.

The left part of **[2]** displays several strings in ASCII format. These strings represent the metadata of the hello_world.ko module. The following is a portion of the metadata found in this section:

- license=GPL
- description=Hello world
- author=Austin Kim <austindh.kim@gmail.com>
- depends=

This metadata gives important information about the module. The license field shows the licensing terms—in this case, GPL (**GNU General Public License**). The description field gives a short explanation of what the module does. The author field shows the name and contact details of the person who created the module. The depends field lists any dependencies the module might require, though it is empty for this example.

What is the source code of the device driver you observed? The following is an example of a simple Linux device driver:

```c
#include <linux/module.h>
#include <linux/kernel.h>
#include <linux/init.h>
static int __init init_hello(void) {
    printk("Hello world.\n");
    return 0;
}
void __exit cleanup_hello(void) {
    printk("Goodbye world.\n");
}
module_init(init_hello);
module_exit(cleanup_hello);

MODULE_AUTHOR("Austin Kim <austindh.kim@gmail.com>");
MODULE_DESCRIPTION("Hello world");
MODULE_LICENSE("GPL");
```

At the bottom of the code, you can see the MODULE_AUTHOR(), MODULE_DESCRIPTION(), and MODULE_LICENSE() macros. These are part of the metadata for the driver. This metadata provides important information about the driver, such as the author, description, and licensing details.

Figure 10.10 illustrates how the code written in the device driver using the MODULE_* macro is placed in the .modinfo section:

```
$ xxd hello_world.ko
00000000: 7f45 4c46 0201 0100 0000 0000 0000 0000  .ELF............
00000010: 0100 b700 0100 0000 0000 0000 0000 0000  ................
[...]
000005a0: 726c 642e 0a00 6c69 6365 6e73 653d 4750  rld...license=GP
000005b0: 4c00 6465 7363 7269 7074 696f 6e3d 4865  L.description=He
000005c0: 6c6c 6f20 776f 726c 6400 6175 7468 6f72  llo world.author
000005d0: 3d41 7573 7469 6e20 4b69 6d20 3c61 7573  =Austin Kim <aus
000005e0: 7469 6e64 682e 6b69 6d40 676d 6169 6c2e  tindh.kim@gmail.
000005f0: 636f 6d3e 0073 7263 7665 7273 696f 6e3d  com>.srcversion=
00000600: 3934 3632 4132 3731 4633 4636 3134 3642  9462A271F3F6146B
00000610: 4639 3146 3039 3300 6465 7065 6e64 733d  F91F093.depends=
00000620: 006e 616d 653d 6865 6c6c 6f5f 776f 726c  .name=hello_worl
00000630: 6400 7665 726d 6167 6963 3d36 2e36 2e34  d.vermagic=6.6.4
00000640: 372b 7270 742d 7270 692d 3237 3132 2053  7+rpt-rpi-2712 S
00000650: 4d50 2070 7265 656d 7074 206d 6f64 5f75  MP preempt mod_u
00000660: 6e6c 6f61 6420 6d6f 6476 6572 7369 6f6e  nload modversion
00000670: 7320 6161 7263 6836 3400 0000 0000 0000  s aarch64.......
```
                                                                        [1]
```
    static int __init init_hello(void) {
        printk("Hello world.\n");

        return 0;
    }

    void __exit cleanup_hello(void) {
        printk("Goodbye world.\n");
    }

    module_init(init_hello);
    module_exit(cleanup_hello);                    [2]

    MODULE_AUTHOR("Austin Kim <austindh.kim@gmail.com>");
    MODULE_DESCRIPTION("Hello world");
    MODULE_LICENSE("GPL");
```

Figure 10.10: The raw data in the .modinfo section and corresponding driver code

These macros help identify the driver and provide essential details for users and developers working with it.

Now that we've explored the ELF format of the kernel binaries, let's examine the key signatures within the kernel binary, specifically in the assembly routines.

Key features of kernel binaries

Binaries executed in the Linux kernel and those in user space share some similarities, especially in their assembly instructions. At a basic level, there are no major differences in how instructions for arithmetic operations or function calls are executed. For instance, instructions for adding numbers or calling functions work the same way in both environments, following the same fundamental principles.

However, binaries for kernel space have key differences compared to those for user space. Kernel binaries include additional instructions for tasks such as managing hardware resources, handling interrupts, and setting up necessary system registers. These tasks are specific to the kernel's role in controlling the system and are not typically required in user space binaries.

In this section, we will examine these differences step by step to better understand the unique characteristics of kernel and user space binaries.

Accessing system registers

The Linux kernel runs at EL1 (Exception Level 1), which has more privileges than EL0. User-space applications, on the other hand, run at EL0. Because the Linux kernel operates at EL1, it can directly access and control hardware resources. This is why kernel binaries include assembly instructions, such as setting up virtual memory, handling interrupts, and configuring important features. These configurations are often performed using system registers.

For example, the following is one example of such an instruction:

```
MSR TTBR0_EL1, X0
```

This instruction updates the TTBR0_EL1 system register with the value stored in the X0 register. The TTBR0_EL1 register holds the base address of the first-page table used during virtual address translation.

Similar instructions are found in the kernel binary because it needs to access system registers. These system registers can be modified at EL1, where the Linux kernel runs. You will not find these types of instructions in user applications because user applications do not have the privilege to directly access system registers or configure hardware resources.

Handling exceptions in the kernel

Another routine found in kernel binaries is the assembly instruction associated with exception handling. As you may know, exceptions are one of the key features of Armv8-A. From the Linux perspective, handling events such as memory aborts, page faults, or interrupts in the kernel is implemented using exceptions. Some engineers consider these routines to be the interface between the Linux kernel and the Arm architecture.

In the Linux kernel, you can find the corresponding exception handler at the vectors symbol, which is seen as follows:

```
ffffffc008010800 <vectors>:
ffffffc008010800: sub   sp, sp, #0x150
ffffffc008010804: add   sp, sp, x0
ffffffc008010808: sub   x0, sp, x0
ffffffc00801080c: tbnz  w0, #14,  ffffffc00801081c
ffffffc008010810: sub   x0, sp, x0
ffffffc008010814: sub   sp, sp, x0
ffffffc008010818: b     ffffffc008011090 <el1t_64_sync>
```

However, you will not find exception-handling routines in user-space binaries. This is because exception handling is system-critical.

Managing sp_el0 and current macro

Looking into a Linux kernel binary, you will often see the instruction that reads sp_el0 in many kernel functions. Here's an example:

```
01 ffffc00080372a60 <put_unused_fd>:
[...]
02 ffffc00080372a6c: stp    x29, x30, [sp, #-48]!
03 ffffc00080372a70: mrs    x1, sp_el0
04 ffffc00080372a74: mov    x29, sp
```

In *line 03*, the value of sp_el0 is copied into register x1. The instruction mrs x1, sp_el0 is often seen in many kernel routines. You might wonder why sp_el0 is accessed so frequently in the kernel binary, even though sp_el0 is typically updated in user space at EL0.

The answer lies in the use of the current macro in the Linux kernel, which reads the value in the sp_el0 register. Why is sp_el0 used? The register is one of the fastest components to access in the system. Another important point is that sp_el0 is not used while the Linux kernel is running.

The current macro is used in many kernel functions and device drivers. It helps the kernel find the starting address of the task_struct structure, which holds information about the process running currently. This macro is very useful because it can be called from any part of the kernel code to get the data of the current process.

Let's take a look at the source code of the current macro:

```
// In arch/arm64/include/asm/current.h
01 static __always_inline struct task_struct *get_current(void) {
02     unsigned long sp_el0;
03
04     asm ("mrs %0, sp_el0" : "=r" (sp_el0));
05
06     return (struct task_struct *)sp_el0;
07 }
08 #define current get_current()
```

Here's a breakdown of how the code works:

- *Line 08*: The current macro is defined to be replaced with get_current
- *Line 04*: In the get_current macro function, the value in the sp_el0 register is stored in the local variable sp_el0
- *Line 06*: The value in sp_el0 is returned after being type-cast to the task_struct structure

When the current macro is called, it reads the value stored in sp_el0, which holds the address of the task_struct structure for the current process.

To understand why sp_el0 holds the address of the task_struct structure, we need to look at the cpu_switch_to function, which is executed during context switching.

Now, let's take a look at a snippet from the cpu_switch_to function:

```
01 ffffffc010085b70 <cpu_switch_to>:
02 ffffffc010085b70:    d281580a    mov  x10, #0xac0
03 ffffffc010085b74:    8b0a0008    add  x8, x0, x10
04 ffffffc010085b78:    910003e9    mov  x9, sp
...
05 ffffffc010085bb8:    9100013f    mov  sp, x9
06 ffffffc010085bbc:    d5184101    msr  sp_el0, x1
07 ffffffc010085bc0:    d65f03c0    ret
```

The cpu_switch_to function is responsible for switching between tasks. When the kernel is ready to switch to a new process, cpu_switch_to is called. In line 06, the address of task_struct for the next process is stored in register x1. This address is then saved to sp_el0 with the instruction msr sp_el0, x1.

This allows the sp_el0 register to hold the address of the task_struct structure for the next process to run. When the current macro is used in any kernel code, it retrieves the address stored in sp_el0, which points to the task_struct structure for the current process. This address remains valid until the process is switched again.

In summary, reading the value of sp_el0 provides the starting address of the task_struct structure for the current process.

Instructions to identify exception levels

When analyzing assembly instructions, you can identify specific instructions that interact with system registers. As you might know, the suffix of a system register provides an important clue: it indicates the lowest exception level required to access system registers. Let's understand this through an example:

```
MRS X0, ESR_EL2
```

The preceding assembly instruction reads the value of the ESR_EL2 register and stores it in the X0 register.

> **Note**
>
> ESR_EL2 is updated with the cause of the exception whenever an exception is taken to EL2. In every exception-handling routine at EL2, the hypervisor reads ESR_EL2 to identify the cause of the exception and properly handle it using the appropriate exception handler.

A common question is what exception level is required to execute this instruction? For this instruction to run successfully, it must operate at EL2 or a higher exception level, such as EL3.

Now, let's analyze another example instruction:

```
MRS X0, ESR_EL3
```

This instruction reads the value of the ESR_EL3 register and places it into the X0 register. In this case, the required exception level is EL3, which is the highest exception level. But what happens if this instruction is executed at EL2? Attempting to execute this instruction at EL2 would result in an access violation, triggering an exception in the system. The reason is the ESR_EL3 register requires at least EL3 to be accessed.

From these examples, we can see that by looking at the instructions that the access system registers, you can figure out the lowest exception level needed to interact with certain registers. To make this clearer, here is a summary of the exception levels and the system registers accessible at each level:

- At EL1: System registers such as ESR_EL1 are accessible
- At EL2 (Hypervisor): System registers such as ESR_EL2 and ESR_EL1 are accessible
- At EL3 (Secure Monitor): System registers such as ESR_EL3, ESR_EL2, and ESR_EL1 are accessible

In other words, the higher the exception level, the broader the range of system registers that can be accessed.

When analyzing assembly instructions, paying attention to the suffix of system registers provides valuable insights into the exception level required to execute those instructions. This understanding is especially important when debugging or working with low-level software because it helps identify the running environment and fix possible access errors.

Understanding the pattern of struct data structures

When analyzing assembly instructions, you may often come across instructions related to data structures. This is common when analyzing unfamiliar data structures in kernel binaries. The Linux kernel has many subsystems that use different data structures.

Many software developers think it is impossible to recreate certain data structures exactly during reverse engineering. While this can be true in some cases, we can often predict or recognize patterns in the instructions that access fields inside a struct—especially if we already know which data types are used or if debug information is available.

In this section, we will explore offsets in struct and examine the instruction patterns used to access fields in struct.

Understanding the offset of fields in struct

Before we dive into the instructions for accessing elements in a struct, let's look at a sample struct and a related function.

```
struct process_struct {
    char task_name[16];
    void *stack;
    unsigned int flags;
    unsigned int state;
};
```

The process_struct structure has several fields, each representing a different data type. To keep things simple, we won't go into detail about each field.

Let's assume that the starting memory address of the process_struct structure is 0x1000. Based on this address, we can identify the memory address of each field as follows:

```
(struct process_struct*)0x1000 = 0x1000 -> (
    [ND:0x1000] task_name = (0, ... 0),
    [ND:0x1010] stack = 0x0,
    [ND:0x1018] flags = 0,
    [ND:0x101C] state = 0
)
```

In this layout, we see that the state field is located at an offset of 0x1C (or 28 in decimal) from the beginning of the structure.

Now that we've introduced the process_struct structure, let's look at a sample function that modifies the state field within the process_struct structure by using a pointer:

```
void set_current_state(struct process_struct *process,
                       unsigned int state_value) {
    process->state = state_value;
    printf("state_value: %u \n", state_value);
}
```

We can analyze the preceding function in the following ways:

- Before explaining what the set_current_state function does, let's examine its parameters. The first parameter, process, is a pointer to a process_struct type. In C programming, struct data types are often managed with pointers, because this makes the code simpler and easier to maintain.

- The main purpose of the set_current_state function is to update the state field in the process_struct structure. The second parameter of the function, state_value, holds the new value that will be assigned to the state field. Bypassing struct as a pointer, the function can change the state field directly in memory.

This way of using pointers is common in C and C++ programs, especially for low-level programming. It helps use memory efficiently and makes the code easier to read and manage.

Instructions for accessing fields in a struct

Let's review the pattern of the process_struct structure and the set_current_state function. Next, we will analyze the disassembled assembly instructions for the set_current_state function. This way, we can understand how the function operates and how it accesses the fields of the process_struct structure.

The following is the assembly code for the set_current_state function:

```
0000000000000814 <set_current_state>:
   814: stp     x29, x30, [sp, #-32]!
   818: mov     x29, sp
   81c: str     x0, [sp, #24]
   820: str     w1, [sp, #20]
```

Let's analyze these instructions line by line:

1. At address 0x814, the values in x29 and x30 are stored on the stack. This is done to preserve these values before the function modifies them. By saving these registers, the program can return to the previous state after the function completes its task.

2. At address 0x81c, the value in register x0 is pushed in the stack area at [sp, #24]. This value represents the address of the process_struct structure.

3. At address 0x820, the value in register w1 is saved in the stack area at [sp, #20]. This value holds the state_value that we want to set for the process_struct structure.

> **Note**
>
> It's important to note that function arguments are passed using registers x0 to x7 in Armv8-A.

From our analysis, we can see that the set_current_state function has two parameters:

- x0 stores the address of the struct process_task
- x1 holds the unsigned integer state_value

Now, let's continue analyzing the next set of assembly instructions:

```
0000000000000814 <set_current_state>:
...
 824: ldr     x0, [sp, #24]
 828: ldr     w1, [sp, #20]
 82c: str     w1, [x0, #28]
 830: ldr     w1, [sp, #20]
```

The key instruction in the preceding assembly routine is the str w1, [x0, #28] instruction at address 82c. Let's analyze the preceding routine, which updates the state field of the process_task structure:

- At address 0x824, the starting address of the process_task structure is loaded into register x0. This means that we are now ready to modify any field in the structure.
- At address 0x828, the state_value (saved in [sp, #20]) is loaded into register w1. This is the new state that we want to assign.
- At address 0x82c, the value in w1 is stored at an address calculated by adding 28 to the address in x0. This address corresponds to the state field of the process_struct structure.

It is particularly important to focus on the instruction at 0x82c. This instruction shows that x0 holds the starting address of the process_struct structure. This address is used as the base to update the state field within the structure.

Now, which field is located at the address that is offset by 28 from the starting address? The answer is the state field. How can we find the offset of the state field? We can use a tool called **pahole**, which shows the structure layout in a C-like format. Here is an example of the pahole output:

```
$ pahole -C process_struct process_task
struct process_struct {
```

```
    char          task_name[16]; /*       0      16 */
    void *        stack;         /*      16       8 */
    unsigned int flags;          /*      24       4 */
    unsigned int state;          /*      28       4 */

    /* size: 32, cachelines: 1, members: 4 */
    /* last cacheline: 32 bytes */
};
```

As you can see, the offset of the state field is 28, which is 0x1C in hexadecimal format. If you want to check the layout of another structure, it is a good idea to use pahole. This tool also shows helpful information such as padding and alignment.

> **Note**
>
> To install it on Debian-based systems (such as Raspberry Pi OS), use this command: `sudo apt install dwarves`. After installation, you can run `pahole -C process_struct <your-binary>`. Your binary must include debug information (compiled with the -g option) for pahole to work.

Looking at the assembly instruction that accesses the state field, we can recall a very important pattern. Let's examine the relevant assembly instructions again:

```
  82c:   b9001c01   str   w1, [x0, #28]
```

The offset 28 represents the position of the state field within the structure.

When you look at assembly instructions such as str and ldr, you may notice that we can sometimes predict the corresponding C code. Here, offsets used with ldr and str instructions often indicate the positions of fields within a structure. Recognizing these patterns can be incredibly helpful in reverse engineering.

Summary

In this chapter, we learned how to analyze kernel binaries. First, we discussed the approach to performing static analysis and highlighted the differences between static and dynamic analysis.

Then, we introduced typical kernel binaries, such as *.ko files and vmlinux, and explained how these files are organized using the ELF format. We also examined common patterns found in kernel binaries. For *.ko files, we looked at the metadata found in the .modinfo section.

We also explored assembly routines that can only be found in kernel binaries. When analyzing kernel binaries, you will see assembly routines that access system resources through various system registers. This pattern is not found in user-space binaries because the kernel runs at EL1, which has the privilege to control hardware resources.

Finally, we discussed the common patterns used to access fields within a struct, a data structure widely used in both kernel and user-space binaries to manage data.

In the next chapter, we will focus on dynamic analysis.

11

Analyzing Program Behavior with Basic Dynamic Analysis

In this chapter, we will continue by exploring how to analyze the call stack and memory dump while running software on an actual target device.

Specifically, we will cover the following topics:

- Introducing dynamic analysis
- Exploring the GDB program
- Understanding the virtual address range
- Analyzing stack memory content
- Return-oriented programming analysis
- Memory corruption: buffer overflow case study

This chapter begins with an explanation of the methodology for dynamic analysis. After that, we will explore the key features of GDB and then move on to a case study focused on memory corruption.

All the materials covered in this chapter are based on real-world issues, such as stack corruption and memory corruption. By understanding the content in this chapter, you will enhance your debugging skills in binary analysis.

Let's begin this chapter by learning about the methodology of dynamic analysis.

Technical requirements

All the code examples for this chapter can be found on GitHub at `https://github.com/ PacktPublishing/Reverse-Engineering-Armv8-A-Systems`.

Introducing dynamic analysis

As mentioned in *Chapter 10*, there are two main approaches to reverse engineering: static analysis and dynamic analysis. In this section, we will focus on dynamic analysis. First, we will explore what dynamic analysis is. Then, we will look at the benefits and limitations of dynamic analysis.

What is dynamic analysis?

Dynamic analysis is a method used to observe how a program behaves while it is running on a device. It provides accurate, real-time debugging information. For example, you can check register values, memory dumps, call stacks, and addresses. This method provides information about what is happening inside the system. As static analysis has certain limitations, dynamic analysis becomes more important for the following reasons:

- **Execution uncertainty**: During static analysis, the assembly instructions or memory addresses you observe might not actually execute when the program runs on a device. With dynamic analysis, you can inspect the contents of memory at specific addresses.

- **Function call flow**: When C code uses function pointers, it is difficult to predict the flow of function calls during static analysis. In contrast, dynamic analysis allows you to track exactly which functions are called during runtime, even when function pointers are used.

- **No address details**: Static analysis does not show the actual addresses of the instructions or the stack area. During dynamic analysis, you can inspect the actual addresses of the process.

By combining static and dynamic analysis effectively, you can gain a deeper understanding of the software's behavior, which makes reverse engineering more successful.

Limitations of dynamic analysis

Dynamic analysis allows you to gather useful information from an actual device. However, it has some limitations:

- **Programs blocking debugging tools**: In some cases, we cannot use a debugging tool on the actual device, as some system configurations may block debugging tools for security reasons. From a security perspective, allowing access to debugging information can be risky. For example, tools such as GDB or similar debuggers might be blocked to improve security. This means we cannot do direct analysis on the device.

- **Address randomization**: Many modern systems use a security feature called address randomization, which changes memory addresses every time a program runs. While this improves security, it makes analyzing memory dumps more difficult because the memory contents appear different with each execution.

- **Limited information**: During dynamic analysis, you are often able to observe only parts of the program. Some functions might run only rarely or under specific conditions, such as when a serious error happens. To overcome this limitation, you can use static analysis to examine the binary object file.

Generally, static analysis is performed before dynamic analysis. In some cases, using both methods together can be more effective.

For example, imagine a program that uses security features, such as address randomization. You could start with static analysis to understand the program's overall structure and functions. Then, during dynamic analysis, you could observe how those functions behave in the actual device and how the program interacts with hardware or other software components.

By combining static and dynamic analysis, you can overcome the limitations of dynamic analysis and gain a deeper understanding of the program.

Introducing basic dynamic analysis

This book covers both basic and advanced dynamic analysis. Here is a description of each:

- **Basic dynamic analysis**: This refers to the traditional method of analyzing binaries in user space, where user applications run. Currently, dynamic analysis mostly focuses on user space binaries.

- **Advanced dynamic analysis**: This involves analyzing binaries that run inside the Linux kernel. It is more complex and focuses on the core parts of the operating system.

EL0	**User space**	Basic dynamic analysis
EL1	**Kernel space**	Advanced dynamic analysis

Figure 11.1: User space binary and kernel space binary

In *Figure 11.1*, the top part shows EL0, which is the user space. In *Chapter 11*, we will look at a binary that runs in user space on a real device. In *Chapter 12*, we will check a binary in the kernel space, which is shown in the lower part of *Figure 11.1*.

In the following section, we will explore the GDB program, which is one of the most commonly used tools for debugging binaries.

Exploring the GDB program

In this section, we will introduce GDB and explain its basic usage, including essential commands. You will also learn about GEF, an extension for GDB.

Introducing GDB

GNU Debugger (**GDB**) is one of the most popular tools for debugging programs. It is used to monitor the internal operations of a process. In real-world projects, many debugging tools are available to inspect memory dumps, register values, and process states. Among these tools, GDB offers several advantages:

- **Open source and free**: GDB is open source, which means it is free for everyone to use. If you are using a Linux distribution such as Ubuntu or Debian, GDB is usually pre-installed. This means anyone can use GDB on devices such as Raspberry Pi or in **Quick Emulator** (**QEMU**). It allows you to analyze user space binaries, inspect registers, and view assembly instructions.

- **Ease of learning other tools**: Once you become familiar with GDB, it becomes easier to learn other debugging tools. Many tools share similar basic features. For example, if you know how to use GDB to inspect a memory dump, you can quickly apply the same skills to other debugging tools such as TRACE32.

- **Widely available and flexible**: GDB can be used in various ways to help with debugging. In real-world projects, when a segmentation fault occurs, a core dump is generated. This core dump file can be opened and analyzed with GDB for debugging.

Next, let's explore two ways to use the GDB program.

Using GDB

Traditionally, GDB has been used for debugging processes directly on a target device. These days, many developers commonly use GDB in two ways:

- **Traditional debugging on the target device**: In this method, GDB runs on the target hardware, such as a Raspberry Pi device. You can debug a program directly as it executes on the device. This is a good approach for beginners who want hands-on experience with debugging real applications.

- **Debugging using a core dump**: The second method involves using GDB with a core dump file. A core dump file is generated when a program crashes, such as during a segmentation fault. This file contains a snapshot of the program's memory at the moment of the crash. By analyzing the core dump with GDB, you can find the cause of the crash without needing to run the program on the real device again. This method is commonly used in real-world projects for crash debugging and fault analysis.

GDB is a powerful tool for debugging crashes and faults in software development.

Running the GDB program

Now, we need to figure out the necessary command to run GDB. First, we will learn about the command to start the GDB program.

Launching GDB

The first step is to launch the GDB program, which you can do in the Linux terminal using the following commands:

- gdb: Launches GDB without loading any debugging or binary file
- gdb program: Starts GDB and loads the specified program file for debugging
- gdb program [core dump]: Launches GDB with the specified program and a core dump file

Setting breakpoints

After launching GDB, the next step is to set breakpoints. You can use the following commands to manage breakpoints in the debugging session:

- break function: Sets a breakpoint at a specific function
- break *address: Sets a breakpoint at a specific memory address
- info breakpoints: Displays a list of all currently set breakpoints in the program
- delete: Removes all breakpoints in the current debugging session

Debugging information commands

When the program hits a breakpoint, it will pause its execution. At this point, you can use additional commands to gather more debugging information:

- p [global variable]: Displays the value of a global variable
- bt: Shows the call stack, which is the sequence of function calls leading to the current point of execution

Inspecting memory contents

To inspect the contents of memory, use the x command, as follows:

```
x/[count][format][size] address
```

This command allows you to examine memory starting from a specified address, with various options to control the output format and size. Components of the x command can be listed as follows:

- count: Specifies the number of memory units to display.
- format: Specifies the output format. Common formats include the following:
  - x: Hexadecimal (default)
  - d: Decimal
  - o: Octal
  - t: Binary
  - c: Character
  - s: String
  - i: Instructions (disassembled)
- size: The unit size that GDB reads from memory.
- address: Specifies the starting memory address to examine.

Now that we have learned about the basic features of GDB, we are ready to move on to the next topic: GEF.

Introducing GEF

Traditionally, GDB has been a widely used tool for monitoring program execution. However, as a command-based debugger, GDB has certain limitations. For this reason, **GDB Enhanced Features (GEF)** is widely used by developers.

In this section, we will explore GEF and understand its advantages.

GEF is an advanced version of the GDB debugger that offers improved **user experience (UX)** features. GEF can monitor instructions and identify potential issues such as stack corruption, stack overflow, and other malfunctions.

To install GEF, you can use the following command in your Linux terminal:

```
$ bash -c "$(curl -fsSL http://gef.blah.cat/sh)"
```

This simple command will install GEF. Since GEF is an extension of GDB, all commands that work in GDB are compatible with GEF. *Figure 11.2* is a screenshot showing GEF running alongside GDB commands:

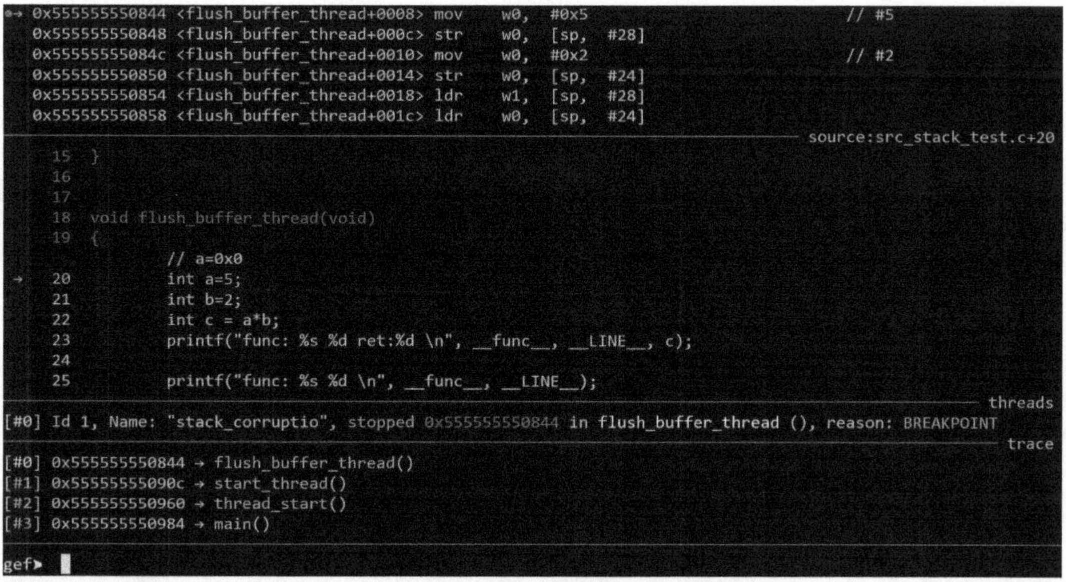

```
0x555555550844 <flush_buffer_thread+0008> mov    w0,  #0x5                            // #5
0x555555550848 <flush_buffer_thread+000c> str    w0,  [sp,  #28]
0x55555555084c <flush_buffer_thread+0010> mov    w0,  #0x2                            // #2
0x555555550850 <flush_buffer_thread+0014> str    w0,  [sp,  #24]
0x555555550854 <flush_buffer_thread+0018> ldr    w1,  [sp,  #28]
0x555555550858 <flush_buffer_thread+001c> ldr    w0,  [sp,  #24]
                                                                     source:src_stack_test.c+20
    15   }
    16
    17
    18   void flush_buffer_thread(void)
    19   {
             // a=0x0
→   20       int a=5;
    21       int b=2;
    22       int c = a*b;
    23       printf("func: %s %d ret:%d \n", __func__, __LINE__, c);
    24
    25       printf("func: %s %d \n", __func__, __LINE__);
                                                                                threads
[#0] Id 1, Name: "stack_corruptio", stopped 0x555555550844 in flush_buffer_thread (), reason: BREAKPOINT
                                                                                  trace
[#0] 0x555555550844 → flush_buffer_thread()
[#1] 0x55555555090c → start_thread()
[#2] 0x555555550960 → thread_start()
[#3] 0x555555550984 → main()

gef➤
```

Figure 11.2: The screenshot of the GEF debugging session

Figure 11.2 displays three key debugging signatures when the software hits a breakpoint at the flush_buffer_thread() function. At the top of *Figure 11.2*, we can observe the assembly instructions that align with the C code. In the middle, the corresponding C code is shown. The lower part displays the call stack. GEF provides these essential debugging signatures on a single screen.

When GEF detects a potentially problematic instruction, it generates a warning message to alert the developer. For this reason, the use of GDB is recommended. Since GDB is one of the most widely used debugging tools, learning about GEF will improve your debugging skills by building on this foundational knowledge.

Now that we have discussed the basics of GDB, let's move to the next topic: virtual address range.

Understanding the virtual address range

To analyze memory content effectively, it is crucial to first understand the virtual address range in the Armv8-A architecture, including how it is structured and how it relates to memory analysis.

Virtual memory system

During dynamic analysis, you may spend a lot of time analyzing memory dumps. A memory dump shows the content of a program's memory at a specific moment, and analyzing it can help you understand how the program works. To find important information, it is important to develop the skill of recognizing patterns in the memory content.

Sometimes, inspecting memory content can be challenging or time-consuming, especially when the source code is not available. What you see are sequences of hexadecimal values in the memory dump. Even though memory content might seem complex, it usually falls into one of the following categories:

- **Process stack**: Represents the active function calls and local variables
- **ASCII code**: Contains readable characters encoded in memory
- **Global variables**: Hold data shared across different parts of the program
- **Machine code**: Represents the instructions

What do we need to know to understand the previous categories of memory content? To analyze memory effectively, we need to understand how virtual memory is configured in the system, particularly from the Armv8-A perspective. The key factors to consider include the following:

- The range of virtual addresses available in the system
- The specific ranges accessible by user space or kernel space

Armv8-A supports three virtual address range configurations, which are as follows:

- VA_39: Utilizes a three-level page table translation
- VA_48: Uses a four-level page table translation
- VA_52: Employs a five-level page table translation

However, it is important to note that modern operating systems typically use either VA_39 or VA_48. The VA_52 configuration is mainly used with large main memory (i.e., 12 TiB or more).

For systems based on VA_39, the virtual address range (page size: 4K) is shown in *Figure 11.3*.

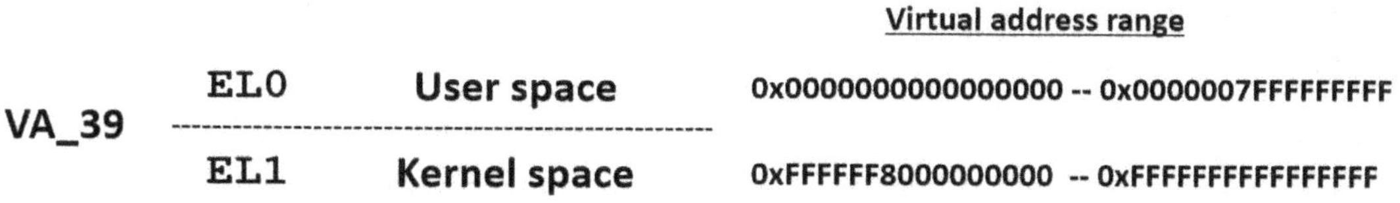

Virtual address range

VA_39	**EL0**	**User space**	0x0000000000000000 -- 0x0000007FFFFFFFFF
	EL1	**Kernel space**	0xFFFFFF8000000000 -- 0xFFFFFFFFFFFFFFFF

Figure 11.3: The address range for VA_39

Similarly, for systems using VA_48, you can find the virtual address range in *Figure 11.4*.

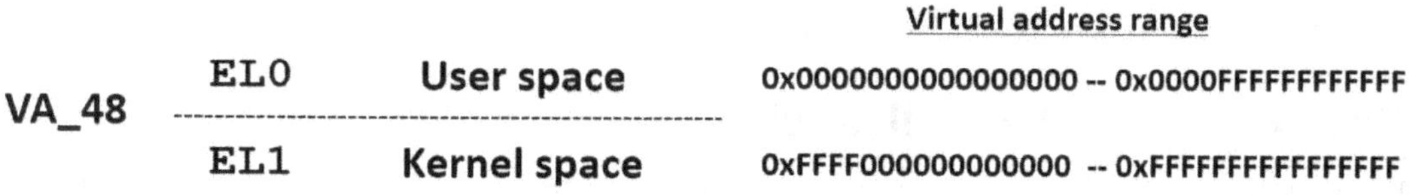

Virtual address range

VA_48	**EL0**	**User space**	0x0000000000000000 -- 0x0000FFFFFFFFFFFF
	EL1	**Kernel space**	0xFFFF000000000000 -- 0xFFFFFFFFFFFFFFFF

Figure 11.4: The address range for VA_48

Understanding these ranges is essential for memory analysis, as it helps you interpret the memory layout of your system.

> **Note**
>
> *Figure 11.3* and *Figure 11.4* illustrate the virtual address ranges accessible by user space and kernel space for better clarity. This book does not delve into the details of page table translation as it is outside the current scope.

Examples of the virtual address pattern

To understand memory content more effectively, let's examine an example of a signature from a memory dump:

```
01  #22 [ffffffc00932bea0] el0t_64_sync_handler at ffffffd174d4da20
02  #23 [ffffffc00932bfe0] el0t_64_sync at ffffffd17421160c
03     PC: 0000007fa528cb20   LR: 0000007fa5237f94   SP: 0000007fc3fc7ad0
04    X29: 0000007fc3fc7ad0  X28: 000000557d72f000  X27: 0000000000000000
05    X26: 000000557d6f5000  X25: 0000007fa5339668  X24: 000000000000000a
...
06     X2: 000000000000000a   X1: 00000055b19f3330   X0: 0000000000000001
07  ORIG_X0: 0000000000000001  SYSCALLNO: 40  PSTATE: 20000000
```

In this example, the output shows a set of general-purpose registers and their corresponding values. On line 03, you can see two virtual addresses: 0x7fa528cb20 and 0x7fa5237f94.

These addresses fall within the user space range, meaning they are being used for program execution at EL0 (user space). The address pattern indicates that the program is actively utilizing these memory locations during its execution.

This skill is especially valuable during dynamic analysis, where interpreting memory addresses can reveal critical details about program execution, potential vulnerabilities, or unexpected behavior.

Analyzing stack memory content

In this section, we will analyze the call stack and stack dump using GDB. We will also discuss vulnerabilities that occur when the stack is corrupted.

Understanding the call stack

How can the execution flow of a process be represented? In many cases, it is represented by the **call stack**. You can view the call stack in the GDB program, and it can also be found in various logs. However, the call stack is a high-level view. To fully understand how the call stack is printed, you need to understand the patterns of the binary data stored in the stack.

You can view the call stack using the **backtrace** (bt) command in GDB. How does GDB display the call stack? Here's how GDB displays the call stack via the bt command, broken down as follows:

1. GDB reads the data stored in the stack area.

2. GDB parses it according to the **Arm Architecture Procedure Call Standard (AAPCS)**.

3. GDB displays the call stack.

To better understand how the call stack is represented, we need to analyze the data in the stack area more closely. Let's now take a look at *Figure 11.5* to examine the call stack and stack dump:

```
gef➤ bt
#0  flush_buffer_thread ()
#1  0x000055555555090c in start_thread ()
#2  0x0000555555550960 in thread_start ()
#3  0x0000555555550984 in main ()

gef➤  x/40ga 0x7ffffffff2f0
0x7ffffffff2f0: 0x7ffffffff310   0x55555555090c <start_thread+96>
0x7ffffffff300: 0x20       0x0
0x7ffffffff310: 0x7ffffffff330   0x555555550960 <thread_start+72>
0x7ffffffff320: 0x3f7f9134c      0x500000002
0x7ffffffff330: 0x7ffffffff350   0x555555550984 <main+24>
0x7ffffffff340: 0x7ffff4e8        0x500000002
0x7ffffffff350: 0x7ffffffff360   0x7ffff7e17740 <__libc_start_call_main+112>
0x7ffffffff360: 0x7ffffffff470   0x7ffff7e17818 <__libc_start_main_impl+152>
```

Figure 11.5: The call stack and stack memory contents

At the top of *Figure 11.5*, you can see the call stack. At the bottom, the memory content of the stack area is shown. Tools such as GEF read this memory content to show the call stack to developers.

Let's take a closer look at a memory dump with a different memory layout, as illustrated in *Figure 11.6*:

```
      Address              Data
0x7ffffffff2f0:  0x7ffffffff310  [1]
0x7ffffffff2f8:  0x55555555090c  → start_thread + 0x60
0x7ffffffff300:  0x20
0x7ffffffff308:  0x0
0x7ffffffff310:  0x7ffffffff330  [2]          gef➤ bt
0x7ffffffff318:  0x555555550960  → thread_start + 0x48   #0  flush_buffer_thread ()
0x7ffffffff320:  0x3f7f9134c                  #1  0x000055555555090c in start_thread ()
0x7ffffffff328:  0x500000002                  #2  0x0000555555550960 in thread_start ()
0x7ffffffff330:  0x7ffffffff350  [3]          #3  0x0000555555550984 in main ()
0x7ffffffff338:  0x555555550984  → main + 0x18
0x7ffffffff340:  0x7fffff4e8
0x7ffffffff348:  0x500000002
0x7ffffffff350:  0x7ffffffff360
0x7ffffffff358:  0x7ffff7e17740
0x7ffffffff360:  0x7ffffffff470
```

Figure 11.6: A memory dump with a call stack in another memory layout

You can notice specific patterns and rules within the memory structure. First, let's look at the section marked **[1]**. By observing the boxes and the direction of the arrows, you can see the location of the previous stack address. In addition, the return address is stored at an offset of +8 from the address where the previous stack address is located.

Next, focus on the sections labeled **[2]** and **[3]**. These sections also contain the previous stack addresses and their corresponding return addresses, following a similar pattern. This way, the GDB tool generates the call stack by analyzing and interpreting the data that has been pushed into the stack area.

You can observe how the previous stack address and return address are pushed onto the stack. But which assembly instructions perform this operation? Let's take a closer look at the beginning of the flush_buffer_thread() function:

```
gef➤   disas 0x555555550844
Dump of assembler code for function flush_buffer_thread:
   0x000055555555083c <+0>:      stp x29, x30, [sp, #-32]!
   0x0000555555550840 <+4>:      mov x29, sp
```

Let's analyze the instruction at the 0x000055555555083c address, which is the entry address of the flush_buffer_thread() function. This instruction pushes the values of the x30 register (which holds the return address) and the x29 register (which acts as the frame pointer) onto the stack.

A similar pattern can be seen in the assembly instructions at the start of other functions, where key register values are stored on the stack for later use. This process follows the rules defined by the AAPCS, which ensures that subroutines can be called independently on different Arm-based systems.

Debugging a corrupted stack

Understanding how registers such as x30 and x29 are saved and restored is essential for debugging and analyzing program behavior. Let's explore this scenario further:

```
gef➤  bt
Backtrace stopped: previous frame inner to this frame (corrupt stack?)
                                                       Corrupted
0x7ffffffff2f0: 0x0000ffffffffffff 0x0000ffffffffffff   0x7ffffffff2f0: 0x00007ffffffff310 0x000055555555090c
0x7ffffffff300: 0x0000000000000020 0x0000000000000000   0x7ffffffff300: 0x0000000000000020 0x0000000000000000
0x7ffffffff310: 0x00007ffffffff330 0x0000555555550960   0x7ffffffff310: 0x00007ffffffff330 0x0000555555550960
0x7ffffffff320: 0x00000003f7f9134c 0x0000000500000002   0x7ffffffff320: 0x00000003f7f9134c 0x0000000500000002
0x7ffffffff330: 0x00007ffffffff350 0x0000555555550984   0x7ffffffff330: 0x00007ffffffff350 0x0000555555550984
0x7ffffffff340: 0x00000007fffff4e8 0x0000000500000002   0x7ffffffff340: 0x00000007fffff4e8 0x0000000500000002
0x7ffffffff350: 0x00007ffffffff360 0x00007ffff7e17740   0x7ffffffff350: 0x00007ffffffff360 0x00007ffff7e17740
0x7ffffffff360: 0x00007ffffffff470 0x00007ffff7e17818   0x7ffffffff360: 0x00007ffffffff470 0x00007ffff7e17818
              (After)                                                    (Before)
```

Figure 11.7: The memory dump for a corrupted stack

Figure 11.7 shows an example of stack corruption:

- On the left side, the stack memory contents are corrupted with a value of 0xffffffffffff
- On the right side, the stack memory contents are shown before the corruption occurred

Why does stack memory corruption happen? Stack corruption can occur in the following common scenarios:

- Writing invalid data to the stack area.
- Loading corrupted data into registers such as X30 (link register) and X29 (frame pointer register).
- Executing the ret instruction, which copies the corrupted value from X30 into the **program counter** (**PC**). For example, if the corrupted value in X30 is 0xffffffffffff (an invalid address that does not belong to the code area), the **Memory Management Unit** (**MMU**) will trigger a fault because the address is not valid. As a result, we can observe the segmentation fault.

When stack corruption occurs, debugging tools such as GDB cannot display the correct call stack. This is because GDB parses the data in the stack area to reconstruct the call stack.

> **Note**
>
> In some cases, you can use advanced debugging tools such as TRACE32 to restore the registers to their correct state before the corruption occurred. This process involves manually setting the registers according to the AAPCS.

So far, we have examined the call stack along with its corresponding stack memory contents. We also observed that the call stack cannot be displayed correctly when the stack is corrupted.

Now, let's look at another signature where the call stack cannot be printed. The following example shows that the GDB program cannot display the correct call stack due to stack corruption (sourced from https://stackoverflow.com/questions/9809810/gdb-corrupted-stack-frame-how-to-debug):

```
Program received signal SIGSEGV, Segmentation fault.
0x00000002 in ?? ()
(gdb) bt
#0  0x00000002 in ?? ()
#1  0x00000001 in ?? ()
#2  0xbffff284 in ?? ()
Backtrace stopped: previous frame inner to this frame (corrupt stack?)
(gdb)
```

At the end of the output, you can see the message (`corrupt stack?`). This indicates that the debugging tool cannot properly display the call stack due to stack corruption.

If the stack is corrupted, how can software developers debug the issue? One effective approach is to analyze the memory dump in the stack area. This can be done by following these steps:

1. Inspect the data in the stack area according to the AAPCS.

2. Identify any corrupted data in the stack.

3. Restore the call stack to its state before the corruption occurred.

By using this method, we can restore the call stack before the stack gets corrupted. This helps developers find the root cause of the problem.

A common example of stack corruption involves deliberately performing an out-of-bound memory copy operation. Consider the following scenario:

```
void function() {
    char data[8];
    memcpy(data, input, 16); //Intentional out-of-bound copy
}
```

Here, the data array has a size of 8 bytes, but the code attempts to copy 16 bytes into it. Since data is a local variable, it resides in the stack memory. As a result, this operation corrupts the stack.

To understand when a segmentation fault or exception occurs, we need to examine the following assembly instructions:

```
01 ldp x29, x30, [SP], #0x10
02 ret
```

These instructions are typically executed at the end of a function:

- Line 01: The x29 (frame pointer) and x30 (link register) registers are updated with values from the corrupted stack.
- Line 02: The ret instruction copies the value in x30 to the PC. For instance, if x30 contains 0xffffffffff, this value is updated to the PC. Since 0xffffffffff is not a valid address, the program crashes.

Exploiting stack corruption

In the previous example, the address holding the frame pointer and return address is shown as 0x0000ffffffffffff. However, if the address containing the return address is corrupted, the Arm core will branch to the modified address after reading data from the stack area.

```
                                        Corrupted
0x7ffffffff2f0: 0x00007ffffffff310 0x0000555555555ddd0    0x7ffffffff2f0: 0x00007ffffffff310 0x000005555555509c
0x7ffffffff300: 0x0000000000000020 0x0000000000000000    0x7ffffffff300: 0x0000000000000020 0x0000000000000000
0x7ffffffff310: 0x00007ffffffff330 0x0000555555550960    0x7ffffffff310: 0x00007ffffffff330 0x0000555555550960
0x7ffffffff320: 0x00000003f7f9134c 0x0000000500000002    0x7ffffffff320: 0x00000003f7f9134c 0x0000000500000002
0x7ffffffff330: 0x00007ffffffff350 0x0000555555550984    0x7ffffffff330: 0x00007ffffffff350 0x0000555555550984
0x7ffffffff340: 0x00000007fffff4e8 0x0000000500000002    0x7ffffffff340: 0x00000007fffff4e8 0x0000000500000002
0x7ffffffff350: 0x00007ffffffff360 0x00007ffff7e17740    0x7ffffffff350: 0x00007ffffffff360 0x00007ffff7e17740
0x7ffffffff360: 0x00007ffffffff470 0x00007ffff7e17818    0x7ffffffff360: 0x00007ffffffff470 0x00007ffff7e17818
              (After)                                                   (Before)
```

Figure 11.8: The memory dump for a corrupted stack with another pattern

On the right side of *Figure 11.8*, you can see that the original return address is 0x000055555555090c. However, an attacker deliberately corrupts the stack area by writing 0x000055555555ddd0. As a result, the PC is branched to 0x000055555555ddd0.

At this corrupted address (0x000055555555ddd0), the attacker places malicious code. This code could perform actions such as privilege escalation or system attacks.

This technique is commonly used by attackers to execute specific functions without explicitly calling them in the C code.

How to identify stack corruption

In real-world projects, identifying the root cause of stack corruption can be challenging, especially when analyzing logs or memory dumps. The main reason is that logs often do not contain the exact signature or message indicating when the stack corruption occurs.

This section introduces a debugging method designed to narrow down the source of stack corruption.

Introducing the debugging patch

Here is an example of debugging code designed for AArch64 (64-bit) in Armv8-A:

```
#define GET_SP_REGISTER_DEBUG() \
    debug_sp_register()

unsigned long sp_value;
unsigned long lr_value;

static inline void debug_sp_register(void)
{
    asm volatile ("mov %0, sp\n" \
                  "mov %1, x30" \
                  : "=r" (sp_value), "=r" (lr_value));

    printf("sp: 0x%lx, x30: 0x%lx \n", sp_value, lr_value);

    printf("[0x%lx]: 0x%lx \n", (unsigned long)sp_value, *((unsigned
long*)(sp_value + 0x0)));
    printf("[0x%lx]: 0x%lx \n", (unsigned long)(sp_value + 0x8),
*((unsigned long*)(sp_value + 0x8)));
```

```
    printf("[0x%lx]: 0x%lx \n", (unsigned long)(sp_value + 0x10),
*((unsigned long*)(sp_value + 0x10)));
}
```

The most important part of this code is the following assembly code block:

```
asm volatile ("mov %0, sp\n" \
              "mov %1, x30" \
              : "=r" (sp_value), "=r" (lr_value));
```

This block of instructions stores the values of the **stack pointer** (**SP**) and the link register (X30) into the sp_value and lr_value global variables.

In the next line, these values are displayed using the printf function:

```
printf("sp: 0x%lx, x30: 0x%lx \n", sp_value, lr_value);
```

The latter part of the code accesses the stack memory to read and display its contents:

```
    printf("[0x%lx]: 0x%lx \n", (unsigned long)sp_value, *((unsigned
long*)(sp_value + 0x0)));
    printf("[0x%lx]: 0x%lx \n", (unsigned long)(sp_value + 0x8),
*((unsigned long*)(sp_value + 0x8)));
    printf("[0x%lx]: 0x%lx \n", (unsigned long)(sp_value + 0x10),
*((unsigned long*)(sp_value + 0x10)));
```

This code uses the printf() function to display data stored at specific stack addresses, allowing developers to analyze the stack contents during debugging.

How to use the stack debugging code

At this point, you might wonder where the GET_SP_REGISTER_DEBUG() macro function should be added.

To use the code we discussed in the previous subsection, you can simply add the GET_SP_REGISTER_ DEBUG() macro before calling a function that is suspected of corrupting the stack. We will explain this further by analyzing the following example code:

```
int add_func(int x, int y)
{
    int result = x + y;

    GET_SP_REGISTER_DEBUG();
```

```
    suspicious_stack_corruption();
    printf("x: %d, y: %d \n", x, y);

    return result;
}
```

Let's suppose that the `suspicious_stack_corruption` function is suspected of causing stack corruption. Add the `GET_SP_REGISTER_DEBUG()` macro right before the line where this function is called.

By adding this macro, you can see a message in the terminal output. This message includes the stack pointer address and the stack memory contents, helping you analyze the state of the stack during debugging.

The following is an example of the log in the terminal:

```
01 sp: 0x7fe564d940 lr: 0x556b5a0b48
02 [0x7fe564d940]: 0x7fe564d960
03 [0x7fe564d948]: 0x556b5a0b48
04 [0x7fe564d950]: 0x6b5a0720
```

The memory dump can be analyzed in the following ways:

- Line `01`: The `sp` is at address `0x7fe564d940`, and the link register (`x30`) holds the value of `0x556b5a0b48`.

- Lines `02-04`: These lines display the data stored at specific stack addresses. For instance, at address `0x7fe564d948`, the value of `0x556b5a0b48` is stored.

A common question is: What happens if the stack is corrupted? If the `suspicious_stack_corruption()` function causes the stack to be corrupted, the output will not be displayed. Instead, a segmentation fault will occur immediately, and the program will stop.

The debugging code introduced in this section can be applied to real-world projects to efficiently detect stack corruption. By adding the `GET_SP_REGISTER_DEBUG()` code, as shown in this section, you can quickly identify and fix issues related to stack integrity.

Mitigation method

To reduce the risk of the PC branching to an address in the stack area, you should enable the address randomization feature. This feature ensures that the address of each function changes every time an application is loaded. By doing so, attackers find it much harder to predict the location of specific functions.

Keep in mind that applications are executed by the loader in the operating system, and many compilers offer options to enable address randomization. It is highly recommended to use the address randomization option whenever possible during development. It is a simple yet effective method to improve the security of your project.

In the next section, we will explore another type of analysis: executing a function without directly calling it in C code.

Return-oriented programming analysis

Return-oriented programming (ROP) is a commonly used technique to execute a specific function without directly calling it in C code. This method is often exploited in security attacks by corrupting the stack area with specific addresses to redirect execution flow.

Key concept of ROP

Consider the following assembly snippet:

```
01 ldp x30, x29, [sp]
02 ret
```

When the ret instruction is executed, the PC is updated with the value stored in the x30 register. This is because the ret instruction copies the return address from x30 into the PC, branching execution to the specified address.

This section provides an example of how a function can be executed without explicitly calling it in the source code. The following shows the content of the example code:

```
#include <signal.h>
#include <stdio.h>

__attribute__((noreturn)) void call_empty() {
    printf("call_empty() called!\n");
}

void sig_handler(int signum) {
    printf("Signal handler called!\n");
    call_empty();
}

void secret_execution(void) {
```

```
        printf("secret_execution called!\n");
}

int main() {
    signal(SIGINT, sig_handler);
    printf("About to raise the signal.\n");
    raise(SIGINT); // Triggers the handler

    printf("Complete: Signal handler executed.\n");
    return 0;
}
```

Let's break down the preceding example code. The actions performed by the example code can be summarized in two tasks:

- The `signal()` function registers the `sig_handler()` function as the handler for the `SIGINT` signal

- When the `SIGINT` signal is raised, the `sig_handler()` function is invoked

Interestingly, when you run this code, the `secret_execution()` function is called, even though there is no explicit call to it in the source code.

What happens if you compile and run the example code provided in this section? The terminal will display the message repeatedly, as follows:

```
secret_execution called!
secret_execution called!
...
secret_execution called!
```

> **Note**
>
> The preceding code was tested on a Raspberry Pi. If you run the same code on another distribution, such as Fedora, it may show an error message once and then cause a segmentation fault.

To understand more, let's analyze the body of the sig_handler function that seems to call the call_empty function:

```
gef➤  disas sig_handler
Dump of assembler code for function sig_handler:
   0x0000555555550850 <+0>:       stp      x29, x30, [sp, #-32]!
   ...
   0x0000555555550864 <+20>:      bl       0x555555550680 <puts@plt>
   0x0000555555550868 <+24>:      bl       0x555555550830 <call_empty>

gef➤  disas secret_execution
Dump of assembler code for function secret_execution:
   0x000055555555086c <+0>:       stp      x29, x30, [sp, #-16]!
   0x0000555555550870 <+4>:       mov      x29, sp
```

As you can see, the sig_handler function ends with bl 0x555555550830 <call_empty>, located at address 0x0000555555550868. When this instruction is executed, X30 is updated to 0x000055555555086c. This happens because the bl (**branch with link**) instruction updates the return address.

Once the call_empty function completes, it executes the following instructions to return, with the return address set to 0x000055555555086c:

```
0x0000555555550848 <+24>:      ldp     x29, x30, [sp], #16
0x000055555555084c <+28>:      ret
```

Let's refer to *Figure 11.9* to understand the execution flow:

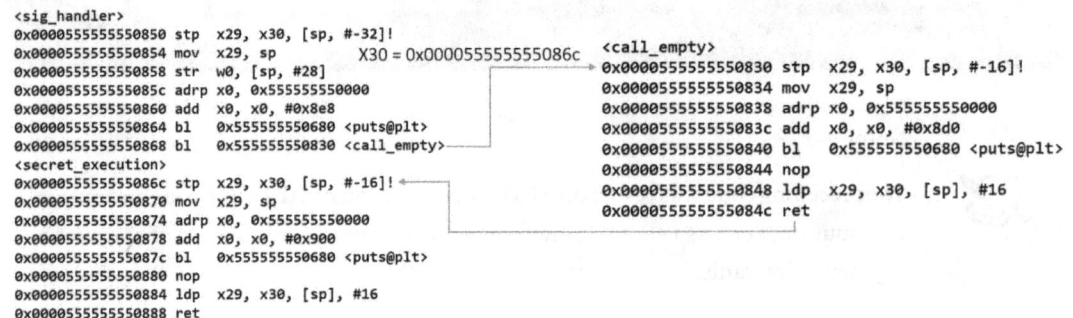

```
<sig_handler>
0x0000555555550850 stp  x29, x30, [sp, #-32]!
0x0000555555550854 mov  x29, sp          X30 = 0x000055555555086c  <call_empty>
0x0000555555550858 str  w0, [sp, #28]                             0x0000555555550830 stp  x29, x30, [sp, #-16]!
0x000055555555085c adrp x0, 0x555555550000                        0x0000555555550834 mov  x29, sp
0x0000555555550860 add  x0, x0, #0x8e8                            0x0000555555550838 adrp x0, 0x555555550000
0x0000555555550864 bl   0x555555550680 <puts@plt>                0x000055555555083c add  x0, x0, #0x8d0
0x0000555555550868 bl   0x555555550830 <call_empty>              0x0000555555550840 bl   0x555555550680 <puts@plt>
<secret_execution>                                               0x0000555555550844 nop
0x000055555555086c stp  x29, x30, [sp, #-16]!                    0x0000555555550848 ldp  x29, x30, [sp], #16
0x0000555555550870 mov  x29, sp                                  0x000055555555084c ret
0x0000555555550874 adrp x0, 0x555555550000
0x0000555555550878 add  x0, x0, #0x900
0x000055555555087c bl   0x555555550680 <puts@plt>
0x0000555555550880 nop
0x0000555555550884 ldp  x29, x30, [sp], #16
0x0000555555550888 ret
```

Figure 11.9: The execution flow of how the secret_execution function is called

A common question is: Why is X30 updated to 0x000055555555086c? This happens because the call_empty() function is declared with the __attribute__((noreturn)) keyword. When a function is declared with this keyword, it informs the compiler that this function will not return to its caller. As a result, the compiler does not generate a ret instruction at the end of the sig_handler() function.

Instead, the return address 0x000055555555086c is set, which is the starting address of the secret_execution() function. This is why the secret_execution() function is called.

Using compiler options to prevent this symptom

We saw how compiler attributes, such as noreturn, can change the execution flow in ways you might not expect. If the secret_execution() function includes dangerous or sensitive actions, it could be a potential security threat.

To avoid these situations, it is recommended to take the following steps:

- Carefully read compiler warnings and messages.
- Use compiler options that help find problems with attributes.
- Test unusual cases to make sure the program works safely and as expected.
- Apply the latest security features, such as PAC, BTI, or MTE, to your system. These features will be explained in *Chapter 15*.

If you first glance at the example code with analysis in this section, you might think that this is just a small and simple example code for practice. But remember, simple examples are often used to help you understand bigger ideas. In this case, the idea of changing the value in X30 can also be used in more advanced ways in real-world programs. The following is an example code:

```
ldr x5, =another_return_address
mov x30, x5
ret
```

When you add this code to any assembly routine, the program will return to the address labeled another_return_address.

In the following section, let's explore another type of memory corruption that can often be found in real-world projects.

Memory corruption: buffer overflow case study

Let's suppose that a variable in your program suddenly has an unexpected value, even though there is no code that sets it to that value. When this kind of issue happens, it can be difficult to troubleshoot.

If this happens accidentally, it is considered a **bug** in your program. However, if memory corruption is caused intentionally using malicious techniques, it is referred to as an **exploit**.

Introducing the example code

Let's start analyzing the memory corruption symptom by looking at the following example code:

```
unsigned int task_state;
void set_task_state(unsigned int new_state) {
    task_state = new_state;
}
```

This code looks simple. The set_task_state function is used to update the task_state global variable. Let's assume that the set_task_state function is only designed to handle two valid states, defined as follows:

```
#define TASK_STATE_SLEEP 0
#define TASK_STATE_RUN 1
```

If you inspect the task_state global variable using GEF, you can identify the value:

```
gef➤  p task_state
$2 = 0x1
```

However, one day, you discover that the task_state global variable has a value of 0xfefe:

```
gef➤  p task_state
$2 = 0xfefe
```

You might find this situation surprising or confusing because there is no routine in the code that directly calls the set_task_state() function with the value of 0xfefe.

Debugging with a patch

If you face a similar issue in a real project, it is a good practice to create a debugging patch to gather more information about the unexpected behavior. For instance, you can modify the set_task_state function by adding a conditional statement, as follows:

```
void set_task_state(unsigned int new_state) {
    if (!(task_state == TASK_STATE_SLEEP ||
          task_state == TASK_STATE_RUN)) {
        abort();
    }
    task_state = new_state;
}
```

The purpose of the patch can be summarized as follows:

- Check the value of task_state: The patch compares the current value of the task_state global variable with expected values, such as TASK_STATE_SLEEP or TASK_STATE_RUN.

- Handle unexpected values: If the value does not match the expected ones, the call to the abort() function is made. This triggers a segmentation fault, which helps identify the issue during debugging.

By applying this patch, you can detect exactly when the task_state variable is assigned an invalid value. This method is useful for isolating and analyzing unexpected behavior in your code.

> **Note**
>
> The abort() function is widely used in Linux system programming to stop a program when an error is detected. In addition, the core dump is generated after the abort() function completes its execution.

After applying the patch, you may notice that a segmentation fault occurs. By loading the core dump file into GDB, you can check the task_state global variable using the following command:

```
gef➤  p task_state
$2 = 0xfefe
```

Here, you can identify that the task_state global variable contains an unexpected 0xfefe value. To gather more details, you can check the memory address of the task_state global variable:

```
gef➤  p &task_state
$1 = (unsigned int *) 0x555555570070 <task_state>
```

You can see that the address of the task_state variable is 0x555555570070.

Next, you can check the memory content near this address by using the `x/10x 0x555555570060` command:

```
gef➤   x/10x 0x555555570060
0x555555570060 <stream_buffer>: 0xf2a317dc      0xfffefffe      0xfefffffff      0xf2f1feff
0x555555570070 <task_state>:    0x0000fefe      0x00000000      0x00000000      0x00000000
```

Figure 11.10: The memory content around the task_state variable

By analyzing the memory addresses at 0x5555555700760 and 0x5555555700770, you may observe another signature. As you can see in *Figure 11.10*, the stream_buffer symbol appears before the task_state variable. The stream_buffer symbol contains data such as 0xfffe and 0xfeff. These values are similar to the 0xfefe pattern found in the task_state variable.

Since the stream_buffer symbol is identified, the next step is to check where this symbol is located in memory:

```
char stream_buffer[BUFF_SIZE];
unsigned int task_state;
void set_task_state(unsigned int new_state) {
    task_state = new_state;
}
```

After reviewing the code, we can see that the stream_buffer[] array is declared before the task_state global variable. By combining the memory dump signature with the code review findings, we can strongly suspect that a buffer overflow has occurred in the stream_buffer[] array.

From this pattern, we can speculate that the overflow from stream_buffer[] might overwrite the value of the task_state variable. *Figure 11.11* shows how memory corruption can happen due to a buffer overflow in the stream_buffer[] array:

```
gef➤   x/30x 0x555555570040
0x555555570060 <stream_buffer>: 0xf2a317dc      0xfffefffe      0xfefffffff      0xf2f1feff
0x555555570070 <task_state>:    0x0000fefe      0x00000000      0x00000000      0x00000000
```

	Address	Data
<stream_buffer>	0x555555570060	0xf2a317dc
	0x555555570064	0xfffefffe
	0x555555570068	0xfefffffff
	0x55555557006C	0xf2f1feff
<task_state>	0x555555570070	0x0000fefe
	0x555555570074	0x00000000

<Memory dump>

Figure 11.11: The memory content as a result of the stream_buffer overflow

The overflow of `stream_buffer` corrupts the data of `task_state`. What we have analyzed is called a **buffer overflow**. It is one of the most common causes of memory corruption in C programming.

What kind of code causes a buffer overflow? A buffer overflow happens when the code writes data beyond the allocated size of a buffer. This often occurs during a copy operation. For example, if you define a buffer and then copy data into it that is larger than the buffer size, a buffer overflow will happen.

Even with extensive analysis, sometimes it can be challenging to identify the routine that corrupts the `stream_buffer` buffer.

Buffer overflow over multiple layers: case study

In real-world systems, many different devices and modules frequently communicate across multiple software layers using buffers. Buffers processed in one software layer can sometimes cause buffer overflows in another layer, especially when multiple layers interact through shared buffers.

In a Linux system, buffers declared in user space can also be accessed from kernel space. For example, memory copy operations can be performed in kernel space. A common question is: What API is used to write values to a buffer in user space from kernel space?

The answer is the `copy_to_user()` function in the Linux kernel.

Buffer overflow from another software layer

When the `copy_to_user` function runs in the Linux kernel, it may modify the contents of the `stream_buffer` buffer. This operation is illustrated in *Figure 11.12*.

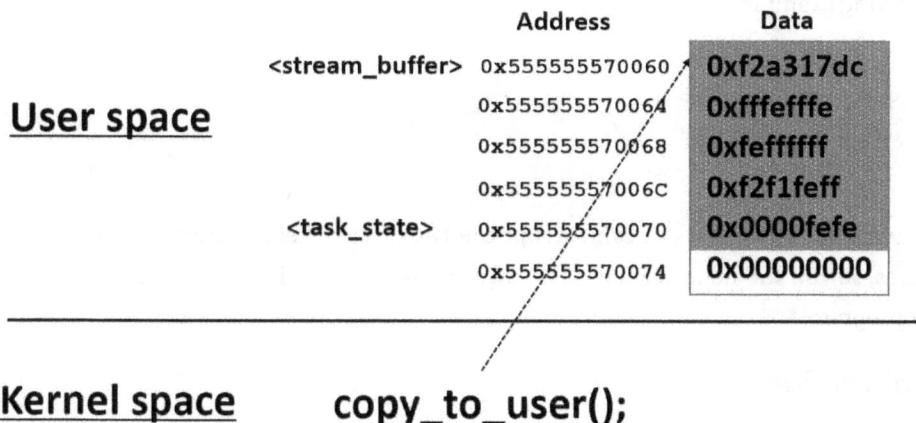

Figure 11.12: The case study of memory corruption

The memory copy operation on stream_buffer may be performed using the copy_to_user function in the Linux kernel. If a buffer overflow occurs during the execution of the copy_to_user function, it may corrupt the data in the stream_buffer[] array.

The buffer size used for the memory copy operation must match in both the user space and kernel space. If the sizes do not match, it may cause a buffer overflow.

The issue of memory corruption is one of the most challenging problems for software engineers. Here is another scenario to consider:

- In user space, a buffer is allocated to handle data for four cores
- In kernel space, this buffer is used for eight cores
- If the code writes to a user space buffer for the fifth or sixth core in the kernel, a buffer overflow can be caused by kernel space

This mismatch can lead to memory corruption. Debugging such issues is particularly challenging when buffers are managed across multiple layers, especially when third-party libraries or components are involved.

Even with thorough code reviews, debugging memory corruption often takes significant time and effort. In real-world projects, developers may spend hours—or even days—identifying the root cause of an issue.

Buffer overflow in a struct

Memory corruption is not limited to global variables; it can also affect fields in a struct. Consider the following example:

```
struct data_handle {
    char stream[BUF_SIZE];
    unsigned int task_state;
};
```

If the stream field overflows, it can corrupt the task_state field. Many C programs use struct structures, so you should also keep this kind of pattern in mind when a buffer overflow occurs in your program.

The mitigation method

Memory corruption, particularly buffer overflows, is dangerous because attackers can exploit it to manipulate memory and execute malicious code. How to protect your program? Let's now discuss methods to prevent memory corruption:

- **Always check the bounds of your buffers**: Use modern compiler features, such as stack protection.

- **Buffer overflow can be caused by a library**: Sometimes, the source of memory corruption is not your code but a library function. In this case, we need to make another plan for debugging this symptom.

- **Using debugging patches**: Debugging patches are practical tools for identifying memory corruption. You are recommended to add a useful debug patch to identify the conditions that trigger segmentation faults.

In real-world projects, issues related to memory corruption are often considered challenging. However, by applying these methods, you can identify the root cause of memory corruption with less difficulty.

Summary

In this chapter, you learned about the basics of dynamic analysis. First, we explained the main benefits of dynamic analysis and also discussed its limitations. Understanding these ideas helps you apply dynamic analysis effectively in real-world projects.

Next, we delve into the basic steps of dynamic analysis, focusing on analyzing user space binaries on a real target device. You also learned about key commands for using GDB, a widely used and open source debugging tool. Additionally, we introduced GEF, the extension for GDB. By practicing with GDB and GEF, you can improve your debugging skills and analyze programs more effectively.

We also explored memory corruption issues, including examples of stack corruption, ROP, and memory corruption related to global variables. These problems can happen in real projects and are often difficult for software developers. You might feel confused or surprised if you face a similar memory corruption issue discussed in this chapter. But once you understand the case studies, you can resolve similar issues in an effective way.

Now that you have a good understanding of this chapter, let's move to the next topic: advanced dynamic analysis.

Join our community on Discord

Join our community's Discord space for discussions with the authors and other readers: `https://packt.link/embeddedsystems`

12

Expert Techniques in Advanced Dynamic Analysis

In this chapter, we will analyze the kernel binary using dynamic analysis. We will do this by debugging important data structures and identifying magic values.

The key topics covered in this chapter are as follows:

- Introducing advanced dynamic analysis
- vmcore and the Crash utility
- Stack area of the process
- Tracking the start address for a struct using the address
- Identifying a structure using a function pointer

First, we will explain what advanced dynamic analysis is and how it is used to analyze the kernel binary. Next, we will introduce the Crash utility, a widely used debugging tool for analyzing Linux kernel memory dumps. Next, we will learn how to examine the stack area, where process execution data is stored. Additionally, we will learn how to trace the starting addresses of frequently used functions in the Linux kernel.

By the end of this chapter, you will have improved your debugging skills in kernel binary analysis, including identifying function entry addresses and structures using the Crash utility.

Let's begin by discussing what dynamic analysis is and why it is important for kernel debugging.

Technical requirements

All the code examples for this chapter can be found on GitHub at `https://github.com/PacktPublishing/Reverse-Engineering-Armv8-A-Systems`.

Introducing advanced dynamic analysis

In this section, we will introduce advanced dynamic analysis and discuss the kernel binary that will be analyzed. We will also learn how to debug the kernel binary and explore different types of kernel binaries. In addition, we will explain how to use the Crash utility, which is a debugging tool for analyzing kernel memory.

What is advanced dynamic analysis?

Advanced dynamic analysis means analyzing a running kernel binary on a real device. In this book, we use this term to describe the process of debugging a kernel binary while it is executing on actual hardware.

Figure 12.1 shows the relevant software layer on the kernel binary.

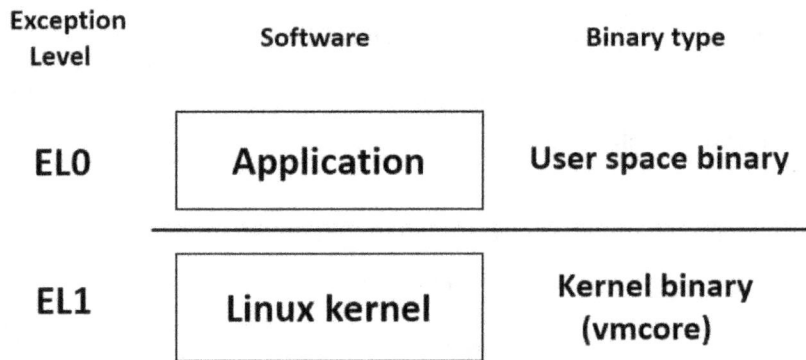

Exception Level	Software	Binary type
ELO	Application	User space binary
EL1	Linux kernel	Kernel binary (vmcore)

Figure 12.1: The kernel binary and software stack

In *Figure 12.1*, you can see the kernel binary (vmcore) that will be analyzed in this chapter. This type of analysis is important because it helps us observe execution flows that cannot be fully understood through static analysis alone.

When analyzing a kernel statically, we only examine the code or object file without running it. In real situations, however, the kernel may behave differently because of hardware behavior, task scheduling, and runtime conditions.

Debugging program for kernel debugging

Now that we understand advanced dynamic analysis, let's explore some commonly used debugging tools for analyzing the kernel binary.

When debugging a kernel binary, how does it differ from debugging a user-space binary? To debug a kernel binary, the software must be executed on an actual target device or an emulator. While different debugging tools offer various features, the general debugging process follows these steps:

1. Set breakpoints at a specific function or address in the code.
2. Execute the software.
3. Analyze the program when execution stops at a breakpoint.

When debugging a kernel binary, several debugging tools are required. Here are three widely used debugging tools for kernel analysis:

- **TRACE32**: A widely used debugger in embedded development. It supports debugging from the bootloader to the Linux kernel. Many embedded software developers use TRACE32 to monitor internal behavior during runtime. By setting breakpoints at kernel addresses, developers can inspect memory contents, the call stack, and local variables. However, TRACE32 is not free to use because it requires a license. Also, the device must have a built-in JTAG interface to connect with the TRACE32 debugger.

- **Quick Emulator (QEMU)**: Open source software that lets one computer system run another system. It is often used to test software without using real hardware. Many software developers use QEMU to test or run Linux on virtual machines, such as Armv8-A or RISC-V systems.

- **Crash utility**: The Crash utility is used for analyzing vmcore files, which contain kernel binary data, for debugging purposes. By using the Crash utility, developers can inspect kernel memory, analyze crashes, and debug kernel-related issues. More details about the Crash utility will be provided in the next section.

These debugging tools are commonly used for dynamic analysis on kernel binaries.

So far, we have explored advanced binary analysis and introduced several debugging tools. Now, we are ready to move to the next topic—analyzing the kernel binary vmcore file using the Crash utility.

vmcore and the Crash utility

In this section, we will discuss different debugging approaches in more detail. Additionally, we will examine vmcore files and how to use the Crash utility to analyze them effectively.

Debugging approaches for the kernel binary

In system software development, there are two widely used methods of debugging:

- **Online debugging**: This method involves running the program on the actual target device. Breakpoints are set, and when the software executes, the breakpoint halts the execution. At this point, debugging is performed. This method requires setting up the debugging tools and directly running the target device.

- **Offline debugging**: This method involves debugging a memory dump extracted from the actual target device. Many chipset developers use this approach to analyze system crashes and unexpected behavior. In Linux, developers can enable a feature called KDUMP to generate a memory dump (vmcore) when a crash occurs. This memory dump captures a snapshot of the kernel's memory at the moment of the crash, allowing developers to examine the system state and identify the cause of the fault or crash.

In real-world projects, we often need to analyze how the kernel operates while running software on a device. In this book, we refer to this approach as **online debugging**.

However, sometimes setting up online debugging can be time-consuming. It requires a physical device and the proper configuration of debugging tools. In some cases, this setup might take much time, especially when dealing with large-scale systems or remote environments. To overcome these challenges, developers often use a different technique called **memory dump debugging**, which is used for offline debugging.

In many situations, analyzing a memory dump is more practical than using the online debugging method. Let's use an example to understand why.

Let's suppose that an automotive navigation system crashes. In this case, it is important to debug the problem efficiently. Instead of performing debugging on the actual device, we can extract the memory dump. When the crash occurs, a Q/A engineer extracts a memory dump from the navigation system. A memory dump provides a snapshot of the system's state at that exact moment. Software engineers do not need to manually reproduce the issue by running the device. Instead, they can analyze the memory dump offline, saving time and effort.

By using memory dump analysis, developers can debug issues without relying on physical devices.

Understanding the KDUMP feature

What is required to get a kernel memory dump from a Linux system? Linux provides a feature called KDUMP. When you enable the KDUMP feature, you can gather a memory dump (vmcore) from the actual device when the crash occurs. Once KDUMP is enabled on the target device, the kernel memory (at the moment of the crash) is saved as a dump file (vmcore) on the device. You can then pull the vmcore file from the device for further analysis.

In this chapter, we will focus on analyzing vmcore, which is a memory dump from a real device. If you're unsure about how to set up KDUMP on a Linux kernel, don't worry. If you download the vmcore and vmlinux files from this book's GitHub, you can follow the debugging steps explained in the *Stack area of the process* section.

Once you have the kernel memory dump, you need to use a debugging tool to examine the vmcore file. To do this, you need to install a debugging tool: the Crash utility. The Crash utility is a popular tool used to analyze kernel memory dump files, such as vmcore.

Analyzing vmcore files using the binary utility

As previously mentioned, the vmcore file is a kernel binary that captures the memory contents of a Linux kernel that was running on the target device when it crashed. In practice, this file is essential for analyzing system crashes and freeze issues.

We will now examine how to check the header of the vmcore file and analyze its layout.

Understanding the layout of the vmcore file

Let's explore the layout of the vmcore file by looking at *Figure 12.2*:

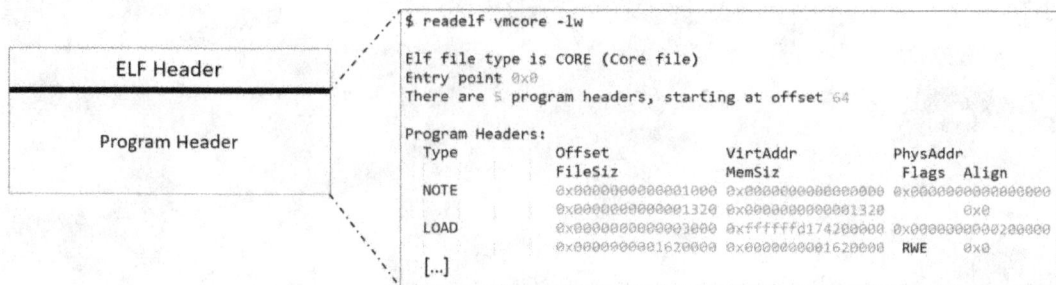

Figure 12.2: The layout of the vmcore file

Here are the key observations from *Figure 12.2*, which shows the layout of the vmcore file, a kernel binary from a real device:

- vmcore is an ELF core dump file used to capture a memory snapshot of the Linux kernel
- Unlike standard ELF files (vmlinux, *.so), vmcore does not contain section headers
- Important system state information is stored in the NOTE section of the program header
- The Crash utility uses this data to reconstruct the kernel's memory state for debugging

Now that we have analyzed the layout of the vmcore file, let's examine its attributes using binary utilities. Whenever you analyze a binary file, it is recommended to check its header information using a binary utility, because the header contains important metadata. Let's continue examining the vmcore file.

To check the type of the vmcore file, we can use the `file` command:

```
$ file vmcore
vmcore: ELF 64-bit LSB core file, Arm aarch64, version 1 (SYSV), SVR4-style
```

This output shows that vmcore is in **Executable and Linkable Format (ELF)**. We can further examine its ELF header using the following command:

```
$ readelf -h vmcore
ELF Header:
  Magic:   7f 45 4c 46 02 01 01 00 00 00 00 00 00 00 00 00
  Class:                             ELF64
  Data:                              2's complement, little endian
  Version:                           1 (current)
  OS/ABI:                            UNIX - System V
  ABI Version:                       0
  Type:                              CORE (Core file)
  Machine:                           AArch64
  Version:                           0x1
  Entry point address:               0x0
  Start of program headers:          64 (bytes into file)
  Start of section headers:          0 (bytes into file)
  Flags:                             0x0
  Size of this header:               64 (bytes)
  Size of program headers:           56 (bytes)
```

```
    Number of program headers:         5
    Size of section headers:           0 (bytes)
    Number of section headers:         0
    Section header string table index: 0
```

As you can see, the structure of vmcore is similar to other ELF files, such as vmlinux or shared libraries (*.so). Here are the key characteristics of vmcore:

- vmcore is a core dump file, not an executable or shared object
- It stores important system information in the NOTE section

Unlike regular ELF binaries, the vmcore file does not contain any section headers. We can confirm this by running the following command:

```
$ readelf --sections vmcore
There are no sections in this file.
```

This is an important characteristic of the vmcore file. Instead of using traditional section headers, the system stores critical information in the NOTE section of the program header.

NOTE section of the program header

vmcore contains important system information in the NOTE section. The Crash utility reads this section to extract key details, such as the following:

- Register values for each CPU core
- System registers such as SCTLR_EL1 and TCR_EL1

These details help locate the correct addresses in vmcore using the corresponding vmlinux file.

To check the program headers, we can run the following command:

```
$ readelf --wide --segments vmcore
Elf file type is CORE (Core file)
Entry point 0x0
There are 5 program headers, starting at offset 64

Program Headers:
  Type           Offset   VirtAddr           PhysAddr           FileSiz
  MemSiz   Flg Align
```

```
   NOTE            0x001000 0x0000000000000000 0x0000000000000000 0x001320
0x001320     0
   LOAD            0x003000 0xfffffffdfe4400000 0x0000000000200000 0x1640000
0x1640000 RWE 0
[...]
```

Here are the key elements of the output:

- The NOTE section starts at offset 0x001000
- The LOAD segments contain memory regions captured in the core dump

To view the contents of the NOTE section, we can use the readelf --note vmcore command:

```
$ readelf --note vmcore
```

The output will display various CORE and VMCOREINFO entries:

```
Displaying notes found at file offset 0x00001000 with length 0x00001320:
   Owner                Data size          Description
   CORE                 0x00000188         NT_PRSTATUS (prstatus structure)
   CORE                 0x00000188         NT_PRSTATUS (prstatus structure)
   CORE                 0x00000188         NT_PRSTATUS (prstatus structure)
   CORE                 0x00000188         NT_PRSTATUS (prstatus structure)
   VMCOREINFO           0x00000c98         Unknown note type: (0x00000000)
```

This confirms that at offset 0x00001000, the vmcore file contains entries related to system state and process status.

To better understand how this data is stored, we can inspect memory contents in hexadecimal format:

```
_____address|_____0_____4_____8_____C
MD:00001000|>00000005 00000188 00000001 45524F43
MD:00001010| 00000000 00000000 00000000 00000000
MD:00001020| 00000000 00000000 00000000 00000000
MD:00001030| 00000000 00000000 00000000 00000000
MD:00001040| 00000000 00000000 00000000 00000000
```

The Crash utility parses this information to properly load the vmcore file and to reconstruct the kernel's memory state.

What are the benefits of understanding the layout of the vmcore file? You can see how the Crash utility loads the vmcore file.

Understanding the Crash utility

The **Crash** utility is an open source debugging tool that works with many Linux distributions, such as Debian and Ubuntu. It was originally developed by Dave Anderson at Red Hat and is now maintained by several key developers.

You can also download the source code, build it, and run it on your Linux system. Before using Crash utility, you need to prepare two important files:

- vmcore: The kernel memory dump file.
- vmlinux: The Linux kernel binary file that matches the vmcore file. Make sure vmlinux is generated with CONFIG_DEBUG_INFO enabled to include the debug symbol table.

Make sure you have these files ready before running the Crash utility.

To use the Crash utility, you first need to install it. The installation process may vary depending on your Linux distribution.

First, we need to install the following packages:

```
$ sudo apt-get install texinfo git build-essential bison zlib1g-dev
libncurses5-dev libncursesw5-dev  pkg-config flex swig libgmp-dev libmpfr-
dev libmpc-dev -y
```

These utilities must be installed before you compile the Crash utility.

Now, let's download the source code from its official GitHub repository:

```
$ git clone https://github.com/crash-utility/crash
```

Once the download is complete, you can see that the crash directory has been created.

> Note
>
> In this chapter, we will analyze a kernel binary based on the Armv8-A architecture using AArch64. To do this, when building the Crash utility, you need to set the target architecture to Armv8-A (AArch64).

The command to install the Crash utility, as introduced in this chapter, should be entered in the Linux terminal. Once you have downloaded the source code, you need to compile it. Run the following commands in a Linux terminal.

For x86-based systems (cross-compiling for Arm64), use the following command:

```
$ cd crash
$ make target=ARM64
```

For Arm64-based systems, use this command:

```
$ cd crash
$ make
```

When compiling the Crash utility on Arm64-based systems, you will see the following message:

```
$ make
TARGET: ARM64
 CRASH: 8.0.5++
   GDB: 10.2
...
  CXXLD  gdb
```

After the build is complete, the `crash` executable file will be generated. You can check the `crash` file with the following command:

```
$ ls -la crash
-rwxr-xr-x 1 root root 104158000 Feb  5 19:40 crash
```

Once the compilation is complete, we can run it with the following command:

```
$ ./crash vmcore vmlinux
```

After you enter the preceding command, the Crash utility will begin execution. The output message when launching the Crash utility will look like this:

```
$ ./crash vmlinux vmcore

crash 8.0.5++

Copyright (C) 2002-2024  Red Hat, Inc.
Copyright (C) 2004, 2005, 2006, 2010  IBM Corporation
...
```

```
       KERNEL: vmlinux  [TAINTED]
     DUMPFILE: vmcore
[...]    NODENAME: raspberrypi
      RELEASE: 5.15.74-v8+
      VERSION: #65 SMP PREEMPT Thu Jan 26 12:00:35 KST 2023
      MACHINE: aarch64  (unknown Mhz)
       MEMORY: 3.9 GB
        PANIC: "Unable to handle kernel NULL pointer dereference at virtual
address 0000000000000000"
          PID: 1591
      COMMAND: "bash"
         TASK: ffffff805d66dac0  [THREAD_INFO: ffffff805d66dac0]
          CPU: 2
        STATE: TASK_RUNNING (PANIC)

crash>
```

A common question is, "when running the Crash utility, how does it extract and display kernel information?" If you analyze the source code of the Crash utility, you can find out how it works.

Fundamentally, the Crash utility works as follows:

1. It reads the kernel binary's memory contents by loading the vmcore file.
2. It then parses the memory content using key kernel data structures and displays the results.

For more information about the Crash utility, you can visit the official GitHub repository at https://crash-utility.github.io/, which includes the reference manual.

Now that we have understood the debugging tools for kernel binaries as well as the layout of the vmcore, let's move on to the next topic: digging into stack memory contents.

Stack area of the process

In this section, we will analyze a kernel binary and check the stack patterns. Specifically, we will look into vmcore to examine how the stack is structured.

Background on the stack of a process

Imagine you are debugging a real-world project. What is the first step in debugging a kernel binary? In most cases, you will perform one or more of the following tasks:

- Analyze the process's stack space (call stack analysis)
- Examine assembly instructions to understand the execution flow
- Inspect key data structures used in kernel operations

While performing such activities, most developers analyze the call stack. Analyzing the call stack is important because it allows developers to view function calls, return addresses, and local variables. For this reason, most debugging tools display the call stack. However, in some cases, you may need to manually analyze the stack contents, especially if the debugging tools do not provide detailed call stack information.

The stack space can be compared to a workspace where a process stores and manages data. What does a process do at the software level? Here are the key operations:

- Arithmetic operations
- Store values in local variables
- Call functions and pass arguments using the stack

To store local variables or call functions, a process utilizes the stack space. During the creation of a process, the Linux kernel assigns a stack memory area for it. The stack size depends on whether the system is 32-bit or 64-bit:

- 64-bit Arm kernel (AArch64): Stack size = 0x4000 bytes (16 KB)
- 32-bit Arm kernel (AArch32): Stack size = 0x2000 bytes (8 KB)

It is important to understand the structure of the stack when analyzing kernel memory and debugging low-level processes. In the next sections, we will explore how to analyze the stack contents of a kernel binary.

The overall layout of the process stack

Take a look at *Figure 12.3* to understand how the process stack is structured:

The lowest address
(0xFFFFFF8008058000)

```
----->  ┌─────────────────────────────────┐
        │                                 │
        │                              ╲   │
        │                                 │
        │                                 │
        │                                 │
        │                                 │
        │       ▲  raw_spin_unlock_irq()  │
        │       ¦  finish_task_switch()   │
        │       ¦  __schedule()           │
        │       ¦  schedule()             │
        │       ¦  rcu_gp_kthread()       │
        │       ¦  kthread()              │
----->  │       ¦  ret_from_fork(asm)     │
        └─────────────────────────────────┘
```

The highest address
(0xFFFFFF800805C000)

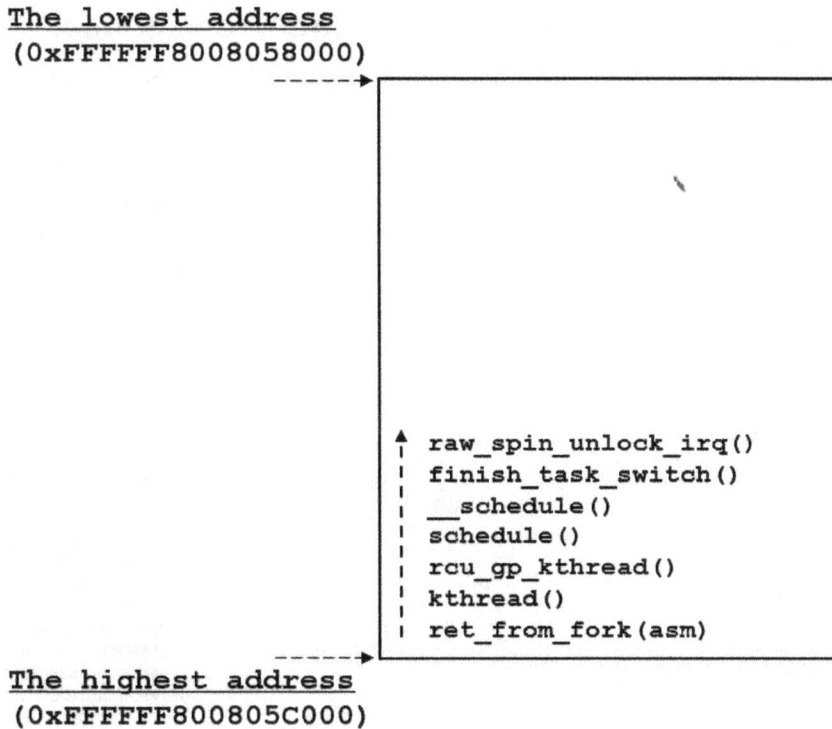

Figure 12.3: The layout of the process stack

The following are the key observations:

- **Stack size:** In *Figure 12.3*, the process stack size is 0x4000 bytes. One key characteristic of the stack is that its size is static. This means the stack does not expand dynamically during program execution. This is different from the heap, which can grow or shrink based on memory allocation needs. Since the stack space is fixed, functions must carefully manage stack usage to prevent stack overflow.

- **Stack growth direction:** The stack grows from a higher memory address to a lower memory address. In most system software development, the stack is set up in this way.

- **Function call symbol:** When a function is called, the BL (branch with link) instruction is executed. During this operation, the return address is updated to X30. After PC jumps to the function, the value in X30 is then pushed into the stack area at the start of the function. This return address in the stack area can be viewed by debugging the program.

This mechanism allows the system to track function calls and return to the address after the function completes its tasks.

Analyzing the memory contents of the process stack

Now, let's analyze the memory contents of the process stack shown in *Figure 12.4*.

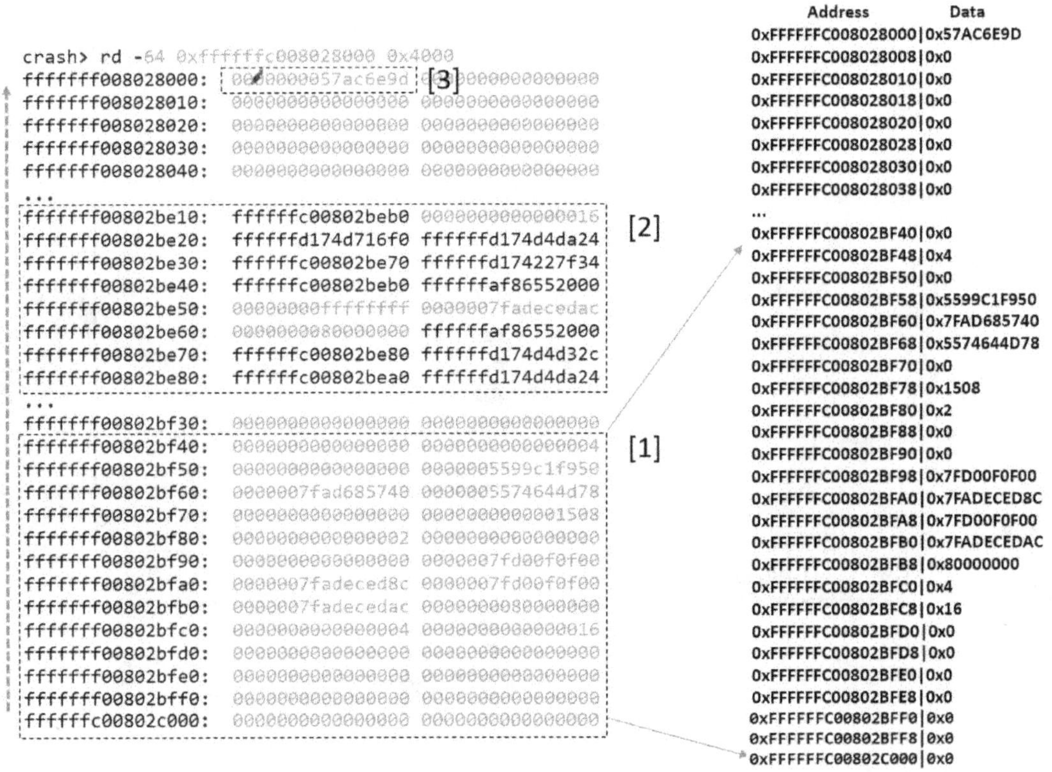

```
                                                              Address        Data
                                                          0xFFFFFFC008028000|0x57AC6E9D
crash> rd -64 0xffffffc008028000 0x4000                   0xFFFFFFC008028008|0x0
ffffffff008028000:  000000057ac6e9d  [3]000000000000000   0xFFFFFFC008028010|0x0
ffffffff008028010:  0000000000000000  0000000000000000    0xFFFFFFC008028018|0x0
ffffffff008028020:  0000000000000000  0000000000000000    0xFFFFFFC008028020|0x0
ffffffff008028030:  0000000000000000  0000000000000000    0xFFFFFFC008028028|0x0
ffffffff008028040:  0000000000000000  0000000000000000    0xFFFFFFC008028030|0x0
...                                                       0xFFFFFFC008028038|0x0
ffffffff00802be10:  ffffffc00802beb0  0000000000000016    ...
ffffffff00802be20:  ffffffd174d716f0  ffffffd174d4da24  [2] 0xFFFFFFC00802BF40|0x0
ffffffff00802be30:  ffffffc00802be70  ffffffd174227f34    0xFFFFFFC00802BF48|0x4
ffffffff00802be40:  ffffffc00802beb0  ffffffaf86552000    0xFFFFFFC00802BF50|0x0
ffffffff00802be50:  00000000ffffffff  0000007fadecedac    0xFFFFFFC00802BF58|0x5599C1F950
ffffffff00802be60:  0000000080000000  ffffffaf86552000    0xFFFFFFC00802BF60|0x7FAD685740
ffffffff00802be70:  ffffffc00802be80  ffffffd174d4d32c    0xFFFFFFC00802BF68|0x5574644D78
ffffffff00802be80:  ffffffc00802bea0  ffffffd174d4da24    0xFFFFFFC00802BF70|0x0
...                                                       0xFFFFFFC00802BF78|0x1508
ffffffff00802bf30:  0000000000000000  0000000000000000    0xFFFFFFC00802BF80|0x2
ffffffff00802bf40:  0000000000000000  0000000000000004  [1] 0xFFFFFFC00802BF88|0x0
ffffffff00802bf50:  0000000000000000  0000005599c1f950    0xFFFFFFC00802BF90|0x0
ffffffff00802bf60:  0000007fad685740  0000005574644d78    0xFFFFFFC00802BF98|0x7FD00F0F00
ffffffff00802bf70:  0000000000000000  0000000000001508    0xFFFFFFC00802BFA0|0x7FADECED8C
ffffffff00802bf80:  0000000000000002  0000000000000000    0xFFFFFFC00802BFA8|0x7FD00F0F00
ffffffff00802bf90:  0000000000000000  0000007fd00f0f00    0xFFFFFFC00802BFB0|0x7FADECEDAC
ffffffff00802bfa0:  0000007fadeced8c  0000007fd00f0f00    0xFFFFFFC00802BFB8|0x80000000
ffffffff00802bfb0:  0000007fadecedac  0000000080000000    0xFFFFFFC00802BFC0|0x4
ffffffff00802bfc0:  0000000000000004  0000000000000016    0xFFFFFFC00802BFC8|0x16
ffffffff00802bfd0:  0000000000000000  0000000000000000    0xFFFFFFC00802BFD0|0x0
ffffffff00802bfe0:  0000000000000000  0000000000000000    0xFFFFFFC00802BFD8|0x0
ffffffff00802bff0:  0000000000000000  0000000000000000    0xFFFFFFC00802BFE0|0x0
ffffffc00802c000:   0000000000000000  0000000000000000    0xFFFFFFC00802BFE8|0x0
                                                          0xFFFFFFC00802BFF0|0x0
                                                          0xFFFFFFC00802BFF8|0x0
                                                          0xFFFFFFC00802C000|0x0
```

Figure 12.4: Key data in the process stack

As you can see, *Figure 12.4* consists of two parts:

- The left side displays the memory contents of the stack using the Crash utility. This is done by executing the rd -64 0xffffffc008028000 0x4000 command. This command reads and prints the memory contents of the stack.

- On the right side, the address and memory contents are displayed in a one-to-one format. Here, the memory contents are shown in 8-byte units. This method makes stack memory analysis more efficient.

In *Figure 12.4*, we can see two key memory addresses:

- The highest address in the stack is `0xffffffff00802c000`
- The lowest address in the stack is `0xffffffff008028000`

These addresses define the range of the process stack. In most systems, the stack grows from higher addresses to lower addresses. This means that when new data is pushed onto the stack, it is stored at decreasing memory addresses.

Breaking down *Figure 12.4* in more detail, there are three types of data stored in the process stack area:

- **[1]**: Near the highest address, we find a set of registers that were used when the process was executing in user space. These registers were stored right after the process entered kernel mode through a system call. They provide a snapshot of the process state in user space just before the transition to kernel execution.
- **[2]**: When the process executes in kernel mode, the stack is used to call functions and store local variables. For example, return addresses are stored in the stack. These return addresses indicate where the process should continue execution after returning from a function call. The call stack displayed by the debugging program is generated by parsing the data. Also, local variables from each function are stored in the process stack area as temporary data.
- **[3]**: At the lowest address, `0xffffffff008028000`, we find a special magic value: `0x57ac6e9d`. This value acts as a signature marking the lowest address in the process's stack.

One important value among the three types of stack data is `0x57ac6e9d`. When you check the kernel binary and find `0x57ac6e9d`, it means you have reached the lowest address of the process stack. The value `0x57ac6e9d` serves as a stack magic value, marking the boundary of the stack.

By identifying this boundary, you can estimate the starting point of the stack memory region. For example, if you see `0x57ac6e9d` in the memory area, you can calculate the highest stack address by adding `0x4000` to it.

In this analysis, the examined stack belongs to the `systemd` process. As a user-space process, `systemd` operates in both user space and kernel space, depending on its execution context.

User process stack versus kernel process stack

Now, let's review *Figure 12.5*, which shows the stack memory contents of two different processes:

Address	Data		Address	Data
NSD:FFFFFFC008028000	0x57AC6E9D		NSD:FFFFFFC008030000	0x57AC6E9D
NSD:FFFFFFC008028008	0x0		NSD:FFFFFFC008030008	0x0
NSD:FFFFFFC008028010	0x0		NSD:FFFFFFC008030010	0x0

...

NSD:FFFFFFC00802BF38	0x0		NSD:FFFFFFC008033F38	0x0
NSD:FFFFFFC00802BF40	0x0		NSD:FFFFFFC008033F40	0x0
NSD:FFFFFFC00802BF48	0x4		NSD:FFFFFFC008033F48	0x0
NSD:FFFFFFC00802BF50	0x0		NSD:FFFFFFC008033F50	0x0
NSD:FFFFFFC00802BF58	0x5599C1F950		NSD:FFFFFFC008033F58	0x0
NSD:FFFFFFC00802BF60	0x7FAD685740		NSD:FFFFFFC008033F60	0x0
NSD:FFFFFFC00802BF68	0x5574644D78		NSD:FFFFFFC008033F68	0x0
NSD:FFFFFFC00802BF70	0x0		NSD:FFFFFFC008033F70	0x0
NSD:FFFFFFC00802BF78	0x1508		NSD:FFFFFFC008033F78	0x0
NSD:FFFFFFC00802BF80	0x2		NSD:FFFFFFC008033F80	0x0
NSD:FFFFFFC00802BF88	0x0		NSD:FFFFFFC008033F88	0x0
NSD:FFFFFFC00802BF90	0x0		NSD:FFFFFFC008033F90	0x0
NSD:FFFFFFC00802BF98	0x7FD00F0F00		NSD:FFFFFFC008033F98	0x0
NSD:FFFFFFC00802BFA0	0x7FADECED8C		NSD:FFFFFFC008033FA0	0x0
NSD:FFFFFFC00802BFA8	0x7FD00F0F00		NSD:FFFFFFC008033FA8	0x0
NSD:FFFFFFC00802BFB0	0x7FADECEDAC		NSD:FFFFFFC008033FB0	0x0
NSD:FFFFFFC00802BFB8	0x80000000		NSD:FFFFFFC008033FB8	0x100005
NSD:FFFFFFC00802BFC0	0x4		NSD:FFFFFFC008033FC0	0x0
NSD:FFFFFFC00802BFC8	0x16		NSD:FFFFFFC008033FC8	0x0
NSD:FFFFFFC00802BFD0	0x0		NSD:FFFFFFC008033FD0	0x0
NSD:FFFFFFC00802BFD8	0x0		NSD:FFFFFFC008033FD8	0x0
NSD:FFFFFFC00802BFE0	0x0		NSD:FFFFFFC008033FE0	0x0
NSD:FFFFFFC00802BFE8	0x0		NSD:FFFFFFC008033FE8	0x0
NSD:FFFFFFC00802BFF0	0x0		NSD:FFFFFFC008033FF0	0x0
NSD:FFFFFFC00802BFF8	0x0		NSD:FFFFFFC008033FF8	0x0
NSD:FFFFFFC00802C000	0x0		NSD:FFFFFFC008034000	0x0

systemd   ## kthreadd

Figure 12.5: Stack signatures of a user process and a kernel process

First, let's examine the data pattern at the highest address of the stack:

- On the left side, we can see a memory dump from the systemd process stack
- On the right side, there is a memory dump from the kthreadd kernel thread stack

In the `systemd` process stack, we observe several pieces of data near the highest address. What does this data represent? They are the registers from user space just before a system call is invoked. Right after a system call is invoked, the set of general-purpose registers from user space is pushed into the kernel-space stack.

Now, let's analyze the stack data from the `kthreadd` process, shown on the right side of *Figure 12.5*. As we can see, there is `0x0` data near the highest address of the stack.

What can we learn from these two binary patterns in the user process or kernel process?

- **User process**: Memory contents are present near the highest address.
- **Kernel process**: No memory contents are present near the highest address. Since kernel processes only run in the kernel space, you cannot find a set of general-purpose registers near the highest stack address.

At the highest address of the process's stack, we find several memory contents. If this data is found, it indicates a user process, and if it is `0x0`, it indicates a kernel process.

When analyzing binaries, if you encounter these patterns, you can confidently identify the process's stack space.

Code review on the stack magic value

`0x57ac6e9d` is stored at the lowest address of a process's stack. This is known as the **stack end magic value**. What are magic values in Linux systems? Magic values are special markers commonly used for validation and debugging.

Let's review the kernel code associated with `0x57ac6e9d`:

```
// include/uapi/linux/magic.h
#define STACK_END_MAGIC    0x57AC6E9D
```

The `STACK_END_MAGIC` macro represents a unique identifier placed at the end of the stack to help monitor stack integrity. When is this value written into the lowest address of a process's stack? It happens during the process creation phase when the `set_task_stack_end_magic` function is called.

Let's review the `set_task_stack_end_magic` function:

```
// kernel/fork.c
void set_task_stack_end_magic(struct task_struct *tsk)
{
    unsigned long *stackend;
```

```
        stackend = end_of_stack(tsk);
        *stackend = STACK_END_MAGIC; /* for overflow detection */
}
```

When running the preceding function, the STACK_END_MAGIC value is stored at the lowest stack address of the process.

A common question is this: "Why is a magic value written at the end of the stack?" The purpose of placing 0x57ac6e9d at the lowest stack address is to detect stack corruption.

The kernel continuously checks whether this magic value remains unchanged. If it detects any changes, the kernel will perform the following actions:

- The kernel assumes that a stack overflow or corruption has occurred
- The kernel triggers a system crash (panic) to reset the system

Another question is this: "When does the kernel check whether 0x57ac6e9d is unchanged?" Every time a process is scheduled, the kernel checks whether the magic value at the end of the stack is still unchanged. This check is performed in the schedule_debug() function. Let's look at the schedule_debug() function:

```
// kernel/sched/core.c
static inline void schedule_debug(struct task_struct *prev, bool preempt)
{
#ifdef CONFIG_SCHED_STACK_END_CHECK
    if (task_stack_end_corrupted(prev))
        panic("corrupted stack end detected inside scheduler\n");
}
```

At the beginning of the function, there is an if statement. If the task_stack_end_corrupted() function returns true, the panic() function is called. This happens if the magic value 0x57ac6e9d at the lowest stack address is corrupted.

Next, let's check the body of the task_stack_end_corrupted() function:

```
// include/linux/sched/task_stack.h
#define task_stack_end_corrupted(task) \
        (*(end_of_stack(task)) != STACK_END_MAGIC)
```

*(end_of_stack(task)) returns the data at the lowest stack address of the process. If the data at this address is not 0x57ac6e9d, the function returns true.

Summary of the magic value inside the binary

Let's summarize the code review we've just done:

- When a process is scheduled in the Linux kernel, the schedule() function is called
- Normally, task scheduling in a Linux system happens at least 30 times per second
- Each time a process enters sleep during task scheduling, the kernel checks whether the magic value 0x57ac6e9d at the lowest stack address has been corrupted

So far, we identified the magic value 0x57ac6e9d at the lowest stack address. Such magic values are often left in memory after being written, without being modified. They can be useful for checking data patterns or verifying the integrity of data structures.

For reference, you can find other magic values in the include/uapi/linux/magic.h header file. You can find different magic values used in the Linux kernel.

In this section, we have explored the stack patterns of a process and learned about magic values. If you open and analyze a kernel dump, you can use the magic value to verify whether the binary you are analyzing is the process stack area.

In the next section, we will explore how to find the start address of the task_struct structure based on the lowest stack address of a process.

Tracking the start address for a struct using the address

In the previous section, we analyzed key stack data patterns and found that the magic value 0x57ac6e9d at the lowest stack address.

Using the lowest stack address, we can determine the starting address of the task_struct structure. In this section, we will learn how to find out the task_struct structure using the Crash utility.

Understanding the task_struct structure

Each process has its own task_struct structure for storing its attributes. The stack field within the task_struct structure holds the lowest address of the process stack. The following is the declaration of the task_struct structure using the Crash utility:

```
crash> struct task_struct
struct task_struct {
    struct thread_info thread_info;
    unsigned int __state;
```

```
    void *stack;
    refcount_t usage;
    ...
    struct thread_struct thread;
}
SIZE: 7744
```

With the struct task_struct command in the Crash utility, you can view the structure definition. Each field, such as thread_info, __state, and *stack, has important properties of the process.

It is important to note that the stack field is declared as a pointer. This means it stores the address, which is the lowest address of the process stack.

Now, let's check the offset of the stack field within the task_struct structure using the struct -o task_struct command:

```
crash> struct -o task_struct
struct task_struct {
    [0x0] struct thread_info thread_info;
    [0x10] unsigned int __state;
    [0x18] void *stack;
}
```

This output shows that the offset of the stack field within the task_struct structure is 0x18. It is important to understand this data structure before starting debugging.

How to find the address of the task_struct structure

Let's continue debugging with the address 0xfffffffc008028000, that is, the lowest stack address analyzed in the previous section. To determine where the lowest stack address of the systemd process (0xfffffffc008028000) is stored, we can use the Crash utility. The Crash utility provides the search command, which allows us to find a specific data value within the kernel's memory. Let's use the search ffffffc008028000 command to search for the stack address:

```
crash> search ffffffc008028000
[…]
ffffff8040238018: ffffffc008028000
```

This result indicates that the value 0xfffffffc008028000 exists at memory address 0xffffff8040238018.

To better understand how the data structure is organized, let's analyze the output of the rd command:

```
crash> rd ffffff8040238018
ffffff8040238018:   ffffffc008028000
```

From this output, you can see that the value 0xffffffc008028000 is stored at memory address 0xffffff8040238018. The rd command shows the memory contents at the specified address.

Next, let's check the offset of the stack field within the task_struct structure. You can do this using the following command:

```
crash> struct task_struct.stack
struct task_struct {
    [0x18] void *stack;
}
```

As shown in the output, the stack field is located at an offset of 0x18 within the task_struct structure. Using this information, we can calculate the base address of the task_struct structure with the following equation:

Base address of task_struct structure = Address of stack field – Offset

0xffffff8040238000 = 0xffffff8040238018 - 0x18

Now, we can see the full contents of the task_struct structure by using the base address:

```
crash > struct task_struct 0xffffff8040238000
struct task_struct {
  thread_info = {
    flags = 0x0,
    {
      preempt_count = 0x100000002,
[...]
    __state = 0x1,
    stack = 0xffffffc008028000,
}
```

From this output, you can see the complete field of the task_struct structure, including the stack field. The stack field points to the memory address 0xffffffc008028000, which represents the stack base for the corresponding process.

Let's examine the memory contents at address `0xffffff8040238000` from another perspective using the rd command:

```
crash> rd -64 0xffffff8040238000 0x20
ffffff8040238000:  0000000000000000 0000000100000002
ffffff8040238010:  0000000000000001 ffffffc008028000
```

The key observation from this output is that the value `0xffffffc008028000` is stored at memory address `0xffffff8040238018`. This value, `0xffffffc008028000`, represents the lowest stack address of the corresponding process.

To better understand how the stack field points to the lowest stack address, you can look at *Figure 12.6*, which shows the full picture:

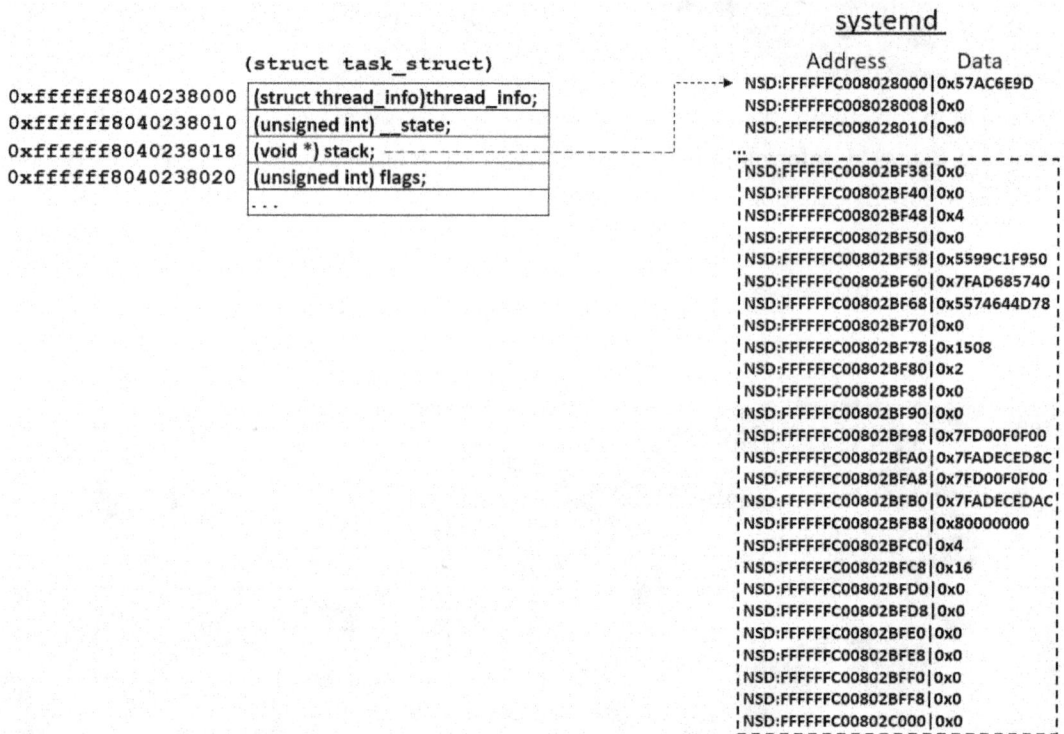

Figure 12.6: The task_struct structure and the process stack layout

Now, let's summarize what we have analyzed in this section:

- The task_struct structure starts at address `0xffffff8040238000`
- The stack field is located at an offset of `0x18` within the task_struct structure

- The stack field stores the lowest stack address (0xffffffc008028000)
- The signature 0x57AC6E9D, which we identified as the lowest stack address, is actually stored in the stack field of the task_struct structure

So far, we have explored how to find the starting address of the task_struct structure using the lowest stack address of a process. Next, let's take a look at another field that represents the process's context information: the thread field.

Reviewing the thread field in the task_struct structure

If you want to inspect the data structure of the thread field inside the task_struct structure, you can use the struct task_struct.thread command in the Crash utility:

```
crash> hex
output radix: 16 (hex)
crash> struct task_struct.thread
struct task_struct {
  [0x1a00] struct thread_struct thread;
}
```

From the output, we can see that the offset of the thread field is 0x1a00. Given that the starting address of the task_struct structure is 0xffffff8040238000, we can deduce that the thread field is located at 0xffffff8040239a00 based on the following rule:

$$0xffffff8040238000 + 0x1a00,$$

where 0xffffff8040238000 is the start address of the task_struct structure, and 0x1a00 is the offset for the thread field.

Let's examine the data stored at 0xffffff8040239a00 using the rd (read memory) command in the Crash utility:

```
crash> rd -64 0xffffff8040239a00 0x10
ffffff8040239a00:  ffffff804226bc80 ffffff8040238000
ffffff8040239a10:  0000000000000001 ffffff8040238000
ffffff8040239a20:  ffffff8041a08000 0000000000000000
ffffff8040239a30:  ffffff8040238658 ffffff8040238000
ffffff8040239a40:  ffffff8040238000 ffffffc00802bd08
```

The thread field is declared as a thread_struct structure. To further analyze how thread_struct is structured, we can use the struct thread_struct command:

```
crash> struct thread_struct
struct thread_struct {
    struct cpu_context cpu_context;
...
}
SIZE: 0x440
```

Additionally, we need to find out how the cpu_context structure is defined since it contains essential information about the context information:

```
crash> struct cpu_context
struct cpu_context {
    unsigned long x19;
    unsigned long x20;
    unsigned long x21;
    unsigned long x22;
    unsigned long x23;
    unsigned long x24;
    unsigned long x25;
    unsigned long x26;
    unsigned long x27;
    unsigned long x28;
    unsigned long fp;
    unsigned long sp;
    unsigned long pc;
}
SIZE: 0x68
```

The cpu_context structure includes multiple fields that represent general-purpose registers in the Armv8-A architecture. When a process is being scheduled, a set of general-purpose registers is stored in the fields of the cpu_context structure. It is important to check these registers because they provide useful debugging information about how the process was running before it was scheduled.

With debugging tools, you can inspect the call stack of a running process in the Linux kernel. The process of retrieving the call stack typically follows these steps:

1. Access the task_struct structure of the target process.
2. Access the thread field in the task_struct structure and access the cpu_context field in the thread structure.
3. Load the register values to reconstruct and display the call stack.

In this section, you learned how to determine the starting address of the task_struct structure using the lowest stack address of a process using the Crash utility.

Many data structures in the Linux kernel are implemented using structures. These structures often contain pointer-type fields that store memory addresses within the structure. If you identify a specific magic value in a memory address, you can use it to trace back to the starting address of the structure that contains it.

By applying these techniques, you can analyze binaries in multiple ways to locate the starting addresses of important structures.

In the next section, we will explore a similar approach using a different example to identify the starting address of the structure in kernel memory analysis.

Identifying a structure using a function pointer

In the previous section, we determined the base address of the task_struct structure by identifying a specific magic value stored at the lowest address of the process stack.

In this section, we will explore a similar approach: finding a structure's base address using a known function address. This method is particularly useful for analyzing kernel memory structures, making it a valuable technique for debugging and binary analysis.

Data structures that store function addresses

In the Linux kernel, many data structures store function addresses to manage various operations dynamically. One example is the stack field in the task_struct structure, which we discussed in the previous section. In many cases, these function addresses serve as function pointers, which are used to invoke function calls during execution.

Now, we will analyze the address of an interrupt handler function and use it to determine the base address of the irq_desc structure.

In this section, we will analyze how to traverse memory to locate the base address of the irq_desc structure using the following information:

- Interrupt handler function: bcm2835_mmc_irq
- Interrupt number: 47

The bcm2835_mmc_irq function is an interrupt handler used to control the **MultiMediaCard** (**MMC**) interface on a Raspberry Pi device.

> Note
>
> Before we move on to a detailed analysis, let's briefly discuss interrupt handlers. If you have experience with device drivers, you may already be familiar with the concept of interrupts.
>
> Why are interrupts used? An interrupt is a signal sent by a hardware device to notify the CPU that an interrupt is triggered. The Linux kernel uses interrupts to handle hardware events efficiently. When an interrupt occurs, the kernel executes a specific **Interrupt Service Routine (ISR)** to process the event.
>
> For example, if you touch the screen on your smartphone, a touch interrupt is triggered to notify the system. Similarly, if you press a key on a keyboard, a keyboard interrupt is triggered to process the keystroke.
>
> Each interrupt is associated with an interrupt handler function, which performs the necessary operation.

Finding the address of bcm2835_mmc_irq

First, let's analyze the function address using the Crash utility. By using the dis bcm2835_mmc_irq command, we can find the address of the bcm2835_mmc_irq function:

```
crash> dis bcm2835_mmc_irq
0xffffffd174b0f6f0 <bcm2835_mmc_irq>:    mov     x9, x30
0xffffffd174b0f6f4 <bcm2835_mmc_irq+4>: nop
0xffffffd174b0f6f8 <bcm2835_mmc_irq+8>: paciasp
0xffffffd174b0f6fc <bcm2835_mmc_irq+12>: stp x29, x30, [sp, #-128]!
0xffffffd174b0f700 <bcm2835_mmc_irq+16>: mov     x0, x1
```

From the output, we can see that the bcm2835_mmc_irq function is located at 0xfffffffd174b0f6f0. Now, let's check where this function address is stored in address using the search command in the Crash utility:

```
crash> search 0xfffffffd174b0f6f0
ffffff80420fc880:  fffffffd174b0f6f0
```

The result shows that the value 0xfffffffd174b0f6f0 is stored at memory address 0xffffff80420fc880. To inspect the memory contents at this address, we need to use the rd command:

```
crash> rd ffffff80420fc880
ffffff80420fc880:   fffffffd174b0f6f0
```

This output confirms that 0xfffffffd174b0f6f0 is stored at the 0xffffff80420fc880 address. The rd command allows us to view the memory contents at a specified address.

Through binary analysis, we can identify the following signatures:

- The bcm2835_mmc_irq function is located at 0xfffffffd174b0f6f0
- The function address 0xfffffffd174b0f6f0 is stored at address 0xffffff80420fc880

Next, let's explore data structures that can serve as useful references for further binary analysis.

Understanding the irqaction structure

To understand why a function address 0xfffffffd174b0f6f0 for bcm2835_mmc_irq is stored in memory, let's examine the relevant data structure.

In the Linux kernel, there is a data structure that is responsible for managing the properties of interrupts and interrupt handlers. This structure is called the irqaction structure. We can inspect its definition using the struct irqaction command in the Crash utility:

```
crash> struct irqaction
struct irqaction {
    irq_handler_t handler;
    void *dev_id;
    void *percpu_dev_id;

    ...
}
```

The handler field is a function pointer that is used to store the address of an interrupt handler. From another perspective, we can see that the first field in the irqaction structure is handler.

Since we previously found that 0xfffffffd174b0f6f0 is located at 0xffffff80420fc880, we can deduce that 0xffffff80420fc880 is likely the starting address of the irqaction structure.

Now, let's examine the contents of the irqaction structure at this memory address using the Crash utility:

```
crash> struct irqaction 0xffffff80420fc880
struct irqaction {
    handler = 0xfffffffd174b0f6f0 <bcm2835_mmc_irq>,
    dev_id = 0xffffff8040bb8d40,
  percpu_dev_id = 0x0,
    [...]
    irq = 47,
    flags = 132,
    thread_flags = 0,
    thread_mask = 0,
    name = 0xffffff80420fc180 "mmc1",
    dir = 0xffffff80420fe6c0
}
```

From this output, we can identify that the handler field in the irqaction structure stores the address of the bcm2835_mmc_irq function.

Finding the address in the irq_desc structure

Now, let's check where the memory address 0xffffff80420fc880 is stored:

```
crash> search 0xffffff80420fc880
ffffff80401fa6a8:  ffffff80420fc880
```

Using the search command, we find that the value 0xffffff80420fc880 is stored at address 0xffffff80401fa6a8. A common question at this point is: Which structure has a field with the type irqaction? To answer this question, we need to inspect the irq_desc structure using the Crash utility:

```
crash> struct irq_desc -o
struct irq_desc {
    [0x0] struct irq_common_data irq_common_data;
    [0x60] struct irq_data irq_data;
    [0x98] unsigned int *kstat_irqs;
    [0xa0] irq_flow_handler_t handle_irq;
```

```
        [0xa8] struct irqaction *action;
[...]
}
```

From this definition, we see that the *action field is a pointer to the irqaction structure and is located at offset 0xa8 from the base address of the irq_desc structure. By subtracting this offset from 0xffffff80401fa6a8, we can calculate the base address of the irq_desc structure as follows:

0xffffff80401fa600 = 0xffffff80401fa6a8 - 0xa8

Now, we can typecast the address 0xffffff80401fa600 to the irq_desc structure to examine its contents:

```
crash> struct irq_desc 0xffffff80401fa600
struct irq_desc {
    [...]
    kstat_irqs = 0xfffffffd175274cd8,
    handle_irq = 0xfffffffd174300ee0 <handle_fasteoi_irq>,
    action = 0xffffff80420fc880,
}
```

The output indicates that the irq_desc structure contains a field named action, which is a pointer to the address of the irqaction structure. This irqaction structure, in turn, stores the function pointer for the bcm2835_mmc_irq function.

Summary of the analysis

Let's take a look at *Figure 12.7* to summarize what we have analyzed in this section:

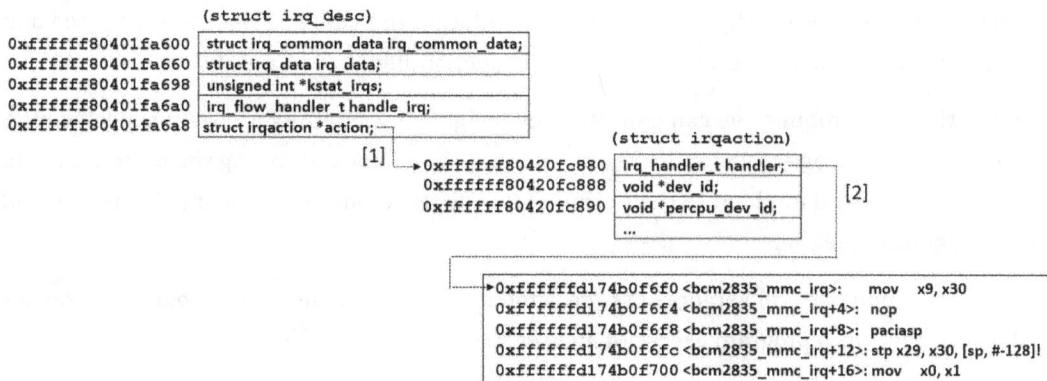

Figure 12.7: The structure relevant to irq_desc and irqaction

Let's break down what we have analyzed:

1. We identified the memory address of the `bcm2835_mmc_irq` interrupt handler.
2. Using the `search` command with this address, we determined the starting address of `irqaction` structure.
3. Finally, we found out the base address of the `irq_desc` structure, which contains a field pointing to the address of the `irqaction` structure.

This step-by-step approach follows a logical debugging method, similar to how developers analyze data structures in the Linux kernel.

By tracing a function pointer back to its containing structure, we determined the base address of the `irq_desc` structure, which manages interrupt information in the Linux kernel.

This method can be applied to analyze other structures and gain a deeper understanding of kernel memory organization.

Summary

In this chapter, we explored different ways to analyze kernel binaries. First, we discussed advanced dynamic analysis, explaining its importance in understanding how a program behaves at runtime. Then, we introduced the Crash utility, a powerful tool used to analyze kernel memory dumps.

Next, we examined how the process stack area is structured. By understanding the stack's data patterns, you can identify a process just by reviewing its memory dump.

We also learned how to determine the address of the `task_struct` structure by using the lowest address of the stack. Many software systems, including the Linux kernel, store addresses using pointer variables. Additionally, we covered how to locate the addresses of the `irqaction` and `irq_desc` structures using the address of an interrupt handler.

Through these techniques, we can gain two key insights: by carefully analyzing specific binary patterns, we can correctly identify kernel structures; and understanding the pattern of data structures helps us relate them to their original C code representation, making debugging and reverse engineering easier.

In the next chapter, we will explore `uftrace`, a modern log-based debugging tool that provides in-depth insights into program execution in user space.

13

Tracing Execution with uftrace

In general, during reverse engineering, we analyze binaries to predict the execution flow of software. However, log-based tracing tools can also be useful for analyzing software behavior.

In this chapter, we will cover **uftrace**, which is a popular open source project. We will cover the following topics:

- Introducing log-based debugging
- Introducing uftrace
- Basic features of uftrace
- Practical features of uftrace

First, let's explore why log-based tracing tools are important. Then, we will introduce uftrace

Technical requirements

To explore more about uftrace, I recommend visiting the following sites:

- `https://uftrace.github.io/slide`
- `https://github.com/namhyung/uftrace`

Introducing log-based debugging

In this section, we will explain why log-based analysis is used for debugging and how it helps software engineers understand system behavior.

Why do we need logs or tracing?

In reverse engineering, it is common to analyze binary files. However, in real-world development and debugging, engineers do not always analyze binaries. Instead, they often use logs to monitor software behavior.

Logs allow us to track what the software is doing over time because they contain timestamps, system events, and error messages. Here are other reasons why logs are useful:

- An error message can be recorded just before an issue occurs
- They identify any unusual system behavior or warnings leading up to the failure
- They show system status indicators such as temperature, battery level, or resource usage

Many Linux distributions provide different types of logs to help developers analyze system behavior. The following are the most well-known logs:

- **Kernel logs**: These provide information about what happens in kernel space
- **System logs**: These contain general system messages and application logs

Let's discuss further why referring to logs is important in real projects.

The importance of logs in real-world projects

In real-world projects, when a new issue is assigned to a developer, logs and tracing files are often the first pieces of debugging information provided. The debugging data we can use depends on the project. But software developers usually check logs first, not memory dumps, when they start debugging the issue.

Log analysis is not a traditional reverse engineering method. However, by referring to logs along with binaries, you can gain a more complete understanding of how the system operates. This approach is especially helpful for debugging complex issues related to performance, stability, or unexpected crashes.

In the next section, we will introduce uftrace, a powerful tracing utility for log-based debugging.

Introducing uftrace

uftrace is a powerful tool for user-space tracing. In this section, we will introduce uftrace and highlight its key features.

Why was uftrace designed?

uftrace was developed by Namhyung Kim and offers powerful features for monitoring the execution of user-space programs.

What is uftrace? The name is a combination of user and ftrace. It is well known that ftrace is used to trace software execution in kernel space. Similarly, uftrace is designed to trace the behavior of software in user space. This debugging utility enables the tracing of user-space activities. However, uftrace offers more advanced features, including argument and return value tracing of the function. It can also trace the function execution flow of libraries used in user space, as well as the behavior in the kernel space.

If you are new to a module with a lot of source code or want to understand the complete structure of a system, uftrace is highly recommended. Here are a few reasons why:

- **Analyzing unfamiliar source code**: When analyzing unknown source code, manually analyzing large amounts of code may take a lot of time. By quickly identifying the function execution flow using uftrace, you can efficiently analyze the call stack patterns.

- **Handling complex software issues**: In real-world projects, the most challenging issues to resolve are often multifunctional. With uftrace, you can analyze the function execution flow across both user space and kernel space.

- **Improving debugging efficiency**: Unlike traditional debugging methods that rely on logs or memory dumps, uftrace provides detailed insights into function execution sequences and performance measurements, allowing developers to debug issues more effectively.

Unlike traditional logs, uftrace provides execution time data in various formats, such as graphs and histograms. These visual representations make it easier to analyze execution flow, helping developers debug issues more efficiently.

Key features of uftrace

uftrace offers the following key features:

- **Supports multiple output formats**: Developers can view execution results in different formats, including graphic and histogram formats.

- **Traces function calls inside user-space libraries**: This helps understand how different software components interact at runtime.

- **Measures function execution time**: This allows for performance analysis and optimization, helping to detect performance bottlenecks. By identifying slow functions, developers can make targeted optimizations.

So far, we have looked at the key features of uftrace. Next, let's learn how to install uftrace.

How to install uftrace

Many modern Linux distributions, such as Debian and Ubuntu, provide a package for uftrace. You can install it using the apt command in the Linux terminal, as follows:

```
sudo apt update
sudo apt install uftrace
```

After installation, you can run uftrace from the terminal. You can enter uftrace commands and see their output directly in the terminal.

Another way to install uftrace is by downloading the source code and building it yourself. To do this, it is recommended to follow these steps:

1. First, let's download the uftrace source code using the following command:

    ```
    $ git clone https://github.com/namhyung/uftrace.git
    ```

2. After downloading, you will see that the uftrace directory is created. Before building uftrace, we need to install some required packages. To do this, navigate into the uftrace directory and run the following command:

    ```
    $ cd uftrace
    $ sudo misc/install-deps.sh
    ```

3. If you run the install-deps.sh shell script, it will automatically find and install the necessary dependencies to build uftrace.

4. Once the installation is complete, we can build and install uftrace using the following commands:

    ```
    $ ./configure
    $ make
    $ sudo make install
    ```

    Once you install uftrace, you can run uftrace in any directories.

In the next section, we will discuss the basic features of uftrace.

Basic features of uftrace

Now it is time to explore the basic features of uftrace. We will start by building a simple "Hello, World" program as a Linux system application. Then, we will examine the output messages generated by uftrace. Additionally, various output formats of uftrace are explained.

Simple "Hello, World!" project

Let's begin with a simple "Hello, World!" program using the following code:

```c
#include <stdio.h>
int main() {
    printf("Hello, World!\n");
    return 0;
}
```

Let's suppose the source file for this code is named hello.c. Before running uftrace to trace the program, we must compile this code with the -pg option. The following is the complete command:

```
$ gcc -o hello -pg hello.c
```

We can use the -pg option to make the compiler insert special instructions, such as mcount(), at the beginning of each function. This option is used by tools such as gprof or uftrace.

Now, we are ready to run uftrace to analyze the execution flow of the hello program. Let's execute uftrace with the hello option:

```
$ uftrace hello
# DURATION     TID        FUNCTION
   1.093 us [   3568] | __monstartup();
   0.462 us [   3568] | __cxa_atexit();
           [   3568] | main() {
   4.408 us [   3568] |   printf();
   4.982 us [   3568] | }
```

When analyzing the uftrace output, you can observe several key pieces of information from left to right:

- DURATION: The execution time of a function. For example, the printf() function in the preceding message takes 4.408 us to execute.
- TID (thread ID): The identifier of the thread executing the function.

Among these, the DURATION field is particularly important because it allows you to measure the elapsed time of a specific function. This information is useful for debugging performance issues by identifying functions that take longer than other functions.

Why -pg is added when compiling the code

How does uftrace capture and display function tracing information? The function is traced using the _mcount symbol. With the -pg option, additional instruction is added in the base address of the subroutine. Let's take a look at the relevant instruction, as follows:

```
0000000000000934 <main>:
...
  944:   d50320ff        xpaclri
  948:   aa1e03e0        mov      x0, x30
  94c:   97ffff91        bl       790 <_mcount@plt>
  950:   90000000        adrp     x0, 0 <__executable_start>
```

You can find the _mcount symbol in this code. Using the _mcount symbol, uftrace provides the sequence of the call stack.

Format of uftrace output

uftrace supports various output formats for saving execution results. Some of the commonly used formats include the following:

- record: Executes a program and saves the trace data
- replay: Displays program execution from the trace data without running the program again
- report: Shows performance statistics from the trace data

For more detailed options, check the tutorial documentation at https://github.com/namhyung/uftrace.

The following section covers the practical features of uftrace, including three use cases.

Practical features of uftrace

uftrace offers powerful debugging features that are not available in traditional debugging tools. It allows tracing the execution flow of various library functions in user space. Additionally, it can trace function arguments and return values.

Library debugging

When debugging Linux systems, analyzing user-space libraries is often necessary. During software development, you may encounter libraries with large amounts of source code. In such cases, uftrace helps by efficiently analyzing execution flow without modifying or rebuilding the libraries.

Let's first examine the libraries used when executing the pwd command with the absolute path. When you run the pwd command, a specific library file located in a directory is executed. To check this in detail, use the which pwd command:

```
$ which pwd
/usr/bin/pwd
```

Here, we can see that /usr/bin/pwd is the actual executable file that runs when the pwd command is executed. The output indicates that executing the pwd command actually runs the /usr/bin/pwd file.

When /usr/bin/pwd is executed, which library functions are called? To answer this question, we need to download the library source code and analyze its functions. However, if you run uftrace with the --force option, you can identify the library functions that are invoked.

Now, let's use the following command to trace the execution of /usr/bin/pwd:

```
$ uftrace record --force /usr/bin/pwd
```

This command includes the --force option, which allows us to view a list of function calls even though we do not have the source code for the executable file.

When running uftrace with the record option, it generates various debugging files inside the uftrace.data directory. These files contain detailed execution logs, which can be seen here:

```
$ cd uftrace.data/
$ ls
1967.dat                 libcapstone.so.4.sym   liblzma.so.5.4.1.sym
perf-cpu2.dat
default.opts             libc.so.6.sym          libm.so.6.sym
perf-cpu3.dat
info                     libdw-0.188.so.sym     libz.so.1.2.13.sym
pwd.sym
ld-linux-aarch64.so.1.sym libelf-0.188.so.sym    perf-cpu0.dat
sid-d3915c5a0393b716.map
libbz2.so.1.0.4.sym       libgcc_s.so.1.sym      perf-cpu1.dat
task.txt
```

Once you run this command, you will notice that several library and text files are generated. After confirming that these files are generated, we can proceed with running uftrace using the replay option:

```
$ uftrace replay
# DURATION     TID       FUNCTION
    7.204 us [    1967] | getenv();
    0.870 us [    1967] | strrchr();
    0.704 us [    1967] | strncmp();
   44.056 us [    1967] | setlocale();
    1.722 us [    1967] | bindtextdomain();
    1.259 us [    1967] | textdomain();
    0.593 us [    1967] | __cxa_atexit();
    3.555 us [    1967] | getopt_long();
    5.723 us [    1967] | getcwd();
    [...]
    0.167 us [    1967] | fflush();
    0.704 us [    1967] | fclose();
```

From this message, we can see that the getenv, strrchr, and setlocale functions are actually called inside the library.

In real-world projects, developers often integrate libraries from other departments within their company or from third-party vendors. Having the ability to quickly analyze different libraries can significantly enhance debugging skills and overall development efficiency.

Argument tracing

When debugging, it is common to check function arguments to understand how a program processes data. But how can we trace the arguments passed to a function? The most basic approach is to insert printf statements into the source code and then recompile the program.

uftrace provides an argument tracing feature, which prints function arguments as messages. This is especially useful for analyzing source code since it allows developers to observe the actual argument values passed to functions during execution.

Now, let's extract the string passed to the printf function in the following hello world code:

```c
#include <stdio.h>
int main() {
    printf("Hello, World!\n");
```

```
    return 0;
}
```

In this case, the printf function takes "Hello, World!" as its argument. Instead of modifying the source code to print this argument, we can use uftrace to display it directly. First, run the command with the appropriate argument option:

```
$ uftrace -A printf@arg1/s hello
# DURATION     TID       FUNCTION
   1.741 us [    2035] |  __monstartup();
   0.667 us [    2035] |  __cxa_atexit();
           [    2035] |  main() {
 211.186 us [    2035] |    printf("Hello world n");
 211.816 us [    2035] |  } /* main */
```

The arg1/s option in uftrace prints the first argument of a function. The s specifier ensures that the argument is displayed as a string. Like the s specifier, uftrace supports various formats to display arguments.

If a function takes only one argument, this method works well. However, many functions take multiple arguments, sometimes more than three.

To analyze additional arguments, you can specify multiple argument options accordingly. If you want to trace three or more arguments passed to a function, you can use the -A option with arg specifiers.

> **Note**
>
> For convenience, uftrace adds argument specifiers for well-known library functions such as printf, strcmp, and others. In this case, we can simply use -A printf without manually providing argument specifiers.

For example, to trace three arguments passed to the example_func function inside the hello program, use the following command:

```
$ uftrace -A example_func@arg1,arg2,arg3 hello
```

This will display the actual values of arg1, arg2, and arg3 when the function is executed.

> **Note**
>
> Unfortunately, several features of arg1 do not work well on ARM platforms due to the mcount ABI.

Now that we have learned how to trace function arguments with uftrace, let's move on to tracing function return values.

Return value tracing

When a function completes execution, it returns a result using the return statement. Many software routines rely on return values to handle error conditions, making it common to check return values during debugging. uftrace provides a return value tracing feature.

Let's take a look at the following example code, where a function returns a value:

```
int add_func(int x, int y)
{
    int result = x + y;
    printf("x:%d, y:%d \n", x, y);

    return result;
}
```

The add_func function takes two arguments and returns the sum of these values using the return result; statement.

Now, how can we check the return value of result using uftrace? To capture function return values, we can use the -R option when running uftrace. To trace the return value of the add_func function, we can use the following command:

```
$ uftrace -R add_func@retval add_func
```

When we execute this command, we will see an output as follows:

```
x:2, y:3, ret:5
# DURATION     TID        FUNCTION
   1.852 us [    2028] | __monstartup();
   0.685 us [    2028] | __cxa_atexit();
```

```
              [   2028] | main() {
              [   2028] |   add_func() {
 17.445 us [   2028] |     printf();
 18.167 us [   2028] |   } = 5; /* add_func */
 19.741 us [   2028] | } /* main */
```

In the output results, what we can see is that the add_func function returns a value of 5. Additionally, we can observe the function call stack and note that the function execution takes 18.167 microseconds with function call stacks.

> **Note**
>
> In Linux and many other systems, error information is typically returned as a negative integer. It is important to pay close attention when a function returns a negative value, as it often indicates an error.

By analyzing function return values, developers can gain valuable insights into program behavior and identify potential issues early in the debugging process.

Summary

In this chapter, we explored uftrace. First, we discussed the importance of using trace logs to predict the execution flow and behavior of software. By combining binary analysis with trace logs, developers can gain a deeper understanding of how a program executes.

We introduced the key features of uftrace and explained how to install and use it. Using a simple Hello World example, we demonstrated how to trace function arguments and return values with uftrace.

Although we only covered the basic features of uftrace, this tool has many powerful features that can greatly help improve debugging skills and software quality. To explore more advanced features, refer to the uftrace GitHub repository at https://github.com/namhyung/uftrace, where you can find additional documentation and examples.

The next chapter will cover **TrustZone**, one of the most widely used security features provided by Armv8-A.

Part 4

Security Features in Armv8-A Systems

In this part, we will dive deeply into the security features available in Armv8-A systems. First, we will take a detailed look at TrustZone. In addition, we will introduce and explain the latest security features in Armv8-A, such as **PAN (Privileged Access Never)**, **PAC (Pointer Authentication Code)**, **BTI (Branch Target Identification)**, and **MTE (Memory Tagging Extension)**.

This part has the following chapters:

- *Chapter 14, Securing Execution with Armv8-A TrustZone*
- *Chapter 15, Building Defenses with Key Security Features of Armv8-A*

14

Securing Execution with Armv8-A TrustZone

The Arm® architecture provides security features known as **TrustZone®**. TrustZone is everywhere. Almost all Arm processors in the IT sector operate with TrustZone enabled.

We will begin by exploring the core features of TrustZone. Next, we will examine the hardware components that enable TrustZone's functionality. Finally, we will review **Arm Trusted Firmware (TF-A)** code to understand how TrustZone-related interfaces are implemented in real systems.

This chapter covers TrustZone with the following topics:

- Introducing TrustZone
- Key concepts of TrustZone
- Secure monitor call
- Implementation of TrustZone in real systems
- Analyzing Arm Trusted Firmware
- Hardware features related to TrustZone

Let's begin this chapter by exploring why TrustZone was introduced.

Technical requirements

To learn more about TrustZone in Armv8-A, you can check the following materials:

- Armv8-A Reference Manual: `https://developer.arm.com/documentation/ddi0487/gb`
- Programmer's Guide for Armv8-A: `https://developer.arm.com/documentation/den0024/latest/`

Introducing TrustZone

TrustZone is a security extension that is widely used across the IT industry. Many modern Arm-based devices, such as smartphones, digital TVs, and automotive systems, rely on TrustZone to improve security.

With TrustZone, chipset manufacturers can create a secure environment where applications run in an isolated, protected space.

Why was TrustZone introduced?

TrustZone was first introduced in 2004 in response to the growing demand for security at the CPU architecture level. At that time, many software companies and system developers realized the need for a secure execution environment.

The main reason for this demand was security threats. As software technology advanced, cyber-attacks also increased. Attackers might exploit software vulnerabilities, making it difficult to rely solely on software-based security solutions. For this reason, many IT companies have requested an execution environment that can provide system security features at the hardware level.

To support this requirement, chipset manufacturers had to integrate dedicated security hardware into their chipsets to support security features. However, a new requirement emerged in the IT industry—security features should be introduced at the architecture level within the CPU itself, eliminating the need to integrate additional security hardware.

To meet this requirement, the Arm company designed TrustZone. TrustZone allows a trusted OS (secure operating system) to run separately from the normal OS, reducing attack surfaces at the architecture level.

With TrustZone, developers can perform the following tasks:

- Protect sensitive data, such as cryptographic keys and authentication processes
- Develop secure applications that operate in an isolated environment
- Establish a trusted computing environment for various applications, including mobile devices, automotive systems, and IoT security solutions

Today, TrustZone is a key security feature in Arm's Cortex-A series processors. In the next section, we will explore the key features of TrustZone in more detail.

What are the primary features of TrustZone?

TrustZone enables the creation of a secure and trusted execution environment within the CPU. This is supported at both the hardware and software levels. With TrustZone, developers can separate normal and secure operations. In TrustZone, the CPU is divided into two execution environments:

- **Secure world**: A security-enhanced execution environment where secure applications and a secure OS run safely. This environment is designed to protect sensitive data and critical operations.
- **Non-secure world**: The normal execution environment where general applications and the main OS run

With the features provided by TrustZone, you can handle security-sensitive data, such as passwords, in the Secure world.

Why we need to learn about TrustZone

Now, let's go over the reasons why we need to learn about TrustZone.

When you first hear about TrustZone, you might think it is only related to security features. For this reason, security developers especially need to learn about it. But what if you are not a security developer? Do you still need to learn about TrustZone? The answer is yes! It is important for all software engineers, especially those working at a low level. It is more than just a security extension—it is a key part of modern system architecture.

By learning about TrustZone, developers can do the following:

- Improve system performance by managing Secure and Non-secure transitions efficiently
- Fix stability issues in the Secure world
- Build a strong foundation for the boot process, including Secure Boot

You already understand why TrustZone was introduced. In the next section, we will explore how TrustZone works by introducing its key concepts.

Key concepts of TrustZone

TrustZone creates two separate environments to protect sensitive data and processes. To understand how this works, we first need to explore the Non-secure world and the Secure world. Next, we need to analyze how execution flows between these two worlds. This transition happens through a special instruction called the **secure monitor call (SMC)**, which will be discussed in the *Secure monitor call* section.

Understanding the Non-secure world

First, let's review *Figure 14.1* to understand the key concepts of TrustZone.

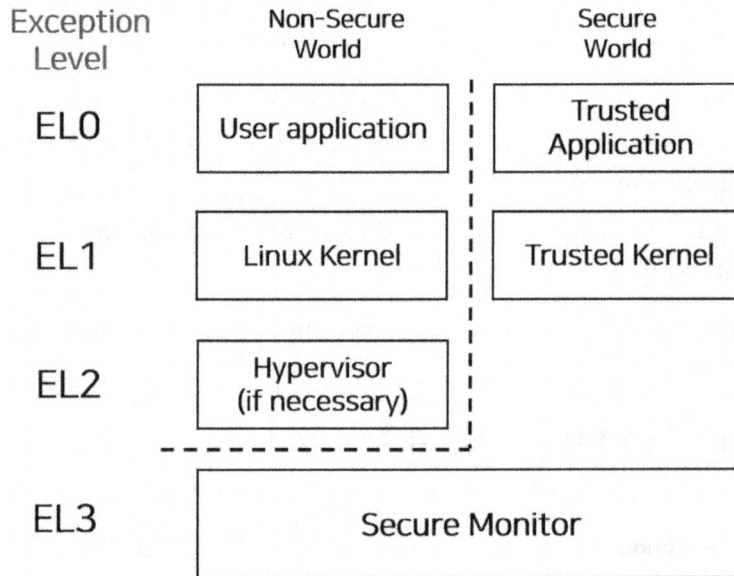

Figure 14.1: The workflow of TrustZone

In *Figure 14.1*, the left side represents the Non-secure world. But what is the Non-secure world? We can explain it as follows:

- In the Non-secure world, the operating system kernel and user applications run. This environment is also called the Normal world.

- In general, most of the software we develop runs in the Non-secure world. This includes standard applications, OS services, and system processes.

On the right side of *Figure 14.1*, you can see the Secure world. What kind of software runs in the Secure world? Here are some examples:

- This environment runs the Trusted Kernel and Trusted Application.

- Security-related features and applications are implemented here to protect sensitive data and operations.

- At EL1, the Trusted Kernel runs. This is often a security-enhanced **real-time operating system (RTOS)** that provides features such as authentication, encryption, and secure communication.

- At EL0, security-related applications are executed.

- At EL3, the Secure Monitor runs. When a transition occurs between the Non-secure world and the Secure world using the SMC instruction, it passes through EL3.

Security-enhanced features, such as cryptographic operations, Secure Boot, and authentication services, can be implemented in either the Trusted Kernel or Trusted Application. By running the Trusted Kernel or Trusted Application, sensitive data and operations can be protected from potential threats in the Non-secure world.

> **Note**
>
> In TrustZone, the term "world" refers to an execution environment or mode, similar to privilege levels in CPU architecture. It distinguishes between Secure and Non-secure processing states.

These days, many people learn new features by reviewing the reference code. Because of this, you may wonder what kind of code actually runs in the Non-secure world.

In the case of the Linux OS, both user applications and the Linux Kernel run in the Non-secure world. To understand this better, let's look at a simple example code running in the Non-secure world:

```
#include <stdio.h>
int main()
{
    printf("hello, world\n");
    return 0;
}
```

This code is a basic Linux system programming example. From the perspective of the Armv8-A architecture, this code runs at EL0. In other words, it executes in user space within the Non-secure world.

Now, let's examine one of the key kernel functions:

```
asmlinkage __visible void __sched schedule(void)
{
    [...]
    if (!task_is_running(tsk))
```

```
        sched_submit_work(tsk);
    __schedule_loop(SM_NONE);
    sched_update_worker(tsk);
}
```

One important example is the schedule() function in the Linux Kernel. This function performs process scheduling, allowing different tasks to share CPU time efficiently. From an Armv8-A perspective, schedule() runs at EL1, which means it executes in kernel space within the Non-secure world.

In general, most of the code you develop—whether it is a user application or part of the Linux Kernel—runs in the Non-secure world. This includes everyday software including system utilities, web browsers, and mobile applications.

Software scenario of the Secure world

In fact, the code of the Trusted Kernel or Trusted Application running in the Secure world is often not open to the public. For this reason, you may wonder what types of software functions or applications should be executed in the Secure world. To better understand this, let's explore some real-world examples. The following are some typical cases:

- **Fingerprint recognition applications**: These applications store and verify fingerprint data to unlock devices or authorize secure transactions
- **Internet banking applications**: Online banking services process sensitive financial information, such as account balances and transactions
- **Critical chipset operations**: Critical functionality such as firmware image authentication ensures that only trusted software runs on a device, preventing unauthorized modifications

Because these applications handle sensitive data and security-critical tasks, they are designed to run in the Secure world.

Now that we have learned about the Secure world and the Non-secure world, the next section will introduce the concept of the SMC. This mechanism enables the system to switch between the Secure and Non-secure worlds.

Secure monitor call

The SMC is an important operation that allows the system to switch between the Non-secure world and the Secure world. To understand how it works, we need to first look at some key components, such as exception levels and exceptions, from the Armv8-A perspective.

Non-secure world to Secure world

Let's take a look at *Figure 14.2*, which illustrates the transition process from the Non-secure world to the Secure world:

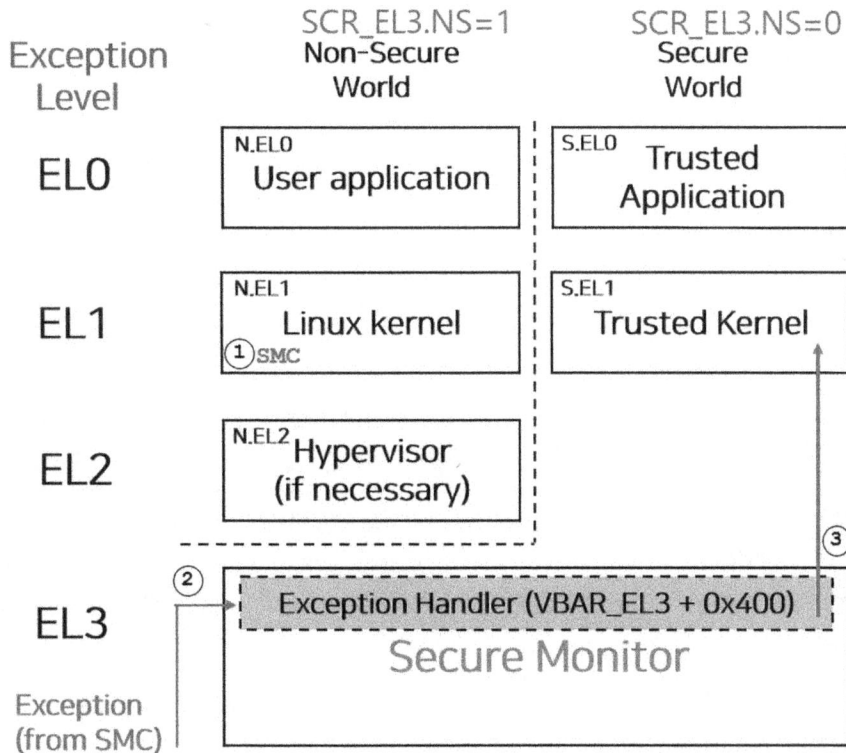

Figure 14.2: The architectural diagram of TrustZone in Armv8-A

On the left side of *Figure 14.2*, you can see the exception levels in the Non-secure world:

- N.EL0: User applications run at EL0.
- N.EL1: The RTOS kernel or Linux Kernel is executed here.
- N.EL2: The hypervisor runs at EL2. In this figure, we assume that the hypervisor is not running. A hypervisor manages the resources of multiple OSs.

Here, N.EL0 refers to EL0 in the Non-secure world, and N.EL1 refers to EL1 in the Non-secure world. As mentioned several times, most software typically runs at N.EL0, N.EL1, and N.EL2. At EL3, the Secure Monitor operates, which handles transitions between the Non-secure world and the Secure world.

Now, let's review the right side of *Figure 14.2*, which represents the Secure world. In the Secure world, we can expect that the following software runs at each exception level:

- S.EL0: Trusted Application runs
- S.EL1: The Trusted kernel operates here

S.EL0 refers to EL0 in the Secure world, and S.EL1 represents EL1 in the Secure world.

The important question is: how can software check whether it is running in the Non-secure world or the Secure world? We can find this information using SCR_EL3.NS, which is shown at the top of *Figure 14.2*:

- SCR_EL3.NS=1 means the software is in the Non-secure world
- SCR_EL3.NS=0 means the software is in the Secure world

The SCR_EL3 register can only be accessed at EL3.

Another important point is how the system switches between the Non-secure world and the Secure world. This transition can be done using the SMC instruction.

In *Figure 14.2*, take a look at **1**. This step shows that the SMC instruction is executed in the Non-secure world at EL1. The execution of the SMC instruction triggers a transition from the Non-secure world to the Secure world. During this operation, the Arm core performs the actions marked as **2** in *Figure 14.2*:

- Switches to EL3 to run the exception handler
- Starts running the Secure Monitor at EL3

3 represents the operation that switches to EL1 in the Secure world (S.EL1). Once the control is transferred to the Trusted Kernel at EL1, security-related features begin to run.

The Secure Monitor plays a key role in the transition between the Non-secure world and the Secure world. So, what is expected to execute in the Secure Monitor? The implementation of the Secure Monitor can vary depending on the specific requirements. However, regardless of the differences in implementation, the general sequence of operations at EL3 is as follows:

- Stores the current set of general-purpose registers at the moment the SMC instruction runs at EL1 into the stack area
- Executes the necessary security operations in the Secure Monitor
- Performs the transition to either the Trusted Kernel (S.EL1) or the Linux Kernel (N.EL1).

The behavior of the Secure Monitor at EL3 depends on its software implementation. For example, the Secure Monitor can handle various tasks, such as decrypting the general-purpose registers, managing access control, and performing system integrity checks.

Secure world to Non-secure world

Once the processor enters S.EL1, the Trusted Kernel starts to execute. The Trusted Kernel is responsible for executing operations associated with security features, such as the following:

- Generating and managing encryption keys
- Running security-sensitive applications, such as internet banking or biometric authentication systems

In the Secure world, software runs in either the Trusted Kernel or Trusted Application. Once a task is completed in the Secure world, execution transitions back to the Non-secure world. This process is marked as **[1]** in *Figure 14.3*.

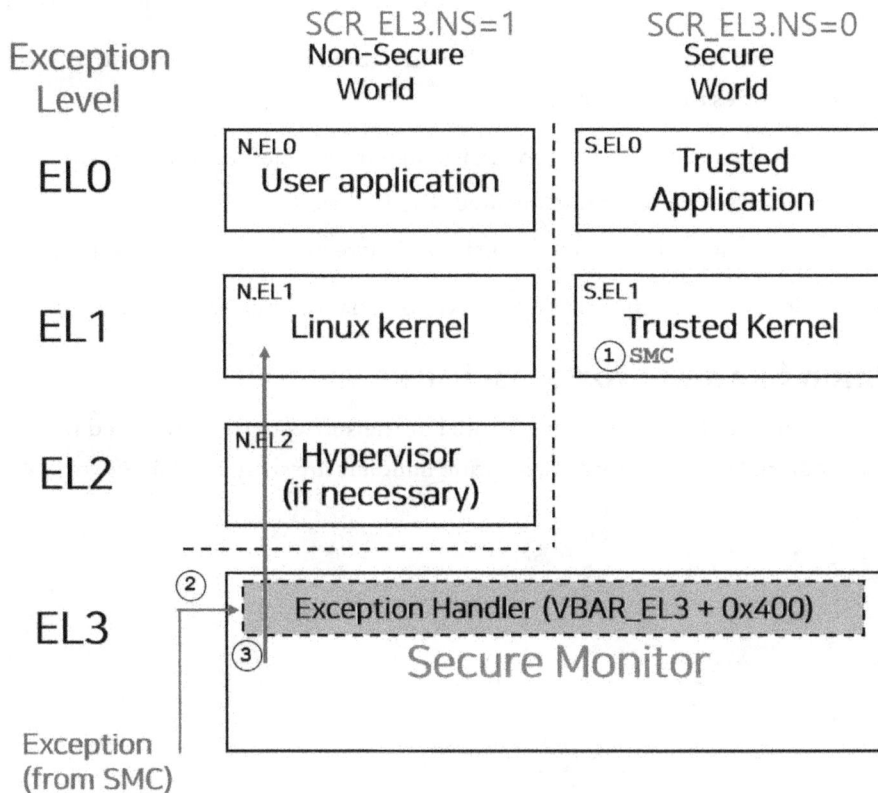

Figure 14.3: The transition from the Secure world to the Non-secure world

Also, the transition occurs when the SMC instruction is executed in the Trusted Kernel at S.EL1. During this process, it performs the following tasks, marked as **2** in *Figure 14.3*:

- Switches EL3 by triggering an exception
- Executes necessary security-related tasks in the Secure Monitor at EL3

[3] represents the operation that transfers execution back to EL1 in the Non-secure world.

Here, we have seen how the software switches between the Non-secure world and the Secure world. Now, let's take a closer look at the responsibilities of EL3. When an SMC instruction is executed from the Secure world, the Secure Monitor at EL3 is a core part of managing the transition. One of its main tasks is to restore the register values of EL1 in either the Non-secure world or the Secure world using the stack or memory area at EL3.

As we have discussed in this section, the Secure Monitor at EL3 acts as a gatekeeper. Every time execution enters or exits the Secure world, it must pass through EL3. This ensures that transitions between the Non-secure world and the Secure world are properly controlled and securely managed.

Understanding this execution flow is essential for designing secure and efficient TrustZone-based applications. It ensures the following:

- Security-sensitive operations remain isolated from general applications.
- Secure world software is only executed when necessary.
- The system efficiently manages transitions between the Secure and Non-secure worlds.

In the next section, we will explore how the exception handler for TrustZone is organized.

Exception handlers for TrustZone

To understand how TrustZone is implemented at the software level, we need to examine the exception handlers. Let's see how the exception handlers are structured in *Figure 14.4*.

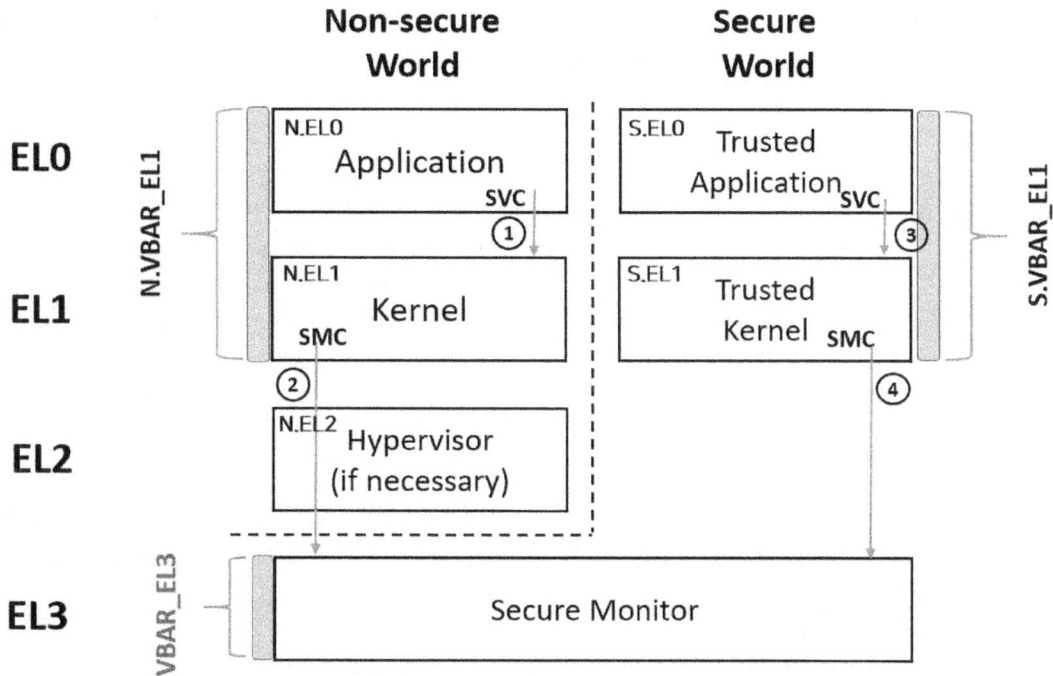

Non-secure World

Secure World

ELO

N.VBAR_EL1

N.EL0
Application
SVC
(1)

S.EL0 Trusted
Application SVC
(3)

S.VBAR_EL1

EL1

N.EL1
Kernel
SMC
(2)

S.EL1 Trusted
Kernel SMC
(4)

EL2

N.EL2 Hypervisor
(if necessary)

EL3

VBAR_EL3

Secure Monitor

- **VBAR_EL3**
  - Current Exception Level: EL3
  - Lower Exception Level: EL1

Figure 14.4: Exception handlers in the Armv8 architecture

At the top left of *Figure 14.4*, VBAR_EL1 represents the base address of the exception vector table for the Non-secure state at EL1. When an exception occurs at EL0 or EL1, the **program counter (PC)** jumps to the exception vector specified by VBAR_EL1.

More specifically, when an exception occurs at EL0 or EL1, the processor refers to VBAR_EL1 to find the correct exception vector address to execute the corresponding exception handler.

> **Note**
>
> The exception vector table is implemented in software to handle exceptions. Each address in the exception vector table contains an assembly routine that works as an exception handler. When an exception occurs, PC jumps to the corresponding exception vector address, allowing the appropriate exception handler to run.

At the bottom left of *Figure 14.4*, VBAR_EL3 represents the base address of the exception vector table at EL3.

When an SMC instruction is executed from either Non-secure EL1 (N.EL1) or Secure EL1 (S.EL1), PC jumps to the exception vector specified by VBAR_EL3. The following operations take place:

- The Secure Monitor at EL3 takes control of execution
- The system performs necessary security operations

Software running at EL3 performs more security-related operations than software at S-EL1. This is because EL3 has the highest privilege level.

On the right side of *Figure 14.4*, the base address of the exception vector table in the Secure world is shown as S.VBAR_EL1. The Trusted Kernel and Trusted Application run in a separate physical memory area, distinct from the physical memory space where the Linux Kernel runs. This ensures isolated and secure execution. The VBAR_EL1 register is also separated: S.VBAR_EL1 is used in the Secure world, while N.VBAR_EL1 is used in the Non-secure world.

When the Trusted Kernel is running in the Secure world, this exception vector table handles exceptions that occur at the following:

- Secure EL0 (S.EL0)
- Secure EL1 (S.EL1)

In S.EL1, the Trusted OS or Trusted Kernel runs, managing secure resources and handling secure exceptions. In S.EL0, trusted applications run to provide services, similar to how regular applications do in the Non-secure world.

We have learned how the transition between the Non-secure world and the Secure world takes place. To understand how the software is implemented, it is essential to explore how the exception vector table is structured. This is because the execution of the SMC instruction triggers an exception. Let's examine the exception vector table shown in *Table 14.1* from the EL3 perspective.

Exception taken from	Offset for exception type			
	Synchronous	IRQ or vIRQ	FIQ or vFIQ	SError or vSError
Current exception level with SP_EL0	0x000	0x080	0x100	0x180
Current exception level with SP_ELx, x>0	0x200	0x280	0x300	0x380
Lower exception level, where the implemented level immediately lower than the target level is using AArch64	0x400	0x480	0x500	0x580
Lower exception level, where the implemented level immediately lower than the target level is using AArch32	0x600	0x680	0x700	0x780

Table 14.1: Specification of the exception vector table in the Armv8-A architecture

(The reference for the exception vector table in *Table 14.1* is https://developer.arm.com/documentation/ddi0487/gb: *Arm Architecture Reference Manual Armv8, for A-profile architecture, Table D1-5 Vector offsets from vector table base address*.)

Before analyzing the structure of the exception vector table, we first need to determine the current **exception level** (**EL**). Once we identify the current EL, we can find the lower EL. From the VBAR_EL3 perspective, the current EL is EL3. The lower exception levels can be EL2, EL1, or EL0 since these levels are lower than EL3.

In the exception vector table (*Table 14.1*), the term *Lower exception level* refers to these exception levels.

Let's break down the exception vector table in *Table 14.1* with a focus on the lower ELs:

- The lower ELs include EL1 and EL2. As for EL0, it does not have the privilege to execute the SMC instruction.
- In systems without a hypervisor, EL1 is typically considered the lower EL. When an SMC instruction is executed at EL1, the processor transitions to EL3 to handle the request. In this case, the software at EL1 is in AArch64.

- PC is branched into the exception vector address by adding an offset of +0x400 to the base address defined by VBAR_EL3 because a synchronous exception occurs during the execution of the SMC instruction.

- Software at EL1 can be either AArch64 or AArch32. For this reason, there are two separate exception vector offsets for EL1, depending on the execution state:

  - If the SMC instruction is executed while the Linux Kernel is running in AArch64, the 0x400 offset is applied to calculate the exception vector address

  - If the SMC instruction is executed while an RTOS is running in AArch32, the 0x600 offset is applied

  These exception vector offsets are designed to support compatibility, as software at EL1 can be configured in various ways.

Having explored the exception handler at the software level, we will now take a closer look at how the Trusted Kernel is implemented in real-world projects.

Implementation of TrustZone in real systems

Chipset vendors and security companies use TrustZone to build secure environments in various ways. This section explains how a trusted OS is designed and operates within TrustZone.

How does a trusted OS run in the Secure world?

In the Non-secure world, an OS kernel such as Linux is executed. But what kind of software runs in the Secure world? The answer is an RTOS designed for security tasks. It is known that an RTOS features task management, interrupt handling, and so on. Trusted kernel has similar components to an RTOS, focusing more on security-related operations, such as secure service handling and access control.

Here are some important points to understand:

- The RTOS in the Secure world does not function independently like a traditional OS. Instead, it cooperates with the Non-secure world and runs only when needed.

- When the kernel in the Non-secure world executes the SMC instruction, it switches execution to the Secure world. There, the trusted OS (RTOS) runs and performs its tasks.

In simple terms, the RTOS in the Secure world behaves similarly to a system call handler. A system call handler does not execute on its own. Instead, only after the system call is invoked using SVC instruction does the system call handler run.

Likewise, when the Non-secure world executes an SMC instruction, the execution flow switches to the Secure world, allowing the RTOS to process secure operations.

Examples of security implementations using TrustZone

When implementing the interface for using the SMC instruction, we can consider the following three common approaches:

- **Using register arguments:** When executing an SMC instruction in the Non-secure world or Secure world, arguments can be passed using the X0 ~ X7 registers in Armv8-A (AArch64). The software in the Secure world reads these arguments and performs different functions based on their values.

- **Restricting access to secure memory:** Certain memory regions can be configured as secure. This means that software in the Non-secure world is not allowed to access these secure memory regions. This restriction blocks unauthorized access. If a process in the Non-secure world tries to access a protected memory region, the system can respond in different ways depending on security policies:

  - Trigger a **Fast Interrupt Request (FIQ)** to notify the Trusted Kernel
  - Reset the system at the hardware level to prevent potential security breaches
  - Generate a fault and deny access to protect sensitive data

  When unauthorized access is detected, we need to check how to handle it.

- **Downloading and running secure code separately:** Secure software that runs in the Secure world can be downloaded from a separate partition. It also runs in a separate physical memory area. This ensures that trusted code remains isolated from the Non-secure world. Additionally, the Trusted Kernel in the Secure world is designed to do the following:

  - Verify and authenticate kernel or firmware images before execution to prevent unauthorized modifications
  - Ensure that only signed and validated software runs, protecting the system from malicious modifications

  This approach is commonly used in Secure Boot mechanisms, ensuring that only authorized firmware and OS components are loaded during system startup.

The way a trusted OS is implemented depends on the system requirements:

- In automotive products, secure software enhances security features for vehicle systems
- In cloud servers, additional security measures are designed based on cloud security requirements

So far, we have explored how the software components of TrustZone are implemented. Next, we will discuss Arm Trusted Firmware, which defines the standard interface for TrustZone-related features.

Analyzing Arm Trusted Firmware

Several chipset manufacturers and security companies aimed to standardize the implementation of TrustZone and its interface. As a result, the Arm Trusted Firmware open source project was initiated. In this section, we will introduce Arm Trusted Firmware and examine its key interfaces to understand how the Secure Monitor at EL3 is implemented. Before analyzing the code, let's first figure out what Arm Trusted Firmware is.

For more details about Arm Trusted Firmware, you can visit the following URL: https://github.com/ARM-software/arm-trusted-firmware.

Analyzing the exception handler at EL3

When the SMC instruction is executed in either the Non-secure world or the Secure world, the EL switches to EL3, triggering the exception handler at EL3.

The exception handler code analyzed in this section is located in bl31/aarch64/runtime_exceptions.S. The corresponding instructions are extracted using a binary utility such as objdump after the ELF file is generated.

In the *Secure monitor call* section, we reviewed the exception vector table in Armv8-A. The exception vector table is shown in *Table 14.2*, from the perspective of EL3.

Exception taken from	Offset for exception type			
	Synchronous	IRQ	FIQ	SError
EL3 with SP_EL0	0xe046000	0xe046080	0xe046100	0xe046180
EL3	0xe046200	0xe046280	0xe046300	0xe046380
EL1 (AArch64)	0xe046400	0xe046480	0xe046500	0xe046580
EL1 (AArch32)	0xe046600	0xe046680	0xe046700	0xe046780

Table 14.2: The exception vector table at EL3

If the current EL is EL3, the lower EL is either EL1 or EL2. This means that any exception occurring at EL1 or EL2 will be taken to EL3 for exception handling. The base address and offset for the exception handler are as follows:

- **Exception handler base address**: 0xe046000 (stored in VBAR_EL3)
- **Offset interval for each exception**: 0x80

To fully understand how exceptions are handled in the Secure Monitor at EL3, it is important to examine the exception vector table and the exception handler structure. Please keep the following points in mind:

- PC branches based on the following rule: *Exception Vector Base Address + Offset Address*
- The VBAR_EL3 register holds the base address of the exception handler in EL3

So far, we have examined how the exception vector table is organized from the perspective of EL3. Let's now move on to explore the overall execution flow.

Exception handler for the SMC instruction

Figure 14.5 illustrates the execution flow when the SMC instruction is executed, along with the corresponding exception vector table at EL3.

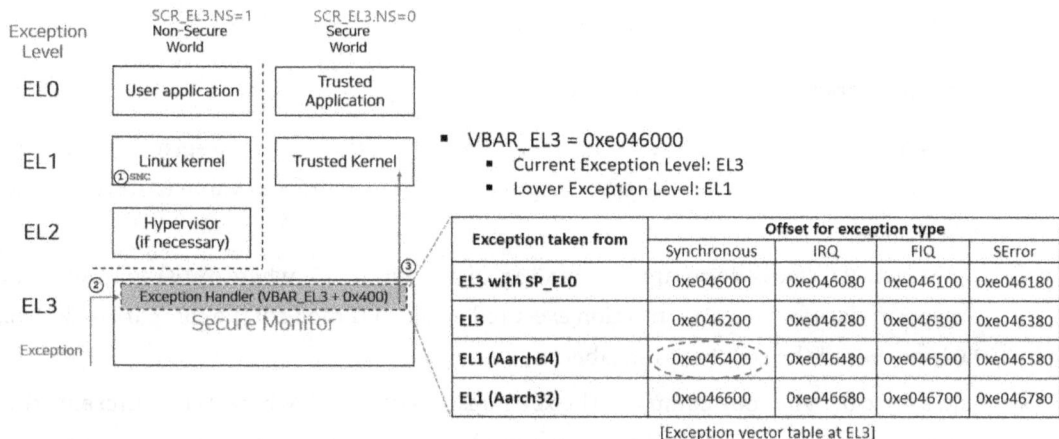

Exception taken from	Offset for exception type			
	Synchronous	IRQ	FIQ	SError
EL3 with SP_EL0	0xe046000	0xe046080	0xe046100	0xe046180
EL3	0xe046200	0xe046280	0xe046300	0xe046380
EL1 (Aarch64)	0xe046400	0xe046480	0xe046500	0xe046580
EL1 (Aarch32)	0xe046600	0xe046680	0xe046700	0xe046780

[Exception vector table at EL3]

Figure 14.5: The workflow with the exception vector table at EL3

From *Figure 14.5*, we can highlight the following important points to remember:

- When the SMC instruction is executed at EL1, which is a lower privilege level than EL3, PC branches to VBAR_EL3 + 0x400

- Since VBAR_EL3 holds the value of 0xe046000, PC branches to 0xe046400, based on the 0xe046000 + 0x400 rule

Another important point is the control flow when switching between the Secure and Non-secure worlds through EL3. It works as follows:

- From N.EL1 → EL3 → S.EL1
- From S.EL1 → EL3 → N.EL1

Now that we have reviewed how the exception vector table is organized, let's look at an example of the exception handler code at the corresponding address:

```
01 0xe046400 <sync_exception_aarch64>:
02     0xe046400:    d50344ff    msr     daifclr, #0x4
03     0xe046404:    f9007bfe    str     x30, [sp,#240]
04     0xe046408:    d53e521e    mrs     x30, esr_el3
05     0xe04640c:    d35a7fde    ubfx    x30, x30, #26, #6
06     0xe046410:    f1004fdf    cmp     x30, #0x13
07     0xe046414:    54ff3220    b.eq    0xe044a58 <smc_handler>
08     0xe046418:    f1005fdf    cmp     x30, #0x17
09     0xe04641c:    54ff3200    b.eq    0xe044a5c <smc_handler64>
10     0xe046420:    f9407bfe    ldr     x30, [sp,#240]
```

Let's explain the important parts of this code:

- Lines 04 to 05: The code reads the [31:26] bits from the esr_el3 register (exception syndrome register) to identify the exception class. The extracted value is stored in the x30 register.
- Lines 06 to 07: The code compares the x30 register with 0x13, where 0x13 represents the exception class for an SMC instruction executed in AArch32 mode. If the comparison is true, PC branches to the smc_handler label.
- Lines 08 to 09: The code compares the x30 register with 0x17, where 0x17 represents the exception class for an SMC instruction executed in AArch64 mode. If the comparison is true, PC branches to the smc_handler64 label.

Here, the exception class represents the cause of the synchronous exception. This is updated to [31:26] in ESR_EL3 when the synchronous exception is taken to EL3. The way the branch to a specific label occurs depends on the mode in which the SMC instruction is executed:

- smc_handler: Handles the SMC instruction if it is executed in AArch32 mode

- smc_handler64: Handles the SMC instruction if it is executed in AArch64 mode

At this point, we need to understand AArch64 and AArch32 at EL1, which is the lower EL, by looking at *Figure 14.6*:

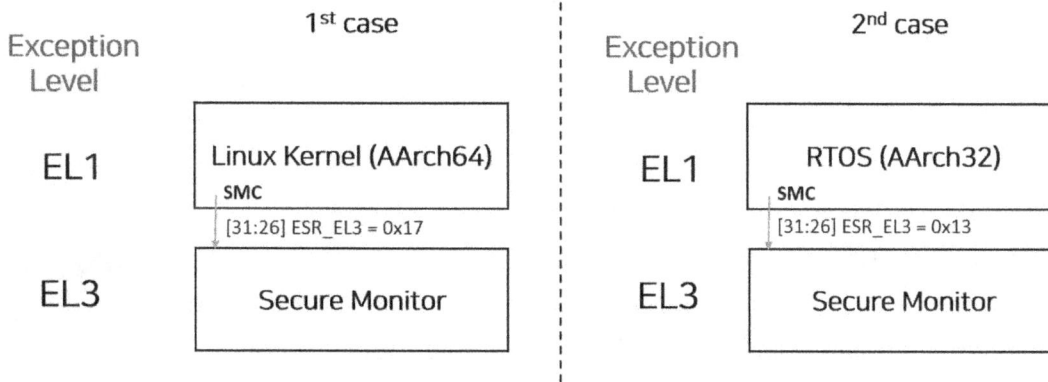

Figure 14.6: How ESR_EL3 is updated depending on the execution state

Let's break down each case in *Figure 14.6*:

- **Case 1:** The Linux Kernel running in AArch64 is operating at EL1. When the SMC instruction is executed, the [31:26] bits of ESR_EL3 are updated to 0x17 during the generation of the synchronous exception. As the subroutine, it branches to the smc_handler64 label.

- **Case 2:** An RTOS running in AArch32 is operating at EL1. When the SMC instruction is executed, the [31:26] bits of ESR_EL3 are updated to 0x13. As the subroutine, it branches to the smc_handler32 label.

This exception-handling design improves compatibility, as the software at EL1 can be either AArch64 or AArch32, depending on the project requirements. From the perspective of Armv8-A, most Linux Kernels today run in 64-bit mode. Therefore, it is particularly important to focus on the smc_handler64 routine for further analysis.

In this section, we examined how the exception handler is executed when an SMC instruction is triggered at EL3. Next, we will dive deeper into the architecture-level security features of TrustZone.

Hardware features related to TrustZone

To fully understand how TrustZone works, it is important to explore the hardware features that support it.

AWPROT and ARPROT signals

Inside a chipset with an Arm processor, many control and data signals are transmitted between different components at the hardware level. The chipset consists of multiple **intellectual property (IP)** blocks, such as Arm processors, memory controllers, and peripherals. In the big picture of a bus system, some components are considered masters, while others act as slaves (targets). The masters initiate transactions, and the slaves respond to them.

Arm defines the **Advanced Microcontroller Bus Architecture (AMBA)** bus protocol, which standardizes how signals are transmitted to enable communication between different IP blocks within a chipset.

By analyzing these hardware-level signals, we can better understand how security features are implemented at the chipset level.

Figure 14.7 shows examples of these signals, which were measured using hardware equipment.

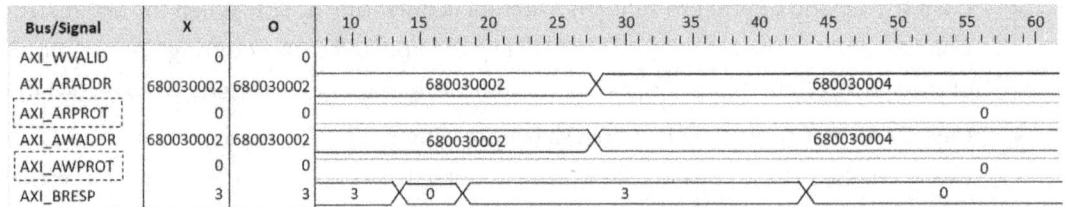

Figure 14.7: An example of the AMBA bus signals

When the Arm processor runs, many signals are transmitted based on the AMBA bus protocol. Among these signals, some are sent from the Arm processor to the bus. Two important signals are AWPROT (write operation) and ARPROT (read operation), which indicate whether a transaction is occurring in the Secure world or the Non-secure world. The reference manual usually refers to AWPROT and ARPROT as AxPROT.

You can find the difference between these signals as follows:

- AWPROT stands for **AXI Write Address PROTection**. It is a signal sent on the write address channel.

- ARPROT stands for **AXI Read Address PROTection**. It is a signal sent on the read address channel.

Using these signals, we can distinguish operations between these two security domains.

The AxPROT signal has three key modes, which are explained in *Table 14.3*.

AxPROT[2:0]	Protection level
[0]	High: Privileged access
	Low: Normal access
[1]	High: Non-secure access
	Low: Secure access
[2]	High: Instruction access
	Low: Data access

Table 14.3: The combination of the AxPROT signal

Let's first review AxPROT[0]. This bit indicates whether the access is privileged or normal:

- If the access is privileged, AxPROT[0] is set to high (1)
- If the access is normal, AxPROT[0] is set to low (0)

Privileged access occurs when the process runs at EL1 or a higher EL. For example, when the Linux Kernel or a Trusted Kernel is running, AxPROT[0] will be measured as high (1).

On the other hand, when a normal application runs at EL0 (user space), AxPROT[0] will be measured as low (0), because user applications do not have privileged access.

Next, AxPROT[1] determines whether the access is happening in the Secure world or Non-secure world:

- If the access is Secure, AxPROT[1] is set to low (0)
- If the access is Non-secure, AxPROT[1] is set to high (1)

Here's an example:

- When the Linux Kernel runs in the Non-secure world, AxPROT[1] is high (1)
- When Trusted Kernel runs in the Secure world, AxPROT[1] is low (0)

The AxPROT[0] and AxPROT[1] signals help identify both the privilege level and the security context of a transaction. By combining these two signals, we can determine whether access is privileged or unprivileged and Secure or Non-secure.

Table 14.4 shows the possible combinations of the software stack based on the AxPROT[0] and AxPROT[1] signals:

AxPROT[0]	AxPROT[1]	Bit combination	Software Stack
Low	Low	- Normal access - Secure	Secure Application (EL0)
Low	High	- Normal access - Non-secure	Non-secure Application (EL0)
High	Low	- Privileged access - Secure	Trusted Kernel (EL1)
High	High	- Privileged access - Non-secure	Non-secure Kernel (EL1)

Table 14.4: The combination of the AxPROT signal with the software stack

By measuring the AxPROT signals, we can identify the pattern of how the software is being executed in *Table 14.4*.

The important question is: How do we use AWPROT or ARPROT signals to implement the security feature? At the hardware level, a hardware filter can be added to the bus line where AxPROT signals are transmitted from the Arm processor. These hardware filters can detect AWPROT and ARPROT signals, allowing the system to enforce different security rules.

By monitoring AxPROT signals, we can create different security environments. Here are some common use cases:

- If the Linux Kernel in the Non-secure world attempts to access a secure memory region, an access error can be triggered
- If software running in the Non-secure world tries to access secure I2C devices, access will be blocked

What happens when an access violation occurs? At the software level, the system's response depends on its security requirements. Some typical error-handling mechanisms include the following:

- Triggering a FIQ to the Trusted Kernel at EL1
- Generating a fault to display an error message, indicating a security violation

These examples show just one possible implementation. The exact design of hardware security features depends on chipset manufacturers and their software development teams.

All security features in TrustZone can be designed and enforced using AxPROT signals. These signals help set up a secure execution environment in TrustZone-enabled systems, ensuring that sensitive operations are protected from unauthorized access.

Hardware features supporting TrustZone

Arm provides several key hardware features to help build secure environments. These features are essential for implementing various security configurations in TrustZone-enabled systems.

Here are some of the key hardware components used for security:

- **Generic Interrupt Controller (GIC)**: Directs external interrupts to the Arm processor and separates Secure and Non-secure interrupts. This ensures that important security events are handled properly. This FIQ is considered a Secure interrupt in Armv8-A.

- **TrustZone Address Space Controller (TZASC)**: Defines secure areas in DRAM and blocks Non-secure transactions from accessing protected memory.

- **TrustZone Protection Controller (TZPC)**: Manages access to registers and memory from both Secure and Non-secure sources. It controls access by hardware masters, such as DMA controllers, rather than the CPU.

- **TrustZone Memory Adapter (TZMA)**: Divides on-chip memory into Secure and Non-secure regions, making sure that sensitive data stored in the chip is protected from unauthorized access.

Among the various hardware features, let's take a closer look at the GIC.

The GIC is the most commonly used interrupt controller licensed by Arm and is responsible for routing interrupts from external I/O devices (such as keyboards or touchscreens) to the Arm processor. The GIC supports a wide range of features. It can be configured to determine which CPU core should receive the interrupt.

One important feature of the GIC is that it allows interrupts to be classified as Secure or Non-secure, and then routes them accordingly to the core. Typically, Secure interrupts are managed by EL3 or S.EL1.

Now that we've discussed these four hardware features, let's remember that these components work together to enforce security policies and protect sensitive data from unauthorized access. By properly configuring these components, you can create a trusted execution environment that enhances overall system security.

A common question is: How are these four hardware features implemented? The remaining four hardware features are typically implemented using Arm's built-in IP blocks or custom designs created by SoC vendors (semiconductor companies). A detailed explanation of these features goes beyond the scope of this book. For more in-depth information, please refer to the Arm reference manual at `https://developer.arm.com/documentation/ddi0487/gb`.

Summary

This chapter presented practical material on TrustZone, focusing on its key concepts and implementations. First, we explored why TrustZone was introduced and how it enhances system security by separating critical processes from less secure operations. We then examined the primary features of TrustZone, including the concepts of the Non-secure world and the Secure world. Next, we learned how software transitions between the Non-secure and Secure worlds using the SMC instruction.

Additionally, we analyzed the assembly code in Arm Trusted Firmware, focusing on how the exception handler at EL3 runs when the SMC instruction is executed at EL1. Also, we explored the hardware features that support TrustZone. One important signal is the AxPROT signal, which is used to control access to Secure and Non-secure memory regions.

TrustZone is the most commonly used security feature in Arm-based processors. It is not only a key security extension but also an important part of system design. By learning about the main features of TrustZone, you gained valuable insights into how it works and its role in enhancing system security.

In the next chapter, we will cover advanced security features in Armv8-A, providing deeper insights into how the architecture enhances system security.

15

Building Defenses with Key Security Features of Armv8-A

When thinking about security features in Armv8-A, many software engineers mention **TrustZone**. But Armv8-A provides even more security features, some of which will be covered in this chapter. We will focus on the latest security features that are used in real systems. Each feature will be explained through case studies and practical examples.

In this chapter, we will explore the following key security topics:

- **Privileged Access Never (PAN)**
- **Pointer Authentication Code (PAC)**
- **Branch Target Identification (BTI)**
- **Memory Tagging Extension (MTE)**

By understanding the security features introduced in this chapter, you will gain useful insights. If you are working on improving the security of your system, this chapter can serve as a helpful reference.

Enabling these security features on your Arm-based device can help reduce the risk of vulnerabilities. Let's begin this chapter with PAN.

Technical requirements

All the code examples and binary files for this chapter are available on GitHub at https://github.com/PacktPublishing/Reverse-Engineering-Armv8-A-Systems.

To learn more about the latest security features of Armv8-A discussed in this chapter, you can check the following materials:

- Armv8-A Reference Manual: `https://developer.arm.com/documentation/ddi0487/latest/`
- Programmer's Guide for Armv8-A: `https://developer.arm.com/documentation/den0024/latest/`
- Armv8.5-A Memory Tagging Extension White Paper: `https://developer.arm.com/documentation/102925/latest/`
- Pointer authentication in AArch64 Linux: `https://docs.kernel.org/arch/arm64/pointer-authentication.html`

Privileged Access Never (PAN)

PAN (**Privileged Access Never**) is a security feature introduced in the Armv8.1-A architecture. The purpose of PAN is to prevent higher-level software (such as the kernel) from accessing memory used by lower **exception levels** (**ELs**) (such as user space). Let's explore what PAN is, why it was introduced, and its main features.

The motivation behind PAN

In the Armv8-A architecture, software running at a higher EL can normally access resources at lower ELs.

Imagine you have developed software that runs at EL0 (user space) and handles sensitive data, such as user credentials or encryption keys. Now, consider what could happen if software running at EL1 (such as an RTOS or the Linux Kernel) attempts to directly access the memory used by the program running at EL0.

If no restrictions are in place, the EL1 software could read or modify the sensitive data stored at EL0. You may not feel comfortable in a system environment where memory access to EL0 is allowed from higher ELs, such as EL1 or EL2.

Additionally, it is hard to predict what will be executed when a hypervisor is running. Hypervisors usually run at EL2 and are responsible for managing multiple operating systems that run at EL1. The EL2 software has higher privileges than EL1, which allows the hypervisor to control and monitor the operating systems running at EL1.

If your software runs at EL0 in this kind of environment, you might not have full control over which hypervisor is managing the system or how it is configured.

This is the main reason why PAN was introduced. Let's take a look at *Figure 15.1*.

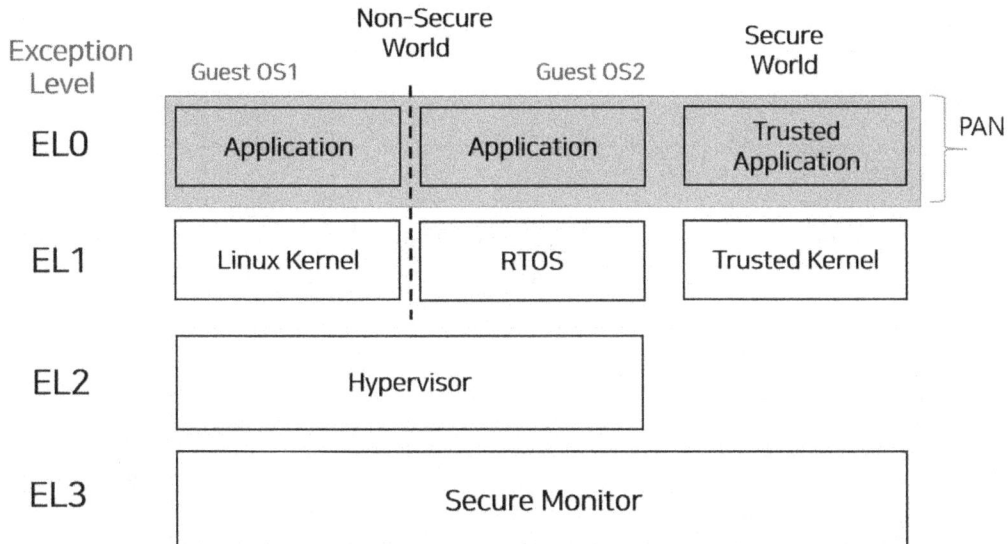

Figure 15.1: The EL with the relevant software stack

As shown in *Figure 15.1*, there is a box that marks the EL0 area. When the PAN feature is turned on, direct access to EL0 memory from higher ELs such as EL1 or EL2 is blocked.

This brings us to an important question: What happens if EL1 or EL2 tries to directly access EL0 memory? In this case, Arm core raises a synchronous exception to halt access, preventing the system from gaining unwanted memory access.

Now that we understand what PAN is, let's understand how to enable PAN.

Registers for configuring PAN

To configure PAN correctly, it is important to understand the two system registers that are used for this feature:

- The PAN system register
- The SPAN field in SCTLR_EL1

The PAN system register

The first register is the PAN system register. When we write the value 1 to this register, the PAN feature is enabled. This register is used to control the PSTATE.PAN bit. Since we cannot change PSTATE.PAN directly, the PAN system register works like an alias (shortcut) to update it.

Starting from Armv8.1-A, the PAN bit flag inside PSTATE is available to support this feature.

> **Note**
>
> PSTATE is an abstraction that holds information about the processor state, such as the current EL. For more information, please see *Chapter 1*.

To set the PAN system register, we can use the **Move to System Register (MSR)** instruction. This instruction allows us to write values to system registers in Armv8-A. We will look at an example of using MSR in the *Code review of PAN initialization in the Linux kernel* section.

The SCTLR_EL1.SPAN field

Another important field is the SPAN field in the SCTLR_EL1 register. This field controls how the PAN system register is updated when an exception is taken to EL1. Based on the value in SCTLR_EL1. SPAN, the Arm core performs the following operations:

- 0b00: The PAN system register is automatically set to 1 when an exception is taken to EL1
- 0b01: The PAN system register value is not changed when an exception is taken to EL1

Next, we will look at the Linux Kernel code that sets up PAN. This example will help us understand how PAN is used in real systems.

Code review of PAN initialization in the Linux Kernel

Reviewing the source code that configures the PAN feature in the Linux Kernel is a useful practice.

Let's review the code for the cpu_enable_pan() function in the Linux Kernel:

```
arch/arm64/kernel/cpufeature.c
01 static void cpu_enable_pan(const struct Arm64_cpu_capabilities *__
unused)
02 {
03     [...]
04     sysreg_clear_set(sctlr_el1, SCTLR_EL1_SPAN, 0);
05     set_pstate_pan(1);
06 }
```

The cpu_enable_pan() function is responsible for enabling PAN in the Linux Kernel, and it is called during the boot process. Let's take a closer look at the key lines:

- **Line 03**: This line clears the SPAN bit in the SCTLR_EL1 register. Clearing this bit is part of the process for correctly configuring PAN. The compiler will translate this line of C code into the msr SCTLR_EL1, x1 assembly instruction. This assembly instruction directly modifies the SCTLR_EL1.SPAN field.

- **Line 04**: This line sets the PAN system register by writing the value 0x1. The corresponding instruction generated by the compiler is msr pan, #0x1. When running this instruction, it sets the PSTATE.PAN bit to 1, which activates the PAN feature.

Once PAN is enabled, it prevents software running at higher ELs (EL1) from accessing memory resources that belong to lower ELs (such as EL0).

This section analyzes the initialization routine, which is part of the PAN feature in the Linux Kernel. For a complete analysis of the PAN feature, please refer to the CONFIG_Arm64_PAN option, where you can find CONFIG_ARM64_PAN in the .config file. This is generated during Linux Kernel compilation.

Now that we understand PAN from the Armv8.1-A architecture's point of view, let's look at how it is used in the Linux system.

Implementation considerations in the Linux system

In real Linux systems, the kernel sometimes needs to access EL0 (user-space) memory. This usually happens when using standard kernel APIs, such as copy_to_user() or copy_from_user().

When PAN is enabled, these functions work as follows:

1. They temporarily disable PAN by writing the value 0 to the PAN system register.
2. They access user-space memory (read or write).
3. They enable PAN again by writing the value 1 to the PAN system register.

For more information about Linux Kernel patches related to PAN, please refer to https://patchwork.kernel.org/project/linux-arm-kernel/patch/1437588354-31278-1-git-send-email-james.morse@arm.com/.

From this analysis, we have learned an important point: if we are writing Linux device driver code at EL1, and we need to access EL0 memory with PAN enabled, we should use standard kernel APIs such as copy_to_user() or copy_from_user().

If you do not use these standard APIs, a synchronous exception may occur during access to EL0 memory.

So far, we have learned about PAN, which is designed to block illegal access from privileged modes to user-space memory. In the next section, we will learn about PAC, which is a more advanced and stronger security feature. It helps protect pointer addresses by adding an authentication code.

Pointer Authentication Code (PAC)

PAC (**Pointer Authentication Code**)was introduced in the Armv8.3-A architecture. It is also called **Pointer Authentication (PAuth)**. PAC is one of the most commonly used features for enhancing a secure environment. Let's begin this section by explaining why PAC was introduced, and then discuss its key features.

Introducing PAC

Cyberattacks often exploit software vulnerabilities to change the program flow. There are two common types of attacks:

- **Return-oriented programming (ROP)**: An attacker can manipulate stack memory that contains a return address. As a result, PC may jump to an address where malicious code is located after the ret instruction is executed.

- **Jump-oriented programming (JOP)**: This attack is similar to ROP but uses the **branch (BR)** instruction instead of ret. It redirects execution flow to unintended locations.

PAC is designed to protect software from ROP and JOP attacks by verifying the integrity of pointer addresses. These pointer addresses include return addresses and the base addresses of structures. This enforces that a program can only return or branch to authorized addresses.

The following PAC features are available:

- Attach a keyed **Message Authentication Code (MAC)** to each pointer
- Only allow the pointer to be used if MAC is valid

In simple terms, each pointer includes an authentication code to ensure that it has not been altered by an attacker.

Now that we've explored what PAC is, let's explore its key feature—the PAC authentication code.

Understanding the PAC authentication code

The PAC feature has the following three components:

- The PAC authentication code, which it generates
- An assembly instruction

- Compiler support

Among these three components, it is important to understand how the PAC authentication code is generated. The main operation of this can be broken down into two parts:

1. The PAC authentication code is created using a PAC key and a modifier (which can be selected).
2. This authentication code is then stored in the upper bits of a virtual address.

Let's look more closely at how the PAC authentication code is generated, as shown in *Figure 15.2*.

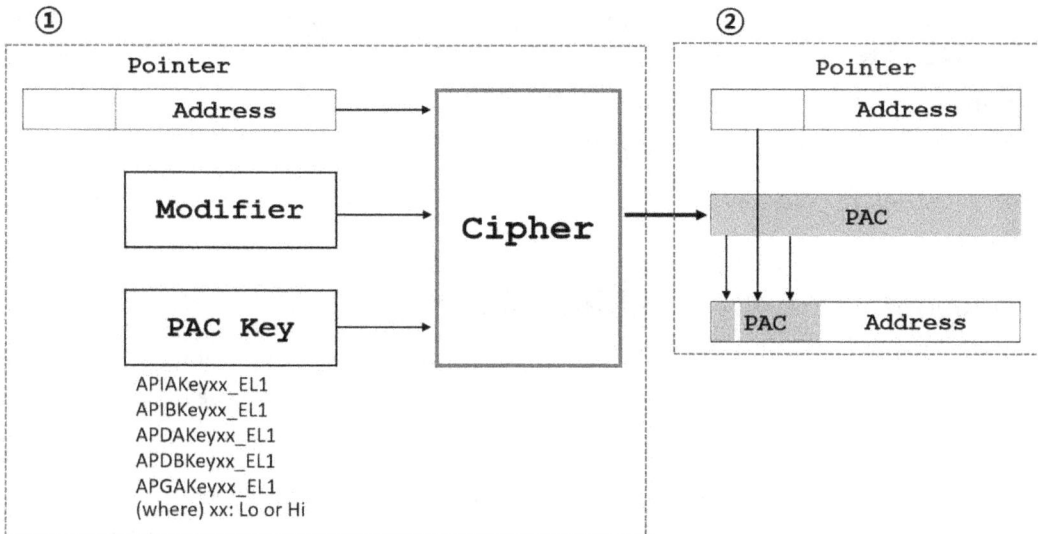

Figure 15.2: The generation of the PAC authentication code

First, let's explore step **[1]** in *Figure 15.2*, which involves generating the PAC authentication code. To generate the PAC authentication code, three inputs are required:

- **PAC key:** This is 128 bits in size. Because of this, the key is stored in two system registers—one for the lower 64 bits and one for the upper 64 bits.
- **Modifier:** This value can be in any general-purpose register or SP value. The modifier is also used as input when generating the PAC authentication code.
- **Pointer address:** An address value.

Using these three inputs, a cipher creates the PAC authentication code. The exact way this cipher works depends on the chipset design and is not shared in public documents. These three components will be analyzed further in the *PAC assembly instructions* section.

Now, let's take a look at step **[2]** in *Figure 15.2*. After the PAC authentication code is created, it is placed in the upper bits of the pointer address. Now, the pointer address consists of two parts:

- The original address value
- The PAC authentication code

Let's imagine that the original pointer address is as follows:

```
0x00007f1234567890
```

After adding the PAC authentication code, the new address looks like this:

```
0xd8087f1234567890
```

By using the PAC authentication code (0xd808), the system can check whether a pointer address is valid. This is used to detect invalid or changed pointer addresses.

Now that we understand how the PAC authentication code is generated, let's learn how it is stored in the virtual address.

The layout of the virtual address for storing PAC

On 64-bit systems, not all 64 bits in the virtual address are used for real memory addresses. Only part of the bits represent actual memory addresses. The PAC feature uses the unused bits in the address to store an authentication code.

Let's review *Figure 15.3*, which shows how the 64-bit virtual address is organized.

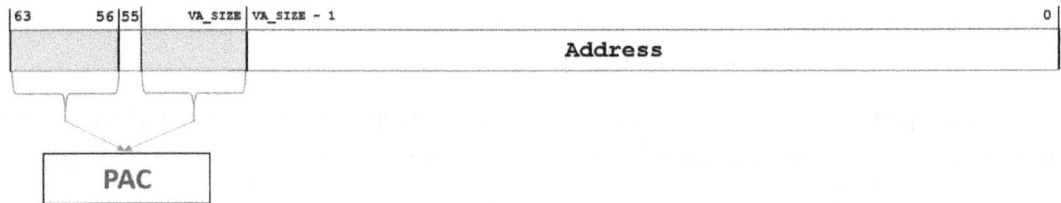

Figure 15.3: Layout of the virtual address with PAC

There are three parts in a virtual address:

- **Bits [0 to (VA_SIZE − 1)]**: These bits store the actual virtual address. The value of VA_SIZE depends on the system settings. For example, VA_SIZE is often 48 or 47.
- **Upper bits**: When the PAC feature is enabled, the [63:56] and [54:VA_SIZE] bit ranges are used to store the PAC authentication code. The exact size and location of the PAC authentication code in these bits can be configured using the TCR_EL1 register.

- **Bit [55]:** This bit is reserved to show whether the address belongs to the high or low part of the virtual address space.

Now that we understand the basic ideas behind the PAC feature, let's look at some use cases where PAC is applied.

How the PAC feature is applied

When we analyze the PAC feature, we focus on how the PAC authentication code is generated. To understand the PAC feature better, we need to look at some common use cases.

First, we will learn how the address is changed when the PAC authentication code is applied. Then, we will understand how the PAC feature works in a branch operation scenario.

A common use case for PAC

Let's look at *Figure 15.4*, which shows a common use case for the PAC feature.

When a function is called, the return address is stored in x30. Before the PAC feature is applied, the value in x30 may look like this:

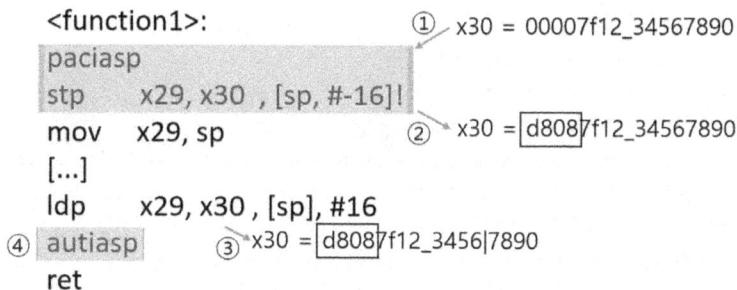

```
<function1>:                    ①  x30 = 00007f12_34567890
paciasp
stp     x29, x30 , [sp, #-16]!
mov     x29, sp                 ②  x30 = d808 7f12_34567890
[...]
ldp     x29, x30 , [sp], #16
④ autiasp       ③ x30 = d808 7f12_3456|7890
ret
```

Figure 15.4: Instructions that add authentication code

Let's take a closer look at *Figure 15.4*:

1. The `paciasp` instruction runs. At this point, the x30 register contains a value of 0x00007f12_34567890. The x30 register is used to hold the return address.

2. Next, the `stp x29, x30, [sp, #-16]!` instruction is executed. In this step, the value in x30 is stored in the stack. However, before it's saved, a PAC authentication code is added to the upper bits of the value. The final value that's saved to the stack becomes 0xd8087f12_34567890, where d808 is the authentication code.

3. The ldp x29, x30, [sp], #16 instruction loads 0xd8087f12_34567890 back into x30 from the stack. This happens when the function is about to return and the return address needs to be restored.

4. Finally, the autiasp instruction runs. This instruction checks whether the authentication code in x30 is correct. If the code is valid, the authentication code is removed, and the program continues. If the code is not valid, an exception occurs because this is considered unauthorized execution.

In C programs, pointers store memory addresses and are commonly accessed using instructions such as **Load Register (LDR)**. If an attacker manipulates a return address, the system may jump to an unintended location, leading to security vulnerabilities. The PAC feature prevents this by ensuring that function return addresses and other critical pointers remain unchanged and secure.

The execution flow when using the branch operation

Let's examine *Figure 15.5* to understand how the PAC feature works from another perspective.

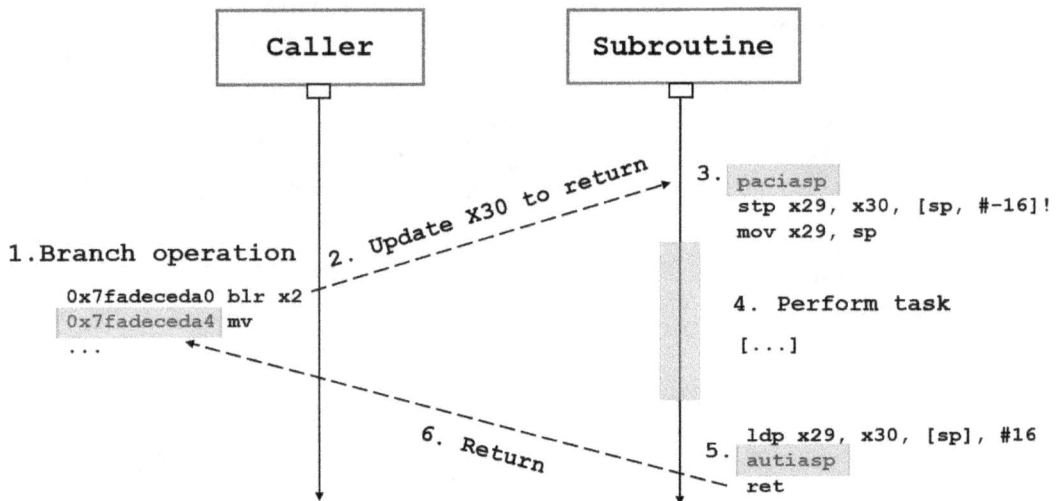

Figure 15.5: Workflow diagram for the PAC feature

Let's take a closer look at the steps involved:

1. **The blr x2 instruction performs**: PC jumps to the address stored in the x2 register.

2. **The return address is saved in x30**: When the blr instruction runs, the return address is updated to the x30 register. In *Figure 15.5*, this return address is 0x7fadeceda4.

3. **The `paciasp` instruction is executed**: If the `paciasp` instruction runs before x29 and x30 are saved to the stack using `stp x29, x30, [sp, #-16]!`, PAC authentication is added to the upper bits of the address in x30. This happens while x30 is being stored on the stack.

4. **The instructions inside the subroutine are executed**: These are the main tasks or logic of the subroutine.

5. **x30 and x29 are restored from the stack**: When running the `ldp x29, x30, [sp], #16` instruction, the values of x29 and x30 are loaded back from the stack. At this point, x30 is expected to hold the data with a valid PAC authentication code. To check whether the PAC authentication code is valid, the `autiasp` instruction must be executed. If the PAC authentication code is not valid—maybe because of an attack—an exception will occur.

6. **The program is returned to the caller**: If the PAC authentication code in x30 is valid, the `ret` instruction is executed. This returns the program to the caller function. In *Figure 15.5*, PC is updated to the `0x7fadeceda4` address.

The `paciasp` and `autiasp` instructions are part of the PAC feature. If PAC is enabled in the compiler, these instructions are inserted in the following manner:

- The `paciasp` instruction appears at the beginning of a function.

- The `autiasp` instruction appears before the function returns, ensuring that execution only continues if the return address is valid.

Now that we've looked at some common use cases, let's explore the assembly instructions for PAC.

Assembly instructions on PAC

Another key feature of PAC is its assembly instructions. There are three main types of PAC instructions:

- PACxx: These instructions compute the pointer's signature and store it in the upper bits of the pointer.

- AUTxx: These instructions check whether the signature of the pointer is valid. If the signature is correct, the instruction removes it.

- XPACxx: These instructions remove the signature without checking whether it is valid. These are rarely used.

Let's take a look at the PACxxx and AUTxxx instructions in more detail.

The components of the PACIASP and AUTIASP instructions

The Armv8.3-A architecture provides many assembly instructions related to the PAC feature. Before looking at the necessary instructions, it is useful to understand the various components of the PACIASP instruction that were mentioned earlier. Let's look at *Figure 15.6*, which shows the components of the PACIASP and AUTIASP instructions.

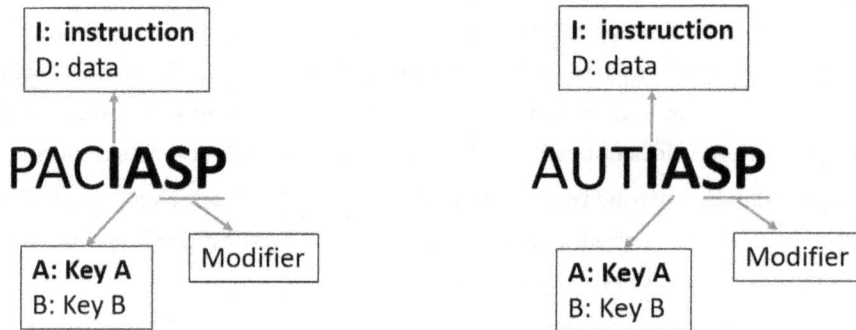

Figure 15.6: The components of the PACIASP and AUTIASP instructions

In the PAC feature, a pointer to either an instruction address or a data address can be authenticated using different encryption keys inside the system. The first thing to understand is the I and D components:

- I: This is used when the pointer is for an instruction address
- D: This is used when the pointer is for a data address

For example, in *Figure 15.6*, I is used because the pointer is an instruction address. The x30 register holds the return address, which is an instruction address.

Next, let's check the key types that are used for encryption:

- A means Key A is used
- B means Key B is used

As shown in *Figure 15.6*, Key A is used to generate the PAC authentication code. In Armv8.3-A, there are five different PAC keys. Two of these keys are called Key A, while another two are called Key B. The fifth PAC key is generic.

> **Note**
>
> You can find these keys in special system registers. We will learn more about these registers later in the *Key system registers for PAC* section.

Lastly, let's look at the modifier. This modifier can be a value from any general-purpose register or SP. This modifier is used as input to compute the PAC authentication code. For example, in the PACIASP instruction, the modifier is the SP value.

When choosing a modifier, it is better to have a modifier value that changes each time. If the same modifier is used again and again, it becomes easier for attackers to predict the PAC authentication code by repeating the PACIASP instruction in the same address.

With that, we have reviewed the components of the PACIASP instruction. To summarize, the PACIASP instruction is used to generate a PAC authentication code for an instruction address and uses the following components:

- Instruction address
- Key A
- The modifier—that is, the SP value

The right-hand side of *Figure 15.6* shows the AUTIASP instruction. The AUTIASP instruction is used to verify whether an address with a PAC authentication code is valid. The components that are used in AUTIASP are the same as those used in PACIASP. This means both instructions use Key A and the SP value as a modifier.

Here are some important points to remember when executing the AUTIASP instruction:

- When checking whether an address with a PAC authentication code is valid using the AUTIASP instruction, it must use the same key (Key A) and modifier (SP) that were used when running the PACIASP instruction.
- If the address that contains the PAC authentication code is invalid, a synchronous exception is generated. If not, the process will continue its execution.

Now that we understand the components of the PACxxx and AUTxxx instructions, let's explore the different instructions supported by the PAC feature.

More PAC instructions

Let's explore the assembly instructions that are commonly used with the PAC feature.

First, we will introduce several instructions that are used to generate a PAC authentication code, along with different options:

- `PACIA Xd, Xn`: Generates a PAC authentication code for the instruction address in Xd, using Key A and the modifier in Xn
- `PACIASP`: Generates a PAC authentication code for the instruction address in x30, using Key A and SP as the modifier
- `PACIAZ`: Generates a PAC authentication code for the instruction address in x30, using Key A and a 0 value as the modifier
- `PACIB Xd, Xn`: Generates a PAC authentication code for the instruction address in Xd, using Key B and the modifier in Xn
- `PACIBSP`: Generates a PAC authentication code for the instruction address in x30, using Key B and SP as the modifier
- `PACIBZ`: Generates a PAC authentication code for the instruction address in x30, using Key B and a 0 value as the modifier

Next, let's look at the list of AUTxxx instructions that are used to authenticate the PAC authentication code in a virtual address:

- `AUTIA Xd, Xn`: Authenticates the instruction address in Xd, using Key A and the modifier in Xn
- `AUTIASP`: Authenticates the instruction address in x30, using Key A and SP as the modifier
- `AUTIAZ`: Authenticates the instruction address in x30, using Key A and a 0 value as the modifier
- `AUTIB Xd, Xn`: Authenticates the instruction address in Xd, using Key B and the modifier in Xn
- `AUTIBSP`: Authenticates the instruction address in x30, using Key B and SP as the modifier
- `AUTIBZ`: Authenticates the instruction address in x30, using Key B and a 0 value as the modifier

For more details about the complete set of instructions related to the PAC feature, please refer to the official Arm Reference Manual at `https://developer.arm.com/documentation/ddi0487/gb` (C3.1.10 Pointer authentication instructions).

Compiler support

A common question is whether developers need to manually add PACxxx and AUTxxx instructions to their code. In practice, developers sometimes need to write these instructions manually.

But, in many cases, they use a compiler that can generate assembly instructions with different PAC features using the appropriate compiler options. This way, developers do not need to add PAC instructions by hand.

Both GCC and Armclang support the PAC feature via the `-mbranch-protection=pac-ret` option. The compiler offers several options to enable the PAC feature:

- `-mbranch-protection=standard`: Enables all available PAC protections
- `-mbranch-protection=pac-ret`: The default option, which protects return addresses
- `-mbranch-protection=leaf`: Extends PAC protection to leaf functions (functions that do not call other functions)
- `-mbranch-protection=b-key`: Uses the B-key for authentication

If you are in a situation where you can enable the PAC feature, you need to check the compiler options shown here. By using these compiler options, you can activate the PAC feature, depending on the requirements of your project.

> Note
>
> Adding PAC to a system may introduce some performance overhead because it adds extra instructions (PACxxx and AUTxxx). However, the trade-off between performance and security must be evaluated carefully. In many security-critical applications, minor performance degradation is acceptable to improve overall security.

How to use PAC in Linux using the GCC compiler

Once you understand the basic operation of the PAC feature and its various compiler options, the next step is to test it in practice. To help you understand this better, we will analyze a simple code example:

```c
#include <stdio.h>
int function2(void)
{
    return 0;
}

int function1(void)
{
    function2();
    return 0;
}

int main()
{
    int ret = function1();
    return ret;
}
```

You can save this code as test.c. To enable PAC during compilation, please use the following command:

```
$ gcc -c test.c -mbranch-protection=pac-ret
```

Here, we are compiling the code using the GCC compiler with the -mbranch-protection=pac-ret option. This option adds extra instructions that are not included in normal compilation. Now, let's compare the assembly instructions from two different compiled versions:

default

0000000000000714 <function2>:
 714: mov   w0, #0x0
 718: ret

000000000000071c <function1>:
 71c: stp   x29, x30, [sp, #-16]!
 720: mov   x29, sp
 724: bl   714 <function2>
 728: mov   w0, #0x0
 72c: ldp   x29, x30, [sp], #16
 730: ret

0000000000000734 <main>:
 734: stp   x29, x30, [sp, #-32]!
 738: mov   x29, sp
 73c: bl   71c <function1>
 740: str   w0, [sp, #28]
 744: ldr   w0, [sp, #28]
 748: ldp   x29, x30, [sp], #32
 74c: ret

-mbranch-protection=pac-ret

0000000000000714 <function2>:
 714: mov   w0, #0x0
 718: ret

000000000000071c <function1>:
 71c: paciasp
 720: stp   x29, x30, [sp, #-16]!
 724: mov   x29, sp
 728: bl   714 <function2>
 72c: mov   w0, #0x0
 730: ldp   x29, x30, [sp], #16
 734: autiasp
 738: ret

000000000000073c <main>:
 73c: paciasp
 740: stp   x29, x30, [sp, #-32]!
 744: mov   x29, sp
 748: bl   71c <function1>
 74c: str   w0, [sp, #28]
 750: ldr   w0, [sp, #28]
 754: ldp   x29, x30, [sp], #32
 758: autiasp
 75c: ret

Figure 15.7: A comparison of assembly instructions: default compile versus PAC-enabled compile

In *Figure 15.7*, the left-hand side shows the disassembled output without the -mbranch-protection=pac-ret option. This is the result of normal compilation. The right-hand side shows the output with the -mbranch-protection=pac-ret option enabled. Additional instructions, such as paciasp and autiasp, appear and are marked with boxes.

The paciasp instruction is placed at the beginning of the function to make sure the return address (X30) is authenticated before it is stored on the stack. At the end of the function, the autiasp instruction is used to authenticate the return address before returning. This shows that we do not need to add these instructions manually. Instead, we can simply apply the appropriate compiler option.

Having looked at the compiler options of the PAC feature, let's move on to another important feature—PAC exception.

PAC exception: Fault on FPAC

As discussed in the previous section, the primary purpose of the PAC feature is to verify the authenticity of a virtual address stored in a register. But what happens if this authentication check fails? In such cases, a synchronous exception is triggered to prevent unauthorized execution. This happens when the **Fault on FPAC** feature is enabled:

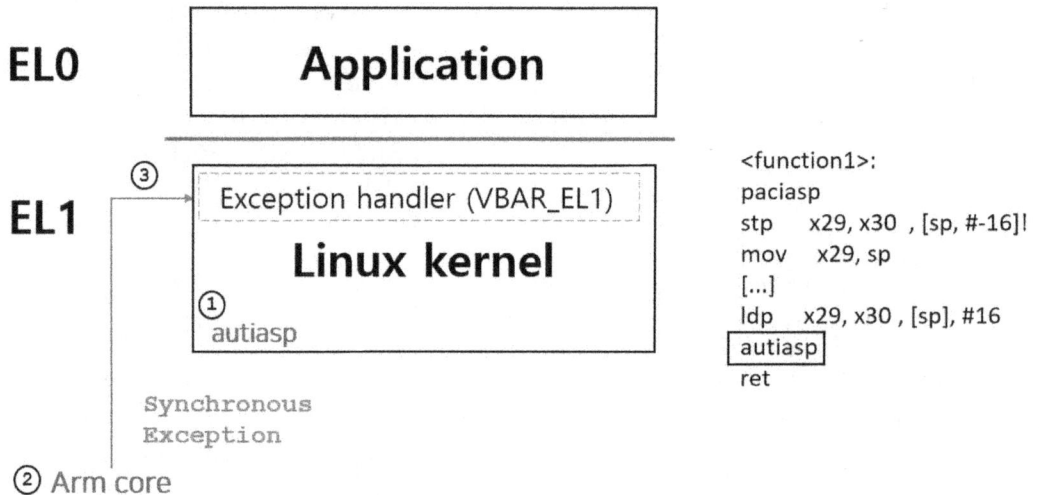

Figure 15.8: Execution flow of a PAC-related exception

Figure 15.8 shows the workflow when authentication fails after the autiasp instruction is executed. Let's look at step **[1]** first. This step shows that the autiasp instruction runs, and the authentication check fails.

As for step **[2]**, the following actions are performed simultaneously:

- A synchronous exception is raised
- The **Exception Class (EC)** bits in [31:26] of the ESR_EL1 register are updated to indicate that the exception occurs due to a pointer authentication error

Step **[3]** shows that PC jumps to the exception vector address.

After PC jumps to the exception vector address, the exception handler starts to run. What the corresponding exception handler does is implemented by system software engineers. For example, in Linux, one of two things occurs:

- If the authentication error occurs in user space, the process that runs the autiasp instruction will be terminated
- If the authentication error occurs in kernel space, a kernel panic may occur

In practice, you may wonder what kind of message is displayed when an exception occurs due to Fault on FPAC. The following is an example of a signature that's observed when a PAC error is detected:

```
Internal error: Oops - FPAC: 0000000072000000 [#1] PREEMPT SMP
Modules linked in:
CPU: 0 PID: 1 Comm: swapper/0 Not tainted 5.19.0-rc3-00132-g78846e1c4757-
dirty #11
Hardware name: FVP Base RevC (DT)
pstate: 20400009 (nzCv daif +PAN -UAO -TCO -DIT -SSBS BTYPE=--)
[...]
```

The Oops - FPAC message reveals that the exception occurs due to Fault on FPAC. For more details about this signature, please refer to https://git.kernel.org/pub/scm/linux/kernel/git/next/linux-next.git/commit/?id=a1fafa3b24a70461bbf3e5c0770893feb0a49292.

Now that we understand the exceptions associated with the PAC feature, let's move on to the next topic—the system registers that contain the five different PAC keys.

Key system registers for PAC

Various system registers are used to provide five different PAC keys. Since each PAC key is 128 bits, two system registers are needed to store the full 128 bits for each key.

Let's check the system registers one by one. First, let's review the system registers used for instruction addresses:

- `APIAKey_EL1`: `APIAKeyHi_EL1` holds bits [127:64], while `APIAKeyLo_EL1` holds bits [63:0]
- `APIBKey_EL1`: `APIBKeyHi_EL1` holds bits [127:64], while `APIBKeyLo_EL1` holds bits [63:0]

Second, here are the system registers used for data addresses:

- `APDAKey_EL1`: `APDAKeyHi_EL1` holds bits [127:64], while `APDAKeyLo_EL1` holds bits [63:0]
- `APDBKey_EL1`: `APDBKeyHi_EL1` holds bits [127:64], while `APDBKeyLo_EL1` holds bits [63:0]

Lastly, the fifth PAC key is generic:

- `APGAKey_EL1`: `APGAKeyHi_EL1` holds bits [127:64], while `APGAKeyLo_EL1` holds bits [63:0]

These five system registers are used to manage the PAC keys.

This section introduced the PAC feature, a security feature commonly used in real-world projects. The main idea of PAC is to store a key value in the unused bits of a virtual address. This idea is also used in MTE, which uses extra bits in virtual addresses to store memory tags.

In the next section, we will learn about BTI, another important security feature introduced in the Armv8.5-A architecture.

Branch Target Identification (BTI)

In Armv8.5-A, the **BTI (Branch Target Identification)** feature was introduced to reduce the risk of attacks that exploit unintended branch targets, such as ROP or JOP.

In this section, we will explore the key features of BTI and review some example code.

Let's start by introducing the motivation behind BTI.

Why was BTI introduced?

Techniques such as ROP allow attackers to redirect execution to addresses that contain malicious code.

To protect against this, the BTI feature was introduced in Armv8.5-A. It is designed to check and control branch operations so that the system can avoid executing dangerous or unknown instructions.

The BTI mechanism is simple:

1.   The compiler places BTI instructions at specific points where valid branch operations are expected.

2.   When running the BTI instruction, it checks whether the branch is valid.

3.   If the branch operation is unexpected or illegal, the Arm core raises a BTI exception, which stops the execution.

Now that we've reviewed the basic concept of BTI, let's understand how BTI works in more detail.

Understanding BTI

To understand how BTI works, it's important to review its instructions, which support branch operations. There are two types of branch instructions:

- **Direct branch instruction:** The BL instruction is considered a direct branch operation. The address to branch to is specified in the BL instruction—for example, BL <target_address>. This target address does not change and is clearly defined.

- **Indirect branch instruction:** The BLR or BR instruction works differently in that it uses a general-purpose register to find the destination address. For example, BLR X3 uses the value in the X3 register as the target address.

The BTI feature mainly supports indirect branch instructions because many invalid or unsafe branch operations occur due to indirect jumps.

Let's take a look at *Figure 15.9*, which shows an indirect branch operation.

```
<irq_thread_fn>
      stp     x29, x30, [sp, #-48]!
      mov     x29, sp
      stp     x19, x20, [sp, #16]
      mov     x19, x1
      mov     x20, x0
      str     x21, [sp, #32]
[1]   ldr     x2, [x19, #32]
      ldr     w0, [x1, #56]
      ldr     x1, [x1, #8]
[2]   blr     x2
      mov     w21, w0
      cmp     w0, #0x1
```

(where) x19 = ffff8001014d9700

```
crash> rd ffff8001014d9700 0x20
ffff8001014d9700:    ffffc00080b0efc8 ffff800101c31580
ffff8001014d9710:    0000000000000000 0000000000000000
ffff8001014d9720:    ffffc00080b0ebd8 ffff800101ca0000
                                    [3]

crash> dis ffffc00080b0ebd8
0xffffc00080b0ebd8 <sdhci_thread_irq>:    mov    x9, x30
```

Figure 15.9: Access to memory before an indirect branch operation

The assembly routine in *Figure 15.9* is related to the irq_thread_fn function in the Linux Kernel.

In this code, the `action->thread_fn` function pointer is used to call another function:

```
kernel/irq/manage.c
static irqreturn_t irq_thread_fn(struct irq_desc *desc,
                                    struct irqaction *action)
{
    irqreturn_t ret;

    ret = action->thread_fn(action->irq, action->dev_id);
```

If we look at the assembly instruction that corresponds to the preceding code, which contains a function call, we'll see the following instruction:

```
blr <Xn>
```

Here, `<Xn>` can be any general-purpose register, such as X2 or X3. Let's analyze each step in *Figure 15.9*:

1. The process loads the function address from memory. At this time, the x2 register (for example) is updated with the target address for the branch.
2. The `blr  x2` instruction performs an indirect branch to the address stored in x2. This is called an indirect branch because the address is not fixed. It can change while the program runs.

Now, let's think about what happens if the memory content is changed on purpose. If an attacker changes the data in memory, x2 may contain an invalid address that points to malicious code. This can cause the program to jump to unexpected code and may cause a security issue.

Unlike the **Branch with Link (BL)** instruction, where the target address is fixed, the `blr` instruction uses the address in the x2 register. The important thing is that the value in x2 can be loaded from different sources. This address might come from memory or be calculated during the program's execution, making it more dynamic and harder to predict.

What happens if an attacker manipulates the address in x2 by changing its source (for example, through a buffer overflow)? If x2 is updated with an invalid address, the program may jump to an unexpected location. This allows the attacker to control the program's flow, which can lead to security vulnerabilities such as unauthorized code execution.

The `BTI` feature helps to reduce this risk as it prevents the process from jumping to unsafe or unintended addresses. If an unauthorized branch is detected, a `BTI` exception is raised, effectively blocking the exploit and maintaining secure execution.

The workflow of BTI

To understand the BTI feature, it is necessary to analyze both the BTI instruction and the PSTATE. BTYPE register. The BTI instruction checks whether the program jumped to its address in a valid way by reading PSTATE.BTYPE.

But how does the processor check whether the jump was valid? The behavior of the BTI instruction is shown in *Figure 15.10*.

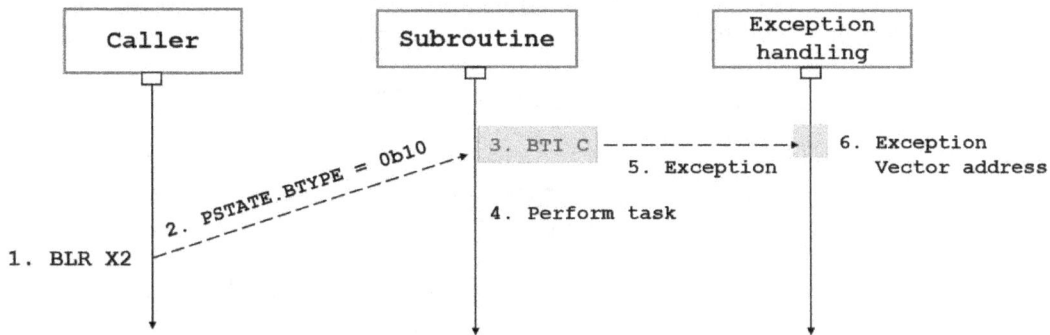

Figure 15.10: Workflow diagram for the BTI instruction

Figure 15.10 shows the main operations of the BTI feature. Let's break this down, step by step:

1. PC branches to the address stored in the X2 register.
2. While the BLR X2 instruction runs, the PSTATE.BTYPE field is updated to 0b10. This value will be checked by the BTI instruction later.
3. The BTI c instruction checks whether the branch is valid.
4. If the BTI c instruction confirms the branch is valid, the next instruction in the program is executed.
5. If the branch is not valid, the BTI c instruction triggers an exception.
6. The exception handler runs to deal with the invalid branch.

The BTI c instruction and the PSTATE.BTYPE field are important parts of the BTI feature. Now that we understand the principle of BTI, let's continue exploring the relevant instructions.

The guarded page

Another important concept that will help us understand BTI is the **guarded page**. A guarded page is a type of memory page that supports the BTI instruction.

Normally, any code that uses a BTI instruction should be stored inside a guarded page. This ensures that the BTI instruction can perform its function correctly.

However, sometimes, a BTI instruction may exist in a non-guarded page. In this case, the BTI instruction may not work as expected. Instead, it will act like a **No Operation (NOP)** instruction, which means it does nothing, and the program continues without performing any special action.

Another reason why the guarded page was introduced is to support backward compatibility. Older versions of Armv8-A, such as Armv8.1-A, do not support the BTI feature, so using guarded pages helps with managing this difference safely when older programs or systems are run.

The BTI instruction and PSTATE.BTYTE

The key features of BTI include the BTI instruction, PSTATE.BTYPE, and BTI exceptions. When the BTI instruction runs, it checks the value of PSTATE.BTYPE. During this process, it decides whether the branch to this location is valid.

Now, let's learn about the assembly instructions used in the BTI feature.

The BTI instruction

The BTI instruction checks whether the program has jumped to the BTI instruction address in a valid way. The BTI <operand> instruction includes an operand represented by 2 bits.

The BTI instruction acts like a placeholder and behaves as a NOP instruction, meaning it doesn't alter the execution flow. However, its main purpose is to mark valid targets for indirect branches.

This operand tells the processor which type of branch operation to check. A 2-bit operand in the BTI instruction consists of four possible values:

- BTI: No branch is allowed to land here (this is not commonly used).
- BTI c: Only calls (marked by c) can land here. This applies to BLR-type instructions.
- BTI j: Only jumps (marked by j) can land here. This applies to BR-type instructions.
- BTI jc: Both calls and jumps are allowed to land here.

In practice, the entry point of a function is typically marked with the BTI c instruction, so only valid function calls can reach it. Meanwhile, the first instruction of a switch-case branch is usually BTI j, allowing jump instructions to land at the beginning of that branch.

Another thing we have to remember is that when the BTI <operand> instruction runs, it checks the value of the PSTATE.BTYPE field. We will learn more about the PSTATE.BTYPE field in the next section.

PSTATE.BTYPE: A new processor state

Starting with the Armv8.5-A architecture, a new bit flag in **Processor State (PSTATE)** called PSTATE.BTYPE was introduced. These 2 bits are used to describe the branch type of the instruction currently being executed.

PSTATE.BTYPE can be set by various instructions and helps describe the context of the current branch. The values of PSTATE.BTYPE can be interpreted as follows:

- 0b00: Running other instructions, including direct branch operations, updates PSTATE. BTYPE to 0b00.

- 0b10: An indirect branch used as a function call updates PSTATE.BTYPE to 0b10. Examples of this are BLR, BLRAA, BLRAAZ, BLRAB, and BLRABZ.

- 0b01: An indirect branch operation, such as in a switch-case statement, updates PSTATE. BTYPE to 0b01. Examples of this are BR, BRAA, BRAAZ, BRAB, and BRABZ:

    - If the instruction is in a guarded page, only the X16 or X17 register is used

    - If the instruction is in any other memory region (non-guarded or guarded), any register may be used

- 0b11: An indirect branch operation in a guarded page updates PSTATE.BTYPE to 0b11 if it uses any register except for X16 or X17. This also typically applies to switch-case style branches. Examples of this are BR, BRAA, BRAAZ, BRAB, and BRABZ.

Most indirect branch instructions set PSTATE.BTYPE to a non-zero value. This includes instructions such as BLR and BR, which are commonly used for indirect branch operations.

Using the BTI option via a compiler

To understand how BTI works, we need to compile a program with BTI enabled and analyze the generated assembly instructions. Let's use the same simple code from the previous section for testing. To compile the code with BTI enabled, use the following command:

```
$ gcc -c test.c -mbranch-protection=bti
```

The -mbranch-protection=bti option enables the BTI feature. When this option is used, additional assembly instructions appear in the compiled code that are not normally present.

Now, let's compare the assembly output before and after enabling the BTI feature:

<u>default</u>   <u>-mbranch-protection=bti</u>

```
0000000000000714 <function2>:              0000000000000714 <function2>:
 714: mov    w0, #0x0                        714: bti   c
 718: ret                                     718: mov    w0, #0x0
                                              71c: ret

000000000000071c <function1>:
 71c: stp    x29, x30, [sp, #-16]!          0000000000000720 <function1>:
 720: mov    x29, sp                         720: bti   c
 724: bl     714 <function2>                 724: stp    x29, x30, [sp, #-16]!
 728: mov    w0, #0x0                        728: mov    x29, sp
 72c: ldp    x29, x30, [sp], #16            72c: bl     714 <function2>
 730: ret                                     730: mov    w0, #0x0
                                              734: ldp    x29, x30, [sp], #16
                                              738: ret
0000000000000734 <main>:
 734: stp    x29, x30, [sp, #-32]!
 738: mov    x29, sp                        000000000000073c <main>:
 73c: bl     71c <function1>                 73c: bti   c
 740: str    w0, [sp, #28]                   740: stp    x29, x30, [sp, #-32]!
 744: ldr    w0, [sp, #28]                   744: mov    x29, sp
 748: ldp    x29, x30, [sp], #32            748: bl     720 <function1>
 74c: ret                                     74c: str    w0, [sp, #28]
                                              750: ldr    w0, [sp, #28]
                                              754: ldp    x29, x30, [sp], #32
                                              758: ret
```

Figure 15.11: Assembly instructions when BTI is enabled

In *Figure 15.11*, the left-hand side shows instructions without the BTI feature. The right-hand side shows disassembled instructions after BTI is enabled:

- **Without BTI (-mbranch-protection=bti not used):** The disassembled code does not include any BTI-related instructions.

- **With BTI (-mbranch-protection=bti enabled):** The disassembled code includes the BTI C instruction at the beginning of each function. This is because the compiler inserts the BTI C instruction at the function entry.

The most commonly asked question here is, why is BTI C inserted? The BTI C instruction marks the function as a valid target for indirect branches, such as those used in function pointers or jump tables. This ensures that only authorized branch targets can be executed.

What happens if an invalid branch operation is detected when running the BTI instruction? In this case, a BTI exception occurs. As a result, the program may terminate or trigger an error, preventing unauthorized code execution.

The following subsection highlights how exceptions are generated when BTI instructions detect an invalid branch operation.

BTI exceptions

If an invalid branch operation is detected, the BTI exception is triggered. *Figure 15.12* shows the workflow for this.

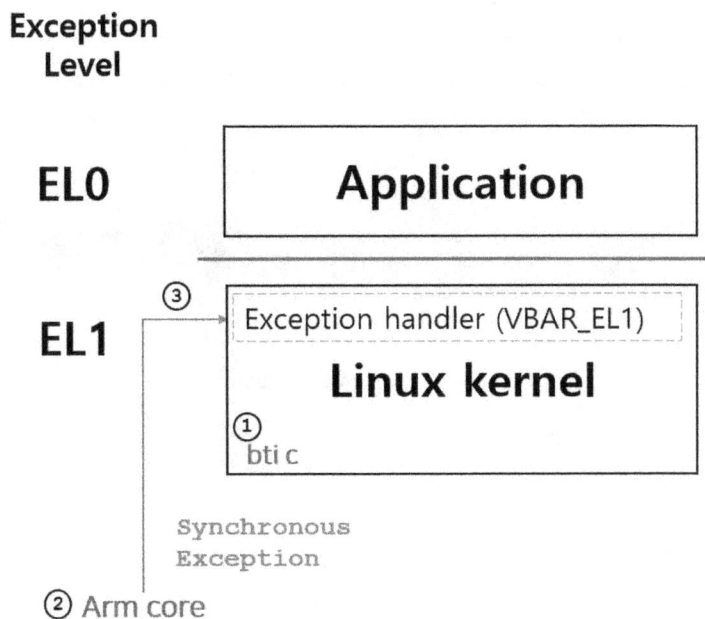

Figure 15.12: Workflow of an exception due to a BTI error

Let's explain how a BTI exception is generated, as depicted in *Figure 15.12*:

1. The bti c instruction runs.
2. If an invalid branch is identified, it does the following:
    - Raises a synchronous exception
    - Updates bits [31:26] of the ESR_EL1 register with the bit representation, indicating that the cause of the exception is a BTI error
3. PC moves to the exception vector address to handle the synchronous exception.

How the system handles the exception depends on the software:

- If the exception happens in EL0 (user space), the process that performs an invalid branch operation is usually terminated
- If the exception happens in EL1 (kernel space), it may cause a kernel panic

The exception handler runs a specific routine. For exceptions in user mode, this routine normally ends the faulty process.

In practice, you may wonder which signature is observed when the exception occurs due to a BTI error. The following is an example signature when a BTI error is detected. This example log signature can be found at https://github.com/NVIDIA/open-gpu-kernel-modules/issues/771:

```
[  165.058515] Internal error: Oops - BTI: 0000000036000002 [#1] SMP
[  165.066266] Modules linked in: nvidia(O+) nft_compat nf_tables mlx5_ib
ib_uverbs ib_core mlx5_core mlxfw ptp pps_core loadpin_trigger(O) fuse
configfs
[  165.079464] CPU: 1 PID: 780 Comm: insmod Tainted: G          O
6.6.72+
 #1
```

As you can see, Oops - BTI is printed. Looking at the Oops - BTI signature in the kernel, you can deduce that this exception happens as a result of a BTI error.

Now that we understand the main features of BTI, let's look at some example code that initializes the BTI feature.

Code review of BTI

In this section, we will learn how BTI is enabled in the Linux Kernel. Let's review the bti_enabled() function to see how BTI is enabled:

```
arch/arm64/kernel/cpufeature.c
static void bti_enable(const struct arm64_cpu_capabilities *__unused)
{
    [...]
    sysreg_clear_set(sctlr_el1, 0, SCTLR_EL1_BT0 | SCTLR_EL1_BT1);
    isb();
}
```

The bti_enabled() function enables BTI when the Linux Kernel boots up. If we run the preceding code, the BT0 and BT1 fields in SCTLR_EL1 are set to 1 using the sysreg_clear_set function. We can find the bit position of BT0 and BT1 in SCTLR_EL1 in the following definition:

```
// tools/arch/arm64/include/asm/sysreg.h
#define SCTLR_EL1_BT1        (BIT(36))
#define SCTLR_EL1_BT0        (BIT(35))
```

So far, we have only reviewed a small part of the implementation of BTI in the Linux Kernel. If you want to explore the full implementation, you can refer to CONFIG_Arm64_BTI in the Linux Kernel source code, where you can find CONFIG_ARM64_BTI in the .config file. This .config file is generated during Linux Kernel compilation.

In this section, we covered BTI. The next section will explain the MTE feature, another popular security feature introduced in Armv8.5-A.

Memory Tagging Extension (MTE)

MTE (Memory Tagging Extension) is a security feature that was introduced in Armv8.5-A to help detect and mitigate memory safety issues, such as buffer overflows and use-after-free vulnerabilities. It provides hardware-assisted memory tagging, which helps developers identify memory corruption issues in development or at runtime.

There is a lot of material to cover regarding MTE since it supports various features at both the hardware and software levels. This section only provides an overview of MTE.

Introducing MTE

In practice, bugs or vulnerabilities can be found when a program accesses certain memory regions. The following are two common types of memory issues:

- **Out-of-bounds access:** This happens when a program tries to read or write memory outside the allowed range. For example, if an array is declared inside a function and the program accesses it with an index that is too large or negative, it may cause unexpected behavior.

- **Use after free:** This issue occurs when the program tries to use memory that has already been freed (released). You may also see this issue in many commit messages that contain bug-fixing patches.

Advanced software, such as the Linux Kernel, includes debugging features to detect out-of-bounds access and use-after-free issues. However, these features cannot catch all memory corruption issues.

From a security point of view, attackers often use out-of-bounds access or use-after-free methods to exploit software. To reduce these risks, the MTE feature was introduced in the Armv8.5-A architecture.

The basic idea behind MTE is simple:

- A memory tag is assigned to a 16-byte memory block.
- When memory is allocated, a random tag is added to the pointer.
- When the program accesses memory, the tag in the pointer is compared to the tag in the memory block. If the tags do not match, an exception is raised.

So, how is the 4-bit tag used in MTE? What exactly is the tag?

The 4-bit tag is used to check whether memory access is correct. The way these tags are stored in physical memory depends on the hardware design. This topic will be explained in more detail in the next section.

How tags are handled

To understand how MTE works, we need to learn about the two types of tags it uses—the address tag and the memory tag. These two tags work together like a key and a lock:

- **Address tag (key):** This is a 4-bit tag that's stored in the upper bits of a virtual address. To use this part of the address, the **Top Byte Ignore (TBI)** feature must be enabled. This allows the processor to ignore the top byte during address translation and use it for tagging.
- **Memory tag (lock):** This is also a 4-bit tag that is assigned to every 16-byte block of physical memory. Each 16-byte unit is called a granule. The way these memory tags are stored depends on the hardware design, and it can vary between different chipset manufacturers.

When a load or store instruction is executed, the hardware compares the address tag (from the pointer) with the memory tag (from the memory block). If the tags match, memory access is allowed. If the tags do not match, the system can either raise an exception or record the mismatch, depending on the configuration settings.

The virtual address layout used to store the address tag

Before learning more about MTE, we need to understand how a 64-bit virtual address is structured. When both the MTE and TBI features are turned on, bits [59:56] of the virtual address are used to store the MTE address tag.

Let's look at an example. The LDR X0, [X3] instruction loads data from the memory address in the X3 register into the X0 register. In this case, the virtual address in X3 has the following layout:

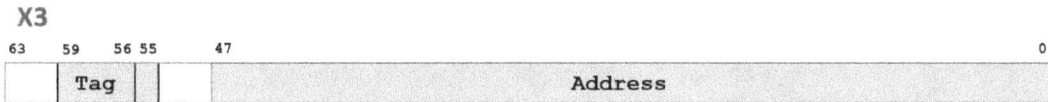

X3

63	59	56 55		47		0
	Tag				Address	

Figure 15.13: Bit position used to store the address tag

The preceding figure shows the bit position that stores the address tag in a virtual address:

- Bits [47:0] are used for normal address translation
- Bit [55] may also be used, depending on the system settings
- Bits [59:56] store the 4-bit tag used by MTE

These upper bits, [59:56] and [55], do not affect the address translation process. This is because the TBI feature tells the processor to ignore the top byte of the address. So, the tag bits are only used for MTE checking, not for finding the memory location.

> **Note**
>
> The virtual address layout in *Figure 15.13* is based on the VA_48 virtual address range. The range of the virtual address depends on a project's requirements.

How is the address tag stored in bits [59:56] of a virtual address? MTE provides special assembly instructions for inserting an address tag into the upper bit of a virtual address. These instructions only work when the MTE feature is enabled, as follows:

- IRG Xd, Xn: This instruction inserts a random tag into the address stored in Xn and stores the result in Xd.
- ADDG Xd, Xn, #<uimm6>, #<uimm4>: This instruction adds a value to the address and also sets a tag. The final result is saved in Xd.

These instructions update the 4-bit address tag in bits [59:56] of a 64-bit virtual address.

Memory tag

A memory tag is a 4-bit value that's assigned to a 16-byte block of memory. This 16-byte unit is called a granule. Memory tags are stored in a special hardware area called tag storage, which is managed by hardware and implemented separately from the data cache, often in system-specific ways. The exact way memory tags are stored can be different, depending on the chipset manufacturer.

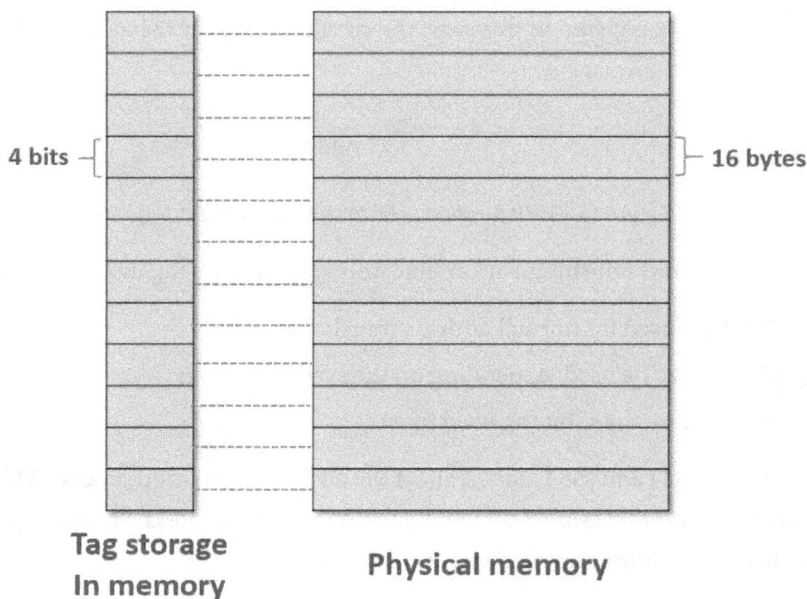

Figure 15.14: Layout of the tag storage in memory

MTE stores the memory tag (from a tagged pointer) into tag storage associated with a memory block. Let's suppose that we run the STG X1, [X0] instruction. Here's are breakdown of this process:

1.   The hardware uses bits [47:0] of the virtual address in X0 to find the physical address. This is done by the **Memory Management Unit (MMU)** using multi-level page table translation.

2.   Once the physical address is found, the system accesses the tag storage connected to that memory block. The address tag is then stored in this tag storage.

This process is performed entirely at the hardware level, so software developers usually cannot observe it directly.

MTE's tag checking operation

Now, let's see how MTE performs tag checking. When an instruction such as **load (LDR)** or **store (STR)** accesses a tagged memory address, the system compares two tags:

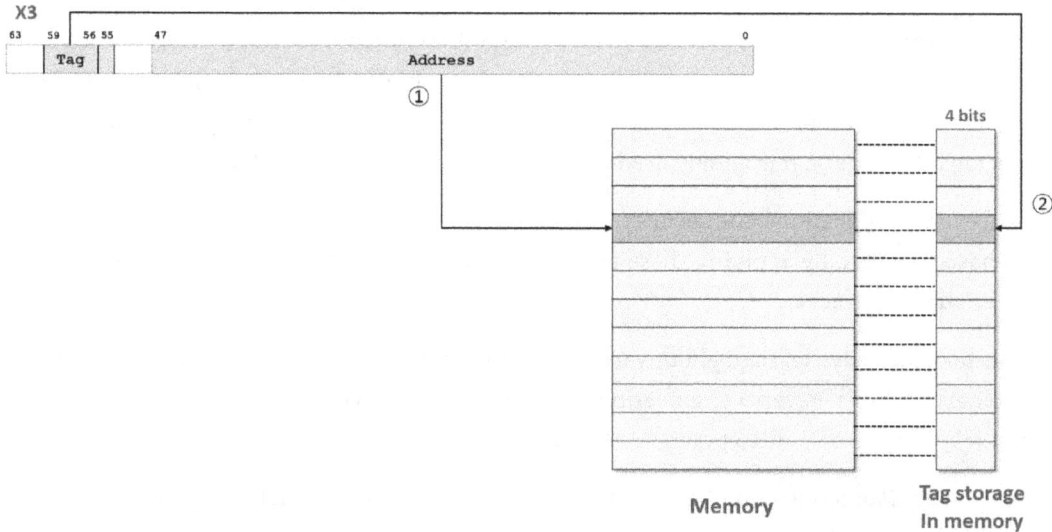

Figure 15.15: Steps for checking memory tagging operations

As you can see, the address tag is located in the virtual address (bits [59:56]).

The memory tag is in the tag storage for that memory block. If the tags match, memory access is allowed. If the tags do not match, the system raises a synchronous exception.

This automatic tag check helps the system catch many memory safety issues during runtime, such as use-after-free issues or out-of-bound access.

Summary

This chapter covered the latest security features introduced in different versions of the Armv8-A architecture. These security upgrades were introduced due to the IT industry's growing need for stronger execution environments that prioritize system security.

First, we explored PAN, a security feature designed to block direct access to EL0, which is the lowest privilege level in Armv8-A. If a user application requires security protection, it is recommended to enable PAN to improve system safety.

Next, we discussed PAC, introduced in Armv8.3-A. PAC helps protect virtual addresses by adding an authentication code to the upper bits of the address before storing it in memory. When the address is later loaded, the system verifies the authentication code. This mechanism helps detect whether the stored address has been modified or corrupted.

Then, we examined BTI, also introduced in Armv8.5-A. BTI helps monitor indirect branch operations and prevents malicious code redirection. Finally, we highlighted MTE, which was introduced in Armv8.5-A. MTE is one of the most powerful security features for enforcing memory access rules using tag information. It is widely used in smartphones and advanced devices.

In real-world applications, the security features covered in this chapter are widely used in many Arm-based devices. By applying these techniques, you can build systems that are more secure and resistant to attacks.

In this book, we have learned about various features of Armv8-A related to reverse engineering and binary analysis. Reverse engineering is a practical skill. If you apply the topics discussed in this book, you will be able to practice analyzing ELF files and binary files.

In particular, *Chapters 10* and *12* explain how to analyze the Linux Kernel binary, which helps you better understand the internal behavior of the kernel.

All the materials in this book are designed to be practical and useful for binary analysis in terms of reverse engineering and debugging tasks. I hope this book serves as a helpful reference when you're examining crash dumps or analyzing unknown binaries.

‹packt›

packtpub.com

Subscribe to our online digital library for full access to over 7,000 books and videos, as well as industry leading tools to help you plan your personal development and advance your career. For more information, please visit our website.

Why subscribe?

- Spend less time learning and more time coding with practical eBooks and Videos from over 4,000 industry professionals
- Improve your learning with Skill Plans built especially for you
- Get a free eBook or video every month
- Fully searchable for easy access to vital information
- Copy and paste, print, and bookmark content

At www.packtpub.com, you can also read a collection of free technical articles, sign up for a range of free newsletters, and receive exclusive discounts and offers on Packt books and eBooks.

Other Books You May Enjoy

If you enjoyed this book, you may be interested in these other books by Packt:

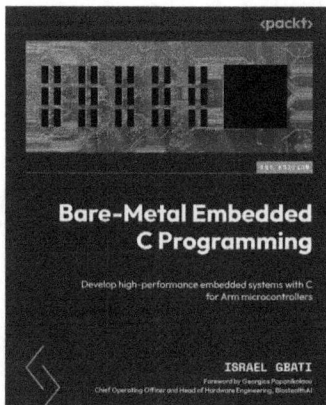

Bare-Metal Embedded C Programming

Israel Gbati

ISBN: 978-1-83546-081-8

- Decode microcontroller datasheets, enabling precise firmware development
- Master register manipulations for optimized Arm-based microcontroller firmware creation
- Discover how to navigate hardware intricacies confidently
- Find out how to write optimized firmware without any assistance
- Work on exercises to create bare-metal drivers for GPIO, timers, ADC, UART, SPI, I2C, DMA, and more
- Design energy-efficient embedded systems with power management techniques

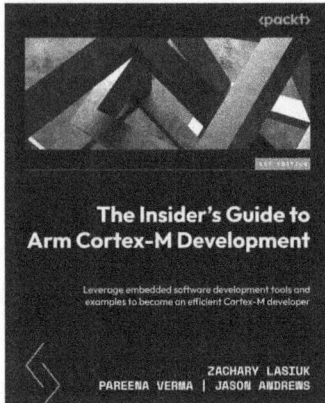

The Insider's Guide to Arm Cortex-M Development

Zachary Lasiuk, Pareena Verma, Jason Andrews

ISBN: 978-1-80323-111-2

- Familiarize yourself with heuristics to identify the right components for your Cortex-M project
- Boot code to efficiently start up a Cortex-M device
- Optimize algorithms with compilers, middleware, and other means
- Get to grips with machine learning frameworks and implementation techniques
- Understand security in the embedded space with solutions like TrustZone and TF-M
- Explore cloud-based development methodologies to increase efficiency
- Dive into continuous integration frameworks and best practices
- Identify future trends that could impact Cortex-M software development

Packt is searching for authors like you

If you're interested in becoming an author for Packt, please visit authors.packt.com and apply today. We have worked with thousands of developers and tech professionals, just like you, to help them share their insight with the global tech community. You can make a general application, apply for a specific hot topic that we are recruiting an author for, or submit your own idea.

Share your thoughts

Now you've finished *Reverse Engineering Armv8-A Systems*, we'd love to hear your thoughts! Scan the QR code below to go straight to the Amazon review page for this book and share your feedback or leave a review on the site that you purchased it from.

https://packt.link/r/1835088929

Your review is important to us and the tech community and will help us make sure we're delivering excellent quality content.

Index

Symbols

.bss section 58

.data section 58

.init section 60

*.ko files (kernel modules) 243
  analyzing 244
  device drivers, types 243
  header information, checking 244-246
  metadata, inspecting in .modinfo
    section 246-250

.rodata section 58

.text section 58

 Ubuntu 22.04 Arm64 cloud image
  reference link 166

A

abort() function 283

ADC instruction 72, 73
  examples 73

add_func function 16

ADD instruction 70
  examples 71

Address Sanitizer (ASan) 196, 197
  need for 196

Add with Carry (ADC) 72

advanced dynamic analysis 263, 290
  kernel binary, debugging 291

advanced static analysis 238, 239
  kernel binaries, debugging program 240
  kernel binaries, features 238, 239
  kernel binaries for analysis, selecting 239

AMBA bus protocol 352

AND instruction 82
  example 83

AND operation 90

Application Binary Interface (ABI) 3

arithmetic operations 70
  ADC instruction 72, 73
  ADD instruction 70
  SBC instruction 75
  SUB instruction 74

Arithmetic Shift Right (ASR) 79

ARM architecture 4, 5
  Cortex® processor and architecture 5

ARM reference manual
  reference link 356

ARM Trusted Firmware
  analyzing 348
  exception handler, analyzing at EL3 348, 349

exception handler, for SMC
    instruction 349-351
reference link 348

ARMv8-A 6

ARMv8-A architecture 3
system registers 14, 15

ARMv8-M 6

ARMv8 profiles 6
ARMv8-A 6
ARMv8-M 6
ARMv8-R 6

ARMv8-R 6

ARPROT signal 352-354

ASR instruction 79

assembly instructions 153, 156, 202
for machine code 154, 155

assembly routines for reverse engineering
analyzing 129
CBNZ instruction 132
CBZ instruction 130
TBZ instruction 133

asynchronous exception 28

AWPROT signal 352-354

B

backtrace (bt) command 270

basic dynamic analysis 263

BIC instruction 86
examples 87

Binary Ninja 203, 240

binary utilities 203, 204
file 204, 205
readelf 205, 206
xxd 205, 207

Binary Utilities (binutils) 148

B instruction 114

Bit Clear (BIC) 86

bit-shift operations 76
ASR instruction 79
case study 80, 81
LSL instruction 76
LSR instruction 78
ROR instruction 80

BL instruction 115

BLR instruction 116

Branch (B) 114

branch instruction 114
B instruction 114
BL instruction 115
BLR instruction 116
BR instruction 116
routine example, analyzing 117

Branch Target Identification (BTI) 376
code review 384
exceptions 383, 384
guarded page 379
need for 376
using, via compiler 381, 382
workflow 379
working 377, 378

Branch to Register (BR) 116

Branch with Link (BL) 115, 378

**Branch with Link and
    Register (BLR) 116, 236**

BR instruction 116

BTI instruction 380

buffer overflow 285
case study 282
code example 282

from software layer 285, 286

in struct 286

mitigation method 286, 287

patch, debugging 282-284

C

call stack 180, 181, 270, 271

CBNZ instruction 126, 127, 132

assembly routine, analyzing 132

corresponding C code, constructing 133

CBZ instruction 126

assembly routine, analyzing 130, 131

corresponding C code, constructing 131

C language 202

CMN instruction 120

example 121

CMP instruction 119

example 120

Compare and Branch if Non-Zero (CBNZ) 126

Compare and Branch if Zero (CBZ) 126

Compare (CMP) 119

Compare Negative (CMN) 120

comparison operations 118

CMP instruction 119

conditional codes 123

condition flags in PSTATE 118

TST instruction 122

compilation process 150, 151

breakdown 151, 152

compiler 152

compiler option 152

linker 152

preprocessor 151

source file types 151

compiler

working 150

conditional branch operations 125

assembly routines for reverse engineering, analyzing 129

CBNZ instruction 126, 127

CBZ instruction 126

TBZ instruction 127-129

conditional codes 123

routine example, analyzing 124, 125

conditional flags 11

condition flags in PSTATE 118

core dump 149

corrupted binary file

case study 209, 210

corrupted stack

debugging 272-274

debugging code, using 276, 277

debugging patch 275, 276

exploiting 274, 275

identifying 275

Cortex® processor and architecture 5

Crash utility 291, 297, 298

reference link 299

Current Program Status Register (CPSR) 11

D

data processing instructions

best practices 91, 92

bit set, clearing 93

else block, handling 94

state, checking 93

variables, initializing 92

Debian 203

debugging methods
  offline debugging 292
  online debugging 292

debugging tools 202

dump analysis 149
  advantages 150
  binary for 149
  limitations 149

dynamic analysis 148, 262
  benefits 262
  limitations 262, 263
  performing 148, 149

dynamic section 59, 60

E

e_entry field 49

e_ident field 46, 47

ELF format 156, 157

ELF header 42
  e_entry field 49
  e_ident field 46, 47
  e_machine field 48, 49
  e_phoff field 49, 50
  e_shoff field 49, 50
  e_shstrndx field 50
  e_type field 47, 48
  exploring 46
  identifying 42, 43
  viewing 44-46

ELR_ELx register 10

else-if statement 214, 215

e_machine field 48, 49

EOR instruction 88
  examples 88

e_phoff field 49, 50

e_shoff field 49, 50

e_shstrndx field 50

e_type field 47, 48

e_type field, types
  ET_CORE 48
  ET_DYN 47
  ET_EXEC 47
  ET_NONE 47
  ET_REL 47

exception 28
  generating 33
  key principles 28
  types 28, 29

exception, component
  branch method 34
  cause, indicating 33
  exception handling 35
  registers, updating 34
  switch method 34

exception handling
  FIQ exception handler 36
  IRQ exception handler 36
  SError exception handler 36
  synchronous exception handler 35
  working 35

exception level (EL) 20, 24, 345, 358
  determining 26
  EL0 with PL0 21
  EL1 with PL1 22
  EL2 with PL2 22
  EL3 with PL3 22
  example 27
  switch instruction 24

exception level (EL), switch instruction
  HVC instruction 26
  SMC instruction 26
  SVC instruction 25

exception link register (ELR_ELx) 10

exception vector table 29, 30
  EL0 (AArch32) 32
  EL0 (AArch64) 32
  EL1 with SP_EL0 31
  EL1 with SPx 31

Exclusive OR (EOR) 88

Executable and Linkable
     Format (ELF) 39, 148, 202, 245, 294
  file layout 41, 42
  learning 40
  overview 40

F

Fast Interrupt Request (FIQ) 12, 347

file utility 204, 205

FIQ exception handler 36

flush_buffer_thread() function 267

for loop 218-221
  with break statement 222-224
  with continue statement 224-226
  with return 0 statement 226, 227

function pointer
  used, for identifying task_struct
    structure 313

G

GDB Enhanced Features (GEF) 266, 267

GDB program
  breakpoints, setting 265
  exploring 264
  information commands, debugging 266

  launching 265
  memory contents, inspecting 266
  running 265

general-purpose registers 7-9

Ghidra 147, 203, 240

global offset table (GOT) 60

GNU Debugger (GDB) 147, 264
  advantages 264
  using 264, 265

GNU General Public License (GPL) 248

GOT section 60

graphical user interface (GUI) 203

guarded page 380

H

hardware components, TrustZone
  Generic Interrupt Controller (GIC) 355
  TrustZone Address Space
    Controller (TZASC) 355
  TrustZone Memory Adapter (TZMA) 355
  TrustZone Protection Controller (TZPC) 355

HVC instruction 26, 137, 138

Hypervisor Call (HVC) 137

I

IDA Pro 203, 240

if-else statement 212, 213

if statement 211, 212
  with return statement 216, 217

instruction analysis, techniques
  control flow analysis, with function calls 235
  line-by-line analysis 235
  static analysis, limitations 236
  static analysis, versus dynamic
    analysis 237, 238

Instruction Set Architecture (ISA) 3

intellectual property (IP) blocks 352

Interrupt Request (IRQ) 12

Interrupt Service Routine (ISR) 314

irqaction structure 315, 316

IRQ exception handler 36

J

jump-oriented programming (JOP) 362

K

KDUMP feature 293

Kernel Address Space Layout Randomization
   (KASLR) 196, 197
   features 196

kernel binaries
   assembly instructions, analyzing 253, 254
   debugging methods 292
   exceptions, handling 251
   features 250
   sp_el0 and current macro,
      managing 251-253
   structure 240
   system registers, accessing 250

kernel binaries structure
   *.ko files (kernel modules) 243
   vmlinux 240

Kernel logs 320

kernel process stack 305
   versus user process stack 304, 305

kernel space 172, 173
   characteristics 173

L

Linux kernel 156, 170
   execution environment 172
   resource manager 171

Linux kernel documentation
   reference link 188

Linux Kernel patches
   reference link 361

Linux Security Modules (LSM) 194-197
   general privileges 194
   root privileges 195

load register halfword (LDRH) 105

load register (LDR) 366

load register (LDR) instruction 98
   assembly routine, analyzing 109, 110
   basic form 98-100
   with offset addressing mode 100, 101

load register signed byte (LDRSB) 105

load register signed halfword (LDRSH) 105

log-based debugging 319
   logs, need for 320
   tracing, need for 320

logical operations 82
   AND instruction 82
   AND operation 90
   best practices 89
   BIC instruction 86
   EOR instruction 88
   ORN instruction 85
   OR operation 90
   ORR instruction 84
   XOR operation 91

Logical Shift Left (LSL) 76

Logical Shift Right (LSR) 78

log output patterns 228

log output routines 229

logs
  need for 320

LSL instruction 77
  examples 77

LSR instruction 78
  examples 78

M

machine code 153
  assembly instruction 154, 155
  example 153

mask flag 12

memory access instructions 107
  assembly routine, analyzing 109, 110
  example code 107-109

memory access operation 105
  secret behind load operations 106
  various load operations 105, 106
  various store operations 106

memory dump debugging 292

memory management 186
  features, in Linux system 186-190
  virtual memory area (VMA) 193
  virtual memory system 190

Memory Management
    Unit (MMU) 5, 190, 272, 388

memory tag 388

Memory Tagging Extension (MTE) 385
  memory issues type 385
  tag checking 389
  tags, handling 386

Message Authentication Code (MAC) 362

microcontroller units (MCUs) 6

mitigation method 277, 278

most significant bit (MSB) 79

move operations 68
  MOV instruction 68
  MVN instruction 69

Move to Register from System (MRS) 26

Move to System Register (MSR) 360

MOV instruction 68
  examples 68, 69

MultiMediaCard (MMC) 314

multiprocess management 182-184

MVN instruction 69
  examples 69, 70

N

National Security Agency (NSA) 203

No Operation (NOP) 380

NOTE section 295, 296

O

offline debugging 292

online debugging 292

ORN instruction 85
  example 85, 86

OR operation 90

ORR instruction 84
  example 84

P

pahole tool 257

PAN system register 359, 360

Parent PID (PPID) 182

p_flags field 65
  PF_R 66
  PF_W 65
  PF_X 65

PLT section 60

Pointer Authentication Code (PAC) 362, 363
  assembly instructions 367
  AUTIASP instruction 368, 369
  compiler support 371
  component 362
  exception 374, 375
  execution flow, with branch
      operation 366, 367
  inputs 363
  instructions 370
  PACIASP instruction 368, 369
  system registers 375, 376
  usage, in Linux with GCC compiler 372, 373
  use cases 365
  virtual address layout for storage 364

Pointer Authentication (PAuth) 362

position-independent code (PIC) 47

p_paddr field 66

printf() function
  call, analyzing 229, 230
  replacing, with puts 230

Privileged Access Never (PAN) 358
  code review, in Linux Kernel 360, 361

considerations, implementing in Linux
      system 361, 362
  features 358, 359
  system registers, configuring 359

Privileged Access Never (PAN), system
      registers
  PAN system register 359, 360
  SCTLR_EL1.SPAN field 360

privilege level 21

Procedure Call Standard for the Arm
      Architecture (AAPCS) 3, 16, 17, 270
  background 16
  BL instruction 18-20
  registers 17

procedure linkage table (PLT) 60

process 177, 178
  call stack 180, 181
  data structure 179, 180
  multiprocess management 181-184
  threads 185

process ID (PID) 180

Processor State (PSTATE) 11, 12, 381

program counter (PC) 10, 192, 272, 343
  scenarios 10

program header 61
  exploring 64
  layout 62-64
  p_flags field 65
  p_offset field 66
  p_paddr field 66
  p_type field 65
  p_vaddr field 66

programs, for static analysis
  Binary Ninja 203
  binary utilities 203
  Ghidra 203
  IDA Pro 203

program status registers 11

PSTATE.BTYTE 381

PT_DYNAMIC 65

PT_INTERP 65

PT_NOTE 65

p_type field 65
  PT_DYNAMIC 65
  PT_INTERP 65
  PT_LOAD 65
  PT_NOTE 65

p_vaddr field 66

Q

Quick Emulator (QEMU) 162, 264, 291
  full system emulation 165-167
  user-mode emulation 163, 164

R

Raspberry Pi 160
  Arm processor profile 161, 162
  features 160

Raspbian 161

readelf utility 205, 206

registers 7
  general-purpose registers 7-9
  program status registers 11
  reverse engineering, performing 16
  special registers 9
  SP_ELx registers 9

return-oriented programming
    (ROP) 196, 278, 362
  compiler options, using to prevent
      symptom 281
  key concept 278-280

return statement 216

reverse engineering 143
  assembly instructions 156
  case study 146
  debugging skills, improving 145
  ELF format 156, 157
  legacy systems 145
  library and firmware debugging 144
  Linux kernel 156
  need for 143

reverse engineering methods 146
  dump analysis 149
  dynamic analysis 148
  static analysis 147, 148

ROR instruction 80

Rotate Right (ROR) 80

S

Saved Program Status Register
    (SPSR_ELx) 11, 13

SBC instruction 75
  examples 75

SCTLR_EL1.SPAN field 360

section headers 50
  exploring 53
  layout 50-53
  sh_addr field 56, 57
  sh_flags field 56
  sh_name field 54
  sh_offset field 57
  sh_size field 57
  sh_type field 54, 55

sections 57
  .bss section 58
  .data section 58
  dynamic section 59, 60
  GOT section 60

.init section 60
PLT section 60
.rodata section 58
.text section 58

secure monitor call (SMC) 138, 338
  Non-secure world, to Secure world 339, 340
  Secure world, to Non-secure world 341, 342

Security-Enhanced Linux (SELinux) 195

security hardening features 194
  Address Sanitizer (ASan) 196
  Linux Security Modules (LSM) 194, 195

SError exception handler 36

sh_addr field 56, 57

sh_flags field 56

sh_name field 54

sh_offset field 57

sh_size field 57

sh_type field 54, 55

sign extension 106

Simplified Mandatory Access
    Control Kernel (SMACK) 195

SMC instruction 26, 138, 139

special registers 9
  ELR_ELx register 10
  Program Counter (PC) register 10

SP_ELx registers 9

stack end magic value 305
  code review 305, 306
  summary 307

stack memory content
  analyzing 270
  call stack 270, 271
  corrupted stack, debugging 272-274
  corrupted stack, exploiting 274, 275

corrupted stack, identifying 275
  mitigation method 277, 278

stack patterns 299
  background 300
  layout 300, 301
  memory contents, analyzing 302, 303
  stack end magic value, code review 305, 306
  user process stack, versus kernel process
      stack 304, 305

stack pointer (SP) 9, 276

static analysis 147, 201, 202
  activities 147
  characteristics 202
  goals, setting 234
  instruction analysis, techniques 235
  methodology 234
  programs 203
  tools 147

store register byte (STRB) 106

store register halfword (STRH) 106

store register (STR) instruction 102
  assembly routine, analyzing 109, 110
  basic form 102, 103
  with offset addressing mode 103-105

struct data structures
  instructions, for accessing
      fields in struct 256-258
  offset of fields 255, 256
  pattern 254

SUB instruction 74
  examples 74, 75

Subtract with Carry (SBC) 75

SVC instruction 25, 136, 137

synchronous exception 28
  handling 35

system call 137, 172
  kernel space 172, 173
  system call handler 176
  system call number 176
  system call operations, monitoring 176, 177
  user space 172, 173
  working 174, 175

system call handler 176

system call number 176

system call operations
  monitoring 176, 177

system control operations 135
  HVC instruction 137, 138
  SMC instruction 138, 139
  SVC instruction 136, 137

System logs 320

system registers 13
  accessing 15
  lowest exception levels 13, 14

T

task_struct structure 307, 308
  address in the irq_desc structure,
    finding 316, 317
  address of bcm2835_mmc_irq, finding 314
  address, tracking 307-310
  analysis 317
  function addresses, storing 313
  identifying, with function pointer 313
  irqaction structure 315, 316
  key elements 180
  thread field, reviewing 311-313

TBNZ instruction 128
  components 128

TBZ instruction 127-129
  assembly routine, analyzing 133
  components 127
  corresponding C code,
    constructing 134, 135

Test Bit and Branch if Non-Zero (TBNZ) 128

Test Bit and Branch if Zero (TBZ) 127

Test (TST) 122

threads 185

Top Byte Ignore (TBI) 386

TRACE32 240, 291

Translation Lookaside Buffer (TLB) 193

TrustZone 138, 333, 334, 357
  AWPROT and ARPROT signals 352-354
  example code, in Non-secure world 337
  exception handlers 342-345
  features 335
  hardware features 352, 355
  key concepts 335
  need for 334
  Non-secure world 336
  Secure world 336, 337
  software scenario, of Secure world 338
  workflow 336

TrustZone, in real systems
  implementation 346
  security implementation examples 347, 348
  trusted OS, running in Secure world 346

TST instruction 122
  example 122

U

Ubuntu 203

Ubuntu Jammy release
  reference link 166

uftrace 320
  installing 322
  key features 321
  need for 321
uftrace basic features 323
  output format 324
  -pg option, adding 324
  project, creating 323
uftrace practical features 324
  argument tracing 326, 327
  library debugging 325, 326
  return value tracing 328, 329
user experience (UX) 267
user process stack 305
  versus kernel process stack 304, 305
user space 172, 173
  characteristics 173

V

virtual addresses
  in kernel space 190, 192
  in user space 190, 192
  software components 192
virtual address layout
  using, to store address tag 387
virtual address pattern
  examples 269
virtual address range 268
  virtual address pattern, examples 269
  virtual memory system 268, 269
Virtual Memory Area (VMA) 188, 193
virtual memory system 190, 268, 269
  key factors 268
  virtual addresses, in user space
      and kernel space 190, 192

vmcore files 150
  analyzing, with binary utility 293
  layout 293-295
vmlinux 240
  generating 240, 241
  header sections, inspecting 241-243

X

XOR operation 91
xxd utility 205, 207
  raw data of binary file, identifying 207, 208
  raw data of text file, identifying 208, 209

Z

zero extension 105

Download a free PDF copy of this book

Thanks for purchasing this book!

Do you like to read on the go but are unable to carry your print books everywhere?

Is your eBook purchase not compatible with the device of your choice?

Don't worry, now with every Packt book you get a DRM-free PDF version of that book at no cost.

Read anywhere, any place, on any device. Search, copy, and paste code from your favorite technical books directly into your application.

The perks don't stop there, you can get exclusive access to discounts, newsletters, and great free content in your inbox daily.

Follow these simple steps to get the benefits:

1. Scan the QR code or visit the link below:

https://packt.link/free-ebook/9781835088920

2. Submit your proof of purchase.
3. That's it! We'll send your free PDF and other benefits to your email directly.

www.ingramcontent.com/pod-product-compliance
Lightning Source LLC
Chambersburg PA
CBHW072009230326
41598CB00082B/6895